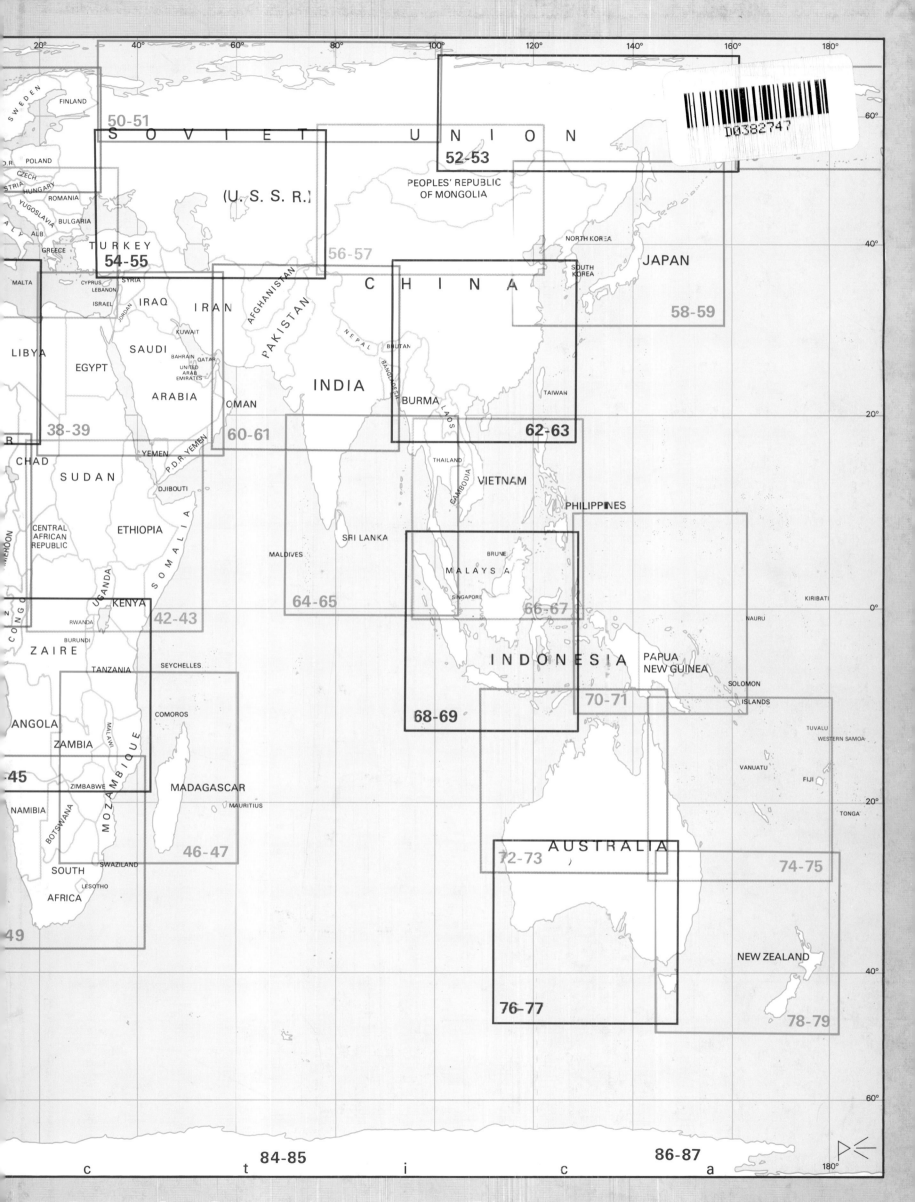

TOPOGRAPHIC MAPS

The contents of the Peters Atlas are identical in all editions produced throughout the world.

PETERS ATLAS OF THE WORLD

1817

Harper & Row, Publishers, New York
Grand Rapids, Philadelphia, St. Louis, San Francisco
London, Singapore, Sydney, Tokyo, Toronto

Contributors and consultants: Dr. E. C. Barrett, Professor Dr. Ulrich Bleil, Michael Benckert, Wolfgang Behr, Professor Heinz Bosse, Professor Walter Buchholz, Dr. Nicola Bradbear, Carol Claxton, Professor Dr. Heinrich Dathe, Hellmuth Färber, Jean Fernand-Laurent, Kurt Ficker, Professor Dr. Fritz Fischer, Karlheinz Gieseler, Professor Dr. Manfred Görlach, Professor Dr. Ulrich Grosse, Dipl.-Geogr. Arnulf Hader, Birgit Hahn, Dipl.-Ing. Max Hann, Dirk Hansohm, Dr. Günther Heidmann, Professor Dr. Dr. Wolf Herre, Karl-Heinz Ingenhaag, Dr. Andreas Kaiser, Toni Kaufmann, Michael Kidron, Professor Dr. Gunther Krause, Dr. Manfred Kummer, Daniel Lloyd, Konrad G. Lohse, Dipl.-Ing. Wolfgang Mache, Dr. Udo Moll, Dr. Aribert Peters, Dipl.-Ing. Werner Peters, Thomas Plümer, D. H. Reichstein, Luise Scherf, Hellmut Schlien, Professor Dr. Hermann Schulz, Ronald Segal, Professor Dr. Axel Sell, Eduard Spescha, Dr. Walter Stützle, Jürgen Wendler, Professor Adolf Witte, Professor Dr. Karl Wohlmuth, Siegfried Zademack, Madeleine Zeller.

Cartography:

Kümmerly + Frey, Bern
Graticules, Coastlines, Borders, Seas, Rivers and Lakes

Oxford Cartographers
Topographic Maps, Thematic World Maps

Cartographic Editor: Terry Hardaker; Editorial Coordination: Penny Watson; Editorial Checking: Ann Leleu, Georg Möller, Anja Peters; Computer Programming: H. Morelli; Topographic Map Compilation: Katharine Armitage, Claire Carlton, John Hall, Hazel Hand, Sheila Hodson, Christine Johnston, Jean Kelly, Tanya Lillington, Angela Morrison, Kay Roberts, Fiona Sutcliffe; Technical Coordination: John Dawson, John Wilders; Map Draughting: Gerhard Engel, Bob Hawkins, Ben Hill, Sally Horn, Robert Hundley, Jeff Jones, David Lewis, Sue Lovell, Colin McCarthy, Michael Oakley, Piet Summerfield; Estimating: Peter Langran, John Williams; Terrain Modelling: David Angus; Terrain Colouring: Terry Hardaker; Indexing: Barbara Croucher, Duncan Croucher, Betty Döppl, Petra Faltermeier, Karin Geier, Franz Huber, Ingrid Kampfhenkel, Hermann Lechner, Lothar Meier, Anton Sommer, Iris Sommer, Margret Suhr, Jürgen Wendler.

Typesetting: Oxford University Press, Getset Ltd Eynsham, Simmering Lilienthal; Photography: Clyde Surveys Ltd Maidenhead, Oxford Litho Plates Ltd; Scanning: Rapidagraphics Ltd London; Manchine Proofing: Colourproof Ltd Swindon; Printing and Binding: Neue Stalling Oldenburg.

ISBN 0-06-016540-5

FOREWORD

A year after the discovery of America the Pope divided up the world outside Europe among the most powerful nations of his own continent. A hundred years later Mercator completed his atlas. By this time the Europeanisation of the earth was already far advanced and his atlas was therefore the first expression of the geographical concept of the world in the age of colonialism.

Since then thousands of atlases have been published differing in many respects from Mercator's Atlas, but all adhering to his Eurocentric view of the world. All of them represent their own country, their own continent, as larger than the non-European countries through the use of different scales. If, together with the age of colonialism, the Eurocentric way of thinking is also to come to an end, we need a new geographical picture of the world based on the equal status of all the peoples of the earth.

This atlas represents all countries and continents at the same scale. Their size and their position in the world can therefore be immediately recognised from the map. This equal presentation of the world is the expression of the worldwide consciousness of solidarity which is beginning to overcome traditional Eurocentric thinking.

The basic change in our picture of the world achieved in this atlas required, in addition to equality of scale, also the projection principle of equality of area and a new, universally applicable representation of relief. All 246 thematic maps are also equal-area world maps, so that this comprehensive presentation of nature, man and society too is based on the same equal-status view of the world as the topogrpahic maps. In this way the atlas can contribute to an understanding of the causes and background of the North-South divide and the tensions between East and West, as an expression of the deep gulf between the poor and rich people and nations, and thus also to an understanding of the profound changes of our times.

Arno Peters

94

a b c d e f g h i j k l m

165°E   170°E   175°E   180°   175°W   170°W   165°W

A R C T I C

C H U K C H I
S E A

1097
Wrangel Island
De Long Strait

Ambarchik   Mal.
Baranikha   Pevek Krasnoarmeyskiy

Cherskiy   Retkucha

Little Anyuy   Ostrovnoy   1641   Mys
North Anyuskiy Mts.   Shmidta

South Anyuskiy Mts.   Ilirney   Plamennyy   Iultin

Great AnyuY   1707   2300
1313   1508

Arctic Circle   1504
Oloyskiy Mts.   Petushkova   Egvekinot

S O V I E T   U N I O N   Chukot Peninsula

Yeropol   Morokovo   Ust'-Belaya   (U. S. S. R.)   1250
2200   Krasnaya
Kolymskiy Mts.   Uel'kal   Yaranga   Uelen   Shishmaref

Anadyr'   Anadyr'   Nunligran   Akkani   Little   Wales   Seward
Markovo   Diomede   Teller
143
Velikaya   Gulf of Anadyr   Providentya   Nome
Penzhino
Berezovo   Tumanskiy   Gambell
Manily   Beringovskiy   Saint Lawrence Island
Koryak Mountains   (U.S.A.)   Alakanuk
Kovrizhka   Maynopil'gyn
2562   Khatyrka   Cape Navarin   Hooper
Dana   Bay   Cheva
Penzhinskiy Mts.   1285 Vatyna   Saint Matthew
Verkh.   Apuka
Pakhacha Chukotskaya   Nunivak
Olyutorskiy
Gulf of Penzhinskaya
Il'pyrskiy Korf   Cape Olyutorskiy

1700 Ossora
Ostrovnoy
Karaginskiy Island

B E R I N G

S E A

Pribilof Islands

Kamchatsk

2412

Podutesnaya
Komandor Islands   Unimak
(U.S.S.R.)
1327

Attu   GUDA

Near Islands
(U.S.A.)   Unimak Pass

Kiska   Andreanof Islands   Atka   Dutch
Rat Islands   Unalaska   Harbor
(U.S.A.)   Amchitka   Adak   Umnak   Fox Islands
A l e u t i a n   I s l a n

n o p q r s t u v w x y z

165°E   170°E   175°E   180°   175°W   170°W   165°W

53

This map shows 1/60 of the earth's surface. Area scale : 1 □ inch on the map ≈ 15,000 □ miles on the ground   1 □ cm on the map ≈ 6000 □ km on the ground

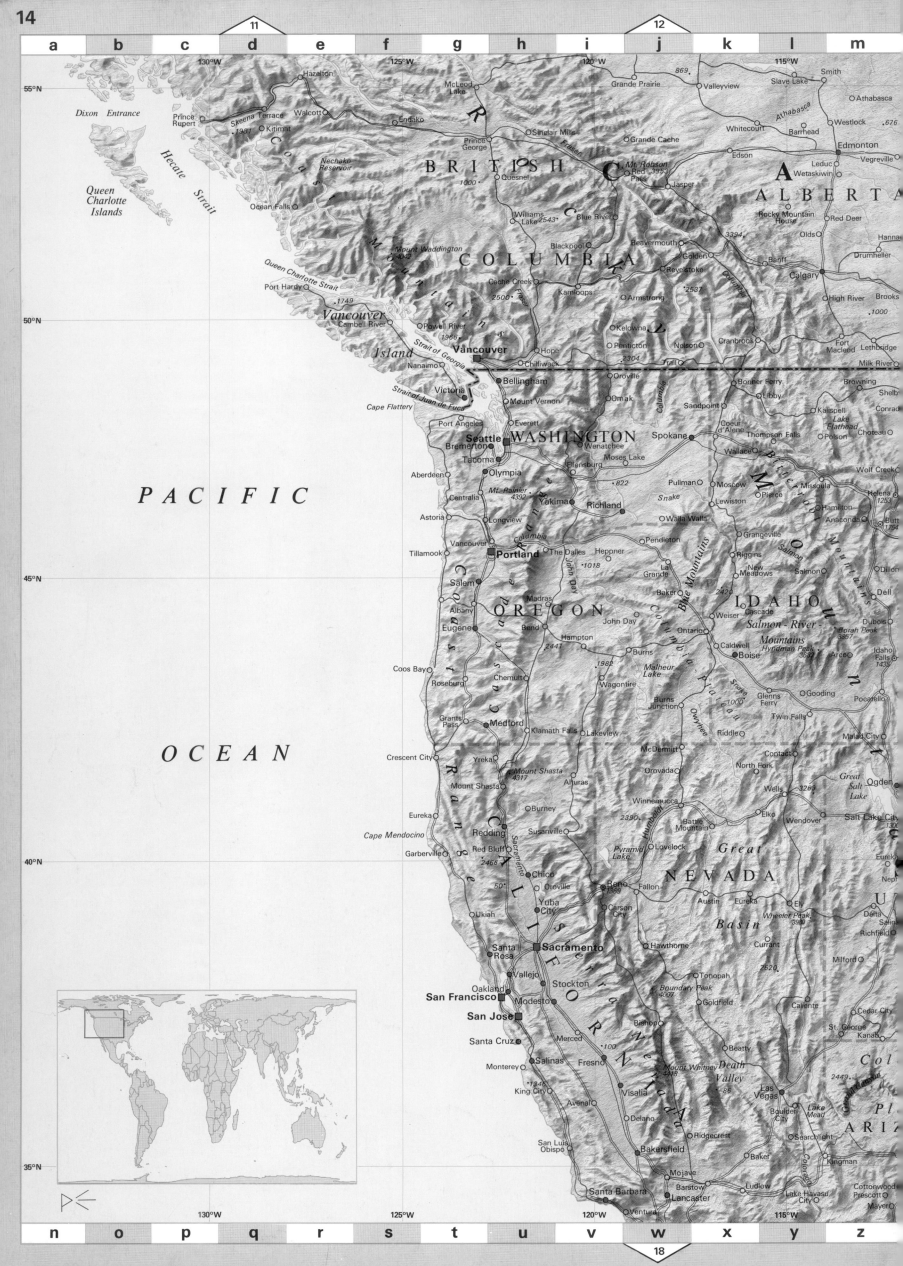

a b c d e f g h i j k l m

11 12

Dixon Entrance

Hazelton

55°N

McLeod Lake

Queen Charlotte Islands

Prince Rupert · Skeena · Terrace · Walcott

1981 · Kitimat · Endako

Hecate Strait

Sinclair Mills

Grande Prairie · Valleyview

869. Slave Lake · Smith

Athabasca

Whitecourt · Barrhead · Westlock

Grande Cache

676.

Prince George · Fraser · Edson

Edmonton

B R I T I S H · C O L U M B I A

Ocean Falls

1000 · Quesnel

Mt. Robson · Red 3953 · Pass

Jasper

Leduc · Vegreville

Wetaskiwin

A L B E R T A

Williams Lake 2543 · Blue River

Rocky Mountain House

Red Deer

Olds

Hanna

Nechako Reservoir

Blackpool · Beavermouth

3394.

Drumheller

Mount Waddington 4042

Cache Creek · 2500 · Kamloops

Golden · Banff

Calgary

Queen Charlotte Strait

1749

Armstrong · 2537.

Revelstoke

High River · Brooks

Port Hardy

Vancouver

Cambell River · Powell River · 1966

Kelowna · Nelson

Cranbrook

1000.

50°N

Penticton · 2304.

Trail

Fort Macleod · Lethbridge

Milk River

Island · *Strait of Georgia* · **Vancouver**

Nanaimo · Hope · Chilliwack

Oroville

Bonner Ferry

Browning

Strait of Juan de Fuca

Victoria · Bellingham

Mount Vernon · Omak

Libby

Shelb

Kalispell

Conrad

Cape Flattery

Port Angeles · Everett

Columbia · Sandpoint

Coeur d'Alene · Thompson Falls

Flathead Lake

Choteau

P A C I F I C

Seattle · W A S H I N G T O N

Bremerton · Wenatchee · Spokane

Wallace · Polson

Tacoma · Moses Lake

Missoula

Olympia · Ellensburg

822.

Moscow · Pierce

Helena 1253.

Aberdeen

Pullman · Snake · Lewiston

Hamilton · Anaconda · Butt 1754

Centralia · Mt. Rainier 4392 · Yakima · Richland

Walla Walla

Astoria

Longview

Pendleton

Grangeville

Wolf Creek

O C E A N

Tillamook

Vancouver

The Dalles · Heppner

1018.

La Grande · Baker

Riggins

New Meadows · Salmon

Dillon

Dell

Portland · *John Day*

Blue Mountains

2420.

I D A H O

Salem

45°N

Cascade

Albany · O R E G O N

Madras · Bend · John Day

Weiser

Salmon River Mountains

Dubois

Eugene

Hampton · 2441.

Ontario · Caldwell · Boise

Hyndman Peak 3682 · Borah Peak 3857

Arco

Idaho Falls 1435

Coos Bay

Chemult · 1982

Wagontire

Burns

Malheur Lake

Owyhee

Snake · 1000.

Glenns Ferry

Gooding

Pocatello

Roseburg

Burns Junction

Twin Falls

Grants Pass · Medford

Klamath Falls · Lakeview

McDermitt

Riddle

Malad City

Crescent City

Yreka

Orovada

North Fork

Contact

Great Salt Lake

Ogden

Mount Shasta 4317

Alturas

Winnemucca · 2390.

Wells · 3263

Mount Shasta

Burney

Wendover

Salt Lake City 131

Eureka

Eureka

Cape Mendocino

Susanville

Pyramid Lake · 2390.

Battle Mountain · Elko

Neph

Redding · Sacramento

Lovelock

Great

40°N

Garberville

Red Bluff · 2466.

Pyramid Lake

N E V A D A

Ely

Wheeler Peak 3980

Delta

Salina

Chico

Reno 1369 · Fallon

Austin · Eureka

Richfield

Ukiah

Oroville

Yuba City

Carson City

Basin

Milford

Santa Rosa

Sacramento

Hawthorne

2620.

San Francisco

Vallejo · Stockton

Tonopah

Goldfield

Cedar City

Oakland · Modesto

Boundary Peak 4007

Caliente

San Jose

Merced · 100.

Bishop

St. George

Kanab

Santa Cruz

Fresno

Mount Whitney 4418 · *Death Valley* -86

Beatty

Las Vegas

Monterey · Salinas

C A L I F O R N I A · *Sierra Nevada*

Visalia

Ridgecrest

Lake Mead

Col

35°N

King City · 1846.

Avenal · Delano

Boulder City · Searchlight

A R I Z

San Luis Obispo

Bakersfield

Baker

Kingman

Mojave · Barstow

Ludlow

Lake Havasu City

Cottonwood · Prescott

Santa Barbara · Lancaster

Ventura

2449.

Mayer

130°W · 125°W · 120°W · 115°W

n o p q r s t u v w x y z

18

This map shows 1/60 of the earth's surface. Area scale : 1 □ inch on the map ≈ 15,000 □ miles on the ground 1 □ cm on the map ≈ 6000 □ km on the ground

a b c d e f g h i j k l m

13

110°W   105°W   100°W   95°W   90°W

55°N

CANADA

Grand Centre
Beaver   Meadow Lake
.747
Lloydminster
Wainwright   North   Adanac
.914   Battleford   Biggar   Saskatoon
Kindersley   Rosetown   Davidson   Central Butte
Medicine Hat   Swift Current   Moose Jaw   Regina
Maple Creek   .1082   Milestone
Shaunavon   Assiniboia   Weyburn
Gladmar   Estevan   .1000

SASKATCHEWAN
North Saskatchewan
South Saskatchewan
Prince Albert   Melfort   Tisdale
Wynyard   Yorkton   Melville
Indian Head
.578   .500

Flin Flon   Wabowden
Lac La-Ronge   .365
Moose Lake
The Pas
Cedar Lake
Hudson Bay   .823
Swan River
Winnipegosis
Dauphin   Riverton
.710   Neepawa   Winnipeg Beach   Pinawa
Minnedosa   Winnipeg
Virden   Brandon   Portage la Prairie   Morden   Middleboro

MANITOBA
Lake Winnipegosis   Lake Winnipeg   Berens River
Lake Manitoba
217.
.305

Norway House
.178
Gods Lake
Island Lake

ONTARIO
Pipangikum Lake
Cat Lake
Red Lake   .359
Lake St. Joseph
Lake Seul
Sioux Lookout
Kenora   Dryden
Lake of the Woods
Fort Frances   Rainy Lake   English River   .500
Trans Canada Highway
Atikokan
International Falls   Upper Red Lake   Lower Red Lake

Bearskin Lake
Sandy Lake
North Caribou Lake
.396
Wunnummin Lake
Albany
Lake St. Joseph
Grand Marais   .646
Thunder Bay

50°N

Westhope   Kenmare   Langdon
Chester   Havre   Malta   Wolf Point   Stanley   Rugby   Grafton
Big Sandy   Glasgow   Culbertson   Williston   Minot   Devils Lake   .300
Milk   Fort Peck Reservoir   Sidney
Vaughn   Missouri   Jordan
Great Falls   Lewiston
Stanford   Glendive   .1108
Miles City   Bismarck

MONTANA
Townsend   Roundup   Forsyth   Baker   .1076   Lemmon
Harlowtown   Billings   Hardin   Ashland   Broadus   Buffalo   Bison
Livingston   Bozeman   Ennis   .3917   Granite Peak
Sheridan   Gillette   Spearfish
Canyon   Cody   Grey Bull   .4016   Cloud Peak
Worland   Newcastle
Moran   Kaycee   Sundance

NORTH DAKOTA
Carrington
Valley City
Jamestown   Fargo   Moorhead
Frederick   .500   Oakes
Mobridge   Selby   Aberdeen
Lake Oahe   Gettysburg
Pierre
Huron   Watertown

SOUTH DAKOTA
Chamberlain   Mitchell
White River   .436
Rapid City   .2184
Black Hills   Cheyenne

Thief River Falls
Crookston
Bemidji   Hibbing   Virginia
Grand Rapids
Fergus Falls   Brainerd   .381   Lake Mille
Alexandria   Little Falls
Sisseton   Ortonville   Willmar   St. Cloud   Rice Lake
MINNESOTA   Pine City
.619   Montevideo   Minneapolis St. Paul
Marshall   New Ulm   Faribault
Brookings   Fairmont   Albert Lea   Austin
Worthington   Mankato   Rochester

Duluth   Superior   Apostle Islands
Lake Superior
Cloquet   Ashland   Ironwood
Rhinelander
Chippewa Falls   Wausau   Merrill
Eau Claire   Ladysmith
River Falls   Red Wing
WISCONSIN
Tomah   La Crosse
Decorah   Portage
Mason City   Madison   .436

45°N

WYOMING
Jackson   .4202   Gannett Peak
Daniel   Lander   Riverton   Casper   .1561   Douglas   Alcova
Kemmerer   Rawlins   Sweetwater   Muddy Gap
Montpelier   Eden
Rock Springs   Laramie   Cheyenne   .1848

UNITED
Chadron   Valentine
Newcastle   Hot Springs   Niobrara
Lusk   Chadron
Alliance   Bassett   O'Neill
Scottsbluff   Thedford   .700
Chugwater   **NEBRASKA**
Sidney   North Platte

Storm Lake
Spencer   Estherville
Webster City   Waterloo
Sioux City   Fort Dodge   Dubuque
IOWA
Randolph   Cedar Rapids   Rockford
Norfolk   Ames   Iowa City   Rochelle
Denison   Newton   Des Moines   Moline
Columbus   Omaha   Council Bluffs   Davenport   Princeton
Knoxville   Oskaloosa   Ottumwa   Burlington   Galesburg
Lincoln   Creston   Shenandoah
Nebraska City   Peoria
Bloomington
ILLINOIS   40°N

Mexican Water   Farmington
Page   Moenkopi   Chinle
NEW   Gallup   Houck
Humphreys Peak   Winslow   .62
Flagstaff   Holbrook   Show Low

MEXICO
Los Alamos   Santa Fe   .2132
Albuquerque   .1509   Grants
Santa Rosa   .1516
Belen   Vaughn
Clovis   Tucumcari
Hereford   Tulia
TEXAS   Amarillo   Shamrock

Steamboat Springs   Walden   Fort Collins   Greeley
Craig   Vernal   .4123 Uinta Mts.   Boulder   .1655   Sterling
Heber City   Green River   Rifle   Glenwood Springs   Denver   .1608
Price   Mack   Grand Junction   **COLORADO**   Limon   Burlington
Green River   Moab   Montrose   .4399 Mt. Elbert   Colorado Springs   .1833
.1500   Monticello   Pikes Peak   .4300   Kit Carson
Lake Powell   Blanding   Durango   Canon City   Pueblo   .1431
San Juan   **Mountains**   Walsenburg   La Junta   Lamar
San Juan   Trinidad   Springfield   Garden City   Dodge City
Raton   Wheeler Peak   .4011   Clayton   Boise City   Liberal
Sangre de Cristo Range   Wagon Mound   Dalhart   Guymon   Perryton

TATES
Norton   Concordia   St. Joseph   Atchison
McCook   Beatrice   Bethany   Kirksville   .300   Quincy   Macon   Jacksonville   Springfield
Republican   .500   St. Joseph   Chillicothe   Hannibal
Junction City   Manhattan   Leavenworth   Litchfield   Alton
Salina   Topeka   Kansas City   Independence   Columbia   Marshall   .307
Hays   Ottawa   Sedalia   Clinton   Jefferson City   Vandalia
KANSAS   Emporia   Lebanon   St. Louis   Festus
Hutchinson   Nevada   Mount Vernon
Pratt   El Dorado   Fort Scott   **MISSOURI**   Ozark   Rolla   Perryville   Cape Girardeau   .540
Bucklin   Wichita   .512   Joplin   Bolivar   Springfield   Cabool   Cairo
Arkansas City   Independence   Aurora   Neosho   Branson   .411   Poplar Bluff
Ponca City   Miami   Dyersburg

35°N

OKLAHOMA
Enid   Oologah Lake   Ozark Plateau
Woodward   Tulsa   Fayetteville   Marshall   Hardy   Newport
Guthrie   Muskogee   Fort Smith   Clarksville   Jonesboro   West Memphis
Oklahoma City   Shawnee   Henryetta   McAlester   Memphis
Clinton   Hobart   Chickasha   Ada   **ARKANSAS**
Canadian   Altus   Lawton   Little Rock   .722   Brinkley   Pine Bluff   White   Mississippi

n o p q r s t u v w x y z

19

110°W   105°W   100°W   95°W   90°W

0   100   200   300 miles
Average linear scale: 1 inch ≈ 125 miles   1cm ≈ 80 km
0   100   200   300   400   500 Km

16

a b c d e f g h i j k l m

95°W 90°W 85°W 80°W 75°W

MANITOBA
55°N

Shamattawa
Fort Severn
Winisk
Hudson Bay
Cape Henrietta Maria
Belcher Islands
Great Whale
Lac l'Eau Claire
Kuujjuarapik
Kanaaupscow

Gods Lake
Bearskin Lake
Big Trout Lake
Winisk
Winisk
Point Louis XIV
James Bay
.168
Chisasibi
La Radisson
Sakami
La Gran

Island Lake
Sandy Lake .276
North Caribou Lake
Wunnummin Lake
Attawapiskat
Akimiki Island
.195

Pipangikum Lake
Cat Lake .396
Attawapiskat Lake
Lake River
Fort Albany
.100
Eastmain
Eastmain
Lake Mistass

Red Lake .359
Lake St. Joseph
Ogoki
Fort Hope 268.
Albany
Moosonee
Hannah Bay
Fort Rupert
Rupert
QUEBEC
Lake Evans .232

Pinawa
Kenora Dryden Trans .317
Armstrong 358.
Lake Nipigon
Nakina
Longlac
Geraldton
Hearst
Fraserdale
Kesagami Lake
Kapuskasing Cochrane
Harricana
Matagami
Chibougamau
Chapais .556

50°N Middleboro
Sioux Lookout
English River
Nipigon .500
Schreiber
Manitouwadge
Marathon
White River
.390
Timmins
Monts Deloge .533
Lake Abitibi
Noranda
Val-d'Or
Senneterre
Gouin Reservoir

Thief River Falls
International Falls Fort Frances
Rainy Lake Atikokan
Thunder Bay
Grand Marais
Isle Royale
Wawa
Chapleau
.640
New Liskeard .693
Kirkland Lake
Témiscaming
Cabonga Reservoir .609

Lower Red Lake 358.
Upper Red Lake
Virginia .416
Lake Superior
Copper Harbor
.665
Blind River
Espanola
Sudbury
Sturgeon Falls
North Bay .796
Mont Laurier

Hibbing
Bemidji 436. Grand Rapids
Duluth Superior
Ashland Ironwood .573
Houghton .603
Marquette
Sault Ste. Marie
Seney
322. Little Current
Manitoulin Island
Tobermory
Parry Sound
Huntsville
Pembroke
Maniwaki .960

Fergus Falls 381.
Brainerd Mille Lacs
Cloquet
Rice Lake .454
Rhinelander
Iron Mountain
Escanaba
Mackinaw City
Petoskey
Alpena
Georgian Bay
Owen Sound
Bancroft .419
Buckingham Hull Ottawa
Montréal
Ste-Agathe-des-Monts St-Jérô

MINNESOTA
Alexandria
Pine City
St. Cloud
Ladysmith Merrill Wausau
Menominee Marinette
Sturgeon Bay
Cadillac
Grayling
Port Elgin
Orillia Lake Simcoe
Midland .573
Barrie
Perth Smith's Falls
Brockville
Cornwall Salaberry-De-Valleyfi
Burlin

Willmar
45°N Minneapolis St. Paul
Minnesota River Falls
Eau Claire Chippewa Falls
WISCONSIN
Stevens Point
Appleton
Green Bay
Manitowoc
MICHIGAN
Bay City Midland Saginaw
Goderich
Kitchener-Waterloo
Hamilton .200
Toronto
Oshawa
Peterborough
Kingston
Belleville
Waterton .637
NEW YORK
Glen Falls .190

15 Marshall New Ulm .510
Faribault
Marshfield
Oshkosh .223
Sheboygan
Luddington
Muskegon
Grand Rapids
Lansing
Flint .385
Sarnia
London
St. Thomas
Buffalo
Niagara Falls
St. Catharines
Rochester Syracuse
Adirondack Mountains
Utica
Schenectady
Albany Pittsfie

Mankato Rochester
Winona Tomah
La Crosse Portage .369
Madison Milwaukee
Racine
Kenosha
Kalamazoo
Battle Creek
Ann Arbor .358
Détroit
Windsor
Lake Erie
Fredonia
Dansville
Seneca Lake
Ithaca Elmira
Binghampton .1284
Catskill Mountains .1269
Kingston Hud

Fairmont
Albert Lea Austin Decorah
Dubuque .436
Janesville Beloit
Rockford
Freeport
Elgin De Kalb
Chicago
South Bend
Toledo
Sandusky
Ashtabula .775
Erie
Meadville .424
Olean Kane Mansfield
Williamsport
Scranton .578
Danbury Bridgepor

Storm Lake Fort Dodge
Webster City
Waterloo
Cedar Rapids
IOWA
Iowa City
Moline
Joliet
Gary
Napoleon
Cleveland
Youngstown
PENNSYLVANIA
Clearfield .424
Altoona
Harrisburg
Reading Trenton
Allentown Newark Elizabeth
Paterson
Newburgh

Omaha
Council Bluffs .290
Newton
Des Moines
Davenport
Rochelle
Morris
Kankakee
Fort Wayne
Findlay
Canton
Mansfield
Johnstown .956 Greensburg .706
New Philadelph

Creston
Shenandoah
Nebraska City
Bethany
Peoria 236.
Bloomington
Lafayette
Rantoul
Kokomo
Lima
Kenton
Pittsburgh
Wheeling
Cumberland .1222
Hagerstown
MARYLAND
Lancaster Wilmington
NEW JERSEY

40°N St. Joseph
Atchison
Kirksville .300
ILLINOIS
Quincy Beardstown Decatur
Champaign
Danville
Muncie
Springfield
Columbus
Anderson
OHIO
Newark .424
Cambridge
Fairmont Clarksburg .1222
Marietta
Bickle Knob .Elkins
Baltimore Washington DC
Annapolis
DELAWARE
Cape May
Atlantic City
Vineland

Leavenworth .367
Kansas City
Independence
Columbia
Macon Hannibal
Jacksonville
Springfield
Terre Haute
INDIANA
Bloomington .322
Cincinatti
Dayton
Richmond
Chillicothe
Athens .412
Parkersburg
WEST VIRGINIA
Spruce Knob .1476
Charlottesville
Arlington Alexandria Cambridge
Culpeper Fredericksburg
Lexington Park Salisbury

Topeka
Ottawa Emporia
Sedalia
Clinton
MISSOURI
Jefferson City
St Louis
Festus
Vandalia
Effingham .322
Bedford
Maysville
Louisville
Lexington
Huntington
Charleston
Richwood
Williamson .1222
Beckley
VIRGINIA .1241
Roanoke
Petersburg
Williamsburg Hampton
Newport News 28°

Fort Scott .300
Nevada
Lebanon
Rolla
Sullivan
Lake Ozark
Cape Girardeau
Cairo
Paducah
Central City
Berea
Hazard
Pikeville .1743
Bluefield
Wytheville Marion Mount Rogers
Martinsville Danville
Lynchburg
Richmond
Norfolk

Independence Parsons
Bolivar
Springfield .510
Caboool
Poplar Bluff
KENTUCKY
Bowling Green Glasgow
Lake Cumberland
Somerset
Kingsport Mount Airy
Mount Rogers .784
Roanoke Rapids
Ahoskie
Elizabeth City

35°N Miami Bartlesville
Neosho Branson
Hardy
Clarksville Dyersburg
Clarksville .307
Nashville
Oak Ridge .1072
Knoxville .2025
Clingmans Dome
Winston Salem
Greensboro Durham
Rocky Mount

Tulsa Tahlequah
Fayetteville Marshall Jonesboro
Blytheville
ARKANSAS
Jackson Columbia
Murfreesboro
TENNESSEE
Clingmans Dome .816
Asheville
Hendersonville
Hickory
Kannapolis
NORTH CAROLINA
Raleigh Roanoke
Greenville
Pamlico Sound
Cape Hatteras

McAlester
Fort Smith Poteau
Henryetta
Little Rock
Brinkley
West Memphis
Memphis .100
Savannah
Lawrenceburg
Fayetteville .878
Chattanooga
Cleveland
Charlotte
Rockingham
Fayetteville
New Bern
Morehead City

95°W 90°W 85°W 80°W 75°W

n o p q r s t u v w x y z

This map shows 1/60 of the earth's surface. Area scale : 1 □ inch on the map ≃ 15,000 □ miles on the ground 1 □ cm on the map ≃ 6000 □ km on the ground

70°W   65°W   60°W   55°W

Lake
Bienville

Caniapiscau

55°N

Scheffervilie

Atikamagen
Lake

N E W F O U N D L A N D

Hopedale

Makkovik

Caniapiscau
Reservoir

640.

Petitsikapau
Lake

945.

Canairiktok

Keyano

Rivière

.914 Nitchequon

Labrador City
Wabush

Twin Falls .562

Smallwood
Reservoir

Lookout Mountain

Naskaupi

North-West River
Happy Valley-Goose Bay

Churchill

Hamilton Inlet

Rigolet

Cartwright

Lake
Melville

.995

Otish Mountains

.1128

Lake
Joseph

Atikonak
Lake
.120

L a b r a d o r

.995

Fox Harbour

Albanel
Lake 713 E

Lake
Plétipi

.948

Gagnon

Manicouagan
Reservoir

Ste.-Marguerite

805.

B E

Natashquan

.125

Romaine

Cape
Whittle

C

Harrington
Harbour

St.-Augustin

St.-Paul

Strait of Belle Isle

St.-Augustin

Flower's Cove

St. Anthony

50°N

Manicouagan

Sept-Îles

Havre-S.-Pierre

Natashquan

Long Range

656.

Rocky
Harbour

806.

Nôtre Dame
Bay

Mistassini

Pipmuacan
Reservoir

Port-Cartier

A

Anticosti Island

.312

Port Menier

Gulf of

Springdale

Corner
Brook

Lewis Hill
.814

.518

Buchans

Windsor

Gander

N E W F O U N D L A N D

Lake
St-Jean
Alma

Baie Comeau

Ste-Anne-
des-Monts

.1268
Mount
Jacques
Cartier

Murdochville

Gaspé

St. Lawrence

Stephenville

.381

Roberval
Chicoutimi
Jonquière

Saguenay

Escoumins

Matane

Mont-Joli
Rimouski

New
Richmond

Chandler

Miscou Point

Magdalen
Islands

Channe -Port-
aux-Basques

St. Alban's

St. John's

Grand
Bank

La Tuque
.166

St.-Siméon

Rivière-
du-Loup

Campbelltown
.493

Mount
Carleton
.820

Bathurst

Cabot Strait

St. Pierre
and Viquelon
(France)

Grand-
Mère
Québec

Montmagny

Édmundston

Van Buren

Newcastle

N E W

Alberton

PRINCE EDWARD
ISLAND

Cape
North

.531

Cape Race

Shawinigan
Ste-Foy
Trois Rivières

Île d'Orléans

Presque Isle

Woodstock

Northumberland

St. Eleanors
.142

Charlottetown

Glace
Bay

Drummondville
St.-Georges

B R U N S W I C K

Strait

Sydney

St.-Hyacinthe

Sherbrooke
.884

1605.

East
Millinocket

Fredericton

Moncton

Amherst

.367

Truro

New
Glasgow

Mulgrave

.331

386.

Dover
Foxcroft

St. Stephen

Saint
John

N O V A
S C O T I A

45°N

Lake
Champlain

Berlin

Rumford

Bangor

M A I N E

Middleton

Halifax

Dartmouth

Waterville

Bay of Fundy

.85

Bridgewater

Barre

Mount
Washington
1917

Augusta

Hulls Cove

Yarmouth

Hanover

Brunswick

Shelburne

Rutland

Lewiston

Laconia

Portland

Cape Sable

Concord

.1164

Rochester

Portsmouth

Wausau

Manchester
Haverhill

A T L A N T I C

MASSACHUSETTS

Boston
Worcester

Springfield

Cape Cod

Hartford

Providence

New Bedford

Waterbury
New Haven

RHODE ISLAND

CONNECTICUT

Calverton

Southampton

Long Island

York

O C E A N

40°N

70°W   65°W   60°W   55°W   35°N

0 100 200 300 miles   Average linear scale: 1 inch≈125 miles 1cm≈30 km   0 100 200 300 400 500 Km

35°N 120°W

Santa Barbara
Santa Cruz
Santa Rosa
San Nicolas
San Clemente
Channel Islands
Santa Catalina

Mojave
Lancaster
San Bernardino
Los Angeles
Long Beach
Anaheim
Santa Ana
Palm Springs
Oceanside
Escondido
El Cajon
San Diego
Tijuana
Rosarito
La Misión
Ensenada

Barstow
Ludlow
115°W
Blythe

CALIFORNIA

Kingman
Cottonwood
Lake Havasu City
Mayer

Flagstaff
Holbrook
110°W
Show Low

Albuquerque 105°W
Belen
Santa Rosa Hereford

ARIZONA

Phoenix
Mesa
Globe

Magdalena
Socorro

NEW

Vaughn
Clovis
Portales

Casa Grande
Safford

UNITED

Alamogordo
Artesia
Hobbs
Carlsbad

Sierra Blanca Peak

Roswell
Levelland

MEXICO

Tucson

Lordsburg Las Cruces
Deming
El Paso

Silver City

Ciudad Juárez

Midland

Guadalupe Peak

Mexicali
Calexico
Yuma
Rio Colorado
San Luis

Colorado
Gila Desert

Sonoyta

Pinacate Desert
Cerro Pinacate

Altar Desert

Sonoyta

Sásabe
Nogales
Sierra Vista
Douglas
Agua Prieta

Ascensión
El Porvenir
Janos
Van Horn
Fort Stockton

Alpine

San Vincente
Colnet
El Chinero
San Felipe
Agua de Chale

Puerto Peñasco
El Socorro
Tajito
Caborca

Tubutama
Magdalena
Santa Ana
Arizpe

Cananea

Bavispe

Nuevo Casas Grandes

Buenaventura

Villa Ahumada

El Sueco

Sanderson

30°N

Rosario de Arriba
Misión San Fernando

Cape Lobos

Angel de la Guarda

Carbó
Hermosillo

Moctezuma

San Lorenzo
Estación Babicora
Madera
Temósachic
Bachinivas

Ojinaga

El Carrizalillo

Emory Peak

Rio Grande

Guadalupe
Punta Prieta
Los Angeles
Rosarito
Tiburón

Sebastián Vizcaino Bay
Cedros

Avispas
Soyapa
Nuri

Yepachic
Yécora

Chihuahua
La Junta
Cuauhtémoc
Meoqui
Delicias
Saucillo

San Guillermo
El Sauz
Aldama

Llanos de los Caballos Mestenos
Las Entimias

Tanque El Revés

La Ojo de Liebre
El Arco
Volcán Tres Virgenes
Santa Rosalía

Ciudad Camargo
La Vibora
Cuatrociénegas

Guaymas
Guásimas
Empalme
Esperanza
Torim
Ciudad Obregón

Macuarichic
Boquilla Reservoir
San Francisco del Oro
Santa Barbara
Guazaparés
Hidalgo del Parral
Villa Ocampo
Jiménez

La Campana

Vizcaino Desert
Laguna San Ignacio
Ballenas Bay

Navojoa
Alamos
Huatabampo
Las Bocas

San Blas
El Fuerte
Guadalupe y-Calvo

Santa Maria
Bermejillo

La Campana
San Pedro de las Colonias

San Juanico
Loreto
Carmen
Santa Catalina
Ahome

Los Mochis
Guasave

Topia
Santiago Papasquiaro

Gómez Palacio
Lerdo
Torreón
Matamoros
Yermo

Ejido Insurgentes
San Carlos
Cape San Lázaro
Los Burros
Quiñones

San José
La Paz
Espíritu Santo
Las Cruces

Pericos
Navolato
Culiacán
El Dorado

Cosalá

La Manch

Durango

Canatlan
Guadalupe Victoria
Nazas

Rio Grand

25°N

Rocas Alijos

La Paz
El Triunfo
Todos Santos
Cape San Lucas
San Lucas

El Salto
La Pañila

Mazatlán
Villa Unión

Dimas

Mezquital

Fresnil

Tropic of Cancer

Escuinapa
Acaponeta

Zacatecas
Jerez

Tecuala
Tuxpan
Santiago Ixcuintla

Mesa del Nayar

Aguascalientes
Tlaltenango

Tres Marias Islands
Maria Madre
Maria Magdalena
Maria Cleofas

Tepic
Compostela
Ixtlán

Juchipila
San Franc del Rinc

160°W
Kauai
Haena
Nihau
Mana
Lihue
Kaula

Oahu
Pearl City
Kaneohe
Waipahu
Honolulu
Molokai
Halawa
Maunaloa
Maunalua
Wailuku
Maui
Lanai
Kahului
Kahoolawe

20°N

Hawaiian Islands

Hawi
Mauna Kea
Kailua
Hawaii
Mauna Loa
Hilo

Naalehu

These islands lie approximately 4000 kilometres to the west of here, in the Pacific Ocean.

160°W

Banderas Bay
Puerto Vallarta
Ameca

Guadalajara
La Pieda
Ocotlan
Lake Chapala
La Barca
Cocula
Sahuayo
Zamora
Tamazula

Tomatlán
Autlán

Sayula
Cd Guzman
Tecalitlan

20°N

Nev. de Colima
Tenacatita
Barra de Navidad

San Benedicto

Revilla Gigedo Islands
Roca Partida
Socorro

Colima
Uruapan

Mazamitla
Apatzingán
Tecomán

Playa Azul

P A C I F I C

Clarión

O C E A N

15°N

115°W 110°W 105°W

This map shows 1/60 of the earth's surface. Area scale : 1 □ inch on the map ≈ 15,000 □ miles on the ground   1 □ cm on the map ≈ 6000 □ km on the ground

OKLAHOMA

Oklahoma City
Henryetta
Poteau
Ada
McAlester
Sherman
Paris

95°W
Fort Smith
Clarksville
Conway
Little Rock
Pine Bluff
Arkadelphia
122

90°W
West Memphis
Memphis
Savannah
Corinth

Newport

Jackson
Lawrenceburg
Florence
Huntsville

TENNESSEE
Cleveland
Chattanooga
Fayetteville
879

85°W
Hendersonville

Asheville
NORTH
Rock Hill
Spartanburg

80°W
Charlotte
Rockingham

35°N

Fort Worth
Irving
Garland
Arlington Dallas
Sulphur Springs

Waco
Temple
Killeen

TEXAS
233

Nacogdoches
Lufkin
Jasper

Tyler
Marshall

LOUISIANA

Shreveport
Natchitoches
Alexandria
113

Minden
Monroe
Vicksburg

Lake Providence
67

MISSISSIPPI
152
Columbus
Winona
149

Jackson
Brookhaven
Hattiesburg
Laurel
Meridian

McComb

Greenville
Tuscaloosa
Bessemer
Birmingham

Selma
Montgomery
Greenville
Andalusia

ALABAMA

Opelika
Phenix City
Columbus
Eufaula
Dawson
Albany

GEORGIA
Macon
425
Warner Robins
Dublin
Statesboro
Tifton

Gadsden
Marietta
Atlanta
College Park
Athens

Decatur
Cullman

Dalton
Gainesville
Anderson
Greenville

SOUTH
CAROLINA
Columbia
Augusta
Clinton Camden
Florence

Lake City
Walterboro
Charleston

Savannah

30°N

Austin
New Braunfels
Gonzales
Bryan
Huntsville
Houston
Baytown
Texas City
Galveston

Victoria
Lake Jackson

Colorado

Beaumont
Lake Charles
Lafayette
New Iberia
Houma

Baton Rouge
Hammond
Slidell
New Orleans

Gulfport
Biloxi
Pascagoula

Mobile
Crestview
Fort Walton Beach
Pensacola

Panama City

Cape San Blas

Marianna
Thomasville
Tallahassee
Chattahoochee

Live Oak
Perry

Apalachee Bay

Valdosta
Waycross
Jesup
Brunswick

Fernandina Beach
Jacksonville

Lake City
Gainesville
Chiefland

Ocala
Crystal River
Leesburg

St. Augustine

Palatka
Lake George

Daytona Beach

Mississippi Delta

Corpus Christi
Kingsville

Three Rivers
50

McAllen
Harlingen
Brownsville
Matamoros

Laguna Madre

25°N

La Carbonera

Laguna Madre

Gulf of

Mexico

Altamonte Springs
Winter Garden
Orlando
Titusville
Cape Canaveral
Melbourne

Tampa
Largo
St. Petersburg
Bradenton
Sarasota

Lakeland
Brandon
Avon Park

FLORIDA

Fort Pierce

Port Charlotte
Cape Coral
Fort Myers

Naples

Cape Romano

Everglades

Lake Okeechobee
Pahokee

West Palm Beach
Fort Lauderdale

Miami

Cape Sable

Florida Bay

Key Largo

Key West

Havana
Matanzas

Pinar del Río
Güines
Colón
Sagua

Cienfuegos

Santa Clara
1156

Trinidad

Isla de Pinos

Ciudad Madero
Tampico
Pánuco

Laguna de Tamiahua

Potrero del Llano
Tuxpan
Poza Rica
Papantla
Huachinango
Martínez de la Torre
Tlapacoyan
Tecolutla

20°N
Teziutlán
Perote
Jalapa
Apizaco
Orizaba
Coscomatepec
Veracruz
Córdoba
Puebla
Alvarado
Tlacotalpan

Desterrada
Pérez

Arenas
Nuevo

Triangulos

Arcas

Bay of

Campeche

Champotón

Río Lagartos
Dzilam de Bravo
Progreso
Motul
Mérida
Izamal
8

Maxcanú
Calkiní
Bolonchén de Rejón
Campeche
Sihochac

Tizimín
Espita

Valladolid

Ticul
Tekax
100
Peto

Cape Catoche
Chiquilá

Puerto Juárez
Cancún
Puerto Morelos

Tulum

Yucatán

Cozumel

Ascensión Bay

Yucatan Channel

Guanahacabibes
Peninsula

Cape Corrientes

Georgetown

Little Cayman
Cayman Islands
(U.K.)

Grand Cayman

San Andrés Tuxtla
1877

Coatzacoalcos
Minatitlán
Villahermosa

Ciudad del Carmen
Frontera
Comalcalco

Laguna de Términos

Mamantel
310

Felipe Carrillo Puerto

Espíritu Santo Bay

Yucatán

Peninsula

Gulf

of

CARIB

Huajuapan de León
Coixtlahuaca
Nochixtlán
Oaxaca
Mitla
1546

Tierra Blanca
Tuxtepec
Acayucan

Isthmus of

MEXICO

Tehuantepec

Macuspana
Balancán
Tenosique
Palenque
Chichén
222

San Cristóbal de las Casas
Comitán

Altamira

Flores

Hondo

Chetumal

BELIZE
Belize

Belmopan

Turneffe Islands

Honduras

Puebla
Onizaba

Jesús Carranza

Morelos

Mazatlán

Tapachula

Tehuantepec

Tierra Colorada

Jesús
Amatenango

Huixtla

Pinotepa Nacional
Puerto Escondido
Puerto Ángel

Gulf of

Tehuantepec

Juchitán
Salina Cruz
Mar Muerto

Arriaga
Tonalá

GUATEMALA
Lago de Izabal

Motagua 90°W

Puerto Barrios

1122

Puerto Cortés
San Pedro Sula

Roatán

Bay Islands
Utila

Tela
La Ceiba

HONDURAS

Guanaja
Trujillo

Cape Gracias á Dios

15°N
95°W

This map shows 1/60 of the earth's surface. Area scale: 1 ☐ inch on the map ≏ 15,000 ☐ miles on the ground 1 ☐ cm on the map ≏ 6000 ☐ km on the ground

75°W 70°W 65°W

35°N

ROLINA
Goldsboro
.50
Fayetteville
New Bern
Jacksonville
Lumberton
Morehead City
Wilmington
Myrtle Beach
Georgetown

A T L A N T I C

30°N

Sargasso Sea

O C E A N

Grand Bahama Island
Great Abaco Island

Nicholls Town
Nassau
Eleuthera

25°N

New Providence
Behring Point
Cat
Andros Islands

San Salvador

BAHAMAS

Rum Cay
Great Exuma Island
Long Island

Great Bahama Bank

Crooked Island

Morón
Acklins
acetas
Ciego de Ávila
piritus
Nuevitas

Mayaguana Island

Camagüey

Grand Caicos

UBA

Victoria de las Tunas
Banes

Turks and Caicos Islands (U.K.)

Holguín

Great Inagua Island

Bayamo
Palma Soriano
Baracoa
Manzanillo
Santiago de Cuba
Guantánamo
Niquero
2005
Port-de-Paix

20°N

DOMINICAN

Cap-Haïtien
Puerto Plata
Santiago
REPUBLIC
Gonaïves
Neiba
La Vega
San Francisco de Macorís
HAITI
St-Marc
3175
San Juan
Virgin Islands
JAMAICA
Anse d'Hainault
Port-au-Prince
2680
Puerto Rico (U.S.A.)
Montego Bay
Spanish Town
Les Cayes
Jacmel
Barahona
Santo Domingo
La Romana
Mayagüez
Bayamón
San Juan
Carolina
May Pen
Caguas
A
1338
Ponce
Kingston
n
t
St. Croix (U.S.A.)
Anguilla
St. Martin Philipsburg
B
i
Netherlands Antilles
Codrington
Barbuda
ANTIGUA AND
E
l
BARBUDA
l
Basseterre
ST KITTS
St. John's
A
e
NEVIS
Antigua
Montserrat (U.K.)
Plymouth
N
s
Guadeloupe (France)
Pointe-à-Pitre
Leeward Islands
Basse-Terre
S E A
DOMINICA
Roseau

15°N

75°W 70°W 65°W

0 100 200 300 miles
Average linear scale : 1 inch ≈ 125 miles   1 cm ≈ 80 km
0 100 200 300 400 500 Km

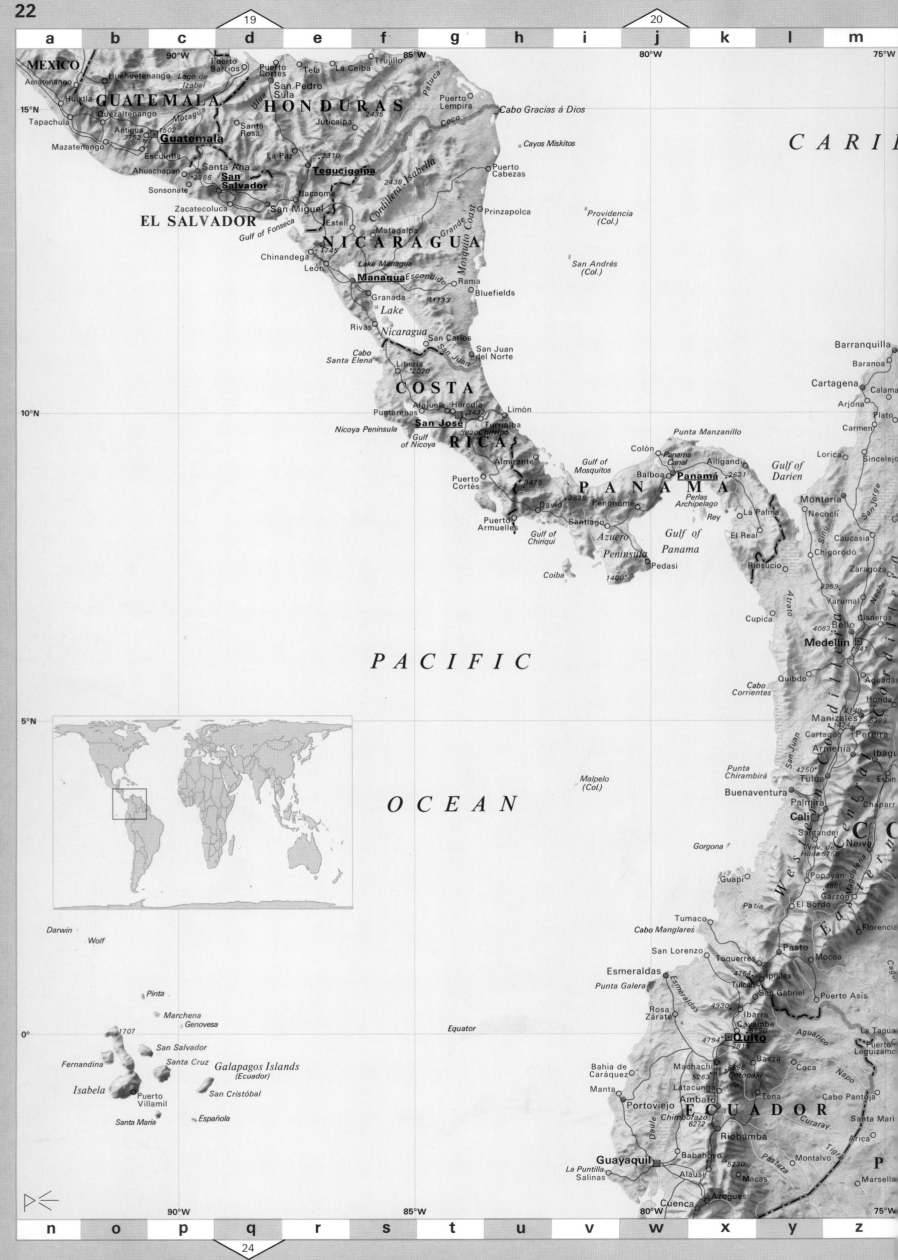

MEXICO

90°W 85°W 80°W 75°W

GUATEMALA HONDURAS

C A R I B

Amatenango
Huehuetenango
Lago de Izabal
Puerto Barrios
Puerto Cortés
Tela
La Ceiba
Trujillo
Patuca

15°N
Huixtla
Quezaltenango
San Pedro Sula
Cabo Gracias á Dios
Tapachula
Antigua ·3752
·1502
Santa Rosa
Motagua
Juticalpa
Puerto Lempira
Coco

Mazatenango
Guatemala
Escuintla
La Paz
·2310
Puerto Cabezas
Cayos Miskitos

Ahuachapan
Santa Ana
Tegucigalpa
·2438
Isabella
Prinzapolca
Providencia (Col.)

Sonsonate
·2386
San Salvador
Nacaome
San Miguel

Zacatecoluca
EL SALVADOR
Estelí
NICARAGUA
Matagalpa
Grande
Mosquito Coast
San Andrés (Col.)

Gulf of Fonseca
·1745
Rama
Bluefields

Chinandega
Lake Managua
Escondido
·1133

León
Managua
Barranquilla
Baranoa

Granada
Lake
Cartagena
Calam
10°N
Rivas
Nicaragua
San Carlos
San Juan del Norte
Arjona
Plato

Cabo Santa Elena
San Juan
Carmen

Liberia ·2020
COSTA
Lorica
Sincelejo

Alajuela
Heredia
Limón
Punta Manzanillo
Gulf of Darien

Puntarenas
San José
·3820
Chirripó
Turrialba
Colón
Panama Canal
Ailligandi
Montería
Necoclí

Nicoya Peninsula
·3432
RICA
PANAMA
Balboa
Panamá
·2621
San Jorge

Gulf of Nicoya
Almirante
Gulf of Mosquitos
Perlas Archipelago
Caucasia

Puerto Cortés
·3475
David
·2826
Penonomé
Rey
La Palma
Gulf of Darien
Chigorodó

Puerto Armuelles
Santiago
El Real
Zaragoza

Gulf of Chiriqui
Azuero
Gulf of Panama
Riosucio
·3959

Coiba
Peninsula
·1400
Pedasi
Cupica
Atrato
Yarumal

Cabo Corrientes
·4083
Bello
Cisneros

PACIFIC
Medellín
·341
Quibdó
Aguadas

5°N
·2140
Manizales
·8389
·1424

Cartago
Pereira
Ibagu

Punta Chirambirá
·4250
Tuluá
Armenia
Espin

Buenaventura
Palmira
Chaparr

O C E A N
Malpelo (Col.)
Cali
Santander
Neiva
Nev. de Huila 575a

Gorgona
Popayán
·4686
Garzón

Guapi
El Bordo
Patía

Tumaco
Florencia

Cabo Manglares
San Lorenzo
Pasto
Mocoa

Esmeraldas
Túquerres
Ipiales
Puerto Asis

Punta Galera
·4764
Tulcán
San Gabriel

Rosa Zárate
·4930
Ibarra
La Tagua

Cayambe
Aguarico
Puerto Leguizamo

0°
Darwin
·4794
Quito
·2819
Baeza

Wolf
Bahía de Caráquez
Machachi
Coca
Napo

Pinta
Manta
·5263
Cotopaxi
Tena
Cabo Pantoja

Marchena
Genovesa
·1707
Portoviejo
Ambato
ECUADOR
Curaray

Fernandina
San Salvador
Santa Cruz
Galapagos Islands (Ecuador)
Chimborazo 6272
Santa Mari

Isabela
Puerto Villamil
San Cristóbal
Riobamba
Arica

Santa Maria
Española
Babahoyo
·5230
Montalvo

Guayaquil
Alausí
Macas
Marsella

La Puntilla
Salinas
Cuenca
Azogues

90°W 85°W 80°W 75°W

This map shows 1/60 of the earth's surface. Area scale : 1 ☐ inch on the map ≈ 15,000 ☐ miles on the ground 1 ☐ cm on the map ≈ 6000 ☐ km on the ground

70°W   65°W   60°W

15°N

DOMINICA   **Roseau**

Martinique-Passage

Martinique
(France)
Fort-de-France

St.-Lucia-Passage

Castries   **SAINT LUCIA**

St.-Vincent-Passage

BARBADOS

SAINT
VINCENT   **Kingstown**   **Bridgetown**
AND
GRENADINES

B E A N   *S E A*

L e s s e r   A n t i l l e s

A T L A N T I C

Saint George's   GRENADA

Cabo
Gallinas   *Aruba*   *Curaçao*
(Neth.)

Willemstad   *Bonaire (Neth.)*
Blanquilla
(Ven.)   *Tobago*
Scarborough
Guajira   *820*   Punto Fijo   *Windward Islands*   *Islas*   **TRINIDAD**
Peninsula   *Paraguaná*   *Los Roques*   **AND**
Peninsula   *(Ven.)*   *Margarita*   La Asunción   **Port**   **TOBAGO**
Riohacha   Maicao   *Gulf of*   Puerto Cumarebo   *Tortuga*   *of Spain*
Santa   *Venezuela*   Coro   Carúpano   340   *Trinidad*
Marta   *Cristóbal Colón*   *Cabo Codera*   Güiria   *O C E A N*
5800   San Rafael   Churuguara   *Tocuyo*   Maiquetía   2765   Cumaná   *Gulf of*   San Fernando
Ciénaga   Maracaibo   Cabimas   Puerto   **Caracas**   *Paria*
Valledupar   La Concepción   San Felipe   Cabello   Maracay   Puerto La Cruz   Carúpito   *Serpent's Mouth*
Ciudad   Carora   Valencia   La Victoria   Barcelona   265
Ojeda   1900   Barquisimeto   La Victoria   San Juan   Piritu   Anaco
Machiques   Carora   do los Morros
Lake   3652   Acarigua   El Sombrero   *Valle de*   Cantaura   Maturín
Mompós   *Maracaibo*   Valera   Boconó   Guanare   El Baúl   Calabozo   *la Pascua*   Zaraza   *Tigre*   Tucupita
El Banco   Catatumbo   *Cordillera de Mérida*   Barinas   *Coledes*   Pariaguán   El Tigre   *Orinoco*
San Carlos   5007   *Guárico*   Barrancas   *Delta*
Ocaña   del Zulia   Mérida   Bruzual   Apure   San Fernando   Boca del   792   *Grande*   *Amacuro*   *Boca Grande*
Badillo   Casigua   Barinas   *Apure*   de Apure   Pao   Ciudad Guayana   *Delta*
2350   Cúcuta   San Cristóbal   Mantecal   Caicara de   Maripa   Upata   San José de Amacuro
Bucaramanga   4100   Pamplona   El Canton   *Arauca*   Orinoco   Ciudad   *Serranía de Imataca*   Hossororo
Barrancabermeja   Málaga   *V E N E Z U E L A*   Bolívar   *Lago de Gurí*
Socorro   5493   Arauca   *Llanos*   La Urbana   1863   1339   El Callao   Marlborough
Puerto   Cravo Norté   *Capanaparo*   Las   La Paragua   *Cuyuni*   Suddie   **Georgetown**
Berrio   La Venturosa   *Mata*   Trincheras   *Guyana*   El Dorado   Peters   New Amsterdam
Puerto   Santa Maria   Fuerto   Mine   Bartica
Boyacá   Sogamoso   Carreño   Sabana de   *Caura*   2100   Mayupa   La Escalera   *Mazaruni*   Rockstone   Linden   Totness
Tunja   Casanare   Puerto   *Tomo*   Cardona   Angel Falls   1399   Cavarayen   2040   Nieuw
Zipaquirá   Yopal   Trinidad   Nuevo   100.   2285   3950   Gran   2810   Tumatumari   *Pakaraima*   **GUYANA**   Nickerie
5644   Orocué   Puerto   *Meta*   San Juan   Arabo   Sabana   Roraima   *Mountains*   Apoera
Bogotá   Villavicencio   Ayacucho   *Ventuari*   El Oso   Santa Elena   1240   Maturuca   *Kabalebo-*
4560   Puerto   *Vichada*   *Meseta del*   2030   *Guayana*   de Uairen   Depósito   *Reservoir*   **SURINAM**
López   San Fernando   *Cerro Jáua*   2579   Catisimiña   Uraricoera   Karanambo   Juliana Top   1026
L O M B I A   San José   de Atabapo   Santa Barbara   *Serra Parima*   Lethem   1230   882
de Ocuné   2396   La Esmeralda   *Irarícoere*   Boa   Kanuku Mts.   Oronoque
Santa   *Guaviare*   Victorino   Boca   *Serra do Apiaú*   Vista   Dadanawa   Isherton   Papai
Rosa   Atrecifal   San Yanaro   San José   Mavaca   1047   *Catrimani*   Rupununi   *Serra Acaraí*
San José   *Inírida*   El Mango   *Serra Curupira*   São José   Caracaraí   Biloku   734   Maloca
del Guaviare   *Guainía*   San Carlos   Serra Tapirapeco   do Anauá   *Branco*   *Kamoa Mts.*
Calamar   Morichal   Uainambi   Vista Alegre   *Casiquiare*   *Pedauiri*   *Anauá*
Mesa de   Vista Alegre   *Demini*
Buenos   *Yambi*   Jibóia   Cucui   3014   São José   Catrimani
Aires   Miraflores   Mitú   *Vaupés*   Pico da   *Araçá*   do Anauá
Cuñaré   *Apaporis*   Neblina   *Jaupari*   Calamaque   100
Puerto   Macuje   Içana   *Negro*   *B R A Z I L*   Santa   Nhamunda
Huitoto   Iuareté   Taracuá   *Uaupés*   Jaupés   Maria   Oriximiná
Palermo   Araracuara   Lérida   São José   Tapuucuara   Faro
100   La Chorrera   *Caquetá*   Barcelos   Tupanacca   Urucará
R U   *Putumayo*   La Pedrera   100   Marcelino   Maraã   Moura   100
El Encanto   Puerto   Vila Bittencourt   Foz do Mamoriá   Fonte Boa   Airão   Urini
Miraña   Tonantins   *Amazon*   *Solimões*   *Jaú*   Santo   *Vatumã*
San Cristóbal   Arica   *Japurá*   *Negro*   Antonio   Parintins   *Amazon*
Santa Clotilde   Santa Clara   70°W   65°W   60°W

n   o   p   q   r   s   t   u   v   w   x   y   z
25   26

0   100   200   300   *miles*   Average linear scale : 1 inch ≈ 125 miles   1cm ≈ 80 km   0   100   200   300   400   500   *Km*

85°W   80°W   75°W

Tumaco
Cabo Manglares
Patia
El Bordo
Florencia
Calamar
Buenos Aires
Miraflores

San Lorenzo
Túquerres
Pasto
Mocoa
C O L O M B I

Esmeraldas
Punta Galera
Tulcán
Ipiales
Puerto Asís
Puerto Huitoto
Cuñaré
Macuje

Rosa Zárate
Ibarra
San Gabriel
La Tagua
Araracuara
Palermo

0° *Equator*
Otavalo
Cayambe
Aguarico
Puerto Leguizamo
La Chorrera

Bahía de Caráquez
Quito
Coca
Napo
Putumayo
El Encanto

Manta
Machachi
Cotopaxi
Baeza
Cabo Pantoja
Arica
Santa María

Portoviejo
Latacunga
Tena
San Cristóbal

Jipijapa
E C U A D O R
Ambato
Curaray
Marsella
Santa Clotilde

Riobamba
Montalvo

Guayaquil
Babahoyo
Macas
Pastaza
Andoas
Sargento Lores
Mazán

La Puntilla
Salinas
Alausí
Azogues
Vargas Guerra
Corrientes
Iquitos
Tamshiyaco

Gulf of Guayaquil
Puná
Cuenca
Puerto Pardo

Machala
Santa Isabel
Santiago
Morona
Borja
Marañón
Bagazán
Yavari

Zarumilla
Tumbes
Zorritos
Loja
Zamora
Sta. Maria de Nieva
Barranca
Concordia
Nauta
Santa Lucia

Máncora
Cariamanga
Orellana
Requena
Elvira

Talara
Las Lomas
San Ignacio
Jeberos
Bretaña

Cabo Pariñas
Sullana
Chulucanas
Bagua
Yurimaguas
Neuva Alejandría
Santa Cruz

5°S Paita
Piura
Huancabamba
Jaen
Rioja
Moyobamba
Santa Isabel

Punta Aguja
Bayóvar
Olmos
Chachapoyas
Dos de Mayo
Ucayali
Rodrigues

Lobos Island
Santa Cruz
Ferreñafe
Bambamarca
Tarapoto
Saposoa
Orellana
Boa Fé

Lambayeque
Chiclayo
Cajamarca
Balsas
Juanjuí
Contamaná
Cruzeiro do Sul

Pacasmayo
San Pedro de Lloc
Bolívar
P E R U
Tiruntán
Juruá

Otuzco
Cajabamba
Tocache Nuevo
Pucallpa

Trujillo
Santiago de Chuco
Tayabamba
Aguaytía
Masisea
Taumaturg

Virú
Huacrachuco
Tingo María

Chimbote
Caraz
Huascaran
Llata
Puerto Inca

Casma
Huaraz
La Unión
Huánuco
Puerto Portillo

10°S
Huarmey
Chiquián
Cajatambo
Ambo
Bolognesi

Pativilca
Cerro de Pasco
Oxapampa
Puesta Varadoro

Huacho
Huaral
La Merced
Atalayá
Urubamba

Chancay
La Oroya
Satipo
Camisea
Fitzcarral

Callao
Matúcana
Jauja
Puerto Rico

Lima
Huancayo
Pampas

Yauyos
Huancavelica
Huanta
Quillabamba

San Vicente de Cañete
Castrovirreyna
Ayacucho
Urubam

Chincha Alta
Chincheros
Huancapi

Chincha Islands
Pisco
Andahuaylas
Abancay

Ica
Chalhuanca

Palpa
Puquio
Coracora
Santo Tomás

San Juán
Nazca
Cotahua

Chala
Caravelí
Chuquibamb

Atico
Ocoña
Camaná

Mollendo

P A C I F I C

O C E A N

15°S

85°W   80°W   75°W

This map shows 1/60 of the earth's surface. Area scale : 1 □ inch on the map ≃ 15,000 □ miles on the ground 1□ cm on the map ≃ 6000 □ km on the ground

a b c d e f g h i j k l m

70°W 65°W 60°W 55°W

VENEZUELA

GUYANA

Mesa de Yambí

Uainambi · San Carlos · El Mango
Mitú · Jibóia · Vista Alegre · Cucúi · Pico de Neblina 3012 · Serra Tapirapecó Curupira · Kamoa Mts. · Serra Acarai · Biloku
Vaupés · Iuareté · Caracarai
Apaporis · Taracuá · Uaupés · Içana · Negro · Demini · Catrimani · São José do Aneuá · Anauá · 734 · Parú do Oeste
Lérida · Uaupés 360 · São José · Tapurucuara · Calanaque · Araça · Catrimani
Caquetá · La Pedrera · Cuiuni · Barcelos · Tupanacca · Jauperi · Mapuera · Trombetas · 0°
Puerto Miraña · Vila Bittencourt · Marcelino · Maraá · Unini · Moura · Santa Maria · Nhamunda · Oriximiná · Óbidos
Arica · Santa Clara · Japurá · Foz do Mamoriá · Fonte Boa · Airão · Santo Antônio · Uatumã · Urucará · Faro · Parintins · Santarém
Puerto San Agustin · Içá · Tontantins · Santo Antônio de Içá · Alvarães · Tefé · Badajós-See · Manacapuru · Anamã · Manaus · Itacoatiara · Tupinambarama · Belterra
Pebas · São Paulo de Olivença · Renascença · Piorini-See · Badajós · Cocajás · Nova Olinda do Norte · Maués · Brasilia Legal · 100
Caballococha · Leticia · Concórcia · Tafé · Coari · Diamantina · Madeira · Mucajá · Itaituba · 5°S
Caxias · Benjamin Constant · Jutaí · Boca do Mutúm · Carauari · Coari · Itaboca · Aiumã · Prato do igapó Açu · Borba · Terra Preta · Laranjal · San Luis de Tapajós · Santa Helena
Três Bocas · Jutaí · Juruá · Liberdade · Jaburu · Piranhas · Boca do Acará · Maricoré · Canumã · Lajinha · Tapajós · Jamaxim
Soledade · Santos Dumont · Tapauá · Aliança · Castanhal · Canumã · Jacareacanga · Sauré · Posto Curuá · 200 · Creporizinho
Eirunepé · Tapauá · Lábrea · Pirapetinga · Sucunduri · Barra do São Manuel · Manuelzinho
Canindé · **BRAZIL** · Marroriá · Manjuriá · Humaitá · Prainha Nova · Samaumá · Recreio · Telles Pires
Tarauacá · Envira · Boca do Moaco · Pauiní · Foz do Pauin · Calama · Jatuarana · Jacaretinga · Arapari · Gêlo · Serra do Cachimbo · 26
Tarauacá · Feijó · Manuel Urbano · Boca do Curequeté · Ituxi · Mucuim · 100 · Porto Velho · Jamari · Tabajara · Theodore Roosevelt · Aripuanã · Cachimbo
Santa Rosa · Sena Madureira · Pôrto Alegre · Bom Jardim · Jaciparaná · Caratianas · Iracema · Serra do Norte · Arinos · Serra dos Apiacás
Esperanza · Iaco · Rio Branco · Manoa · Abunã · Ariquemes · Jarú · Aarão C · 200 · Serra · Pôrto do Cajueiro
Balta · Canamaria · Acre · Taquaras · Villa Bella · Rondônia · Serra do Tombador · Carmem
Alerta · Xapuri · Brasiléia · Madre de Dios · Guajará Mirim · Serra dos Pacaas Novos · 800 · Presidente Hermes · Pimenta Bueno · Acampamento de Indios · Pôrto dos Gauchos · Pouso Alegre · Pôrto Atlântico · Marape · Lucas
Iñapari · Cobija · Porvenir · Puerto Rico · Riberalta · Serra dos Parecis · José Bonifácio · Fontanillas · Serra Formosa
Las Piedras · Iberia · Fortaleza · Fortaleza · Santo Antônio · Vilhena · Juruena · Uiariti · Providencia
Manú · Puerto Maldonado · Puerto Heath · Cavinas · Lago Rogoaguado · San Joaquin · Mategua · Pimenteiras · Ponta da Pedra · Diamantino · Mato Grosso Plateau
Quince Mil · Astillero · Madidi · Lago Rogagua · Magdalena · El Carmen · Puerto Alegre · Santa Isabé · Campo dos Parecis · 702 · Rosario Oeste
Cuzco · Urcos · Macusani · Sandia · Cerros de Bala · Reyes · Santa Ana · Lago de San Luiz · Blanco · La Esperanza · Serra de Huanchaca · Guaporé · Tapirapua · Várzea Grande · Cuiabá
Ayaviri · Huancané · Apolo · San Borja · San Ignacio · Trinidad · Perseverancia · La Noria · 1595 · Mato Grosso · Cáceres · Poconé · Jaciara
Juliaca · Puerto Acosta · Santa Ana · Llanos de Mojos · Loreto · Concepción · Salinas · Pôrto Esperidião · Descalvados · São Lorenço
Puno · Lake Titicaca · Achacachi · Coroico · Ascensión · San Javier · San Ignacio · San Matías · 283 · Pôrto Jofre
Arequipa · La Paz 3577 · Chulumani · Todos Santos · Puerto Villarroel · Montero · El Cerro · San José de Chiquitos · Laguna Uberaba · Itiquira
Moquegua · Viacha · Cochabamba · Portachue · 614 · Laguna Concepción · Pedro Gomes
Tacna · Calacoto · Sicasica · Totora · Santa Cruz · Serra de Santiago · Amolar
Arica 70°W · Oruro · Aiquile · Cordillera · Llanos de Chiquitos · Robore 60°W 55°W

n o p q r s t u v w x y z

23

0 100 200 300 miles
Average linear scale: 1 inch = 125 miles 1 cm = 80 km
0 100 200 300 400 Km

23

VENEZUELA

60°W

Caura
Mayupa
2100
1890
La Escalera
Nazaruni
Rockstone
New Amsterdam
Linden
Totness
55°W
Paramaribo
Mana

Cavanayen
Puricama
Tumatumari
Coutantyne
Nieuw Nickerie
Groningen
Paranam
Moengo
St. Laurent
Sinnamary

Gran Sabana
2040
Roraima 2810
Apoera
Brokopondo
Apatou
Kourou
Cayenne

Arabelo
Caroni
Paragua
Santa Elena de Uairen
Maturuca
1240
Depósito
Essequibo
Apoteri
Prof. van Blommestein Lake
Aurora
694
Grand Santi
Montsinery
Kaw
Cabo Orange

Catisimiña
Meseta del Cerro Jaua
Pacaraima Mountains
Guiana
SURINAM
1026
Bakrakondre
710
Patience
Grand Santi
FRENCH
Régina
St. Georges
Oiapoque

Serra Parima
Uraricoera
Karanambo
Juliana Top 1230
882
Intelewa
658
Saul
GUIANA
Vila Velha

Serra Chimipa
1047
Boa Vista
Lethem
Kanuku Mts.
Dadanawa
Oronoque
Tapanahoni
Kawatop
635
Cunani
Calçoene

Serra do Apiau
Isherton
Papai
Maloca Velha
690
Serra Lombarda
Lorenço
Amapá

Serra Tapirapeco
Caracarai
Biloku
Kamoa Mts.
Serra Acaraí
Pôrto Poet
Tumucumaque
Maracá
Cabo Norte

734
Meriruma
Araguari
Aporema

São José do Anauá
Maloca
Terezinha
Serra do Navio
Ferreira Gomes

Catrimani
Malaripó
315
Acampamento
Pôrto Grande
Janaucú

0°
Calanaque
Branco
Jauaperi
Trombetas
Paru de Oeste
Jari
Pôrto Santana
Macapá
Caviana

Cuiuni
Barcelos
Tupanacca
Moura
Mapuera
Morro Grande 629
Monte Dourado
228
Boca do Jari
Queimada
Afuá
Chaves
Mexiana
Cabo Maguarinho

Unini
Airão
Santa Maria
Nhamunda
Oriximiná
Óbidos
Mulata
305
Ramos
Almeirim
Grande de Gurupá
Anajás
Souré
Marajó Bay
Vigia

Jaú
Santo Antônio
Faro
Prainha
Monte Alegre
Pôrto de Moz
Breves
Cachoeira do Arari
Pará
Castanha
Belém

Tefé
Lago Badajós
Manacapuru
Urucará
Santarém
Curua-Uná
Portel
Abaetetuba
Moju

Lago Piorini
Badajós
Anama
Manaus
Amazon
Itacoatiara
Parintins
Belterra
Pacoval
Victoria
Belo Monte
Pindobal
Capim
Mocajuba
Tomé-Açu

25
Piorini
Codajós
Borba
Tupinambarama
Brasilia Legal
Caima
Altamira
Tuéré
Baião
Capim

Tefé
Coari
Diamantina
Nova Olinda do Norte
Mucajá
Maués
Itaituba
Rurópolis
229
Tucuruí
Gurupizinho

5°S
Coari
Itaboca
Arumã
Madeira
Terra Preta
Maués
Laranjal
Pôrto Alegre
Iriri
Lontra
Sem-Tripa
Jatobá
Jatobal
Jacundá
Itinga

Jaburu
Piranhas
Novo Aripuanã
San Luis de Tapajós
Xingu
José Rodrigues
São Félix
399
Serra dos Carajás

Tapauá
Boca do Acara
Manicoré
Lajinha
Santa Helena
Forte Veneza
Carajás
Marabá
São João de Araguaia

Aliança
Castanhal
Canumã
Jacareacanga
Tapajós
Posto Curuá
Araras
São Félix do Xingu
Tucumã
Tocantinópolis

Lábrea
Pirapetinga
Sucunduri
Sauré
Creporizinho
Cajueiro
Jojoca
Posto Cocraimore
Xinguara
Babaçulândia

Humaitá
Prainha Nova
Barra do São Manuel
Manuelzinho
Gorotiré
Araguaína

Calama
Jatuarana
Samaumá
500
Garimpo Cumaru
Redenção
Guarai

Pôrto Velho
Jamari
Recreio
Serra do Cachimbo
Conceição do Araguaia

Jaciparaná
Caratianas
Jacaretinga
Araparí
Gêlo
Cachimbo
Campo Alegre
Santana do Araguaia
Araguacema

Ariquemes
Iracema
Aarão
Aripuanã
Plara-Açu
Barreira do Campo
Miracema do Norte
240

10°S
Antuerpia
Jarú
Serra do Norte
Serra dos Apiacás
Xingu
São José do Xingu
Paraíso do Norte de Goiás
Tocantin

Serra dos Pacaas Novos
Rondônia
Fontanillas
Pôrto do Cajueiro
Posto Alto Manissaua
Campo de Diauarum
Santa Teresinha
Cristalandia
Pôrto Nacional

800
242
Presidente Hermes
Pimenta Bueno
Acampamento de Indios
Pôrto dos Gauchos
Pôrto Atlântico
Xingu
Pôrto Alegre
Fátima
Gurupi

Fortaleza
José Bonifácio
Pouso Alegre
Serra Formosa
Carmem
São Félix
Ilha do Bananal
Natividade

Costa Marques
Santo Antônio
Juruena
Uariti
Marape
Tamitatoala
Pôrto dos Meinacos
Peixe

San Joaquin
Mategua
Vilhena
Ponta da Pedra
Lucas
Pôrto Artur
Garapu
Alvorada
1566

Magdalena
Puerto Alegre
Pimenteiras
Campo dos Parecis
Teles Pires
Mato Grosso Plateau
635
São Miguel do Araguaia
Porangatu
Araguaçu

BOLIVIA
El Carmen
Santa Isabel
60°W
55°W
50°W
Alto Paraíso de Goiás

28

This map shows 1/60 of the earth's surface   Area scale : 1 ☐ inch on the map ≈ 15,000 ☐ miles on the ground   1 ☐ cm on the map ≈ 6000 ☐ km on the ground

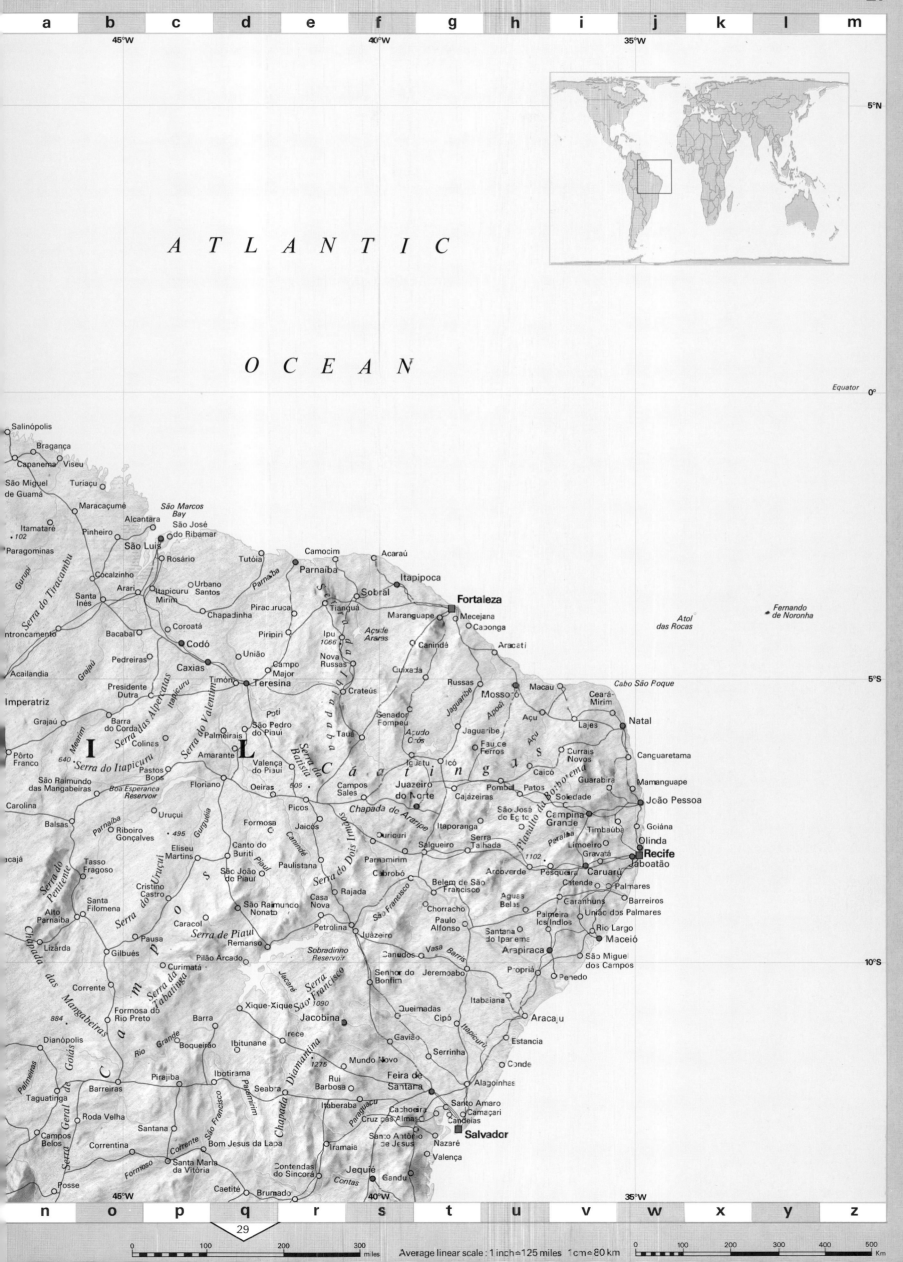

45°W   40°W   35°W

5°N

A T L A N T I C

O C E A N

Equator   0°

Salinópolis
Bragança
Capanema   Viseu
São Miguel
de Guamá   Turiaçu
Itamataré   •102
Pinheiro   Maracaçumé   Alcântara   *São Marcos Bay*
Paragominas   São José
do Ribamar
Cocalzinho   São Luís
Santa   Arari   Rosário   Tutóia   Camocim   Acaraú
Inês   Itapicuru   Urbano   *Parnaíba*   Parnaíba   Itapipoca
ntroncamento   Mirim   Santos   Piracuruca   Sobral   **Fortaleza**
Bacabal   Chapadinha   Tianguá   Maranguape   Mecejana
Coroatá   Piripiri   Ipu   Caponga
Codó   União   1066   *Açude Araras*   Canindé   Aracati
Pedreiras   Campo   Nova
Acailandia   Caxias   Major   Russas   Quixada
Grajaú   Timón   Teresina   Crateús   Russas   Macau   Ceará-
Presidente   Crato   Mossoró   Mirim
Imperatriz   Dutra   Poti   Senador   Apodi   Açu   Natal
Grajaú   Barra   São Pedro   Fompeu   Jaguaribe   Lajes
Pôrto   do Corda   do Piauí   Taua   *Açude Crós*   Jaguaribe   Açu   Currais
Franco   640   Colinas   Palmeirais   Fau ce   Novos   Cançuaretama
São Raimundo   *Serra do Itapicuru*   Amarante   Valença   Icó   Ferros   Caicó   Guarabira
das Mangabeiras   Boa Esperança   do Piauí   505   Campos   Patos   Mamanguape
Carolina   Reservoir   Floriano   Oeiras   Sales   Juazeiro   Cajázeiras   Pombal   Soledade   João Pessoa
Balsas   Picos   do Norte   Campina   Goiána
Uruçui   495   Formosa   Jaicós   *Chapada de Araripe*   Itaporanga   São José   Grande   Olinda
acajá   Riboiro   Canto do   Ouricuri   Salgueiro   do Egito   Timbaúba   **Recife**
Gonçalves   Buriti   Paranamirim   Serra   1102   Limoeiro   Jáboatão
Eliseu   Paulistana   Talhada   Gravatá
Tasso   Martins   São João   Cabrobó   Arcoverde   Caruarú
Fragoso   do Piauí   Belem de São   Pesqueira   Catende   Palmares
Cristino   Casa   Rajada   Francisco   Aguas   Garanhuns   Barreiros
Alto   Castro   Nova   Chorracho   Belas   Palmeira   União dos Palmares
Parnaíba   Santa   São Raimundo   Paulo   los Indios   Rio Largo
Filomena   Nonato   Petrolina   Alfonso   Santana   Maceió
Caracol   Juázeiro   do Iparema   Arapiraca
Lizárda   Pausa   Remanso   Vasa Barris   Propriá   São Miguel
Gilbués   Pilão Arcado   Sobradinho   Canudos   dos Campos
Curimatá   Reservoir   Senhor do   Jeremoabo   Penedo
Corrente   Bonfim   Itabaiana
Formosa do   Xique-Xique   1090   Queimadas   Aracaju
884   Rio Preto   Barra   Jacobina   Cipó   Estancia
Dianópolis   Boqueirão   Irece   Gavião   Serrinha   Conde
Taguatinga   Ibitunane   Mundo Novo
Barreiras   Pirajiba   Ibotirama   1275   Rui   Feira de   Alagoinhas
Roda Velha   Seabra   Barbosa   Santana
Santana   Santo Amaro   Camaçari
Campos   Correntina   Itaberaba   Cachoeira   Candeias
Belos   Bom Jesus da Lapa   Cruz das Almas   **Salvador**
Posse   Santa Maria   Iramaia   Santo Antônio   Nazaré
da Vitória   de Jesus   Valença
Contendas   Jequié
do Sincorá   Gandu
Caetité   Brumado

ILL

Fernando
de Noronha

*Atol
das Rocas*

Cabo São Poque

5°S

10°S

45°W   40°W   35°W

0   100   200   300 miles
Average linear scale : 1 inch≏125 miles   1 cm≏80 km
0   100   200   300   400   500 Km

a b c d e f g h i j k l m

PERU
BOLIVIA
ARGENTINA
PARAGUAY
CHILE
URUGUAY

PACIFIC OCEAN

Abancay
Chalhuanca
Aurangate 6394
Urcos
Macusani 5852
Sicuani 5443
Ixiamas
Reyes
Lago Rogagua
Lago de San Luis
El Carmen
Puerto Alegre
Ponta da Pedra
Campo dos Parecis
Diamantino

Santo Tomás
Yauri
Ayaviri
Sandia
Palomani 5999
Apolo
Rapulo
Santa Ana
San Ignacio
Perseverancia
La Noria
Serra de Huanchaca
1095
Mato Grosso
Tapirapua
Rosario Oeste
Várzea Grande

Cotahuasi
Chuquibamba
Chivay
5641
Huancané
Juliaca 5443
Huancané
Puerto Acosta
Illampu 6485
Ancohuma 6388
Coroico
Puerto Marquez
Ascensión
Salinas
1150
Pôrto Esperidião
1283
Cáceres
Pocoñé
Cuiabá

Corupuna 6425
Chuquibamba
Camana
Arequipa 2304
Tacora 5988
Tambo 5593
5761
Lake Titicaca
La Paz
Viacha
Guaqui
Illimani 6402
Chuluman
Todos Santos
Puerto Villarroel
Ichilo
Montero
Concepción
San Javier
San Ignacio
Descalvados
Itiquira
Pôrto Jofre

Mollendo
Moquegua
5213
Calacoto
Umala
Sicasica
Quillacollo
Cochabamba
Totora 3209
Comarapa
Santa Cruz
El Cerro
Laguna Concepción
San José de Chiquitos
Robore
Santa Ana
Lagoa Uberaba
Grand

Ilo
Tacna
Putre
Guallatiri 6060
Sajama 6542
Corque
Oruro 5383
Aiquile
Rio Valle Grande
Llanos de Chiquitos
Banados del Izozog
Santo Corazón
Amolar
Pantanal

Arica
Cuya
Nama
Sabaya
Challapata
Sucre 2790
Tarabuco
Lagunillas
Cabezas
Yuti
Fortín Ravelo
Fortín Max Parades 727
Puerto Suárez
Corumba
Aquidauana
Aquidaur

Pisagua
Huara
Sillaguay 5995
Lago de Coipasa
Rio Mulatos
Potosí
Azurduy
Camiri
Charagua
Fortín Gral. Eugenio Garay
998
Timane
Bahia Negra
Pôrto Esperança
Guaicurus

Iquique
5218
Salar de Uyuni
Uyuni
Vitichi
Macharetí
Fortín Garrapatal
Fortín Madrejón
Fuerte Olimpo
Bonito

Pintados
Collahuasi 5739
4320
Cotagaita
Tupiza
Pilaya
Villa Montes
Fortín Hernandarias
Mariscal Estigarribia
Pôrto Murtinho
Bella Vista

Lagunas
Ollague
6045
5865
Alota
San Pablo 5695
Mojo
Yacuiba
Dr. Pedro P. Peña
Filadelfia
Puerto Piñasco
Jardim

Quillagua
Chuquicamata
Tocopilla
Maria Elena 2293
Calama
5680
Tocorpuri 5833
Villazón
La Quiaca 5029
Tartagal
Bermejo
Fortín Juan de Zalazar
Puerto Sastre
Ponta Pora 700

San Pedro de Atacama
Licancabur 5921
Abra Pampa
Rosario
San Ramón de la Nueva Orán
Juan Sola
Ingeniero Guillermo
Nueva Juárez
San Pedro
Concepción
Lima
Ypé Jhú

Mejillones
Carmen Alto
6050
Humahuaca
Embarcación
Los Blancos
Fortín General Diaz
Pozo Colorado Monte

Antofagasta
Varillas
Salar de Atacama
5890
Catua
Salinas Grandes
Chani 6200
Libertador Gral. San Martín
San Pedro
Las Lomitas
Rozo del Tigre
Benjamín Aceval
San Estanislao

Caleta el Cobre
Augusta Victoria
Pular 6225
5594
San Antonio de los Cobres
San Salvador de Jujuy
General Güemes
Las Lajitas
Palo Santo
Villa Hayes
Asunción

Paposo
Los Vientos
Socompa 6031
Llullaillaco 6723
Salar de Arizaro
Cachi 6720
Salta
Joaquín V. González
Pirané
Clorinda
Coronel Oviedo

25°S
Taltal
Salar Punta Negra
6050
Salar de Pocitos
Cachi
Metán
Palo Santo

Santa Catalina
5700
San Salvador
Salta
Joaquín V. González

Diego de Almagro
El Salvador
Antofalla 6440
Salar de Antofalla
5070
Colorados
6049 Antofagasta de la Sierra
Santa María
Rosario de la Frontera
Monte Quemado
Castelli
Tres Isletas
Formosa
Villarrica
Caazapá

Chañaral
Inca de Oro
Nevada 6400
Cafayate
San Miguel de Tucumán
Termas de Rio Hondo
Pampa de los Guanacos
Presidencia Roque Sáenz Peña
Pilar
San Juan Bautista

Caldera
Copiapó 6080
Ojos del Salado 6880
4920
Concepción
Monteros
Hondo Reservoir
Santiago del Estero
Charata
Presidencia de la Plaza
Resistencia
Corrientes
Posadas

Carrizal Bajo
Castilla
Pissis 6858
Bonete 6872
San Miguel
Belén
La Banda
Suncho Corral
Villa Angela
Empredrado
Apóstoles

Huasco
Vallenar
5830
Fiambala
Tinogasta
Catamarca
Salar de Pipanaco
Andalgala
Frias
San Martín
Bandera
Tostado
Reconquista
Bella Vista
Goya
Santo Tomé
São Bo

Cabo Bascuñan
Domeyko
Mejicana 6250
Chilecito
Chumbicha
Recreo
Pinto
Villa Guillermina
Mercedes
Yapeyú
Uruguaiana

La Higuera
La Serena
Copiapó
Tortolas 5332
Villa Unión
La Rioja
Villa Ojo de Aqua
Vera
Corrientes
Curuzú Cuatiá
Quarai
Ibicuy

Coquimbo
Olivares 6282
5510
San José de Jáchal
Chamical
Cruz del Eje
Deán Funes
Ceres
San Cristóbal
Esquina
Bella Unión
Artigas

30°S
Ovalle
5620
Patquía
Laguna Chiquita
Morteros
San Justo
La Paz
Chajari
Salto
Arapey

Maitencillo
Combarbala
Olivares
San Juan
San Agustín de Valle Fértil
Villa Dolores
2880
San Francisco
Rafaela
Esperanza
Concordia
Salto
Tacuarembó
Rive

Illapel
Salamanca
Mercedario 6710
Zanjón
Quines
Santa Rosa del Conlara
Oliva
Santa Fe
Paraná
Villaguay
Paysandú
Negro Reservoir

Chincolco
San Felipe
Aconcagua 5989
Villa Media Agua
San Juan
Río Tercero
Villa Maria
Diamante
Concepción del Uruguay
Durazno

La Calera
Valparaíso
Santiago
Tupungato 6800
Mendoza
San Martín
La Paz
San Luis 1599
Río Cuarto
La Carlota
Vanado Tuerto
Rosario
Gualeguaychu
Carmelo
Cardona
Florida

San Antonio
San Bernardo
5830
Tunuyán
Mercedes
Vicuña Mackenna
San Nicolás
San Pedro
Pergamino
Gualeguay
Zárate

Santa Cruz
Rancagua
5290
San Rafael
Buena Esperanza
Laboulaye
Lincoln
Chacabuco
Martínez
Buenos Aires
C. del Sacramento
La Plata

Santa Cruz
San Fernando
Curico
5160
4860
Diamante
Salado
General Alvear
Huinca Renancó
General Villegas
Chivilcoy
Lobos
Montevide

Constitución
Union
River Plate
Magdalena
Canelone

15°S
20°S
25°S
30°S
35°S

70°W
65°W
60°W

n o p q r s t u v w x y z

This map shows 1/60 of the earth's surface. Area scale: 1 □ inch on the map ≈ 15,000 □ miles on the ground 1 □ cm on the map ≈ 6000 □ km on the ground

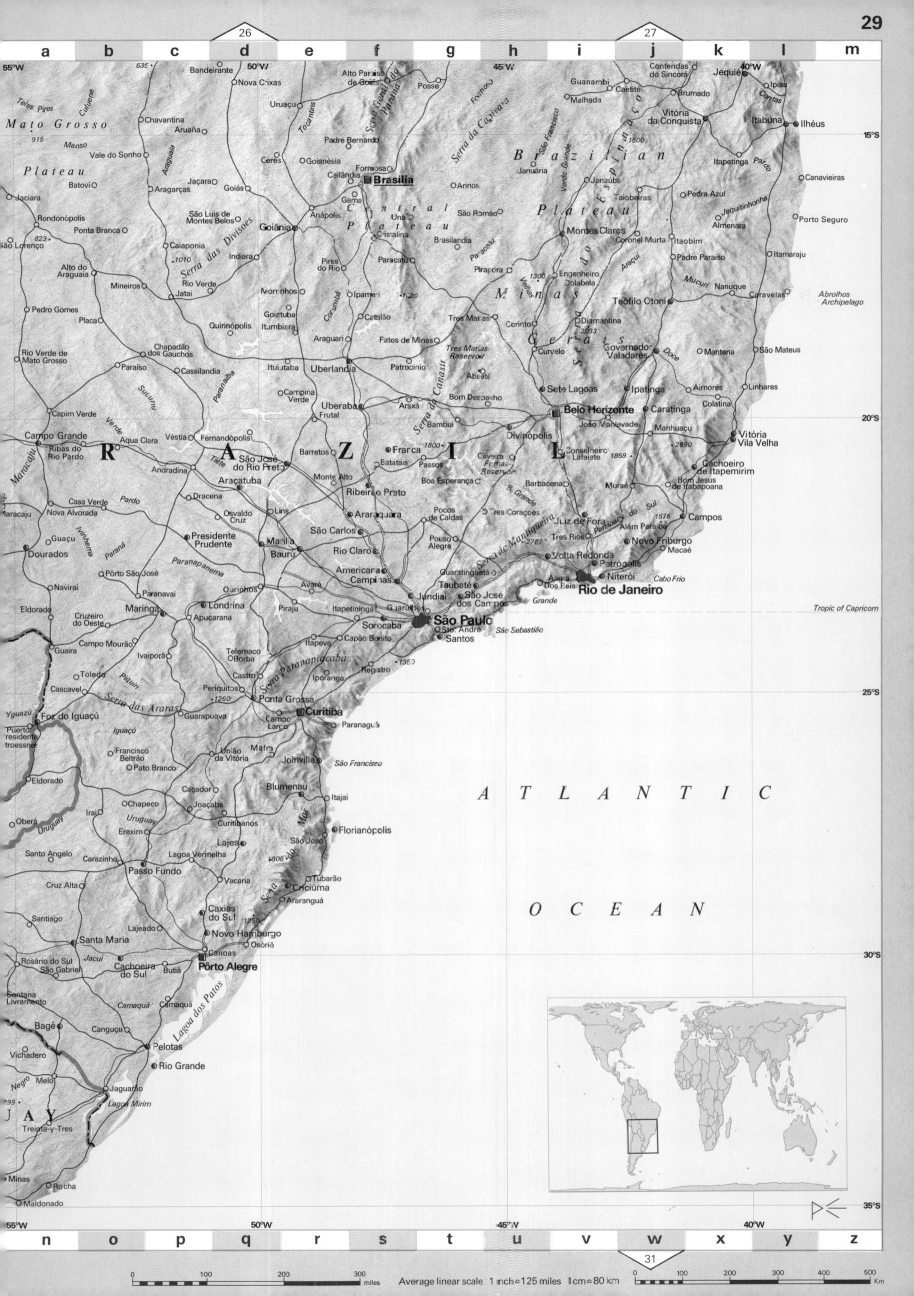

a b c d e f g h i j k l m

80°W   75°W   70°W   65°W

Juan Fernández Islands
(Chile)
Alejandro   Robinson
Selkirk   Crusoe

35°S

P A C I F I C

40°S

O C E A N

45°S

50°S

55°S

Valparaíso
Santiago
San Bernardo
San Antonio
Rancagua
Santa Cruz
San Fernando
Curicó
Constitución
Maule
Talca
Malargüe

Talcahuano
Concepción
Punta Lavapié
Chillán
Los Angeles
Lebú
Victoria
Temuco
Villarrica
Valdivia
Lago de Ranco
Osorno
Lago Llanquihue
Puerto Montt
Ancud
Chiloe
Castro
Cabo Quilán
Gulf of Guafo
Gulf of Corcovado
Chaitén
Esquel
Chonos Archipelago
Puerto Cisnes
Magdalena
Puerto Aisén
Coihaique
Tartao Peninsula
San Valentín 4058
Lago Gen. Carrera
Penas Gulf
Cochrane
San Lorenzo
Campana
Wellington
Lago o'Higgins
Lago Cardiel
Murallón 3600
Lago Viedma
Lago Argentino
Hanover
El Calafate
Lago del Toro
Yacimiento
Nelson Strait
Puerto Natales
Río Turbio
Magellan Str.
Desolación
Punta Arenas
Santa Inés
Brunswick Peninsula
Magellan Straits
Porvenir
Tierra del Fuego
Lago Fagnano
Sarmiento Pen.
Ushuaia
Hoste
Cape Horn

Tupungato 6800
San Martín
Río Cuarto
La Carlota
San Luis
Mercedes
Vicuña Mackenna
Laboulaye
Tunuyán
La Paz
Justo Daract
San Rafael
Diamante
Salado
Buena Esperanza
Huinca Renancó
General Villegas
Rivadavia
General Pico
Eduardo Castex
Union
Victorica
Santa Rosa
General Alvear
Algarrobo del Aguila
Santa Isabel
Barrancas
Chos Malal
Colorado
Chacharramendi
General Acha
Carhue
Cerros Colorados Reservoir
Catriel
Puelches
Villa Iris
Neuquén
Zapala
Plaza Huincul
Cutral-Co
Limay
General Roca
Chelforó
Río Colorado
Picún Leufú
Ezequil Ramos Mexia Reservoir
Choele Choel
San Martín de los Andes
Junín de los Andes
Paso Limay
Sierra Colorada
General Conesa
Carmen de Patagones
Viedma
San Carlos de Bariloche
Los Menucos
Valcheta
San Antonio Oeste
Lago Nahuel Huapi
Maquinchao
Puerto Lobos
Punta Norte
El Maitén
Ingeniero Jacobacci
Gastre
Telsen
Puerto Madryn
Valdés Peninsula
Nuevo Gulf
Punta Delgada
Gangán
Tecka
Las Plumas
Trelew
Rawson
Chubut
Florentino Ameghino Reservoir
José de San Martín
Paso de los Indios
Gran Laguna Salada
Camarones
Chico
Facundo
Lago Musters
Lago Colhué Huapi
Malespina
Río Mayo
Sarmiento
Comodore Rivadavia
Gulf of San Jorge
Chile Chico
Perito Moreno
Las Heras
Caleta Olivia
Cabo Tres Puntas
Bajo Caracoles
Pico Truncado
Jaramillo
Deseado
Puerto Deseado
Gobernador Gregores
El Salado
Lago Cardiel
Puerto San Julián
Tres Lagos
Chico
La Julia
Piedrabuena
Puerto Santa Cruz
Santa Cruz
Esperanza
Bahía Grande
Gallegos
Río Gallegos
Laguna Blanca
Punta Delgada
Cerro Sombrero
Grande
Río Grande
Cabo San Diego
Staten Island

Sierra del Nevado
Neuquén
ARGENTINA
Meseta de Somuncura
San Matías Gulf
Banados del Atuel

This map shows 1/60 of the earth's surface. Area scale : 1 ☐ inch on the map ≏ 15,000 ☐ miles on the ground   1 ☐ cm on the map ≏ 6000 ☐ km on the ground

n o p q r s t u v w x y z

80°W   75°W   70°W   65°W

a b c d e f g h i j k l m

60°W   55°N   50°N   45°W

Gualeguay
San Nicolas
Mercedes   Duranzo
Venado
Tuerto
Pergamino
San
Pedro   Carmelo   Cardona   Treinta-y-
Tres
Zárate   Florica
Martinez   C. del
Luján   Sacramento   San Jose
de Mayc   Minas
ufino
Junin   Mercedes   **Buenos**   Canelones   Rocha
Lincoln   Chacabuco   **Aires**   Lanús
al. Viamonte   Chivilcoy   Lobos   La Plata   **Montevideo**   Maldonado
Magdalena
9 de Julio   San Miguel
del Monte   Chascomús
Pehuajó   Saladillo
Samboronbón
Bay
enque
auquen   Las Flores   Salado   Dolores   Punta Norte
San Carlos
de Bolivar
Azúl   Rauch
Guamini   Olavarría   Ayacucho   General Juar Madariaga
Coronel
Suárez   Tandil
igüe   Coronel
Pringles   .1243   Benito
Juárez   Mar del Plata
Tres   Loberia
Bahía Blanca   Arroyos   Miramar
Cnel. Dorrego
Punta
Alta   Necochea

URUGUAY

*Bahía
Blanca*

River Plate

A T L A N T I C

O C E A N

35°S

40°S

45°S

50°S

Falkland Islands / Islas Malvinas
(U.K.)
*West
Falkland*   *East
Falkland*   Port Stanley

South Georgia Islands
(U.K.)

55°S

60°W   55°W   50°W   45°W

n o p q r s t u v w x y z

0   100   200   300
miles
Average linear scale : 1 inch ≃ 125 miles 1cm ≃ 80 km

0   100   200   300   400   500
Km

Greenland
(Denmark)
Scoresby Sound
○ Scoresbysund
20°W
15°W
10°W
Jan Mayen
(Norway)
5°W
0°
70°N

A R C T

Denmark Strait

O C E A N

Cape Horn
Arctic Circle
Fontur
○ Isafjördur
Húna Bay
○ Akureyri
Breidhi Fjord
I C E L A N D
•1765
65°N
Vatnajökull
○ Djúpivogur
1400
Akranes ○
Faxa Bay
2119 •
Keflavik ○
● Reykjavik
Reykjanes

Faeroe Islands
(Denmark)

Shetland
Islands
Lerwick ○

60°N

O C E

A T L A N T I C

Orkney
Islands
Cape
Wrath
Pentland Firth
● Thurso

N O R T

Lewis
Minch
Moray Firth
Hebrides
Inverness ●
Elgin
Loch
Ness
Highlands
•1305
Skye
Aberdeen
S C O T L A N D

90

Fort William •1343
● Dundee
Mull
Perth ●
Stirling ●
Islay
Edinburgh ●
Glasgow ●
Berwick
upon
Tweed

GREAT BRITAIN
Ayr ●
Newcastle
upon Tyne ●

55°N
Londonderry ●
North Channel
AND
Carlisle ●
Sunderland ●
NORTHERN
IRELAND
● Belfast
NORTHERN IRELAND
Middlesbrough ●

O C E A N

Donegal
Bay
Lough Neagh
Portadown ●
Sligo ●
Isle of
Man
○ Douglas
Dundalk ●
Leeds ●
York ●
Kingston upon Hull ●
Westport ●
Blackpool ●
I R I S H
Irish Sea
Manchester ●
Athlone ●
Liverpool ●
Sheffield ●
Galway ●
Holyhead ●
Stoke-on-
● Dublin
Anglesey
886
Trent
Nottingham ●
Roscrea ●
1986
Derby ●
Arklow ●
R E P U B L I C
Limerick ●
Birmingham ●
Leicester ●
Norwich ●
1920
Wexford ●
W A L E S
Coventry ●
Cambridge ●
Aberystwyth ●
Ipswich ●
Killarney ○
Waterford ●
Oxford ●
Luton ●
Cork ●
Fishguard ●
St. George's Channel
Southend-
Swansea ●
Thames
on-Sea
Cardiff ●
Reading ●
● London
Dover
Ostend
Bristol ●
Dover
Cape Clear
Bristol
Channel
Southampton ●
Brighton ●
Strait of
Calais
Bournemouth ●
Gher
Exeter ●
Isle of
Wight
Lille
Valenciennes
Plymouth ●
50°N
English Channel
Abbeville
Land's End
Penzance ●
Amiens
Cherbourg ●
St. Quer
Guernsey
Le Havre ●
Rouen
Channel Islands
(U.K.) Jersey
Caen ●
Compie
Gulf of St Malo
Seine
Granville ●
Évreux ●
Brest ●
● Paris
St. Brieuc ●
Alençon ●
Chartres ●
Rennes ●
Le Mans ●
Orleans
F R A N C
Lorient ●
Loire
Auxerr
St. Nazaire ●
Angers ●
Tours ●
Nantes ●

This map shows 1/60 of the earth's surface.   Area scale : 1 □ inch on the map ≏ 15,000 □ miles on the ground 1 □ cm on the map ≏ 6000 □ km on the ground

5°E 10°E 15°E 20°E 25°E *North Cape* 30°E

Cape Kiberg

ICELAND

NORWAY SWEDEN FINLAND

Hammerfest · Alta · 1139 · Lakselv · 623 · Kirkenes · 70°N
Tana · Tana · Pečenga

Sörōya · Söröya

Senja · Tromsö · Skibotn · Lake Inari · Ivalo · 636 · Lotta · Paduhskoye More
Vesterålen · Ar.döya · 155G · Lappland · Kolari · SOVIET
Lofoten Islands · Langöya · Narvik · Kebnekaise · 2117 · Kiruna · 507 · Muonio · Kemijärvi · 263 · Lake Pyaozero
Vest Fjord · Bodö · 2090 Sarek · Gällivare · Torne · Kolari · Kemi · Kalevala · UNION · 65°N
Svartisen 1599 · Lönsdal · 1906 · Hornavan 697 · Piła · 396 · Tornio · Kemi · Kuusamo · Reboly
Mo-i-Rana · 1693 · Arjeplog · 211 · Oulu · Lake Pielis
Mosjöen · 915 · Lake Udd · Luleå · Raahe · Kajaani · 355
Kvigtind 1703 · Skelleftea · Skellefteå · Kokkola · Joensuu · 279
Vikna · Storg · 1390 · Storuman · Lycksel · Ume · Jakobstad · Lake Oulu
Steinkjer · Grorg · Strömsund · 530 · Umeå · Vaasa · 125 · Kyvjärvi · 239 · Kuopio
Trondheimsfjord · Åre · Lake Stor · Östersund · Örnsköldsvik · Lake Näsi · Jyväskylä · FINLAND · Sortavala
Kristiansund · Trondheim · 736 · Kramfors · Parkano · Lake Saimaa · Imatra
Molde · Oppdal · Lake Stor · 1009 · Sundsvall · Lake Päijänne · Lappeenranta
Ålesund · Åndalsnes · Tynset · Sveg · 430 · Hudiksvall · Pori · Tampere · Lake Ladoga
Mālöy · Dombås · 2469 Galdhöpiggen · 2183 · Söderhamn · Hämeenlinna · Vyborg
2038 · Övre Årdal · Lillehammer · 774 · Gävle · Åland Islands (Finland) · Turku · Espoo · Vantaa · Kotka · 179 · 60°N
Sognefjord · Gudvangen · Hamar · Lake Siljan · Borlänge · Uppsala · Mariahamn · Helsinki · Leningrad · Kolpino
1662 · Gol · Lake Mjösa · Kongsvinger · Dal · Västerås · Harkö · Tallinn · Narva · Chudovo
bergen · Eidfjord · Hönefoss · Karlstad · Örebro · Stockholm · ESTONIA · Luga
1660 · Grungedal · Drammen · Oslo · 279 · Södertälje · Hiiumaa · Tartu · Lake Peipus (L. Chud) · Novgorod
augesund · Evje · Larvik · Fredrikstad · Lake Väner · Norrköping · Saaremaa · Pärnu · 145 · Lake Pskov · Lake Ilmen
Stavanger · Arendal · Uddevalla · Lidköping · Linköping · Valga · Pskov · Staraja Russa
Egersund · Kristiansand · Lake Vätter · Västervik · Visby · Riga · 311 · R.S.F.S.R. · Lovat · 50
Cape Skagen · Jönköping · Borås · 377 · Gotland · Gulf of Riga · Ostrov · Opochka
Skagerrak · Frederikshavn · Växjö · LATVIA · Velikije Luki
Ålborg · Kattegat · Halmstad · Kalmar · Öland · Ventspils · Liepaja · Jekabpils · Dvina · Nevel
Holstebro · Randers · Helsingborg · Karlskrona · Kristianstad · SOVIET UNION · Vitebsk
Jutland · Århus · Helsingör · Siauliai · 229 · Panevėžys · Polotsk · 259 · 55°N
DENMARK 173 · Kolding · Copenhagen · Malmö · 207 · Klaipeda · LITHUANIA · Postavy
Esbjerg · Odense · Zealand · Ystad · Bornholm (Denmark) · Verian · Sovetsk · Kaunas · Vilnius · Molodetschno · 342 · Borisov
Flensburg · Fünen · Lolland · Falster · Cape Arkona · Rügen · Kaliningrad R.S.F.S.R. · Chernyakhovsk · Lida · Minsk
Heligoland Bight · Kiel · Lübeck Bay · Stralsund · Pomeranian Bay · Słupsk · Gdynia · Gulf of Danzig · Suwałki · Grodno · WHITE
Frisian Islands · Wilhelmshaven · Kiel · Lübeck · Rostock · Wismar · Greifswald · 476 · Koszalin · Gdansk · Elbląg · Lomza · Białystok · Baranovichi · Bobruysk
Groningen · Bremerhaven · Emden · Schwerin · Neubrandenburg · Szczecinek · Olsztyn · Slonim · RUSSIA · Dovsk
Leeuwarden · Bremen · GERMAN · Szczecin · Stargard · Bydgoszcz · Torun · Grudziadz · 313 · Grodno · Slutsk 192 · Krichev
Emmen · Hamburg · Wittenberge · Neuruppin · Gorzów-Wlkp. · Włocławek · Kutno · POLAND · Brest · Pinsk · Pripet · Gomel
HERLANDS · GERMAN · Hannover · Potsdam · Berlin · Frankfurt · Poznan · Warsaw · Siedlce · Marshes · Mozyr · Chernigov
Amsterdam · Enschede · Osnabrück · Brunswick · Magdeburg · 162 · Oder · Werta · Łódź · Kalisz · Lublin · Kovel · Nezhin
Utrecht · Arnhem · Münster · Göttingen · DEMOCRATIC · Dessau · Halle · Leipzig · Leszno · 299 · Piotrków · 240 · Lutsk · Korosten · Kiev Reservoir
Rotterdam · Essen · Dortmund · 840 · Kassel · Cottbus · Legnica · Wrocław · Częstochowa · Radom · Rovno · Kiev
eda · Eindhoven · Düsseldorf · REPUBLIC · Dresden · Kielce · Zamość · Novograd-Volynskiy · 252
Antwerp · Cologne · Aachen · Weimar · Erfurt · Gera · Marx-Stadt · 1603 · Wałbrzych · Katowice · Rzeszów · L'vov · Zhitomir · UKRAINE · Belaya Tserkov
Brussels · Bonn · Bad Hersfeld · 983 · Plauen · 1244 · Hradec Králové · Kraków · Przemyśl · Ternopol' · Khmel'nitskiy
GIUM · FEDERAL · Koblenz · Wiesbaden · Karlovy Vary · CZECHOSLOVAKIA · Ostrava · Bielsko-Biala · 617 · Ivano-Frankovsk · Vinnitsa
Liège · Charleroi · 689 · 774 · Frankfurt · Main · Prague · Kolín · Plzen · Olomouc · Žilina · Prešov · Košice · Uzgorod · Kolomyya · Cherkassy
LUXEMBOURG · Trier · 816 · Würzburg · Bamberg · Nuremberg · České Budějovice · Jihlava · Brno · Znojmo · 1592 · 2043 · Mukachevo · Dniester · Kamenets-Podol'skiy · Uman'
Luxembourg · Saarbrücken · REPUBLIC · Regensburg · 1457 · Plzen · Passau · Linz · Danube · 1603 · Bratislava · Miskolc · Chernovtsy · Mogilev Podol'skiy · Pervomaysk
Thionville · Metz · Mannheim · Nuremberg · Zvolen · Košice · Nyíregyháza · Baia Mare · 2305 Pietrosu · Bel'tsy
Nancy · Karlsruhe · Stuttgart · Danube · Augsburg · Munich · Vienna · AUSTRIA · 2075 · Salzburg · Dachstein 2996 · Leoben · HUNGARY · Satu Mare · MOLD · AVIA · Orgejev
Reims · Strasbourg · Freiburg · Memmingen · Lake Constance · Zugspitze 2963 · Innsbruck · 2713 · Győr · Vác · Budapest · Debrecen · ROMANIA · South Bug
Chaumont · Mulhouse · 1493 · SWITZERLAND · Bàsle · Zürich · Zugspitze · Inn · 2076 · Danube · Suceava · Prut
Troyes · Dijon · Besançon · 5°E · 10°E · 15°E · 20°E · 25°E · 30°E

FEDERAL REPUBLIC

BALTIC SEA

Gulf of Bothnia

Gulf of Finland

n o p q r s t u v w x y z

0 100 200 300 miles
Average linear scale: 1 inch = 125 miles   1 cm = 80 km
0 100 200 300 400 500 Km

a b c d e f g h i j k l m

5°W · 5°E · 10°E

GREAT BRITAIN
Southampton · Dover
Bournemouth · Brighton · Strait of Dover · Calais · Gent · Brussels · BELGIUM · Cologne · Bad Hersfeld · Erfurt · Gera · G.
Plymouth · Exeter · Isle of Wight · Lille · Valenciennes · Liège · Aachen · Bonn · Karl-Marx-Stadt · Flauen
Land's End · Penzance · English Channel · Abbeville · Amiens · St Quentin · Sedan · LUXEM-BOURG · Trier · Koblenz · Wiesbaden · Frankfurt · Karlovy Vary
50°N
Cherbourg · Le Havre · Rouen · Compiègne · Reims · Thionville · Luxembourg · Saarbrücken · Mannheim · Würzburg · Nuremberg · Bamberg
Channel Islands (U.K.) · Guernsey · Caen · Seine · Évreux · Paris · Chartres · Metz · Nancy · Strasbourg · Karlsruhe · Stuttgart · GERMAN FEDERAL · Regensburg · 145
Jersey · Gulf of St. Malo · Granville · Alençon · Chaumont · Rhine · Danube · Augsburg · Munich
Brest · St. Brieuc · Rennes · Le Mans · Orléans · Troyes · Dijon · Besançon · Basle · Zürich · Freiburg · Lake Constance · Memmingen · Zugspitze 2963 · Innsbruck
Lorient · Angers · Tours · F R A N C E · Chalons-sur-Saône · Lucerne · Vaduz · LIECHTENSTEIN · Landeck
St. Nazaire · Nantes · Loire · Poitiers · Moulins · Mâcon · Geneva · Berne · SWITZERLAND · Chur · Bolzano · Dolomites
A T L A N T I C · 288 · Limoges · Clermont-Ferrand · St. Étienne · Lyon · Lake Geneva · Mont Blanc 4807 · Monte Rosa · Bernina · Bergamo · Lake Garda
La Roche-sur-Yon · 1885 · Massif · Aosta · Novara · Milan · Verona · Vicenza · Padua
O C E A N · La Rochelle · Angoulême · Central · Grenoble · Pelvoux 4102 · Alessandria · 3847 · Turin · Po · Brescia
Bay of · Saintes · Brive · Le Puy · Valence · Maritime Alps · Cuneo · Piacenza · Parma · Ferrara · Ravenna
45°N · Bordeaux · Dordogne · Aurillac · Rhône · Cévennes · Digne · Nice · Genoa · Modena · 2120 · Bologna · Rimini
Biscay · Agen · Lot · Nîmes · Avignon · Imperia · Gulf of Genoa · La Spezia · Florence · SAN MARINO
Adour · Garonne · Toulouse · Montpellier · Arles · Aix-en-Provence · MONACO · Livorno · Pisa · Arezzo · Perugia
Bayonne · Pau · Narbonne · Marseilles · Toulon · LIGURIAN SEA · Siena
Gijón · Santander · San Sebastián · Carcassonne · Gulf of Lion · Bastia · Elba · Grosseto
Corunna · Oviedo · 2417 · Cantabrian Mountains · Bilbao · Pau · Tarbes · 2504 · Perpignan · Corsica (France) · 2710 · Civitavecchia · Viterbo · Ter
Cape Finisterre · Santiago de Compostela · Ponferrada · 2533 · Vitoria · Pamplona · Jaca · Pico de Aneto 3404 · ANDORRA · 2923 · Gerona · Costa Brava · Ajaccio · Rome
Orense · León · Logroño · Huesca · Saragossa · Lérida · Bonifacio · Str. of Bonifacio · Latina
Vigo · Miño · Burgos · Soria · Ebro · Barcelona · Sassari · Olbia · TYRRHEN
Braga · Zamora · 2142 · Calatayud · Tarragona · Nuoro · Sardinia (Italy) · SEA
Oporto · Douro · Valladolid · Duero · Segovia · Guadalajara · Tortosa · 1834 · Oristano
Aveiro · 1382 · Salamanca · 2430 · Teruel · Castellón · Balearic Islands · Menorca · Cágliari
40°N · Guarda · Ávila · Madrid · 2020 · Alcudia · Cape Teulada
Coimbra · 2592 · S P A I N · Talavera de la Reina · Toledo · La Almarcha · Valencia · Mallorca · Palma
Leiria · Cáceres · Trujillo · Ciudad Real · Guadiana · Júcar · Albacete · Ibiza · M E D I T E R
Lisbon · Santarém · Mérida · Puertollano · Segura · Gandia · Cabo de la Nao · Costa Blanca
Setúbal · Badajoz · Alicante · Murcia · 2036 · Úbeda · Lorca · Cartagena
Évora · Sierra Morena · Córdoba · Jaén · Baza · Águilas
Sines · Beja · Aracena · Guadalquivir · Écija · Granada · 3478 · Sierra Nevada · Almería
Odemira · Mértola · Algarve · Huelva · Sevilla · Antequera · Motril · Dellys · Bejaia · Skikda · Annaba · Tabarka · Tunis
Sagres · Cape St. Vincent · Lagos · Faro · Gulf of Cádiz · Jerez de la Frontera · Málaga · Algiers · Tizi Ouzou · Constantine · Setif · 586 · Beja · Gulf of Tunis · Cape Bon · Kélibia
Cádiz · Algeciras · Gibraltar (U.K.) · Costa del Sol · Ténès · Blida · Medea · Bordj Bou Arreridj · Souk-Ahras · Le Kef · Tebourouk · Zaghouan · Pantelleria (Italy)
35°N · Tangier · Str. of Gibraltar · Ceuta (Sp.) · Tétouan · Mostaganem · Cheliff · 1983 · Tell Atlas · M o u n t a i n s · Batna · Aïn Beïda · Kairouan · Sousse · Linosa · Pelagie Islands (Sicily)
Asilah · Chechaouen · Oran · Mohammadia · Relizane · Tiaret · Metlili Chaamba · 1357 · Khenchela · Tebessa · Kasserine · El Djem · Mahdia · Cape Kaboudia · Lampedusa
Al Hoceima · Melilla (Sp.) · Sidi-bel-Abbes · Chellala · 767 · Bou Saada · 2326 · Fériana · Sfax · Kerkenna Islands
M O R O C C O · Ksar el Kebir · Beni Saf · Tlemcen · A t l a s · P l a t e a u x · Djelfa · Biskra · Gafsa
Aknoul · Oujda · Marhoum · Hauts · Monts des Ouled Nail · Chott Melrhir · Tozeur · Djerba
Ouerrha · Chott ech Chergui · Aflou · Ouled Djellal · Chott Djerid · Kebili · Zarzis
Bougtob · 1977 · Messaad · 40 · El Meghaier · Médenine · Gulf of Gabès
Méchéria · El Bayadh · Laghouat · Diamaa · El Oued · Ben Guerdane
A S a h a r a n · A L G E R I A · Touggourt · 238 · Zuwara · Al Aziziya
2236 · Brézina · Tilrhemt · Guerara · Hassi Messaoud · Bordj Bourguiba · Ghariy · Jadu
Aïn Sefra · Ghardaia · Ain Oussera · Ouargla · 145 · Bir Zar · Nalut · 688
Chebka du Mzab · Guerara · 306 · Great Eastern Erg · Remada · Mizda
Great Western Erg · 502 · El Goléa · Sinawen · LI

This map shows 1/60 of the earth's surface. Area scale: 1 □ inch on the map ≈ 15,000 □ miles on the ground 1 □ cm on the map ≈ 6000 □ km on the ground

n o p q r s t u v w x y z

a b c d e f g h i j k l m

POLAND

Dresden 15°E
Wałbrzych
Wrocław
Częstochowa
20°E
Kielce
Zamość
Lutsk
Rovno
Kcrosten
Kiev Reservoir
Nezhin
Sumy
30°E
Priluki
Akhtyrka
35°E
Prague
Hradec Králové
Kolin
Katowice
Kraków
Rzeszow
Przemyśl
L'vov
Novograd-Volynskiy
Zhitomir
Kiev
SOVIET UNION
Lubny
Poltava
Khar'kov
Valki
Plzen
Olomouc
Ostrava
Bielsko-Biala
Zakopane
Vistula
Ternopol
Khmel'nits'kiy
Vinnitsa
Belaya Tserkov'
Cherkassy
Kremenchugskoye Reservoir
Pereshchepino
České Budějovice
Žilina
Gerlachovsky 2663
Prešov
Stryy
Ivano-Frankovsk
Kolomyya
Kamenets-Podol'skiy
Uman'
Znamenka
Kremenchug
Dnprodzerzhinsk
Novomoskovsk
CZECHOSLOVAKIA
Jihlava
Znojmo
Brno
Zvolen
Košice
Užgorod
Mukachevo
Chernovtsy
Mogilev-Podol'skiy
UKRAINE
Kirovograd
Dnepropetrovsk
Passau
Linz
Danube
2043
Pervomaysk
Krivoy Rog
Nikopol
Zaporozh'ye
AUSTRIA
Vienna
Bratislava
Györ
Danube
Vác
Nyíregyháza
Satu Mare
Baia Mare
Pietrosu 2305
Suceava
Botoşani
Bel'tsy
MOLDAVIA
Orgejev
Melitopol
salzburg
Dachstein 2996
Leoben
2075
Budapest
Veszprém
HUNGARY
Debrecen
Oradea
Dej
2103
Iaşi
Kishinev
Tiraspol
Kakhovskoye Reservoir
dgastein
Klagenfurt
Graz
Balaton Lake
Cluj Napoca
Tirgu Mureş
Bacau
Siret
Odessa
Kherson
Novaya Kakhovka
Maribor
Varaždin
Nagykanizsa
Pecs
Szeged
Békéscsaba
Arad
Deva
Sibiu
Braşov
Belgrad
Kharkinitskiy Bay
Dzhankoy
18.
Sea of Azov
2863
Ljubljana
Zagreb
Osijek
Subotica
Zrenjanin
Timişoara
ROMANIA
Negoiu 2548
Galaţi
Mouths of the Danube
Tulcea
Belgorod
Simferopol
Feodosiya
45°N
lrieste
Rijeka
Pula
Cres
Karlovac
Novisad
Vršac
2509
Tirnu-Severin
P teşti
Poieşti
Sevastopol
1259
Jalda
Crimea
Zadar
Bihać
Banja Luka
Brod
Mitrovica
Belgrade
Danube
Smederevo
Craiova
Resiori
Bucharest
Ruse
Constanţa
Šibenik
Split
Zenica
2107
Sarajevo
Titovo Užice
Morava
Vidin
Danube
Roşiori
BLACK
Pag
Brac
Hvar
Korčula
Jablanica
2387
YUGOSLAVIA
Niš
Pirot
Vraca
Pleven
Kolarovgrad
Varna
SEA
Ancona
Monte Corno 2914
Pescara
Pelješac
Dubrovnik
Ivangrad
Priština
2693
Leskovac
Turnovo
Sliven
ADRIATIC SEA
Titograd
Kumanovo
Prizren
2375
Sofia
Stara Zaçora
Burgas
Avezzano 2793
Campobasso
Shkodër
2747
Skopje
Musala 2925
Plovdiv
Blagoevgrad
BULGARIA
Cape Ince
Foggia
Durrës
Tiranë
Titov Veles
Rhodope 2191
Kürdžali
Edirne
Sinop
Caserta
Benevento
Bari
ALBANIA
Ohrid Lake
Bitola
Sërra
Komotini
Luleburgaz
Bosporus
Ereğli
Karabük
Kastamonu
Samsun
aples
Salerno
Potenza
Brindisi
Taranto
Lecce
Korca
Prespa Lake
Edessa
Kavalla
Tekirdağ
Istanbul
Üsküdar
2565
2068
N
Monte 2248
Gulf of Taranto
Vlorë
Kozani 2533
Thessaloniki
Chalkidike
Thasos
Sea of Marmara
Izmit
Bandirma
Bursa
Bilecik
2543
Adapazari
Bolu
Gerede
Corum
Turhal
Sapri
Capo Santa Maria di Leuca
Corfu
Corfu
Jánina
Trikala
Lárisa
Imbros
Lemnos
Troy
Çanakkale
Balikesir
Eskişehir
Ankara
Kirikkale
40°N 54
Cosenza
Corigliano
Pindus
Larisa
AEGEAN
Canakkale
Ayvalik
Manisa
2446
Afyon
Kütahya
Yozgat
2345
Catanzaro
Volos
Northern Sporades
Lesbos
SEA
Akhisar
TURKEY
Kayseri
Lipari Islands
lermo
Messina
Reggio
Etna 3340
Riposto
Levkas
Lamia
Euboea
Chíos
Izmir
Alaşehir
3916
Sicily
Enna
Catania
Agrinion
Delphi
Chalkis
Sámos
Aydin
Anatolia
Lake Tuz
Akşehir
Konya
Niğde
altanissetta
Agrigento
Gela
IONIAN
Cephalonia
Patras
Gulf of Corinth
2224
Athens
Piraeus
Andros
Tinos
Menderes
Denizli
Lake Eğridir
Lake Beyşehir
Ereğli
3488
cata
Ragusa
Noto
SEA
Zante
Korinth
Pyrgos
Tripolis
Cyclades
Náxos
Muğla
Karaman
Kozan
Adana
Geyhan
Ka amai
Mílos
Cape Akritas
Southern Sporades
Fethiye
3085
Antalya
Alanya
Mersin
Iskenderun
Gozo
Valletta
Cape Matapan
Cape Malea
Kithira
Sea of Crete
Kárpathos
Rhodes
1215
Rhodes
Finike
Gulf of Antalya
Silifke
Anamur
Cape Anamur
Antakya
1795
MALTA
Kánea
Meambes 2456
Iráklion
Crete
CYPRUS
Nicosia
Famagusta
Latakia
Cape Andreas
35°N
R
Cape Arnauti
Olympus 1951
Larnaca
Tartus
Paphos
Limassol
Tripoli
3087
LEBANON
Beirut
Zahle
Damascus
Al Bayca
Darrah
Quneitra
Golan Heights
Dar'a
poli
Khoms
Al Marj
682
Benghazi
Al Jabar al Akhdar
Al Abyar
Haifa
Hadera
1241
Tarhuna
Misurata
Qaminis
Tobruk
ISRAEL
Tel-Aviv-Jaffa
Zarqa
Amman
Gulf of Sirte
Al Adam
169
Al Burdi
Nile Delta
Baltîm
Jerusalem
Dead Sea
Beni Walid
Buerát el Hsun
Sidi Barrani
Mersa Matruh
Rosetta
Dumyat
Gaza
Beer Sheba
Al Karak
Sirte
LIBYA
Sallum
Fuka
Alexandria
Damanhûr
Al Mansura
Port Said
Suez Canal
Ar Arish
15°E
20°E
EGYPT
25°E
30°E
35°E

0 100 200 300 miles
Average linear scale: 1 inch = 125 miles 1cm = 80 km
0 100 200 300 400 500

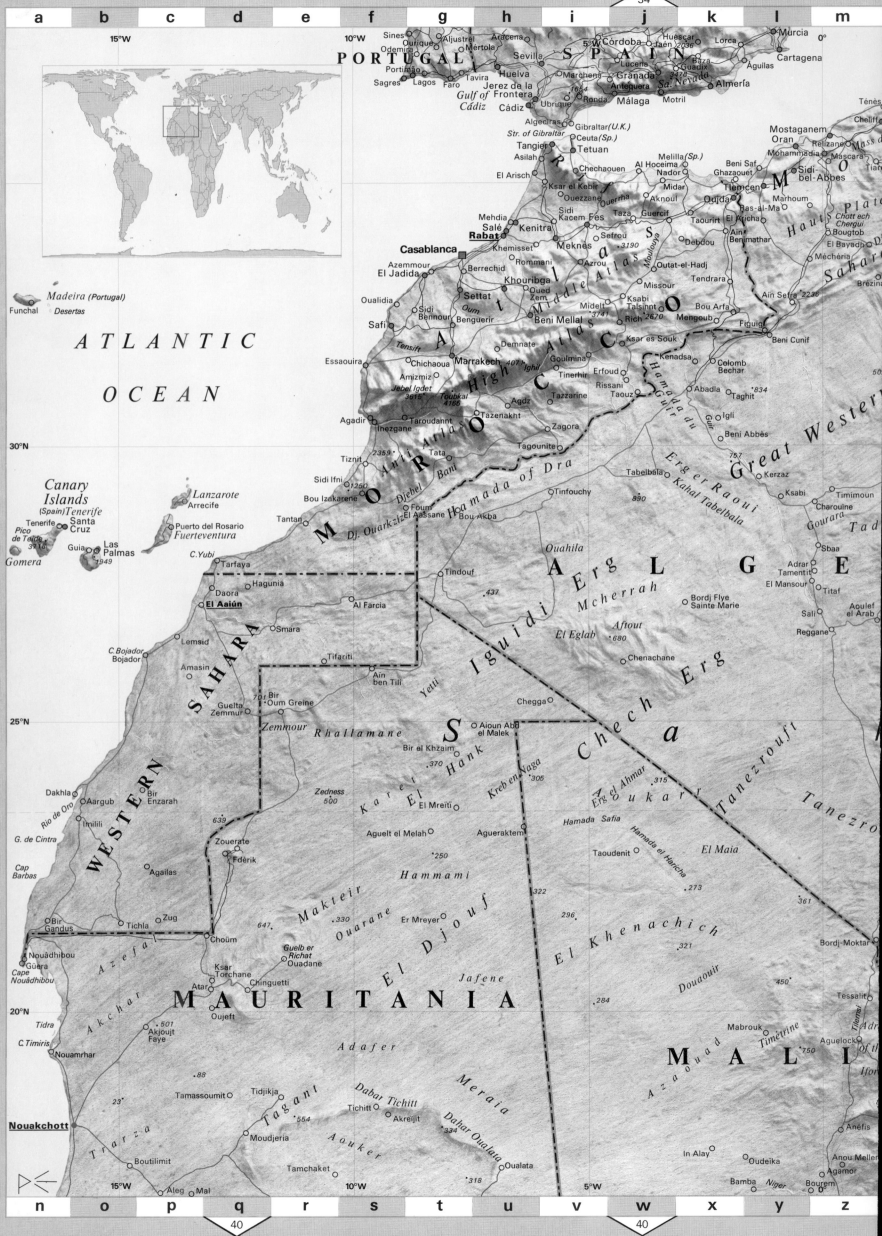

ATLANTIC

OCEAN

PORTUGAL
SPAIN

Sines
Odemira
Ourique
Aljustrel
Mértola
Aracena
Córdoba
Jaén
Huéscar
Baza
Guadix
Lorca
Murcia
Cartagena
Sevilla
Marchena
Lucena
Granada
Sa. Nevada
Almería
Águilas

Portimão
Lagos
Faro
Tavira
Huelva
Jerez de la Frontera
Ubrique
Ronda
Antequera
Málaga
Motril

Sagres
Gulf of Cádiz
Cádiz
Algeciras
Gibraltar (U.K.)
Ceuta (Sp.)

Str. of Gibraltar

Tangier
Asilah
Tetuan
Chechaouen
Al Hoceima
Melilla (Sp.)
Nador
Midar
Beni Saf
Ghazaouet
Tlemcen
Oran
Mostaganem
Mohammadia
Relizane
Mascara

El Arisch
Ksar el Kebir
Ouezzane
Ouerrha
Aknoul
Oujda
Ras-al-Ma
Marhoum

Mehdia
Salé
Rabat
Kenitra
Sidi Kacem
Fès
Taza
Guercif
Taourirt
El Aricha
Ain Benimathar
Chott ech Chergui
Bougtob

Casablanca
Khemisset
Meknès
Sefrou
Azrou
Debdou
Missour
Tendrara
El Bayadh
Méchéria

Azemmour
El Jadida
Berrechid
Rommani
Khouribga
Oued Zem
Ksabi
Talsinnt
Bou Arfa
Ain Sefra
Brézina

Oualidia
Settat
Benguerir
Demnate
Beni Mellal
Midelt
Rich
Mengoub
Figuig

Safi
Sidi Bennour
Marrakech
Goulmina
Ksar es Souk
Kenadsa
Beni Cunif

Essaouira
Chichaoua
Amizmiz
Tinerhir
Erfoud
Colomb Béchar

Jebel Igdet
Toubkal
Agadir
Taroudannt
Tazenakht
Tazzarine
Taouz
Abadla
Taghit

Agadir
Inezgane
Agdz
Zagora
Hamada du Guir
Igli

M O R O C C O

High Atlas
Middle Atlas
Anti Atlas

A L G E R I A

Tiznit
Tata
Bani
Hamada of Dra
Tabelbala
Kerzaz

Sidi Ifni
Bou Izakarene
Foum el Aassane
Bou Akba
Tinfouchy
Great Western

Tantan
Dj. Ouarkziz
Bou Akba

C. Yubi
Tarfaya
Hagunia
Al Farcia
Tindouf
Erg Iguidi
Bordj Flye Sainte Marie

Daora
El Aaiún
Smara
Lemsid
Tifariti
Ain ben Tili
Yetti
Chegga
Erg Chech

C. Bojador
Bojador
Amasin
Bir Oum Greine
Zemmour
Rhallamane
El Hank
Aioun Abd el Malek

Guelta Zemmur
Bir el Khzaim
Karet

WESTERN SAHARA

Dakhla
Aargub
Bir Enzarah
Kreb en Naga
Erg el Ahmar
Tanezrouft

Rio de Oro
Imilili
Zedness
El Mreiti
Hamada Safia

G. de Cintra
Zouerate
Aguelt el Melah
Agueraktem
Taoudenit
Hamada el Haricha
El Maia

Cap Barbas
Fdérik
Agailas
Hammami

Bir Gandus
Tichla
Zug
Choûm
Makteir
Ouarane
Er Mreyer
El Djouf
El Khenachich
Bordj-Moktar

Nouâdhibou
Güera
Ksar Torchane
Chinguetti
Guelb er Richat
Ouadane
Jafene
Douaouir
Tessalit

Cape Nouâdhibou
Azefal
Akchar
Atar
Oujeft

M A U R I T A N I A

M A L I

Tidra
Tamassoumit
Akjoujt
Faye
Adafer
Azaouad
Mabrouk
Timétrine
Aguelock

C. Timiris
Nouamrhar
Tamassoumit
Tidjikja
Dahar Tichitt
Meraia
In Alay
Oudeika
Anou Meller
Agamor

Nouakchott
Tichitt
Akreijit
Dahar Oualata
Oualata
Bamba
Bourem

Trarza
Boutilimit
Moudjeria
Tamchaket
Niger

Madeira (Portugal)
Funchal
Desertas

Canary Islands (Spain)
Tenerife
Santa Cruz
Pico de Teide
Gomera
Guia
Las Palmas

Lanzarote
Arrecife
Puerto del Rosario
Fuerteventura

This map shows 1/60 of the earth's surface   Area scale : 1 □ inch on the map ≃ 15,000 □ miles on the ground   1 □ cm on the map ≃ 6000 □ km on the ground

MEDITERRANEAN

SEA

ITALY

Egadi
Marsala
Corleone
Sciacca
Agrigento
Licata
Gela
Ragusa
Sicily
Etna 3340
Adrano
Enna
Caltanissetta
Noto
Riposto
Catania
Syracuse
Pachino
Bova Marina

15°E

Pantelleria (It.)

Linose
Pelagie Islands
(Sicily)
Lampedusa

Gozo
Valletta
MALTA

35°N

20°E

Algiers
Dellys
Boufarik
Blida
Medea
Cherchell
Khemis
Miliana
Ksar el
Boukhari
Ouarsensis
767
Djelfa
Monts des Ouled Nail
Messaad
Laghouat
Aflou
977
Atlas
Tizi Ouzou
Bejaia
Djidjelli
Skikda
Constantine
Setif
Bordj-Bou-
Arreridj
Batna
2326
Khenchela
Biskra
Tolga
Ouled
Djellal
Bou Saada
Metlili Chaamba

Annaba
Binzert
Mateur
Tabarka
Beja
585
Guelma
Souk-
Ahras
Aïn Beïda
Tebessa
Le Kef
135
Kasserine
Fériana
Redeyef
Metlaoui
Gafsa
Chott Melrhir
40
Tozeur
Nefta
Chott
Djerid

Gulf of
Tunis
Cap Bon
Kélibia
Tunis
Hammam Lif
Zaghouan
Sousse
Msaken
Mahdia
Kairouan
El Djem
Sfax
Cape Kaboudia
Kerkenna Islands
Gulf of Gabès
Gabès
Kebil
Djerba
Zarzis
Médenine
Ben Guerdane

TUNISIA

Sicilian Channel

El Oued
Guémar
Touggourt
Temacine
Djamaa
El Meghaier
Guerara
Dzioua
Berriane
Ghardaia
Ain Oussera
Ouargla
145
Hassi Messaoud
306
El Goléa
Hassi
Maroket
249
Hassi
Inifel
Hassi
Touareg
Bordj
Messouda
535
Hassi
bel Guebbour
Dhanet
Bordj Omer Driss
In Amenas
Tiguentourine
Edjele
718
Tarat
Illizi
Irharharene
Amguid
1772
1684
Arak Bordj
2330

238

Bordj
Bourguiba
Bi-Zar

Nalut
688
Sinawan
Ghadames
Darj
628

Remada
Jadu
Al Aziziyah
Gharyian
Beni Walid
Mizda

Zuwarah
Jarzur
Tajura
Tarhuna

Tripoli
Khoms
Zliten
Misurata

Benghazi
Qaminis

Gulf of Sirte

Tripolitania

Hamada el Homra

Al Qariya
As Shwayrif
Bu Ndjem
357

Buerát el Hsun
Sirte
111
Sirte Desert
147

Ajdabiya
Al Aqaylah

30°N

Ez Zemoul el Akbar

Tinrhert Hamada

Hamadat
Tingharat
Awayrat Wanin
652
Sukrah
Waddan
Hun
Zella
Tlisen
Maradah

El Fugha

Harudj el Asued
1200

RIA
636
In Salah
idikelt
879
kabli
Ahnet
1731
1420
In Ekker
In Amguel
1100
Ahaggar
2918
Atakor
Abalessa
Tit
Silet
Tamanrasset
Amsel
581
Timeiaouine

A

Tassili-n-Ajjer

2158
Fo-t
Gardel
Djanet
El Barcat
Ghat
Anai
1441
In Aseleh
In Ekker
2455
Djebel
Tahat Telertheba
Djebel Serkout
Hirafok
2306
Ideles

Idri
Brak
Semnu
Umm el Abid
Sabha
Ubari
Jarma
Murzuq
Zuwaylah
Timsah
Terbu
Qatrur
Tajarhi

LIBYA

Fezzan

Wau el Kebir

Wau en
Namus

Tmed Bu
Haschischa

38

25°N

Mangueni
Plateau
1054
Tu nu
1022
840
Ramlat Rabyana

Tropic of Cancer

1260

In Ebeggi
952
564
Ténéré du
Tafassâsset
Djado
Plateau
Madama
Auzu
Jabal Nub y
3376
Aozi

Tassili Oua-n-Hoggar
Ténéré
In Azaoua
Djado
Dao Timmi
Seguedine
Yeggueba
Cheffadene
Pic Toussidé
3265
Bardai
Zouar
Sherda
Yebbi Bou
Tibesti
Tarso Ahon
3325
Emi Koussi
3415
Gouro

CHAD

479
Borkou

1944

20°N

Bouressa
Timeiaouine
In
Azarat
In Abalene
Tin
Zaouatene
In Guezzam
Assamakka
Talak
400
Iférouane
Timia
NIGER
Aïr
2022
Bagzane
Aoude as
Agadez
In Azaoua
579
Tachi
Erg du Ténéré
Zoo Baba
Dibella

Grand Erg de Bilma
Achénoumma
Dirkou
Bilma
Aney
Djado
Kichi Kichi
Faya
234
Yarda

5°E
10°E
15°E
20°E

0 100 200 300 miles
Average linear scale 1 inch=125 miles 1 cm=80 km
0 100 200 300 400 500 Km

a b c d e f g h i j k l m

35

20°E 25°E 30°E 35°E

GREECE

Kithira
Cape Maléa
Sea of Crete
Rhodes
1215
Finike
Gulf of Antalya
Cape Anamur
2540
30°E
Cape Andreas
1795
TURKEY
Aleppo
Antakya
Idlib
Maskana
Silifke

Kárpathos
Rhodes
35°E
SYR
Cape Arnauti
CYPRUS
Latakia
1385
Hama
1279

35°N
Nicosia
Olympus 1951
Famagusta
Larnaca
Tartus
Homs
Tall Kalakh
Tadmur (Palmyra)
1405

Paphos
Limassol
Tripoli
Baalbek 2659
Sab Abar

MEDITERRANEAN
Beirut
Syrian
308
Nabk

LEBANON
Damascus
Zahla

SEA
Sur
Qunaitra
Golan Heights
1735
833

Nile Delta
Haifa
Hadera
Irbid
1247
Mafraq

Baltim
Dumyat
Tel-Aviv-Jaffa
Zarqa
Amman

Rosetta
Port Said
Gaza
850
Jerusalem
Beer Sheba
Dead Sea
Al Hadithah

Alexandria
Damanhûr
Al Mansura
Suez Canal
Ar Arish
Al Karak
Wadi as Sirhan

Fuka
Tanta
Zagazig
Great Bitter Lake
1641
Bayir
Al Isawiyah

Mersa Matruh
Al Alamein
Al Hammam
Ismâilîya
Nakhl
1515
Ma'an
Al Isawiyah

Sîdi Barrâni
Lower Egypt
Cairo
Suez
Wadi al Arish
Petra
Al Mudawwara

Libyan Plateau
Shubra al Kheima
Giza
Helwân
Sudr
Elat
Aqaba
Al Mughairah

Al Mekhily
Tobruk
Al Burdi
Qattara-Depression
Pyramids
Memphis
Ain Sukhna
Sinai
Nuweiba
1626
Al Bir
Al Qaliba

Benghazi
Al Adam
Sallûm
Qara
123
Al Faiyûm
Beni Suef
Gulf of Suez
Peninsula
Katherina 2637
Dahab
2580
Al Bad
Tabuk
Wadi al Akhdar

Qaminis
169
Marmarica
Siwa
Siwa Oasis
Ras Ghârib
Ofira
Ras Muhammad
Ash Sharmah
Taim

Ajdabiyah
Cyrenaica
Beni Mazâr
Gemsa
1990
Duba

30°N
30
Wadi al Hamim
Fort Qarain
Bahariya Oasis
Bawîti
Al Minyâ
Hurghada
Mada in Salih

Awjilah
Al Jaghbub
Jaghbub Oasis
Dairût
Port Safaga
Al Wajh

Jalu
Jalu Oasis
113
Farafra
Farafra Oasis
Asyût
Abu Tig
Akhmîn
Wadi Qena
Marsa Alam

LIBYA
EGYPT
Sohâg
Port Safaga
Al Wajh

Qasr
Al Balyana
Qena
Qusair

Dakhla Oasis
Mût
Al Khârga
Thebes
Qus
Karnak
Luxor
Arabian Desert

Tazirbu 184
Al Khârja Oasis
Isna
Idfu
Ras Abu Madd
1814

Zighan
Bâris
Upper Nile Egypt
Kom Ombo
Yanbu al Bahr

37
Kufrah Oasis
Wadi Garara
Berenice
1977
Ras Banas

Rabyanah
Al Jawf
1st Cataract
Aswân
Wadi Hadari
Bir al Hasa

625
Tropic of Cancer
Gilf Kebir Plateau
Lake Nasser
Wadi Allaqi
Wadi Ibib
Ras Abu Dara

25°N
Libyan Desert
Abu Simbel
Halaib
2217
Ras Hadarba

1893 Uweinat
2nd Cataract
Wadi Halfa
Wadi Oko
Dungunab
Ras Abu Shaga
Muhammad Qol

Kosha
Nubian Desert
2218 Erba

20°N
Ounianga Kebir
Erdi
Kerma
Abu Hamed
2260 Oda
Port Suda

Dongola
3rd Cataract
Umm Mirdi
Amur
Suakin

CHAD
SUDAN
Karima
4th Cataract
5th Cataract
Sinkat

Mourdi Depression
Al Khandaq
Merowe
Musmar

Fada 545
Ennedi
Debba
Korti
Berber
Haiya
Karor

Archei
Haouach
Howar
Baiyuda
Atbara
Derudeb
Adarama
Nakfi

al Milk
White Nile
Atbara
Mitatib
738

Shendi
Ker

Wadi Seidna
6th Cataract
517

20°E
25°E
30°E
Omdurman
Khartoum North
35°E
ETHI

n o p q r s t u v w x y z

42

This map shows 1/60 of the earth's surface. Area scale : 1 □ inch on the map ≃ 15,000 □ miles on the ground 1 □ cm on the map ≃ 6000 □ km on the ground

a b c d e f g h i j k l m

54

Countries: IRAQ, IRAN, SAUDI ARABIA, KUWAIT, BAHRAIN, QATAR, UNITED ARAB EMIRATES, OMAN, YEMEN, PEOPLE'S DEMOCRATIC REPUBLIC OF THE YEMEN

40°E 45°E 50°E 55°E

35°N 30°N 25°N 20°N

Raqqa, Al Hasakah, Sinjar, Tall 'Afar, Mosul, Arbil, Saqqez, Qojur, Qazvin, Takestan, Amol, Ghaem Shahr, Damghan, Mayamey

Suwar, Tall 'Afar, Sharqat, Kirkuk, Sulaimaniyah, Baneh, Bijar, Rezan, Karaj, Tehran, Semnan, Torud

Dayr az Zawr, Wadi ath Tharthar, Tikrit, Tuz Khurmatu, Sa'andaj, Kangavar, Hamadan, Qareh Su, Daryacheh-ye-Namak, Qom, Kashan, Khor, Tabas

Abu Kamal, Euphrates Anah, Al Hadithah, Jalaula, Karand, Bakhmaran, Eslamabad-e-Gharb, Borujerd, Arak, Mahallat, Ardestan, Anarak, Nain, Aliabad

Jabal at Tinef, Ar Ramadi, Baghdad, Ba'qubah, Ilam, Mehran, Khorramabad, Azna, Meymeh, Najafabad, Isfahan, Ardakan, Yazd, Darband

Ar Rutbah, IRAQ, Al Aziziyah, Dehloran, Dezful, Shush, Shahr-e-Kord, Qomsheh, Izadkhast, Mehriz, Bafq, Ravoro

Turaif, Karbala, Al Hilah, Al Kut, Keshvar, Masjed-e-Soleiman, Ahwaz, Abadeh, Shiraz, Anar, Zarand, Kerman

An Najaf, Ad Diwaniyah, Ar Fifah, Al Amarah, Ramhormoz, Behbahan, Dehbid, Rafsanjan, Baghin, Bam

Al Jalamid, Ar'ar, As Samawah, Al Qurnah, An Nasiriyah, Hawr al Hammar, Bandar-e-Khomeini, Abadan, Saadatabad, Hoseinabad, Sirjan, Laleh Zar, Baft

Nabk Abu Qasr, Ad Duwaid, As Salman, Al Busaiyah, Basra, Umm Qasr, Al Faw, Bubiyan, Bandar-e-Rig, Kazerun, Persepolis, Daryacheh-ye-Tashk, Dowlatabad

Sakakah, Al Jawf, Rafha, Ansab, NEUTRAL ZONE, Jahra, KUWAIT, Ahmadi, Bandar-e-Rig, Bushehr, Borazjan, Daryacheh-ye-Bakhtegan, Neiriz, Aliabad

An Nafud, Jubbah, Linah, Al Qaisumah, Ad Dibdibah, Al Wafra, Mina Saud, Safaniyah, Ras Halileh, Firuzabad, Fasa, Jahrom, Juyom, Hajiabad, Qotbabad

Ha'il, Al Maiyah, Bir Shari, Qaryat al 'Ulya, Abu Hadriyah, Al Jubayl, Zeydan, Kangan, Mand, Lar, Bandar-e-Lengeh, Minab

Tabah, Samirah, Buraidah, Az Zifi, Sarar, Ash Shumlul, Dhahran, Damman, Manama, BAHRAIN, QATAR, Doha, Gavbandi, Bastak, Bandar Abbas, Qeshm

SAUDI ARABIA, Ad Artawiyah, Al Majm'ah, Ushairah, Abqaiq, G. of Bahrain, Dukhan, Karana, Ar Ruwais, Ras al Khaimah, Sharjah, Dubai, OMAN

Hulaifah, Uqlat al Suqur, Unaizah, Shaqra, Khuff, Khurais, Al Hufuf, Al Ucailiyah, Umm Sa'id, Salwa, Abu Dhabi, Jebel Ali, Fujairah, Dibba

Khayber, Al Hanakiyah, Al Qurain, Durma, Riyadh, Sulaimaniyah, Haad, Marawah, Abu al Abyad, As Sila, UNITED ARAB EMIRATES, Al Ain, Shinas, Sohar

Buwatah, Medina, Badr Hunain, Afif, Ad Dawad mi, Muhairiqah, Jabal adh Dhanna, Tarif, Al Khaznah, Bu Hasa, Habshan, Ibri, Bahla

As Sidr, Mahd adh Dhahab, Zalim, Halaban, Al Hilah, Taraq, An Nashash, Liwa Oasis, Umm al Samim

Masturah, Jeddah, Mecca, Taif, ARABIA, Layla, As Sawadah, Ar Rub' al Khali, Wadi Aswad

Ras al Aswad, Arafat, Turabah, Ar Rauda, As Suq, Jabal Tuwayq, Ad Dahna, Al Uruq al Mutaridah

Mastabah, Al Lith, Ban Sar, Qal'at Bishah, Wadi ad Dawasir, As Sulaiyil, Al Khamasin, Al 'Uruq al Mu'taridah

Al Ulaya, Tathlith, Sauqira Bay

Al Qunfudhah, An Nimas, Asir, Dhofar, Sharbithat, Ras Sharbithat

Ras Kasar, Khay, Abha, Ad Darb, Khamis Mushait, Hima', Sanaw, Thamarit, Jabal al Qara, Salalah, Mirbat, Ras Mirbat, ARABIAN SEA

Mersa Teklay, Mitsiwa, Dahlak Islands, Zahran, Najran, Sa'dah, PEOPLE'S DEMOCRATIC REPUBLIC OF THE YEMEN, Jabal al Qamar, Raisut, Kuria Muria Islands

Farasan Is., Jizan, Midi, YEMEN, Al Hazm, Thamud, Al Ghaydah, Camar Bay, Ras Fartak

Hajjah, Huth, Wadi al Jawf, Haynan, Sayun, Wadi Masilah, Wadi al Jiz

n o p q r s t u v w x y z

43

60

ARABIAN GULF, Str. of Hormuz, Musandam Pen., Ash Sha'am, Gulf of Oman

Scale: 0 100 200 300 miles — Average linear scale: 1 inch=125 miles 1cm=80 km — 0 100 200 300 400 500 Km

a   b   c   d   e   f   g   h   i   j   k   l   m

15°W

Moudjéria
Boûmdeïd
Tamchaket
Boutilimit
Aleg   Mâl
Mederdra
Rosso   Senegal   Bogué
Dagana
St. Louis
Louga
Kiffa
Mbout
Kankossa
Kobenni
Hamoud
Maghama
Sélibabi

Aoukâr

600
Montagnes
de l'Affolé
Ayoûn el Atroûs
Oualâta
Néma
Bassikounou
Amourj
Timbedgha
Nioro du Sahel
Ballé
Nara
Sokolo
Nampala

In Alay
Oudeïka
Bamba
Bourem
Tombouctou
Goundam
Niafounké
Lake Faguibine
Lac Débo
Doro
Hombori
1155

MAURITANIA

Trarza

Irîgui

Tuare

S   a   h   e

Macina

15°N
Dakar
Cape Verde
Thiès   Mbaké
Mbour   Diourbel
Kaolack

SENEGAL

Ferlo

Linguère
Fourdou
Matam
Birou
Kidira   Kayes
Koniakari
Diéma
Didiéni
Diamou   Bafoulabé
Bamba
Tambacounda
Koumpentoum
Malème-Hodar

Banjul   Georgetown
Sere Kunda   GAMBIA   *Gambia*
Brikama   Basse   Santa Su
Bignona   Dialakoto
Karang   Dialafara
Casamance   Kolda   Niokolo   Saraya
Ziguinchor   Farim   Koba   Kédougou
Koundara

GUINEA-BISSAU

Mansôa   Bafatá
Bissau   *Corubal*
Gaoual   1538
Bissagos Islands   Catió   Boké   *Kogon*
Boffa   Fouta   Djalon   Labé   1264   Pita   Télémélé
Frie   Konkouré   Dalaba   1015   Dabola
Kindia   Mamou   1094   Sanouyah
Forécariah   Kabala   Faranah
Conakry   Kambia   Makeni   Koidu
Kamsar   *Little Scarcies*   *Rokel*

Sokolo
Mopti
Bandiagara
Djibo
Ouahigouya
Djenné
Ségou   *Niger*
San   *Bani*

MALI

BURKI

FAS

Ouagadougou

Yako   Kaya
Boulsa
Tenkodog
Toéssé   Po   Zabré
Léo   Bawk

Tougué
Dinguiraye   Siguiri
Kpuroussa
Kankan
Bafing
1028

GUINEA

Koundougou
Houndé
Bobo-Dioulasso   505
Sikasso   820
Banfora
Gaoua
Tumu   Navrongo   Walewal
Lawra   Bolgatanga   Gambaga
Wa   Yala   Pigu
Ga   *Black Volta*
Tamale

Bougouni
Garalo
Manankoro
Samatiguila
Odienné
Boundiali
Pogo
Ouangolodougou
Ferkéssédougou
Baouna
Kong   430
Koutouba
Sawla
Bole
Maluwe
Salaga

Kéouané
Bako
Morondo
Kani   Koro
Korhogo
Kanawolo
Katiola
Bondoukou
Goumeré   700
Bamboï
Kintampo
Techiman   Atebubu
Berekum
Sunyani
Mampong

GHANA

Kolda   Saraya

Mansôa
Bafatá
Bissau

Bohodou
Kissidougou
Kérouané
Macenta   1656   Beyla   1257   Tibé   1504
Guéckédou   Nzérékoré   1752   Man   1189
Zorzor
Loma   Mts.   1948

SIERRA   LEONE

Freetown
Bo   Pendembu
Kenema
Pujehun   *Sewa*   *Moa*   *Loffa*
Sherbro Island
Mano   River   *Mani*
Bomi   St. Paul   Gbarnga   Ganta
Hills   Bong   Danané
Tapeta   Guiglo
Toulépleu
Tchien

LIBERIA

Monrovia
Buchanan   *Cess*
Greenville
Juazohn
Plibo   Grabo
Harper   Tabou

Grain Coast

Biankouma
Séguéla
Bouaké
Danané
Duékoué   Daloa
Bouaflé
Yamoussoukro
Dimbokro   Abengourou
Toumodi
Akoupé
Agboville
Sassandra   Gagnoa   Lakota
Soubré
Tai   *Sassandra*
Bandama
Niénokoué   396
San Pédro   Sassandra
Cavally
Grand-Lahou
Dabou   Grand-Bassam
Abidjan
Prestea
Tarkwa
Sekondi-Takoradi

IVORY   COAST

Kossou Reservoir

Agnibilekrou
Kumasi
Kononglo
Nkawkaw
Obuasi   Koforidua
Dunkwa   Oda
554
Tano   *Komoé*
Awaso
Accra
Cape Coas

Ivory   Coast

Gold Coast

10°N

Conakry

5°N

A   T   L   A   N   T   I   C   O   C   E   A

Equator

15°W   10°W   5°W

n   o   p   q   r   s   t   u   v   w   x   y   z

This map shows 1/60 of the earth's surface.   Area scale : 1 ☐ inch on the map ≈ 15,000 ☐ miles on the ground   1 ☐ cm on the map ≈ 6000 ☐ km on the ground

a b c d e f g h i j k l m

5°E 10°E 15°E

Agamor
Anou Mellene ·500
Vallée de L'Azaouak
Azaouak
Tegguidda-n-Tessoum
Aouderas
Akrereb
10°E
Dibella
Toro Doum

Gao
In Talak
·500
Agadez
Mazalet
Ouyu Bezze Denga
Homodji
Agadem

Ansongo
Ménaka
Tillia
Tchin-Tabaradene
Termit N
Massif de Termit ·710
Ngourti
Moul
·280

N I G E R
Abala
Tahoua
Aderbissinat
Task
Idaye
·255
Nokou
Rig-Rig
15°N

·550
Niger
Tillabéri
Ouallam
Filingué
Illéla
Madaoua
Tanout
Gouré
Goudcumaria
Nguigmi
Lake Chad
Kanem
Mao
Mondo
Am Raya
Moussoro

Téra
·302
Matankari
Burni-Nkonn
Tessaoua
Zinder
Maïné-Soroa
Komadugu
Bosso
Baga
Ngouri
Massakori

Niamey
Torodi
Dogondoutchi
Illela
Maradi
Dungas
Nguru
Gashua
Geidam
Mainé-Soroa
Monguno
Djermaya
Karmé
Ngoura

NA
Say
Dosso
Sokoto
Katsina
Hadejia
Damakar
Dikwa
296 Fort-Foureau
N'Djamena
·442
CHAD

O
Kantchari
Koulou
Argunçu
Talata Mafara
Kaura Namoda
Kano
Potiskum
Damaturu
Maiduguri
Bama
Chari
Massenya

Fada-Ngourma
Diapaga
Gaya
Birnin-Kebbi
Anka
Gusau
Faskari
Funtua
Wudil
Faggo
Kari
Buni
1141
Mokolo
Guélengdeng
Bousso

Dapango
Tanguiéta
·550
Béroubouay
Kandi
Zuru
Yelwa
Zaria
Zalanga
Gongola
Gombe
Biu
Mubi
Maroua
Bongor
Ham

Sansanné-Mango
Natitingou
Bembéréké
Niger
Kontagora
Birnin Gwari
Kacuna
·1594 Goura
Bauchi
Bara
Wuyo
Moutouroua
10°N

BENIN
Boukombé
Djougou
Wawa
Tegina
Minna
Kafanchan
·1625 Kagora 1518 Pankshir
Jos
Numan
Garoua
Pala
Kelo
Lai

Lama-Kara
Parakou
Yashikara
Kaiama
Jebba
Bida
Abuja
Akwanga
Wamba
Zamko
Jalingo
Yola
Guidjiba
Moundou
Doba

Bassari
·772 Sokodé
Bassila
Igbetti
Ilorin
Niger
Baro
Lafia
Ibi
Beli
Poli
Tchollire
Toubore
Koumra

TOGO
Kilibo
Agoaré
Oyo
Ede
Lokoja
Benue
Wukari
Mbé
Gore

Blitta
Savé
Isevin
Oshogbo Ilesha
Makurdi
Takum
Adamaoua Highlands
Béka
Ngaoundéré
Bélel
Baïbokoum
Béboura
Bocaranga

Kpessi
·845
Savalou
Iwo Ife
Ado Ekiti
Kabba
Okene
Ayangba
Oturkpo
Banyo
Doualayel
Béké
Bétaré Oya

Lake Volta
Atakpamé
Abomey
Ibadan
Ikerre
Akure
Owo
Ondo
Ogoja
1850
Ntambe
Tibeti
Meiganga
Bozoum
Bossangoa

Kpandu
Nuatja
Iaro
Ijebu Ode
Lekki
Benin City
Enugu
Nkom
3008
Bamenda
Mamfe
Garoua Boulaï
Baboua
Bouar
Bombalé
CENTRAL

Kpalimé
Tsévié
Porto Novo
Lagos
Sapele
Onitsha
2700
Foumban
Bétaré Oya
Carnot
AFRICAN

Lomé
Ouidah Cotonou
Slave Coast
Warri
Afikpo
Cross
Uschang
Bafoussam
Yoko
Kenzou
Berbérati
Bania
REPUBLIC

Tema
Ugheli
Aba
2050
Bafang
Nkongsamba
Bafia
Ndjole
Bertoua
Batouri
Nola
5°N

Brass
Bonny
Port Harcourt
Calabar
Mt. Cameroon 4100
Buea
Yabassi
Sanaga
Nanga Eboko
Bangya

Malabo 2890
Limbé
Douala
Edéa Eséka
Yaoundé
Abong Mbang
Yokadouma
Bayanga

Luba ·2662
Bioko Island
Nyorg
Mbalmayo
Dja
Lokomo
Bomassa

N
Gulf
of
Guinea
Principe
Ebolowa
Sangmélima
Moloundou

SÃO TOMÉ
AND PRINCIPE
EQUATORIAL GUINEA
Ebebiyin
Bitam
Ntam
Souanké
Ouesso

Bata
Niefang
Oyem
1200 Tembo
937
Sembé
Liouesso

Mbini
1200
Mbini
Nkolabona
Mékambo
Pikounda

Cocobeach
Mitzic
Makokou
CONGO

São Tomé
São Tomé 2024
Libreville
Kougouleu
Lalara
·950
Booué
Likouala
Makoua

Pagalu (Equa. Guinea)
Ndjolé
Gabon
Lastoursville
Ewo
Boundji
Okoyo
Mossaka

GABON
Port-Gentil
Lambaréné
875
Okondja
Kellé
500
Owando
Kouyou
Zaïre

Ogooué
Lake Onangué
Koulamoutou
Moanda
Francevile
ZAÏRE
Omboué
Mouila
Mimongo
Ombona

n o p q r s t u v w x y z

0 100 200 300 miles
Average linear scale: 1 inch≈125 miles 1cm≈80 km
0 100 200 300 400 500 Km

20°E   25°E   30°E   35

CHAD

SUDAN

CENTRAL AFRICAN REPUBLIC

ZAÏRE

CONGO

UGANDA

TANZANIA

RWANDA

Ennedi

Bodélé

Fada

Koro Toro

Salal

Biltine

Abéché

Oum Hadjer

Ati

Mongo

Mangalmé

Guedi .1506

Bitkine

1613

Abou Deia

Mêlfi

Zakouma

Am Timan

Kendégué

Haraze Mangueigne

Sarh

Koumra

Maro

Kabo

Batangafo

Ouandago

Kaga Bandoro

Mbrés

Bossangoa

Bouca

Dékoa

Sibut

Bambari

Bogangolo

Damara

Bossembélé

Bangui

Bimbo

Zongo

Mbaïki

Zinga

Boyabo

Libenge

Enyélé

Dongou

Impfondo

Mbandaka

Ruki

Ingende

Kalamba

Bikoro

Lake Tumba

Yandja

Bolia

Inongo

Kiri

Ntadembele

Lake Mai-Ndombe

al Junayna

Adré

Kebkabiya

El Fasher

Zalingei

Jebel Marra .3071

Menawashei

Kass

Nyala

'Idd al Ghanam

Rahad al Berdi

Goz Beïda

Birao

Tiroungoulou

Ouadda

Ouanda Djallé

Ndélé

Yalinga

Bria

Bambari

Alindao

Kouango

Kongbo

Gambo

Bangassou

Rafaï

Dembia

Zémio

Obo

Li Yuba

Tambura

Doruma

Yambio

Maridi

Umm Keddada

Dam Gamad

Wad Banda

El Obeid

Er Rahad

al Nahûd

Abu Zabad

al Udaiya

al Fûla

Babanusa

al Muglad

Kadugli

Dilling

Ghubeish

al Da'ain

Sumaih

Aweil

Wau

Raga

Sopo

Pongo

Busseri

Toni

Rumbek

Mvolo

Mundri

Medi

Juba

Yei

Aba

Faradje

Khartoum

Omdurman

Khartoum North

Wadi Seidna

Shendi

Adarama

6th Cataract

El Hasaheisa

Wad Medani

El Gezira

Sennar

Singa

Rabak

Kosti

El Jebelein

Renk

Ed Damazin

Lake Roseires

Kurmuk

Paloich

Malakal

Tonga

Bentiu

Nasir

Dembidolo

Gambela

Akobo

Kongor

Bor

Pibor Post

Ngangala

Kapoeta

Torit

Kajo Kaji

Lokichok

Kakama

Nimule

Laropi

Arua

Gulu

Kitgum

Kotido

Moroto

Lira

Amudat

Masindi

Soroti

Hoima

Nakasongola

Kamuli

Mbale

Iganga

Tororo

Kampala

Jinja

Entebbe

Kisumu

Lake Victoria

Bukoba

Musoma

Tarime

Kigali

Gisenyi

Kayonza

Kabale

Kyaka

Lake Kivu

Lake Edward

Lake Albert

Lake Kyoga

Bunia

Beni

Butembo

Lubero

Walikale

Masisi

Goma

Mambasa

Komanda

Isiro

Watsa

Rungu

Baranga

Poko

Bambesa

Niangara

Dungu

Medje

Wamba

Nepoko

Zambeke

Kole

Bomili

Nia Nia

Banalia

Kisangani

Boyoma Falls

Yangambi

Bengamisa

Batama

Opiene

Ubundu

Punia

Lubutu

Kindu

Opala

Ikela

Yomboto

Monkoto

Yalifafu

Bosanga

Ikela

Befori

Samba

Yali

Djolu

Befale

Boende

Watsi

Watsi-Kengo

Bolomba

Lulonga

Waka

Basankusu

Bongandanga

Busu-Djanoa

Basoko

Aruwimi

Yahuma

Yambuya

Isangi

Madula

Lingomo

Yekana

Bumba

Lisala

Mongola

Budjala

Kungu

Gemena

Businga

Bosobolo

Gbadolite

Mobayi-Mbongo

Yakoma

Abumonbazi

Bondo

Angu

Bili

Api

Ango

Ese

Titule

Buta

Aketi

Dulia

Bodala

Modjamboli

Ibembo

Gombari

Isiro

Watsa

This map shows 1/60 of the earth's surface. Area scale : 1 ☐ inch on the map ≙ 15,000 ☐ miles on the ground 1 ☐ cm on the map ≙ 6000 ☐ km on the ground

41

a b c d e f g h i j k l m

Derudeb · Mersa Teklay · Jizan · Sa'dah · Thamud · Al Ghaydah

·2589 · 40°E · 45°E · 50°E

Mitatib · Nakfa · Farasan Islands · Midi · Huth · al Hazm · Haynan · Sayun · Wadi al Jiz · Makrah · Qamar Bay · Ras Fartak

·738 · Barka · Red · Sea · Hajjab · al Mahdad · Sir'wa · Bawda · Wadi Masilah

Kasala · Keren · 2617 · Mitsiwa · Dahlak Islands · San'a · YEMEN · PEOPLE'S DEMOCRATIC REPUBLIC OF THE YEMEN · 15°N

hashm al Girba · Akordat · Asmara · 2374 · Dekemhare · Az Zaydivan · ·2242 · Hadramaut · Sayhut

Showak · Adi Quala · Adi Keyih · Hodeida · Isba · Dhamar · Manar · al Baida · Ba'wda · Riyan · 2185 · al Mukalla · al Shihr

Gedaret · Humera · Aksum · Adwa · Mekele · Kwiha · Ba't al Faqih · Zabad · Ibb · Manar ·3350 · Lawder · Abyan

·699 · Adi Arkay · Adigrat · Lake Assale · Hays · Ta'izz · Ahwar

Mesfinto · Ras Dashen ·4550 · Maychew · Ramlu ·2130 · al Mukha · Turbah · Ghedir · Aden

Metema · Gonder · Abune Yoset · Danakil · Aseb · Musa Ali · Bab al Mandab · Gulf of Aden

Gorgora · ·2223 · ·4190 · Kobbo · 850 · Lahej

Guba · Lake Tana · Addis Zemen · Debre Tabor · Weldiya · Asayta · Randa · Tadjourah · Abd al Kuri

·3131 · Beleya · Bahir Dar · Tisisat Falls · Guna · Betehor · Tendaho · 1783 · Arta · DJIBOUTI · Cape Guardafui · Bereda

Bure · ·4052 · Dese · Kembolcha · Lake Abbe · Ali-Sabieh · Djibouti · Hodde ·1400 · El Gal

Dangla · 2960 · Ethiopian · Debre Markos · Bati · Dikhil · Bosaso · 2200

Gimbi · Highlands · Dejen · Karakore · Cewane · ·1789 · Berbera · Mait · al Mado · Las Koreh · Erigavo · Carcar Mountains · Ras Hafun

Amara ·3146 · Fiche · Debra Birhan · Dire Dawa · 3292 · Buramo · Arde ·1858 · Las Dave · Wadi Giahel

Nekempt · Hagere Hiywot · Addis Ababa · ·2408 · Sheno · Miaso · Harer · Babile · Jijiga · Hargeisa · Burao · Bur Anod ·1097 · Gardo · Bender Beila

Arjo · Ghion · Debre Zeit · Nazret · Awash · Asbe Tafari · 2084 · Kirit · El Dab · Las Anod · Sinugif · Garoe · Eil

Bedele · Welkite · 3719 · Gugu ·3060 · Ahmar Mountains ·1856 · Rabableh

Metu · Gore · Agaro · Jima · Lake Ziway · Asela · Fik · Degeh Bur · SOMALIA · Baduen · El Hamurre

Maigudo ·2386 · Lake Abiyata · Lake Langano · Kaka ·4190 · Hamarre Hadad · Sigbell · Galca · Berdale

Bonga · Sodo · 2743 · Awasa · ·2115 · Imi · Kebri Dehar · Ghelinsor · Mirsale

Shishinda · Mizan Teferi · Dila · Wendo · Mendebo Mountains · Megalo · Warder · Godinlave · Dusa Mareb

Maji · Jinka · Lake Abaya · Lake Chamo · Kibre Mengist · Gode · Shilabo · Kelafo · Sinedogo · Obbia

Key Afer · Gidole · Konso · ·1441 · Negele · Hargele · Mustahil · Ferfer

Kelem · Yabelo · Filtu · Dawa · Lema Shilindi · El Kere · Belet Huen · El Bur · 5°N

okwo · Chew Bahir Lake · Bokol Mayo · Yet · Maas · El Dere

odertang · Banya Fort · Mega · Dolo · Hoddur · Tigieglo · Bulo Burti · INDIAN

okitaung · Lake Turkana · Moyale ·1260 · Ramu · Mandera · Luuq Ganana · Calie Corar ·566 · OCEAN

alekol · North Horr · Sololo · Bur Acaba · Baidoba ·600 · Mahaddei Uen · Acale

Lodwar · Chalbi Desert · Buna · El Wak · El Uach · Dinsor · Uanle Uen · Giohar

Lorukumu · Loiyangalani · Bardera · Afgoi

Lokichar · Marsabit · Tarbai · Saco Uen · Coriolei · Mogadishu

Lokori · Nyiru ·2752 · South Horr · Wajir · Duguma · Shibeli · Merca

Baragoi · Laisamis · ·2375 · Habaswein · Afmadu · Gelit · Giamama

Kapedo · Maralal · Kisima · Archer's Post · Mado Gashi · Balad Cogani · Araara

tale · Eldoret · Baringo Lodge · Isiolo · Meru · Garba Tula · Liboi · Hagadera · Kisimaio

apsabet · Nyahururu ·2360 · Nanyuki · Kenya ·5200 · Saka · Equator · 0°

Nakuru · KENYA · Garissa

Kericho · Gilgil · Embu · Kolbio

Naivasha · 3994 · Kijabe · Thika · Mwingi · Tana

Narok · Nairobi · Kitui · Hola

Machakos · Mutomo · Mokowe · Patta Island

Lake Natron · Magadi · Kajiado

40°E · 45°E · 50°E

n o p q r s t u v w x y z

45

0 · 100 · 200 · 300 miles · Average linear scale: 1 inch≈125 miles 1 cm≈80 km · 0 · 100 · 200 · 300 · 400 · 500 Km

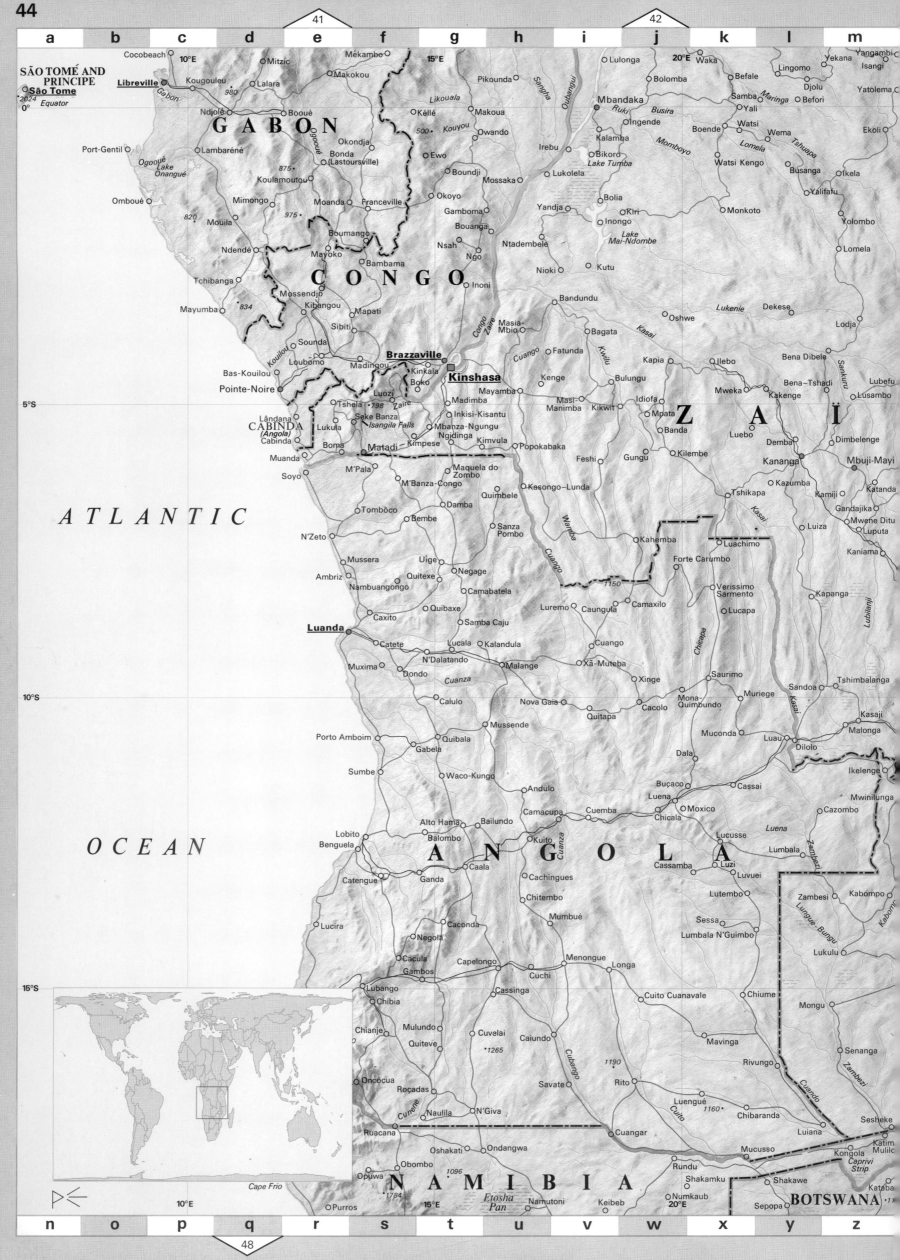

a b c d e f g h i j k l m

SÃO TOMÉ AND PRINCIPE
São Tome
2024
0° Equator

Cocobeach 10°E
Libreville Kougouleu
Ndjolé Mitzic
Lalara
Booué
Makokou Mékambo 15°E
Pikounda
Kéllé Makoua
Likouala
Kouyou 500
Okondja Owando
Ewo
Boundji
Okoyo Mossaka
Gamboma
Bouanga
Ngo
Inoni
Nsah
Ntadembele

Lulonga 20°E Waka
Bolomba Befale Lingomo Yekana
Yatolema Isangi
Mbandaka Ruki Busira Samba Maringa Djolu
Ingende Yali Befori
Irebu Boende Watsi Wema Ekoli
Kalamba Lake Tumba Watsi Kengo Tshuapa
Bikoro Busanga
Bolia Monkoto Yalifafu
Yandja Kiri Ikela
Inongo Yolombo
Lake Mai-Ndombe Lomela

GABON 980

Port-Gentil
Omboué
Mouila 820
Mayumba 834
Tchibanga

Lambaréné
Mimongo 875
Moanda Franceville 975
Boumango
Mayoko
Bambama

CONGO

Mossendjo
Kibangou Mapati
Sibiti
Sounda
Loubomo Madingou
Bas-Kouilou
Pointe-Noire

Brazzaville
Kinkala
Boko Kinshasa
Madimba
Inkisi-Kisantu
Mbanza-Ngungu

Masia-Mbio
Bandundu
Oshwe Lukenie Dekese
Bagata Lodja
Cuango Fatunda Kasai
Kenge Kapia Ilebo Bena Dibele
Bulungu Bena-Tshadi Lubefu
Masi-Manimba Kikwit Idiofa Mweka Kakenge Lusambo
Mpata Banda Luebo Demba Dimbelenge
Kazumba Kananga Mbuji-Mayi
Kamiji Katanda
Gandajika Mwene Ditu

ZAÏ

ATLANTIC

Muanda
Soyo
N'Zeto

Lândana
CABINDA
(Angola)
Cabinda
Lukula
Boma Matadi
Tshela 798
Seke Banza
Isangila Falls
Kimpese
Zaire
Luozi

M'Pala
Tombôco
Bembe
Mussera
Ambriz
Nambuangongo

Maquela do Zombo
M'Banza-Congo
Damba
Quimbele
Uige Negage
Quitexe
Camabatela

Kimvula
Popokabaka
Feshi
Gungu Kilembe

Sanza Pombo
Luremo Caungula Camaxilo
Forte Carumbo 1150
Kahemba Luachimo
Verissimo Sarmento Kapanga
Lucapa

Kasaji

Luiza
Kaniama

Chitapa
Lubilanji

OCEAN

Luanda
Catete
Muxima
Dondo
Porto Amboim
Sumbe

Caxito
Quibaxe
Samba Caju
N'Dalatando Malange
Cuanza
Calulo
Quibala
Gabela
Waco-Kungo

Lucala Kalandula
Xá-Muteba
Cuango
Xinge
Nova Gaia Quitapa Cacolo
Mussende
Andulo

Saurimo
Mona-Quimbundo
Muconda Muriege Sandoa Tshimbalanga
Dala Luau Kasaji
Buçaco Cassai Malonga
Luena Dilolo
Moxico Cazombo
Chicala Ikelenge
Mwinilunga

ANGOLA

Lobito Balombo
Benguela Caala
Catengue Ganda
Lucira

Alto Hama Bailundo
Kuito
Caála

Camacupa
Cuemba
Lucusse
Lumbala
Cassamba Luzi Luvuei
Cachingues
Chitembo
Mumbué

Luena
Lutembo
Zambesi Kabompo
Lungue-Bungu
Lukulu

Kabompo

Negola
Cacula
Gambos
Capelongo
Cuchi
Menongue Longa
Sessa
Lumbala N'Guimbo

Caconda

Lubango
Chibia
Chianje
Mulundo
Quiteve
1265

Cassinga
Cuvelai
Caiundo

Cuito Cuanavale
Chiume
Mongu

Cubango 1190
Mavinga
Rivungo
Senanga

Cuando
Zambesi

NAMIBIA

Oncócua Roçadas
Cunene
Naulila N'Giva
Ruacana
Oshakati Ondangwa
Opuwa Obombo 1096
Purros
Cape Frio

Savate
Rito Luengue 1160
Chibaranda
Luiana
Mucusso
Rundu Shakamku
Shakawe
Numkaub Keibeb
Sepopa

Cuangar Caprivi Strip Kongola Katima Mulilo Sesheke
BOTSWANA Kataba

1784
Etosha Pan
Namutoni 20°E

n o p q r s t u v w x y z

This map shows 1/60 of the earth's surface. Area scale: 1 □ inch on the map ≃ 15,000 □ miles on the ground 1 □ cm on the map ≃ 6000 □ km on the ground

a b c d e f g h i j k l m

43

UGANDA

KENYA

SOMALIA

Kisangani
Madula
Boyoma Falls
Ubundu
Pene-Tungu
Opienge
Beni 5109
Port Portal
Kasese
Kyanjojo
Kavanga
Iganga
Kaliro
Tororo
Eldoret
Loruk
Baringo Lodge
Archer's Post
Mado Gashi
Afmadu
Belesc Cogani
Butembo
Kasindi
Kampala
Entebbe
Mubende
Jinja
Kakamega
Kapsabet
Nyahururu
Meru
Garba Tula
Hagadera
Liboi
Kisimaio
Equator 0°
Lubero
Lake Edward 2341
Lake George 2197
Masaka
Kisumu
Kericho
Nakuru
Gilgil
Nanyuki
Mt. Kenya 5200
Saka
Garissa
Walikale
Rutshuru
Kabale
Isheshe River
Kikagati
Musoma
Kisii
Kilkoris
3100
Naivasha
Kijabe
Thika
Mwingi
Hola
Patta Island
Masisi
Karisimbi 4507
Goma
Ruhengeri
Gisenyi
Kayonza
Bukoba
Tarime
Mara
Narok
Nairobi 1662
Kitui
Machakos
Mutomo
Mokowe
Kigali
Gitarama
Kavumu
Bukavu
Cibitoke
Kayanza
Nyakanazi
Geita
Ngudu
Ukereve Islands
Banagi
Magadi
Kajiado
2775

RWANDA

BURUNDI

Bujumbura

Lake Victoria

Mwanza
Shinyanga
Manonga
Mbulu
Makuyuni
Arusha
Meru 4556
Kilimanjaro 5895
Moshi
Manyami
Malindi
Kilifi
Mombasa

TANZANIA

Lake Tanganyika

Dodoma

Nzega
Ibologero
Tabora
Singida
Kondoa Irangi
Korogwe
Handeni
Segera
Tanga
Pemba Island

INDIAN

OCEAN

Lake Rukwa
Mbeya
Iringa
Dar-es-Salaam
Zanzibar
Zanzibar Island
Bagamoyo
Chalinze
Kisarawe
Morogoro
Kibiti
Mafia Island
Kilindoni
Mohoro

Lake Malawi

MALAWI

Lilongwe
Blantyre
Zomba
Lake Chilwa

ZAMBIA

Lusaka

ZIMBABWE

Harare

MOZAMBIQUE

Nampula
Nacala
Quelimane

Kariba Reservoir
Victoria Falls
Livingstone

Average linear scale : 1 inch = 125 miles, 1 cm = 80 km

25°E · Kaloko · Luvua · Sange · Moba · Lake Tanganyika · Mpanda · Kitunda · Rungwa · Kilosa · Morogoro · Chalinze · Bagamoyo 40°E · Dar-es-Salaam

Kaniama · Kabongo · Manono · Kiambi · Kapona · 2460 · Rungwa · 2287 · 2646 · Kisarawe

1060 · Mulongo · Marungu Mountains · Namanyere · Lake Rukwa · Mbuyuni · Mikumi · Kibiti · Mafia Island

Pidi · Kikondja · Malemba Nkulu · Mukana · 2418 · Sumbawanga · Kipembwe · Iringa · 2576 · Ifakara · Mohoro · Kilindoni

ZAIRE · 1139 · Pweto · Sumbu · Kasanga · Makongolosi · Chunya · Sao Hill · 2072 · Mahenge · Luhombero · Nangurukuru

Kamina · Lake Upemba · Mitwaba · Chiengi · Mpulungu · Mbala · Chimala · Mbeya · Uyole · Makambako

Kabondo Dianda · Lake Mweru · Nchelenge · Mporokoso · 2559 · Tunduma · Nakonde · Itungi · Njombe

Kamba · Mukana · Kawambwa · Kasembe · Kapatu · Kasama · Isoka · Karonga · Lukumburu · Songea · Lindi · Mingoyo · Mtwara

Busanga · Bunkeya · Kasenga · Munungu · Luwingu · Mbesuma · Chilumba · Gumbiro · Nachingwea · Masasi

Kolwezi · Luambo · Likasi · Minga · Mansa · Lake Bangweulu · 1475 · Chinsali · 2606 · Livingstonia · Tunduru · Nangomba · Newala · Diaca · Mocimboa da Praia

ZAMBIA · Kambove · Samfya · Chisoso · Chama · Rumphi · Mzuzu · Chamba · Ruvuma · Mueda

Mwinilunga · Chisasa · Solwezi · Chembe · Mpika · Chilonga · Nkhata Bay · Maniamba · 1836 · Litunde · Marrupa · Macomia

Kipushi · Lubumbashi · Mukuku · Chibembe · Lundazi · Jenda · Mzimba · Lichinga · Malanga · Nantulo

Chililabombwe · Mokambo · Kapalala · Chipata · Mchinji · Dwangwa · Massangulo · Nungo · Montepuez · Metoro · Pemba

Chingola · Mufulira · **Lake Malawi** · Nkhotakota · Kasungu · Lúrio

Kitwe · 1350 · Ndola · Kanona · Serenje · Chibembe · Katete · Salima · **Lilongwe** · Namapa

1261 · Luanshya · Chifwefwe · Nyimba · Petauke · Dedza · **MALAWI** · Mandimba · Cuamba · Nacaroa · Nacala

Kabompo · Kasempa · Kapiri Mposhi · Kabwe · Kachalola · Chitunde · 2035 · Mangochi · Mutuali · Ribauè · Namialo · Lumbo · Moçambique

Kaoma · Lubungu · Mumbwa · Landless Corner · Fingoé · Bene · Balaka · Gurué · Nampula · Monapo

15°S · Rufunsa · Cabora-Bassa Reservoir · Songo · Zomba · Molócuè · Liupo

1220 · Namwala · Mazabuka · **Lusaka** 1279 · Zambezi · Zumbo · Chiúta · 560 · **Blantyre** · Limbe · Errego · Angoche · Nameti

Sesheke · Choma · Kariba Reservoir · Mkumbura · Tête · Mulanje · 3000 · 200 · Moma

Katima Mulilo · Livingstone · Kariba · 1204 · Karoi · Mhangura · Mount Darwin · Nyamapanda · Changara · Tambara · Nsanje · 2054 · Mocuba · Mucubela · Pebane

Kazungula · Victoria Falls · Binga · Nembudziya · Banket · Mvurwi · Bindura · Mutoko · Guro · Vila de Sena · **MOZAMBIQUE** · Namacurra

Kataba · 1108 · Hwange · Dete · Gwai River · Mutoko · 2592 · Inyanga · Catandica · 1862 · Caia · Quelimane

Pandamatenga · **ZIMBABWE** · Kadoma · Chegutu · **Harare** 1472 · Rusape · Mopeia · Inhaminga · Chinde

Gwai · Kenmaur · Kwe Kwe · Chivhu · 1447 · Dorowa · Mutare · Chimoio · Gorongosa · 105 · Dondo

1000 · Nkayi · Gweru · Chatsworth · Nyanyadzi · Chimanimani · 2436 · Beira

Basotho · Tsholotsho · 1028 · Masvingo · Chipinge · Nova Golegã · Sofala Bay

20°S · Kanyu · Nata · Bulawayo 1345 · Zvishavane · Zimbabwe · Rupisi · Espungabera

Tsoe · Makgadikgadi Pans · Mosetse · Plumtree · Antelope Mine · Gwanda · Tuli · Chiredzi · Macane · Jofane · 502

Xhumo · Letlhakane · 974 · Tlalamabele · Francistown · Mwenezi · Rutenga · 500 · Massangena · Mabote · Mapinhane · Inhassoro · Bazaruto

BOTSWANA · Serule · Selebi-Phikwe · Beitbridge · Bubye · Tswiza · Chicualacuala · Machaila · Mapai · Chigubo · Funhalouro · Massinga

Metsiamonong · Shoshong · Mahalapye · Pontdrift · Messina · Pafuri · 438 · Panda · Inhambane

Kikao · Soje · Marken · Louis Trichardt · Shingwedzi · Limpopo · 132 · Quissico

Molepolole · Jwaneng · **Gaborone** · Thabazimbi · Pietersburg · Tzaneen · Phalaborwa · Massingir · 169

Kanye · Lobatse · 2085 · Nylstrom · Warmbad · Steelpoort · Sable · Magude · Macia · Xai-Xai

25°S · Zeerust · Dwarsberg · Groblersdal · Lydenburg · Witrivier · Skukuza · Manjacaze

SOUTH AFRICA · Rustenburg · **Pretoria** 1733 · Witbank · Middelburg · Waterval Boven · Komatipoort · **Maputo**

Lichtenburg · Roodepoort · **Johannesburg** 1661 · Benoni · Springs · Carolina · Nelspruit · 515 · **Mbabane** · Namaacha · Bela Vista

Delareyville · Potchefstroom · 1253 · Germiston · Bethal · Ermelo · Manzini · **SWAZILAND** · Catuane

Klerksdorp · Vereeniging 1440 · Standerton · 25°E · 30°E · 35°E · 40°E · **Maputo**

This map shows 1/60 of the earth's surface. Area scale : 1 □ inch on the map ≈ 15,000 □ miles on the ground 1 □ cm on the map ≈ 6000 □ km on the ground

45°E   50°E   55°E   60°E

Aldabra Island

10°S

I N D I A N   O C E A N

Moroni
COMOROS

Comoros Islands

Moheli   *Anjouan*

○Dzaoudzi
Mayotte (France)

○Antsiranana

Nosy-Bé
Hell-Ville○

○Ambilobe

○Iharañe

Tsaratanana
2876
Mountains

○Sambava

Mozambique

○Andapa

Antsohihy○

○Antalaha

15°S

Befandriana Av.○
1214
Maroantsetra○

○Ambohitralanana

Mahajanga○
Port-Bergé-○
Vaovao

○Mahalevona

Mandritsara○

Betsiboka

Marovoay○   ○Mampikony

○Mananara

Mahavavy

1301

Nosy Boreha

Miarinarivo○

1325

M A D A G A S C A R

Maevatanana○

Andriamena○

1545

○Morafenobe

Voridiala○
Toamasina○

○Ankazobe

○Antsalova

Antananarivo
1384

Tsiroanomandidy○

2643

Mandoto○

Manambolo

Mahanoro○

○Tsimafana

Betafo○
Antsirabe○

Morondava○
Mahabo○

Tsiribihina
2140

○Fandriana

20°S

Port Louis
MAURITIUS

○Ambositra

○Mancabe

Mananjary○

Mangoky

Fianarantsoa○

○Ironoro

Isalo Mountains

Saint-Denis
3063
Réunion (France)

○Morombe

Ambalavao○
Manakara○

2658

○Ankazoabo

1348

Ihosy○

○Ivohibe

○Manombo

Mananara

○Farafangana

Toliara○
Andranovory○

Betroka○
1824

○Vangaindrano

Tropic of Capricorn

○Betioky

Ampanihy○

1957

Antanimora○

○Taolañaro

Tsihombe○
Ambovombe○

25°S

45°E   50°E   55°E   60°E

0   100   200   300 miles

Average linear scale : 1 inch ≈ 125 miles   1 cm ≈ 80 km

0   100   200   300   400   500 Km

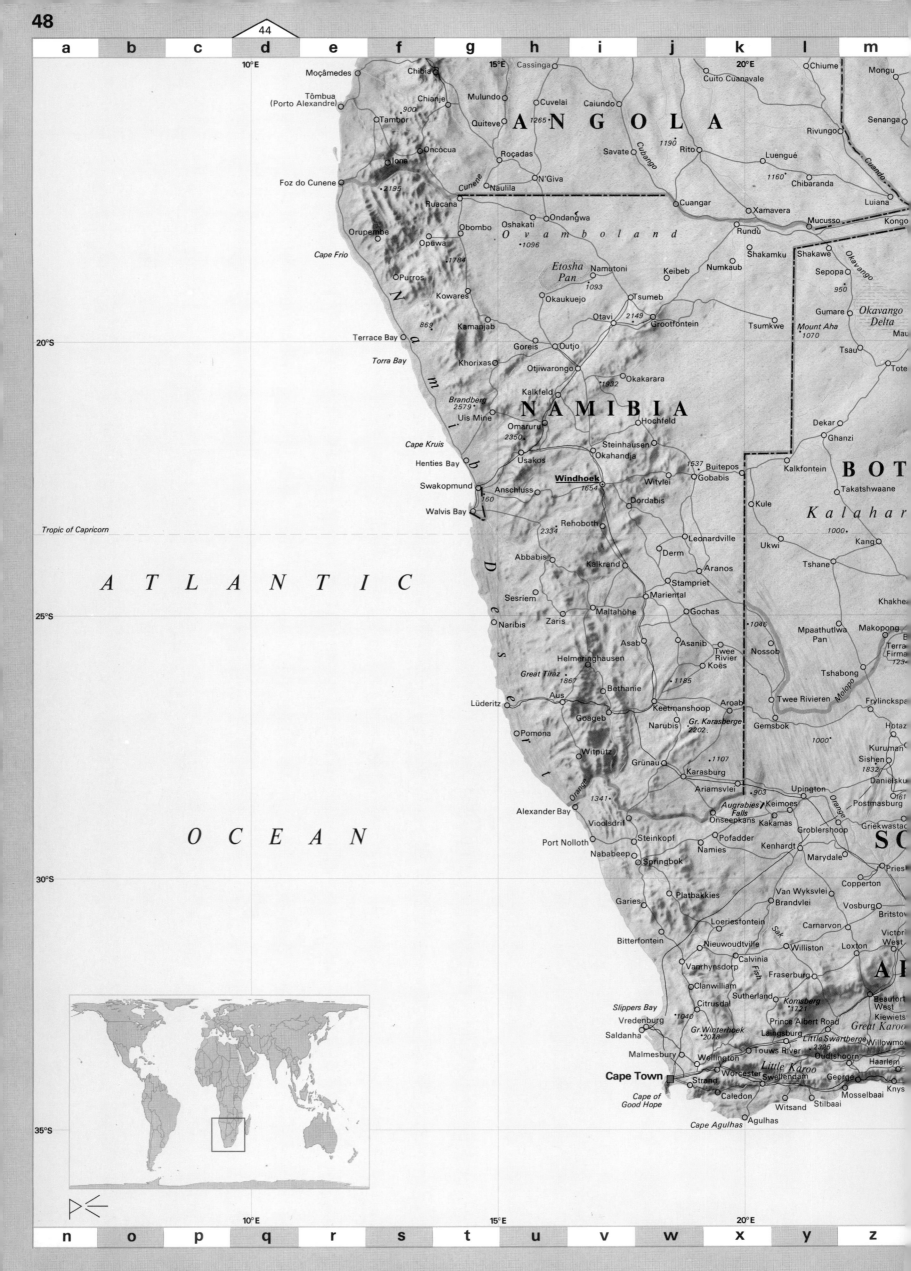

a   b   c   d   e   f   g   h   i   j   k   l   m

10°E   15°E   20°E

Moçâmedes
Chibia   Cassinga   Chiume   Mongu
Tômbua   Cuito Cuanavale
(Porto Alexandre)   Chianje   Mulundo   Senanga
          .900   Cuvelai   Caiundo
Tambor   Quiteve   .1265   A N G O L A   Rivungo
                                          .1190
Oncócua   Roçadas   Savate   Rito   Luiana
Iona   .1160   Chibaranda
Foz do Cunene   Cunene   N'Giva   Luengué
          .2195   Naulila   Mucusso
Orupembe   Ruacana   Ondangwa   Cuangar   Xamavera
              Obombo   Oshakati   Ovamboland   Rundù
Cape Frio   Opuwa   .1096   Shakamku   Shakawe   Okavango
              .1784   Sepopa
Purros   Etosha   Namutoni   Keibeb   Numkaub   .950
              Kowares   Pan   .1093   Numkaub   Okavango
Z   Okaukuejo   Tsumeb   Gumare   Delta
          .869   Otavi   .2149   Tsumkwe   Mount Aha
Terrace Bay   Kamanjab   Goreis   Outjo   Grootfontein   .1070
          a   Tsau
Torra Bay   Khorixas   Otjiwarongo   Dekar   Tote
          m   .1932
Brandberg   Kalkfeld   Ghanzi
2579   N A M I B I A   Hochfeld
Uis Mine   i   Omaruru   B O T
Cape Kruis   2350   Steinhausen   Kalkfontein   Takatshwaane
          b   Usakos   Okahandja   K a l a h a r
Henties Bay   Anschluss   Windhoek   Witvlei   Buitepos
Swakopmund   1654   Gobabis   .1000   Kang
          .160   Dordabis   Kule
Walvis Bay   Derm   Leonardville   Ukwi
          Rehoboth   Tshane
Tropic of Capricorn   .2334   Derm
                                    Aranos
A T L A N T I C   Abbabis   Kalkrand   Stampriet
                    D   Sesriem   Mariental   .1046   Makopong
          25°S   Naribis   Zaris   Maltahöhe   Gochas   Nossob   Mpaathutlwa
                                                Pan
          Asab   Asanib   Tshabong
          e   Helmeringhausen   Twee   .1000
          Great Tiras   Rivier   Koës   Twee Rivieren   Frylinckspa
          1867   Bethanie   .1185
O C E A N   s   Aus   Gr. Karasberge   Gemsbok   .1000   Hotaz
          Lüderitz   Goageb   Narubis   2202   Kuruman
          Pomona   Narubis   Sishen
          Witpütz   .1107   1832
          e   Grünau   Daniëlsk
          Karasburg   Upington   Ori
          Orange   Ariamsvlei   .903   Keimoes   Postmasburg
          l   .1341   Augrabies   Keimoes
Alexander Bay   Falls   Kakamas   Groblershoop   Griekwastad
          Vioolsdrif   Onseepkans   Kenhardt   S C
Port Nolloth   Steinkopf   Pofadder
          Pofadder   Namies   Kenhardt   Marydale   Pries
Nababeep   Springbok   Copperton
          30°S   Van Wyksvlei
          Garies   Platbakkies   Brandvlei   Vosburg   Britsto
                        Loeriesfontein   Carnarvon   Victor
          Bitterfontein   Nieuwoudtville   Williston   Loxton   West
                        Calvinia
                    Vanrhynsdorp   Fraserburg
          Clanwilliam   Sutherland   Komsberg   Beaufort   A
          Slippers Bay   Citrusdal   1721   West
          Vredenburg   .1040   Kiewiets
          Saldanha   Gr. Winterhoek   Prince Albert Road   Great Karoo
                    .2078   Laingsburg   Little Swartberge
          Malmesbury   Touws River   2325   Oudtshoorn   Willowmo
                    Wellington   Little Karoo   George
          Cape Town   Worcester   Swellendam   Knys
                    Strand   Caledon   Mosselbaai
          Cape of   Witsand   Stilbaai
          Good Hope   Agulhas
          Cape Agulhas

n   o   p   q   r   s   t   u   v   w   x   y   z

10°E   15°E   20°E

This map shows 1/60 of the earth's surface. Area scale : 1 □ inch on the map ≏ 15,000 □ miles on the ground 1 □ cm on the map ≏ 6000 □ km on the ground

25°E · Mumbwa · Reunsa 30°E Fingoè · Chiúta · Zomba Gurué Nampula Moçambique

Lusaka · 1279 Zambezi Zumbo Cabora Bassa - Reservoir Songo MALAWI Lmbe · 1000 Molócuè Errego Liupo · 200

1220 · Namwala Lake Kafue Mazabuka · 560 Elantyre Mulanje Nametil

ZAMBIA Kariba Ka iba Mkumbura Tete Zambezi 2054 · Nsanje · 760 Mocuba Mucubela Angoche

Reservoir Karoi Mhangura Mount Changara Tambara Moma

Choma · 1204 Darwin Nyamapanda Guro Vila de Sena Namacurra

Kalomo Binga Banket Bindura Mutoko · 142C Caia Mopeia Quelimane

Sesheke Livingstone Gokwe Chegutu Harare Invanga 2592 Catandica Inhaminga · 105 Chinde

Katima Victoria Falls Hwange Kadoma Rusape Mutare Chirroio Gorongosa

Mulilo Kazungula Dete Gwai River ZIMBABWE Chivhu Dorowa Beira

Kataba · 1108 Kenmaur Kwe Kwe · 1447 Nyanyadzi Chimanimani Dorodc Sofala Mozambique

Pandamatenga Bulawayo 1343 Gweru Chatsworth Masvingo Rupisi Chipinge Nova Golegã Bay 20°S

Shorobe Basotho · 1000 Tsholotsho Plumtree Zvishavane Espungabera

Kanyu Nata Mosetse · 1028 Gwanda Rutenga Macane Save

Tsoe BOTSWANA Tlalamabele Antelope Mine Mazunge Bubye Tswiza Massangena · 167 Pambarra Bassas da India (France)

Xhumo 974 Letlhakane Selebi- Tuli Beitbridge Chicualacuala Machera Mabcte Bazaruto

WANA Serule Phikwe Pontcrif Messina Pafuri · 438 Mapai Mapinhane

Metsiamonong Serowe · 1000 Palapye Louis Shing veczi Chigubo Massinga Europe Island (France)

Kikao Kalamare Mahalapye Trichardt Funhalcuro

Soje Marken Tzaneen Phalaborwa Massingir Panda Inhambane

Dutlwe Ellisras Pietersburg 2128 · Satara Guija · 159 MOZAMBIQUE

Letlhakeng Mosomane · 2085 Potgietersrus · 1856 Skukuza Manjacaze

Jwaneng Gaborone Vaalwater Nylstroom Steelpoort Sable Magude Xai-Xai Quissico 25°S

Kanye 1479 Thabazimbi Warmbad Wtrivier Macia 46

Lobatse Dwarsberg Grobersda Lydenburg Komatipoort

Molopo Zeerust Middelburg Waterval Nelspruit · 515

Morokweng Mmabatho Rustenburg 1338 Boven Maputo

Pretoria Witbank Carolina Mbabane Namaacha

Delareyville Lichtenburg Roodepoort 1753 Benoni Witbank Ermelo Bela Vista

Vryburg Johannesburg Germiston Springs SWAZI Manzini Catuane

Schweizer Potchefstroom Vereeniging 1667 Bethal Standerton LAND Lavumisa

Reneke Wolmaransstad Parys 1440 Vaal Piet Retief

Reivilo Klerksdorp Heilbron Frankfort Volksrust 2277 Pongde Mkuze

Warrenton Christiana Bloemhof Kroonstad Reitz Utrecht · 1533 Lake St. Lucia

Barkly West Reservoir Winburg Newcastle Vryheid Mtubatuba

Kimberley Bultfontein Bethlehem Ladysmith Ulundi

Bloemfontein 4426 Ficksburg Harrismith Dundee Eshowe Richards Bay

Luckhoff Maseru 3096 Clocolan Estcourt Greytown

Fauresmith Wepener Mont aux Himeville Pietermaritzburg INDIAN

Trompsburg Smithfield LESOTHO Sources 3482 Ixopo 1000 Durban 30°S

Colesberg Aliwal North Zastron Moyen Kokstad Umzinto

De Aar Hanover Burgersdorp Lady Grey Mount Port Shepstone

Middelburg 2052 Barkly East Fletcher Mount Frere Port Edward

Steynsburg Elliot 1677 Maclear

RICA Cradock Lady Frere Umtata Port St. Johns

Graaff Reinet Queenstown Icutywa Coffee Bay

Somerset Stutterheim

East 500 King William's Town

Fort Beaufort East London

Grahamstown Bell

Steytlerville 1627 Kirkwood OCEAN

Uitenhage Port Alfred 35°S

Port Elizabeth

Jeffreys Bay

Mozambique Channel

0 100 200 300 miles   Average linear scale : 1 inch ≈ 125 miles 1cm ≈ 80 km   0 100 200 300 400 500 Km

85°N
35°E 40°E 45°E 50°E 55°E 60°E 65°E

A R C

Alexandra Land *George Land* Salisbury I. Jackson I. Rudolf I. Yeva-Liv
Karla-Aleksandra
Luidzhi La Rons'yer
Hooker I. McClintock I. Hall I. Wilczek Land Graham Bell
80°N *F r a n z* *J o s e f* *L a n d* Sal'm Island
Zem

• 1052

Russkaya Gavan

75°N Smidovich

N o v a y a *Z e m l y a* **K A R A   S E A**

Sedova
Stolbovoy 1115
• 260 Litke

B A R E N T S   S E A Krasino

Proliv Karskiye Vorota

Pechora Sea • 162 Cape Uengan
Vaigač
70°N Amderma *Baidara*

Kolgujev Chernaya Pay-Khoy Ust'-Kara
166 Dresvyanka Yangarey
Cape Kanin Nos • 201 Khal'mer-Yu • 1218

• 242 Nar'yan *Bol'shezemel'skaya* *Tundra* Vorkuta
Kanin Mar Kolva Koreyver Yeletskiy
Peninsula • 106 Makarikha Pay-yer • 1499
Češa Velikovisochnoye Abez' Labytnangi
Bay Trosh *Usa* Safekaro
Volonga Inta
Mezen' Nonburg • 155 Kosyu Kashg
Gulf Ust'Tsil'ma Fedulki
Mezen' Stafonovo Izhma Pechora *Narodnaya*
Arctic Circle Kadzherom 1894
65°N Azopol'ye *T* Kedva 164 Saranpaul Vanzevat
Kola • 463 *i* Voyvozh
Murmansk Pinega *m* Ukhta *N* Patrasuy North Sosva Berezovo
Mončegorsk Politovo *a* *o* Muligort
• 1191 *Mezen'* Shomvukva *n* Vey Vozh Kyrta 1617
Kirovsk Vendenga *R* Nyaksimvol
Kandalakša Loptyuga *i* Zheleznodorozhnyy • 324 *r* Sergino
Severodvinsk *d* Mikun **S** Troitsko-Pechorsk *t*
White Archangelsk *North Dvina* Irta Puzla *h* Khangokurt
Sea *g* • 259 *Vym* **S O** V I E Porog *e*
Belomorsk Pinega Syktyvkar *Vyčegda* Suyevatpaul Pol'yano
Onega Bay Verkhnyaya Ust'Kulom Kur'ya 1108 *r* Sovetskiy
Onega Toyma 303 Komsomol'skiy
Segeža Kizema Kotlas Vizinga • 1027 Polunochnoye Pionerskiy
• 417 Vel 239 *Uvaly* Cherdyn 1493 Ivdel'
Medvežjegors Konoša *Vaga* Velikiy Kazhim Denezkin Kamen Mulym'y
Kargopol Ustyug • 213 *Kolva* • 162 • 78
Lake *Sukhona* *U* *Kama* Krasnotur'insk
Onega Noshul' Pyatigory Solikamsk Lobva
Petrozavodsk Totma Nikol'sk *Northern* Kirs Berezniki Sos'va
Kudymkar Gubakha 883
Podporoze *Vel* Murashi Kamskoje Dobryanka 321
60°N Tichvin *Vetluga* Reservoir Verkhniy Tura
Nizhniy Kirov Glazov Krasnokamsk 100
Yenangsk Novo-Vyatsk Perm' Nizhniy Tagil
Čerepovec Vologda Vetluzhskiy Kotel'nich Kez *Tavda*
Rybinsker • 292 Pizhma Igra Kungur Turinsk
Reservoir Bui Uren Nolinsk Pervoural'sk Artemovskiy Tavda
Rybinsk Kostroma Yaransk Sverdlovsk
Vyšni Voloček Kinešma Krasnyye-Baki Votkinsk Krasnoufimsk Talitsa
• 343 Kalyazin Kil'mez Izhevsk Bogdanovich
Ostashkov Ivanovo Yoshkar Malmyzh Sarapul Degtyarsk Yalutorovsk
Torzhok Dubna Ola 217 Agryz Sysert' Kamensk-
Kalinin Klin Dmitrov Arsk Neftekamsk Nyazepetrovsk Ural'skiy Shadrinsk
Nelidovo Staritsa Volokolamsk *Volga* Cheboksary Izevsk Kasli
Ržev Zagorsk Vladimir Gor'kiy Yadrin Naberezhnyje KTyumen
Moscow Mytišči Dzerzhinsk *Oka* Kazan' Čelny
Odintsovo Elektrostal Murom Mamadysh

35°E 45°E 50°E 55°E 65°E

This map shows 1/60 of the earth's surface. Area scale : 1 □ inch on the map ≃ 15,000 □ miles on the ground 1 □ cm on the map ≃ 6000 □ km on the ground

Byrranga Mountains
Vezdekhodnaya
75°N
Laptev Sea

Lake Taimyr
Bol. Balakhnya
Begichev
Nordvik
Cape Nordvik
Khorgo
Uele
Dunay
Turkannakh
Sagastyr
Antipinskiy
Korennoye
Kozhevnikovo
Uryung-Khaya
Suolama
Ust'-Olenëk
Stannakh-Khocho
Ary
·52
Trofimovsk
Orto-Ayan
Novyy
Novoryonye
Sagyr Khatanga
Lukunskiy
Novay
Bychez
Fomich
Popigay
Popigay
Saskylakh
Anabar ·268
Amakinskiy
·128
Bor-Yuryakh
Ot-Siyen
Pur Sklad
211· Taymylyr
405·
Tit-Ary
·921
Tiksi
Buorkhaye Bay
Khatanga
Star. Kayakhnyy
Kuoyka
Khasalakh
Chekurovka
Kyusyur
Tas-Tumus ·982
Kotuykan
Popigay ·536
Dzhelinde
70°N
Central
Ulgumun
Siktyakh
Govorovo
Sakhandzha ·1291

Tukalan
Kirbey
Mongolo
Lena Kel'
Dzhardzhan
Molodo
Sutun'-Yu
Yessey
Ylas-Yuryakh
Dzhara
Kirbey
Kyuekh-Bulung
Ukukit
Sukhana
Motorchuna
Menkere
Sencha
Dzhelon
Kotui
Moyero
Arga-Sala
Siligir
Olenëk
Muna
Menkere ·2389
Tirekh
Murukta
Siberian
Olenëk
S O V I E T
Kystatyam
Zhigansk
Batamay
Ekonda
Vilyuy Mountains
Eyakit-Tërdë
Udachnyy
Onkuchakh
Eyik
Tyung
Khoronnokh
Bakhynay
Endybal
Toyon-Tirekh
Uplands
Aykhal
Markha
Andyngda
Amysakh
Borolgustakh
Linde
Tungus-Khaya
65°N
Vilyuy
Kochechum ·823
Yeyka
Markoka
Tyulkyan
Engerdyakh
Bagadzha
Mastakh
Kyrgyday
Dalgoye
Siege Kyug
Niznaya Tunguska
Kananda
Ygyatta
Malykay
Ulgumdzha
Vilyuy
Khampa
Kobya
Amo ·501
Yukta
Ankacho
Kysyl-Yllyk
Nyurba
Verkhnevilyuysk
Vilyuysk
Ebe
Ilbenge
Tyugene
Kangalassay
Tyungul
Chuyengo
Ilimpeya
Simenga
Chernyshevskiy
Novyy
Khordogoy
Sheya
Khochot
Kiriyestyakh
Yakutsk
Taimura
Tunor
Bugorkan
Viljujskoje Reservoir
Mirnyy
Almaznyy
Suntar
Oleng-Sala
Tongulakh
Kerekyano
Pokrovsk
May
Čunja
Ayan
Yerbogachen
R U S S I A N
Tenke
Neleger
Strelka-Čunja
Dzhunkun
Tas-Yuryakh
Ergedzhey
Atakh-Yuryakh
Yet-Kyuyel'
Sinyaya
Kytyl-Zhura
Kachikattsy
Sosna
Chamcha
Nyuya
Lena
Sangyyakhtakh
Khoronkhu
51
Vanavara
Kulinda
Khomokashevo
Yerema
Ulakhan Botuobuya
Dulga-Kyuyel'
Lensk
Nyuya
Olekminsk
Uritskoye
Taloye
Tegyulte-Tërde
60°N
Tëtere
Ust'-Chayka
Nyuya
Khabalakh
Khamra
Bol. Patom
Patom
Cherendey
Tuolba
Chemdal'sk
Kamanga
Ayan
Nepa
Tolon
Tokko
Andreyevskiy
Berezovskaya
Kudu-Kyuyel'
Khoppuruo
Amga
Ugoyan
Verkhnyaya Amga
Mon'ot
Panovo
Kata
Ika
Nepa
Vitim
Chuya
·1639
Patomskoye Plateau
Polovinka
Chara
Olakma
Dikimdya
Tommot
Ust'-Timpton
Ugun Chagda
Angara
Bur
Cherkashina
Kureyskaya
Vorontsovka
Kropotkin
Chara
Torgo
Tokko
Aldan
Usmun ·1612
Suon-Tit
Chyul'be
Ust'Ilimsk
Volokon
Ichera
Vitimskiy
Severomuysk ·1771
Berezovka
Yenyuka
Bol. Khatymy
Gynym ·186
Vorob'yeva
Lena
Kirensk
Bodaybo
Sinyuga
Lake Nichatka
Khani
Taluma
Neryungri
Berkakit
·1870
Gonam
Garmenka
Romanova
Ust'-Kut
Gorno-Chuyskiy
Mama
Vitim
Oron
Chara
Udokan
Ust'Nyukzha
Sutam
Ilimsk
Riga
Injaptuk ·2579
Uoyan
Tonnel'nyy
Ust'-Muya ·2467
Taluma
Lopcha
Larba
Nagornyy
Chapa ·24
Bratsk
Vidim
Suvorka
Orlinga
Kazachinskoye
Yukhta
Nizhneangarsk
Bambuyka
Sredniy Kalar
Vetekhtina
Tynda
Stanovoy Mountains
Bratskoye Reservoir
North Baykal Plateau
Baykal'skoye
Baunt
Kadali
Kalakan ·1592
Ugagli
Zeyski
55°N
·763
Atalanka
Žigalovo
Sugdža
Oron
Vitim Plateau
Mogojto
Bagdarin
Ust'-Karenga
Koltovkinda
Gulya
Belen'kaya
Zeya Un'ya
Ust'-Kada
Sosnovka
·2573
Jeleninskij
Bugunda
Zel'onoye Ozero
Tupik
Bam
Solov'yevsk
Urusha
Ogoron
Loksi
Zima
Zalari
Balagansk
·2069
Bol. Onguren
Barguzin
Ust'-Dzilinda
Chulugli
Mogoča
Amazar
Skovorodino
Zeya
Oktyabrskiy
Malyuti
Čeremchovo
·774
Manzurka
·2049
Romanovka
·1911
Silka
Dzhalinda
Magdagachi
Byssa
Usolje Sibirskoje
Ust'-Ordynskij
Maksimicha
Isinga
Telemba
Narga
Ust'-Karsk
Mosëgda ·1249
Luoguhe
Gulian
Ershiyizhan
Ushumun
Petropavlovka
·3266
Kyrën
Angarsk
Selichov
Irkutsk
·2304
Chaim
·1322
Uda
Chita
Cernyševsk
Versino-Darasunskij
Sretensk
Nerchinskiy Zavod
Kurleja
Yimuhe
Qiqian
Walagan
Novorossiyka
Shimanovsk
Sl'ud'anka
Listv'anka
Kamensk
Ulan-Ude
Chorinsk
Šilka
Ingoda Baley
Borshchovochnyy Mountains
Ergun
Jinhe
Linhai
Huma
Novokiyevskiy
Tanchoj
Selenga
Petrovsk Zabajkal'skij
Chilok
Darasun
Karymskoje
Nerchinskiy Zavod
Mordaga
Kalaqi
Orogen Zizhiqi
Amur
Belogorsk
Gusinoozersk
Tanga
Ila
Olov'annaja
C H I N A
·827
Zakamensk
Džida
Chilok
·1248
Gol
Priargunsk
Tulihe
Ergun Yuoqi
Amur
105°E
110°E
115°E
120°E
125°E
130°E

This map shows 1/60 of the earth's surface. Area scale : 1 □ inch on the map ≈ 15,000 □ miles on the ground 1 □ cm on the map ≈ 6000 □ km on the ground

94

a b c d e f g h i j k l m

135°E 140°E 145°E 150°E 155°E 160°E

New Siberian Islands

Bennetta

Bel'kovskiy Kotel'nyy

75°N

Kotel'nyy
320

Ambardakh

Stolbovoy

Mal. Lyakhovskiy

Bol'shoye
Zimov'ye

Novaya Sibir

East Siberian Sea

Fedorovskiy

Bot. Lyakhovskiy

Kigilyakh

Chay-Povarnaya
420

Laptev Strait

Kr.arstan

Chikhacheva

Cape
Buorkhaya

Uyëdey

Star. Dom

Balagannakh

Khroma

Kokuora

Kisaleva

Tabo

Ulovo

Kolesovo

70°N

Dzhamm

Kuogastakh

Kazach'ye

Yana

Tumat

Tenkel

Boru

Ukta

Indigirka

Alekseyevo

Chokurdakh

Kondakovo

*Kolymskiy
Plain*

Kular

Saydy

Tirakhtyakh

Uyanc
1221

Oyun-
Kyuyel'

Deputatskiy

Uyandina

Bvyangnyr

Ozhogino

Tenalr

Ilimnir

Kharā-Tala

314

Chukochye

*Lake
Nerpich'ye*

Keriske

Oyun-Yurege

Tas-Kumsa

Bytantay

Orto-Kyuyel'

Chibagalakr

Syagannakh

Druzhina

Shestakova

Urdakh

Kyrbana

Balagannakh

Mys

Cherskiy

Volochsk

Gorelova

*Lake
Ozeogino*

Ali-Bagata

Batagay

Verkhoyansk

omtor

1726

U N I O N

Suordakh

Khobolchan

1919
Tuostakh

Tuostakh
1926

Okhastakh

Bertes

Mayor-Krest

Khongsev

Srednekolymsk

Ozhogino

Arge

Malaya

Oysurdakh

Zhirkova

Chernyy
Mys

Berezovka

Omolon

Arctic Circle

Zatish'ye
721

Shcherbakovo

Tokuma

Qlom

C h e r s k o g o

Khonu

Udanna

Mama

Kycham-
Kyuyel'

Erozionnyy

Yuzo-Tala
Zyryanka

Pastakh

Sededema

65°N

Kusagan-
Olokh

Ulaga

Khara-
Tas

Nel'gese

Astakh

Cheulik

Adycha

Cribagalakh

2703

Tyubelyakh

Udanna

3147

Ozhogino

Ressokha

Oroyek

Korkodon

Korkodon

Bulun

Mountains

Bilir
1135

Komelek

1627

Alvesk tovyy

Ust'-Nera

M
Nara

Motyk

2558

M o u n t a i n s

Khongo
Razdolnoye

Kolyma

im Chapyeva

Ust'-Sugoy

Abkit

Shcherbakovo

Munugudzhak

Mountains

Marshal'skiy

Tirgelir
2341

Oymyakon

Knuzdzhakh

2038
1347

Sordongnokh

Seymchan

Omolon
1550

Suglan

Tompo

Kysyl-
Suluo

Tomtor

Arkagsla

Kolymskiy

Omsukchan

Galimyy

Aldan

Khara-Aldan

Dal'stroy

Dyalinnya

Byuchennakh

Adygalakh

Eurkhala

Debir

Orotukan

1830

Gizhiga

Bysyttakh

Tyry

1714

Gvardeyets

Khatyngnakh

Pik Aborigen
2586

Stelka

Mountains

Ytyk-Kyuyel'

Khandyga

2933

im Gaste

Vetrenyy

Myakit

Viliga-
Kushka

Nayakhan

Sayylyk

Kennya

Kolyma

Atka

60°N

Churapcha

S. F. S. R.

Okhotskiy
Perevoz

Burgakhchan

Ust'Omchug

Kandychan

Tumany

*Cape
Taygonos*

Amga

El'dikan

Zolotoy

Allakh-Yun'
Ancha

Kencha

Inye
1585

Ugulan

*Gulf of
Shelekhova*

Khatyngnakh

Ust'-Maya

Ayaya

Ynykchanskiy
Yudoma

2350

Neter

Palatka

Malkachan

Lesnaya

Ust'-Mil'

Ulukuut

Yugorenok

Yudoma-
Krestovskaya

Arka

Bulun

Star.
Khezdzhan

Kuntuk

Talon

Arman

Majadan

Yama

Srednly

Palana

el'kachi

Aim

Sordongnokh

Maya

Arka

Urak

Okhotsk

Shilkan

Inya

Balagannoye

Metyklleyka

Nyurchan

Yamsk

*Cape
Tolstoy*

Kurun Uryak

Ingili

Kaval'kan

Alachakh

Khanyangda

543

Sivuch

*Cape
Alevina*

Ust'-Tigil'

Tigil

Khakhar

Chigul'bach

Nel'kan

Enkan

D z h u g d z h u r   M o u n t a i n s

Utkholok

Mountains

2531

Chasovnya-
Uchurskaya

Topko
1906

Kemkara

Ust'-Belogolovoye

Kekuk

Batomga

Maymakan

Ayan

*Sea of
Okhotsk*

Ust'-Sopochnoye

Kiyuchi

Esso

Atlasovo

4750

Nemuy

*Ichinskaya
Sopka*

Icha
3621

Ob
lukovino

Tvayan

1500

*S. *
Maya

Chumikan

Shantar

Mil'kovo

Kronok

Udskoye

Burandzha

Tugur

Cape
Yelizavety

Nyvrovo
602

Kirovskiy

Pymta

Pushchino

Zhupanovskiy

Uda

Shevli

Tugur

Litke

*Lake
Orel*

Bol.
Vlas'evo

Okha

Oktyab'skiy

1870

Malka

Nalychevo

Baladek

Ekimchan

Usal'gin

Nikolayevsk
na-Amure

Paromay

Paratunka

Petropavlovsk-
Kamchatskiy

139

2295

Guga

Yashkino

Tyr

Bol'sheretsk

Polovinka

Sofiysk

Gaktsynka

Bcgorodskoye

Boatasyn

Sakhalin

*Lake
Chukehagirskoye*

1462

Marinskoye

Sofiysk

Nysh

Ust' Niman
Bolodzhak

Duki

Kondon

Sizim an

Alexandrovsko-
Sakhalinskiy

1609

Tymovskoye

Urgal

2010

Boktor

Amur

Novoilinovka

Gomy

Paramušir

Chekunda

Mogdy

Komsomol'sk-
na-Amure

155°E

10

0   100   200   300
miles

Average linear scale : 1 inch ≈ 125 miles 1 cm ≈ 80 km

0   100   200   300   400   500
Km

n o p q r s t u v w x y z

135°E 140°E 145°E 150°E 155°E 160°E

50

a b c d e f g h i j k l m

35°E 40°E 45°E 50°E 55°E

Ostashkov
Nelidovo
Torzhok
Rzev Staritsa
Kalinin
Dubna
Dmitrov
Jaroslavl'
Ivanovo
Kineshma
Krasnye-Baki
Uren
Yaransu
Kilmez
Izevsk
Votkinsk
Sarapul
Agryz

Smolensk
Dnieper
Vyaz'ma
.320
Gagarin
Volokolamsk
Klin
Zagorsk
Balashikha
Noginsk
Gor'kiy
Volga
Cheboksary
Yoshkar Ola
Malmyz
.217
Neftekamsk

Moscow
Mytisči
Odintsovo
Mozhaysk
Obninsk
Orechovo-Zujevo
Vladimir
Oka
Murom
Arzamas
Yadrin
Sergach
Kanash
Kazan'
Mamadysh
Naberezhnyje
Celny
Al'met'yevsk

Podolsk
Kolomna
RUSSIAN
S. F. S. R.
Kuybyshevskoje
Reservoir
Oktyabr'skiy
Davlekanovo

Roslavl
Obninsk
Serpuchovo
Kaluga
Chekalio
Tula
Novomoskovsk
Skopin
Troyekurovo
Kadnoye
Shatsk
Morshansk
Temnikov
Saransk
Inza
Ul'yanovsk
Alatyr
Baryshi
Kuznetsk
Syzran
Togliatti
Kuybyshev
Chapayevsk
Krotovka
Buguruslan
Sharlyk

Bryansk
Karchev
Navlya
Orel
Belev
Zmiyevsk
Plavsk
Yelets
Lipetsk
Michurinsk
Tambov
Kirsanov
Rtishchevo
Penza
Maryevka
Maryevka
Bol'shaya
Glushitsa
Andreyevka
Sorochinsk
Bulanovo

Klintsy
Desna
Shostka
Khomutovka
Seym
Kursk
Gorshechnoye
Oboyan
Staryy
Oskol
Voronezh
Rogachevka
Borisoglebsk
Tugolukovo
Mordovo
Atkarsk
Vyzakova
Balakovo
Orenburg
Ilek
Ural

Konotop
Priluki
Lubny
Sumy
Akhtyrka
Belgorod
Alekseyevka
Kamenka
Pavlovsk
Buturlinovka
Kalininsk
Balashov
Saratov
Engel's
.122
Pushkino
Dergachi
Ural'sk
Aksay
Sol Iletsk

Khar'kov
Valki
Poltava
Valuyki
Kantemirovka
Veshenskaya
Mikhaylovka
Log
Volga
Kamyshin
Nikolayevsk
Kaysatskoye
Rovnoye
Novo
Uzensk
Furmanovo
Antonovo
Mergenevo

UKRAINE
Kremenchugskoye
Reservoir
Izyum
Don
S O V I
Lake
Aralsor
Masteksay

Kremenchug
Znamenka
Kirovograd
Pereshchepino
Novomoskovsk
Pavlograd
Dnepropetrovsk
Stakhanov
Kamensk-
Shakhinskiy
Morozovsk
Volgograd
Krasnoslobodsk
Kapustin-Yar
Elton
.67
Primorsk
Inderborskiy

Dneprodzerzhinsk
Днепропетровск
Gorlovka
Voroshilovgrad
Solodniki
Chernyy
Yar
Mikhaylova
Caspian Depression
Kulagino

Krivoy Rog
Nikopol
Zaporozh'ye
Kakhovskoye
Reservoir
Makeyevka
Donetsk
Shakhty
Novoshakhtinsk
Novocherkassk
Volgodonsk
Tsimlyanskoye
Reservoir
Kotel'nikovo
Dubovskoye
Kharabalio
Volga
Sarychik
Makat
Sagiz

Melitopol'
Berdyansk
Taganrog
Zhandov
Rostov
Bataysk
Sal'sk
Krasnyy-Yar
Astrakhan
Zelenga
Gur'yev
Iskine
.27
Kul'sary

Kherson
Novaya
Kakhova
18
Yeysk
Sosyko
Lake
Manych
Gudilo
Elista
Yashkul'
Utta
Canyushikino
Zhagaly
Oporniy
Porva

Karkinitskiy
Bay
Dzhankoy
Sea of
Azov
Primorsko-
Akhtarsk
Tikhoretsk
Divnoye
Mumra
Zelenga
Kultay
Karaton

35
Crimea
Kerch'
Kavkaz
Kuban
Kropotkin
Kugulta
Ulan-Khol
Kulaly
Bayne
Us

45°N
Simferopol'
.1259
Feodosiya
Armavir
Stavropol'
Kuma
Velichayevskoye
Kochubey
Fort-Sevčenko
.44
Say-Utes
Pte

Sevastopol'
Jalda
Novorossiysk
Krasnodar
Maykop
Čerkessk
Pjatigorsk
Terek
Kiz'lar
.25
Kulaly
Shetpe
Ševčenko
.132

Tuapse
2867
.3238
Kislovodsk
Prochladnyy
Nal'čik
Groznyi
CASPIAN
Kyzyk
Fetisovo

Soči
Elbrus
5642
Ordzonikidze
Machačkala
SEA
.70

BLACK
Suchumi
Caucasus
.5047
Kazabegi
.4151
Derbent
Kyzyl

SEA
Poti
Kutaisi
GRUZIYA
Chasuri
Kura
S.S.R.
Tbilisi
Rustavi
Kazachi
Kuba
Bekdaš
Kara-Bogaz-
Gol
Kara-Bogaz-Gol

Cape Ince
Sinop
Batumi
Hopa
Marneuli
Mingecaurskoje
Reservoir
.2205
Sumgait

Kastamonu
Karabük
Pontine
Samsun
Fatsa
Trabzon
Ardahan
Leninakan
.1332
Kirovakan
Kirovabad
Jevlach
Achsu
Baku
Žioj

Gerede
.2565
Çorum
Gümüşhane
.3065
Kars
Kegizman
ARMENIA S.S.R.
AZERBAYDZHAN
S.S.R.

40°N
Ankara
Sivas
Erzincan
Erzurum
Askale
Aras
Yerevan
Lake
Sevan
Agdam
Saljany
Krasnovodsk
Čeleken
.1881
Nebit
Dag

TURKEY
Kırıkkale
Yozgat
.2345
.2740
Kara Dag
Divriği
Aras
.5156
Ağri
Nachičevan
Araks
Ožalilabad
Ogurčinskij

Anatolia
Kayseri
.3916
Gurun
Patnos
Maku
Ahar
Astara
Ardebil
Gorgan
Ghaem-
Shahr

Aksaray
Niğde
Malatya
.2500
Ağ Dağ
Bingöl
.4484
Lake
Van
Van
Khoy
Marand
Tabriz
.1962
.4811
ELBURS
Ramsar
Amol
Damavand
.5771
Mountains

Konya
Ereğli
.3488
Maraş
Kozan
Gaziantep
Elazig
Diyarbakir
Kurtalan
Hakkâri
.4168
Oroumieh
Lake
Urmia
Marageh
Miáneh
.3050
Bandar Anzeli
Rasht
.3713
Qazvin
Gonbad
e-Kavus

Anamur
Adana
Mersin
Zagros
İskenderun
.1795
Urfa
Nusaybin
Tigris
Al Hasakah
Sinjar
Tall
'Afar
Mosul
Saqqez
Qojur
Zanjan
Elburz
Mountains

Cape Anamur
Silifke
Antakya
Aleppo
Maskana
Raqqah
Euphrates
SYRIA
Idlib
Sharqat
Baneh
Bijar
Takestan
Karaj
Tehran
Damgha

MEDITERRANEAN
SEA
Cape
Andreas
Latakia
.1463
Tall
Afar
IRAQ
Arbil
Less
Zab
Sulaimaniyah

CYPRUS
Cape
Andreas
35°E
40°E
45°E
50°E

39

n o p q r s t u v w x y z

This map shows 1/60 of the earth's surface. Area scale : 1 □ inch on the map ≈ 15,000 □ miles on the ground 1 □ cm on the map ≈ 6000 □ km on the ground

Kungur · Pervoural'sk · 60°E · **Sverdlovsk** · Talitsa · 65°E · Yalutorovsk · Ishim · 70°E · Tevriz · Irtysh · 75°E · .142

Krasnoufimsk · Nyazepetrovsk · Degtyarsk · Bogdanovich · Kamensk-Ural'skiy · Shadrinsk · Golyshmanovo · Panovo · .122 · Tara · Biaza · .124

Ufa · Asha · Min'yar · Suleya · Zlatoust · **Chelyabinsk** · Shumikha · Kurgan · Makushino · Petukhovo · Presnovka · **Petropavlovsk** · Isil'kul · Lyubinskiy · **Omsk** · Kalachinsk · Chistoozernoye · 55°N · Lake Chany · Barabinsk · Pokrovka · Tatarsk

Chernikovsk · Ust' Kata · Plast · Troitsk · Ust'-Uyskoye · Dem'yanovka · Mar'yevka · Volocarskoye · Krasnoarmeyesk · Kzyltu · Cherlak · Kupino · Karasuk

Krasnousol'skiy · Sterlitamak · Beloretsk · Verkhneural'sk · **Magnitogorsk** · Varna · Kartaly · Kustanay · Uritskiy · Peski · Kokchetav · .887 · Stepnyak · Aksu · Bestobe · Shuga · Lake Azhbulat · Kachiry

Kumertau · Baymak · .447 · Bredy · Dznetygara · Dzhambul · Naurzum · Yesil · Dzhaksy · Zhaltyr · Zholymbet · Yermentau · Karashoky · Ajryk

Troitskoye · Saraktash · Krasnoyarskiy · Terensay · Askarga · Derzhavinsk · Arkalyk · .391 · Novoishimskiy · Sabyndy · **Tselinograd** · Novodolinka · Maykain · Pavlodar · Jamyševo · Yermak · Ekibastuz

Mednogorsk · Martuk · Orsk · Dombarovskiy · Tolybayš · Aksuat · Lake Tengiz · Kurgal'dzhino · Aktau · Temirtau · Saran · Karaganda · Ul'yanovskoye · .621 · 50°N

E T U N I O N · Aktyubinsk · Khrom-Tau · Karabutak · Turgay · Shenber · **Kazakh** · Korobovskiy · Kiikkaškan · Kajnar

Alga · Uil · .316 · Temir · Emba · Akkabak · Kabyga · Saga · Erali · Ulutau · Kyzyl-Dzhar · Atasu · Dar'inskiy · Uspenskiy · Nuru · Agady · Myylybu ak · Karagayly · **Uplands**

Karaulkeldy · Irgiz · Shakh-ty · Kyzyluy · Nikol'skiy · Baykonyr · Dzhez-azgan · Ayshirak · .633 · Zhamshi · Dagandely

K A Z A K H S T A N · S. S. R. · Kulakshi · Chushakyl' · .343 · Akespe · Togyz · Béleutty · Soraysu · Kiik · Mointy · Balkhash · Sajak

Sokyrbulak · Aral sk · .59 · Lake Arys · Bet-Pak-Dala · **Betpak-Dala Steppe** · Kashkanteniz · Tomar · Karabas · Lake Balkhash

Kyushe · Kulanoy · Kokaral · Bugun · Kazalinsk · Leninsk · Dzhusal · Čam-kaly · Karazhingil · Karoy · .603 · Uštobe

Aral Sea · Barsa-Kel'mes · Vozrozhdeniya · Z-anay · Erimbet · Kyzyl-Orda · Aksumbe · ČU · Mynaral · Kuyygan · Burylbaytal · 45°N · 56

Urt · Uzynkair · Svrdaria · Chilli · Algatart · Furmanovka · Khantau · Aktogaj · Saryozek · Taldy-Kurgan

teau · Šatlyk · Muinak · Kazakdarya · .146 · Yany-Kurgan · .2176 · Uyuk · Ču · .1506 · Kapčagajskoje Reservoir · Čilik

Urga · Karaozek · Chimbay · Kentau · Turkestan · Kara Tau · Tatty · Ču · Čemolgan · **Alma Ata**

Lake Sudočje · Kungrad · **Kyzyl Kum** · .335 · Mynbulak · Uchkuduk · Arys' · Džambul · Legovoi · Frunze · Kaškelen · **Ala Tau**

Lake Sarykamyškoje · Bol'ševik · Kun'a Urgenč · Chodzeili · .473 · Cimkent · .3817 · Kara-Balta · Bubačie · Lake Issyk-Kul' · Przeval'sk

Tašauz · Turtkul' · Zarafshan · **KIRGIZIYA** · .4503 · Toktogul · Cajek · Ottuk · Shan

Urgenč · **UZBEKISTAN** · Cardara · Cr-čik · **Tashkent** · Namangan · Taš-Kumyr · Naryn · Taragay · Karasaj

Lebap · **S. S. R.** · Carderinskoje Reservoir · Jangijul' · Angren · Andižan · Kok-Jangak · Lake Catyrk ol · Pik Dankowa · Toxkan He

TURKMENIYA · Gorel'de · .2165 · Gulistan · Kokand · Margilan · Oš · .4641 · Gul'ča · Čatyrtaš · Sari Bulak · Akqi

Darvaza · .81 · Gizhduvan · Navoi · Leninabad · Ferana · Sugun · Sanchakou

S. S. R. · Jerbent · **Kara Kum** · Kazakly · .224 · Buchara · Kaçan · Džzat · Bekabad · Ura-Uba · **TADZHIKISTAN** · 40°N

Kazandžik · Bachardok · Alat · Kattakurgan · **Samarkand** · Mubarek · .5509 · Daraut Kurgan · Irkeštam · Kashgar

Kizyl-Arvat · Arčman · Čardžou · Karši · Šachrisabz · Džirgatal · Lenina · Lake Karakul · Opal · Yopurga · Markit

.68 · Repetek · .4643 · Novabad · Mt Communism · **S. S. R.** · Bulunkol · Shache

Sarlauk · Maraveh-Tappeh · .2243 · Aščabad · Tezejet · Mary · Bajram Ali · Nička · Denau · Viščary · Arkbajtal · Murgab · Kungur · Shache

Dašti · Bojnurd · Quchan · Dušak · Karakumskiy Canal · Keriči · .295 · Ušanbe · Ku'ab · .6083 · **P a m i r** · Mamazai · **CHINA**

Mayamey · Sabzevar · Nishabur · **Mashhad** · Aryk · Tedžen · Sarakhs · Ardkhoy · Termez · Khum · Kurgan-T'ube · Qust · Fa dzabad · .7719 · **PAKISTAN**

N · Takhta Bazar · Maimana · Aqcha · **Mazar-i-Sharf** · Taliqan · Zebak · Kunar · K2 · Gilgit · Bonda

AFGHANISTAN · Sheberghan · Sari-i-Pul · Aibak · Kunduz · Baghlan · Tirich Mir · Chitral · Yarkant He · Misgar

60°E · Qaisar · Doāb-i Mikh-e Zarin · Bala Murghab · 65°E · M'aimana · Qaisar · 70°E · Drosh · Chilas · Indus · 75°E

0 100 200 300 miles · Average linear scale: 1 inch=125 miles 1cm=80 km · 0 100 200 300 400 500 Km

S O V I E T

R U S S I A

M O N G

C H

KAZAKHSTAN S.S.R.

KIRGIZIYA S.S.R.

Novosibirsk

Tomsk

Krasnojarsk

Barnaul

Semipalatinsk

Alma Ata

Pavlodar

Urumchi

Vasyuganye

Kulundinskaya Steppe

Altai

Abakan Mts.

Sajan Mountains

Tannu Mountains

Tarbagataj Mts.

Tien Shan

Borohoro Shan

Junggar Pendi

Tarim Basin

Takla Makan Desert

East Turkestan

Altun Shan

Tsaidam Basin

Bei Shan

Kunlun Shan

Lake Balkhash

Lake Issyk-Kul

Lake Chany

Lop Nur

Onegva Yar
Kolpashevo
Staritsa
Belyy Yar
Yeniseysk
Lesosibirsk
Strelka
Galanino
Rodina
Boguchany
Oktyabr'isk
L'vovka
Mogochin
Čulym
Vorozheyka
Altat
Vydrino
Nevanka
Baturino
Asino
Tegul'det
Meletsk
Birilyussy
Predivinsk
Asansk
Shelayevo
Biaza
Komsomol'sk
Moryakovskiy Zaton
Mariinsk
Bogotol
Achinsk
Pamyat
Shivera
Aban
Kansk
Pokrovka
Chumakovo
Yurga
Anzhero-Sudzhensk
Kemerovo
Nazarovo
Uzhur
Krasnojarsk
Uyar
Borodino
Zamzor
Tayshet
Nizneudinsk
Barabinsk
Chulym
Ob'
Tsentral'nyy
Čulym
Mina
Sum
Gutara
Chistoozernoye
Ordynskoye
Cherepanovo
Krasnobrodskij
Kisel'ovsk
Novokuzneck
Sira
Bellyk
Kuraginо
Art'omosk
Pokrovsk
Kupino
Kamenna-Obi
Suzun
Tal'menka
Prokopjevsk
Sorsk
Černogorsk
Minusinsk
Burgon
Karasuk
Pavlovsk
Mezdurečensk
Abakan
Birikčul
Sušenskoje
Khabary
Len'ki
Rebricha
Bijsk
Mundybaš
Taštyp
Sajanogorsk
Kazyr
Sevi
Pavlodar
Blagovščenka
Troickoje
Taštagol
Abakan
Ak-Dovurak
Kyzyl
Saryg-Sop
Us'-Bel'dir
Yermak
Rodino
Alejsk
Turočak
Cadan
Sagonar
Kyzyl-Chem
Jamyševo
Pospelicha
Alel
Altejskij
Čodro
Ak-Dovurak
Malčin
Balgazya
Scerbakty
Rubcovsk
Čaryšskoje
Lake Teleckoje
Kyzyl-Chaja
Orög Nuur
Uvs Nuur
Samagaltaj
Naryn
Ajryk
Molgary
Dolon
Gorn'ak
Semonaicha
Inja
Koš-Agač
Turgen
Baruun Turuun
Bajan-Uul
Cagaan Uul
Kiikkaskan
Bel'agaš
Tuekta
Kuraj
Kyzyl-Chaja
Cagaan Nuur
Chirgis Nuur
Ojgon Nuur
Kajnar
Semipalatinsk
Ust'-Kamengorsk
Katun'
Argut
Cagaan Nuur
Erdene Büren
Ulgij
Ofgij
Telmen Nuur
Čarsk
Serebr'ansk
Georgiievka
Bol'šenarymskoje
Lake Markakol
Korti Linchang
Cagaan Gol
Altaj
Kobdo
Char Us Nuur
Jaruu
Uliastaj
Madenijet
Ajaguz
Belaja Škola
Zajsan
Buran
Ertix He
Burqin
Beitun
Attay
Altaj
Manchan
Döröö Nuur
Aldar
Teelin
Karaaul
Žarma
Zajsan
Zajsan
Muz Tau
Ulungur Hu
Fuyun
Mönch Chajrchan
Dzereg
Bujant
Taskesken
Urdžar
Tacheng
Toli
Utubulak
Sarbulak
Ovoot
Cagaan-Olom
Delger
Sajak
Aktogaj
Urho
Ulungur
Ertai
Bulgan
Tamc
Türgen
Beger
Im Frunze
Lepsy
Žarsuat
Ebinur Hu
Manas Hu
Bugat
Altaj
Dzachuj
Bajan-Ondor
Ustobe
Taldy-Kurgan
Wenquan
Bole
Jinhe
Usu
Shihezi
Jiangjumiao
Gov'Chonin
Altaj
Aktogaj
Saryozek
Panfilov
Ining
Nilka
Manas
Changji
Ganhezi
Qitai
Santanghu
Nom
Kapčagaj
Ili He
Qapqal
Tekes
Xinyuan
Narat
Urumchi
Bogda Feng
Qijiaojing
Barkol Hu
Barkol Kazak
Čemolgan
Alma Ata
Zhaosu
Houxia
Baiyanghe
Qiquanhu
Liaodun
Hami
Yiwu
Karlik Shan
Kaskalen
Kegen
Narynkol
Tekes
Baiyanghe
Ewirgol
Turpan
Shanshan
Liushuquan
Mergol
Rubcоje
Ananjevo
Prževal'sk
Bulguntay
Yandun
Mingshui
Gongpoquan
Ottuk
Pik Pobedy
Keyi
Yengisar
Qarqi
Yanqi Huizu Zizhixian
Bosten Hu
Weiya
Xingxingxia
Jiangjuntai
Naryn Tarabaj
Kuqa
Dalaoba
Korla
Yuli
Daquan
Hongliuyuan
Jiangquanzi
Pik Dankowa
Yakrik
Xinhe
Tarim
Kongi
Anxi
Qiaowan
Čotyrtaš
Toxkan
Aksu
Karayulgun
Tarim Liuchang
Zhangjiaquan
Shule
Choushuidan
San Bulak
Akqi
Awat
Aral
Yengisu
Kumkuduk
Dunhuang
Dongbatu
Sanchakou
Bachu Liuchang
Ikanbujmal
Luobuzhuang
Donglük
Shazaoyuan
Jiayuguan
Sugun
Yarkant
Hotan
Tarim Basin
Miran
Ruoqiang
Aksay
Obo Liang
Changma
Jiuquan
Yopurga
Markit
Tongguzbasti
Takla Makan Desert
Aktaz
Waxxari
Xorkol
Niubiziliang
Lenghu
Suhai Hu
Huahaizi
Hasalbag
Yecheng
Koxlax
Qiemo
Hadilik
Tura
Ayakkum Hu
Youshashan
Tsaidam Basin
Iqe
Har Hu
Muji
Zawa
Qira
Minfeng
Andirlangar
Aqqikkol Hu
Gas Hu
Mangnai
Shaliangzi
Da Qaidam
Delingha
Zangguy
Hotan
Yutian
Karasay
Bostan
Tekiliktag
Aktag
Nur Turu
Dabsan Hu
Qarhan
Xitieshan
Holt Taria
Ulan
Mazar
Yarkant
Karakax
Pulu
Muztag
Boluntay
De Juh
Golmud
Nomhon
Dulan
Kangxiwar

80°E 85°E 90°E 95°E
55°N 50°N 45°N 40°N

This map shows 1/60 of the earth's surface. Area scale : 1 □ inch on the map ≈ 15,000 □ miles on the ground 1 □ cm on the map ≈ 6000 □ km on the ground

a b c d e f g h i j k l m

100°E · Kova · 105°E · Volokon · Lena · 110°E · Vit mskiy · 115°E · 120°E · Yenyuka

636 Karamysheva · Ust'Ilimsk · Kirensk · Gorno-Chuyskiy · Bodaybo · Taluma
Vorob'yeva · Garmenka · Romanova · Ilimsk · Ul'kan · Kirenga · Yermaki · Sinyuga · Berezovka · Ust' Nyukzha
Bratsk · Suvorka · Vidim · Ust'-Kut · Riga · Orlinga · Injaptuk 2579 · North Baykal Plateau · Tonnel'nyy · Okkana
Chunskiy · Bratskoye Reservoir · Angara · Nizhneangarsk · Uoyan · Vitim Plateau · Bukačača · Ust'-Karsk · 1249 · Yimuhe · Gulian · Luoguhe

UNION

Tulun · 763 Ust'-Kada · Žigalovo · Sugdža · Baykal'skoje · Baunt · Oron · Jeleninskij · Veršino-Darasunskij · Cernyševsk · Sretensk · Kurleja · Mangui
Zima · Balagansk · 774 · Massimicha · Isinga · 1322 · Talembas · Uda · Chita · Šilka · Ingoda · Balev · Nerchinsky Zavoid · Argun · Mordaga · Jinhe

Borshchovochny Mts

Čeremchovo · Usolje Sibirskoje · Ust'-Ordynsk · Lake Baykal · Tataurovo · Chorinsk · Darasun · Karymskoje · Klin · Priargunsk · Argun Zuoqi · Kalaqi
Angarsk · Irkutsk · Selichov · Ulan-Ude · Chilok · Petrovsk-Zaba kal'skij · Tanga · Ula · Olov'annaja · 1248 · Onon Gol · Borzya · Argun Youqi · Tulihe
Mondy · 3266 · Kyren · Listv'anka · Kamensk · Gusinoozersk · Urluk · Narasun · Solovjevsk · Manchouli · Qagan · Chen Barag Qi · Yuanlin · Yakeshi · 1395
Rinčin Lchumbe · Chanch · Sl'ud'anka · Tanchoj · 2394 · Selenga · 2523 · Chapčeranga · Uldz Gol · Gurvan Ozagal · Hailar · Hailar · 50°N
Chövsgöl Nuur · Zakamensk · Süchbaatar · K'achta · Penza · Bajan-Uul · Chevirga · Huluun Nuur · 1474 · Goukpu

MONGOLIA

Chatgal · Möron · Tarialan 2263 · Darchan · Charaa · Onon Gol · Norcvin 1595 · Cojbalsan · Xin Barag Youqi · Xin Barag Zouqi
Chutag · Erdenet · Orchontuul · Mandal · Bajan Ovoc · Bulgar 1260 · Öncör · Buyr Nuur · Handgai 1712
Ulan Bator 1309 · Cencher Mandal · Cherlen Gol · Yirshi · Xikou · Dashizhai
Lün · 1843 · Bajan · Tariat · Öndör Chaan · Ar Dzargala · Tamsagbulag · 58
Bajan Baraat · 1706 · Tüvšinširee · Bajšint · Qahan Qulut · Shun ougou 1394 · Horqin Youyi Qianqi
Delgerchaan · Sümber · Calandžargalan · Erdene Cagaan · Bulag Sum · Dong Ujimqin Qi · 1950 · Nungnain Sun · Tuquan
Sajnšend · Etap Bajanmönch · 1750 · Xar Hudak · 45°N

Orog Nuur · Bujart-Ovoo · Mandach · Erdene · Xi Ujimqin Qi · Jarud Qi
Bajanleg · Chovd Mandal-Ovoo · Cogt-Ovoo 1521 · Manlaj · 1150 · Xilin Qagan Obo · Abag Qi · Jirin Sum · 510 · Yolin Mod
Bulgan · Chövsgöl · Erenhot · Xilin Hot · Linxi · Kailu He
2631 · Dalandzadgad 1791 · Chan Bogd · Orgon Tal · Qagan Nur · Yarud Sum · Hexigten Qi · Bairin Youqi · Xar Moron · Tongliao
Ovoot Chural · Nomgon · Sular Chee · Baixingt · Ongniud Qi · Baixingt · Naiman Qi
Qen · Sogo Nur 1395 · Suj · Ondor Sum · Zhenglan Qi · Chifeng · Fusin
Saxun Nur · Gaihan Toroi · Ejin Qi · Bayan Obo · Zhenghuang Qi · Shangdu · Taibus Qi · 1081 · Weichang · Jianping · Yi Xian
Ximiao · Hanggin Houqi · Wuyuan · Guyang · 2174 · Tsining · Shangyi · Fengning · Longhua 1941 · Chinchow · Chinsi
Tiancang · Bayan Mod · Linhe · Shiguaigou · Huhehot · Changkiakow · Suanhwa · Chenteh · Harqin · Yingkow
Tiancheng · Badain Jaran · Urad Qianqi · Huang He · Togtoh · Huai'an · Miyun 1677 · Kuancheng · Gai Xian
Dengkou · Dongsheng · Tatung · Yu Xian · Peking (Beijing) · Lulong · Qinhuangdao · Fu Xian · Wudao
Otog Qi · Juntuliang · Pianguan · Laiyuan · Tangshan
Badain Jaran 1766 · Suhait · Vauda 2149 · Shihtsuishan · Shenmu · Xi Xian · 3054 · Pacting · Ba Xian · Tientsin · Lüda (Dalian)
Alashan Desert · Dongzhen · Alxa Zuoqi · Yinchuan · Shuo Xian · Ding Xian · Cangchow · Po Hai · Maiodao Islands
Dongle · Shandan · Jinchang · Wuzhong · Nangsin Sum · Yulin · 2831 · Shihkiachwang · Yangchuan · Yanshan · Penglai
5020 Minle · Wuwei · Zhongwei · Dingbian · Taiyuan · Yutze · Tehchow · Laichow Bay · 220 · Yantai
Manyuan · Great Wall · Tianshui · Suide · Taigu · 2069 · Boxing · Shanjung
Gangca · Datong · Sining 2244 · Yondeng · Tongxin · Wuqi · Zichang · Huo Xian · Singtai · Linqing · Tsinan · Tzepo · Weifang · Laiyang
Qinghai Hu · Dashuiqiao · 4832 · Gonghe · Minhe · Jingyuan · Lanchow 1508 · Guyuan · Yan'an · Hantan Fengfeng · Anyang · Tai'an · 120°E · Jiao Xian · Tsingtao

Average linear scale: 1 inch ≈ 125 miles 1 cm ≈ 80 km

n o p q r s t u v w x y z

Ingoda
Baley
Klin
Nerchinsky Zavod
Nerchinsky Zavod
120°E
Jinhe
Linhai
Shimanovsk
Svobodnyy
Novokiyevskiy Uval
Urgal
Ust'Niman
Chegdomyn
Bolodzhak
Kondon
Bokto
Duki

SOVIET UNION
Borzya
Priargunsk
Argun Zuoqi
Mordaga
Kalaqi
827
Shisanzhan
Hume
Belogorsk
Zeya
RUSSIAN S.F.S.R.
Bureya
Chekunda
Mogdy
Gornyy
Komsomol'sk-na-Amure

Chen Barag Qi
Nerchimsky Zavod
Argun Zuoqi
Argun Youqi
Tuliihe
Oroqen Zizhiqi
1212
Dayangshu
Huolongmen
Heihe
Blagoveshchensk
188
Zavitinsk
Raychikhinsk
Bureya
Talandzha
Ust'Tyrma
Tyrma
1381
SOVIET UNI
Amursk

50°N
Hulun-Nur
Manchouli
Qagan
Hailar
Yuanlin
1395
Xiao'ergou
Morin Dawa
Nenjiang
Longzhen
Bei'an
Xunke
Arkhara
Izvestkovyy
Birobidzhan
Khabarovsk
Kruglikovo

Xin Barag Youqi
Xin Barag Zuoqi
Hailar
Yakeshi
1474
Arun Qi
Nehe
Yi'an
701
Wuyiling
Jiayin
1014
Luobei
Tongjiang
Amur
Fuyuan
Khor
Chuken

Buyr-Nur
Handgai
1712
Yirshi
Great Khingan Mts.
Longjiang
Zalantun
Nen Jiang
Fuyu
Baiquan
Yichun
1150
Hokang
Nancha
Kiamusze
851
Schwangyashan
831
Bikin
Kotikova
Sinn
Luchegorsk
Svetlovodnaya

Tamsagbulag
MONGOLIA
Xikou
Tsitsihar
(Qiqihar)
Dorbod
Qing'an
Suihua
Fangzheng
Qitaihe
Dongfanghong
Dal'nerechensk
Bikin
Velikaya Kema
1448

Gobi
Dashizhai
Tailai
Daqing
Laoxi
Manchuria
Suihua
Harbin
Shangzhi
1060
Linkou
Muling-He
Hulin
Lesozavodsk
Sidatun

Inner
Bulag Sum
Horqin Youyi Qianqi
Baicheng
1394
Zhaoyuan
Shuangcheng
Lalin He
Sungari
Xiachengzi
Kisi
Lake Khanka
Kirovsky

CHINA
Nungnain Sum
1950
Tuquan
Tao'an
Qian Gorlos
Yushu
1322
Mutankiang
Ning'an
Dongjingcheng
Spassk Dal'niy
Terney

45°N
Dong Ujimqin Qi
Qagan Qulut
Jarud Qi
Tongyu
Dehui
Xiachengzi
Suifenhe
Ussuriysk
1855
Margaritovo

Xi Ujimqin Qi
Jirin Gol
510
Xinkai He
Horqin Zuoyi Zhongqi
1397
Ning'an
Dongjingcheng
Artem
Kavalerovo

Holt Sum
Jarud Qi
Yolin Mod
Changchun
Kirin
(Jilin)
Jiaohe
Emu
Wangqing
1498
Hunchun
Vladivostok
Nakhodka

Xilin Hot
2029
Bairin Zuoqi
Xar Moron
Kailu He
Tongliao
Shwangliao
2404
Huinan
Jiaohe
Dunhua
Yenki
Hoeryong
Tumen
Najin

Zhenglan Qi
Linxi
Bairin Youqi
Naiman Qi
Baixingt
Szeping
Liaoyuan
Jingyu
Liuhe
Paektu-san
2744
Chuuronjang
Ch'ŏngjin

Hexigten Qi
Chifeng
1081
866
Fusin
Xinmin
Qingyuan
Tunghwa
Linkiang
Changpai Shan
Hyesanjin
Kapsan
Kimchaek

Ongniud Qi
Weichang
Fushun
Mukden
(Shenyang)
Tunghwa
Huanren
Manp'ojin
1823
Pukch'ong

40°N
Luan He
1941
Jianping
Yi Xian
Penki
Liaoyang
Anshan
Kuandian
Yalu
2522
Kimchaek
SEA OF

Longhua
Harqin
Chinchow
Liaoyang
Huanren
940
1132
Hüich'on
Hamhung
JAPAN

Fengning
Chengteh
Kuancheng
1677
Chinsi
Yingkow
Gai Xian
Antung
(Dandong)
Sinŭiju
NORTH
Anju
Wŏnsan

Miyun
Great Wall
Lulong
Qinhuangdao
Wudao
Fu Xian
Gushan
KOREA
Korea Bay
Pyongyang
Hwangju

Peking
(Beijing)
Tangshan
Qinhuangdao
Chinnamp'o
Ich'ŏn
Sokch'o
SEA OF

Tientsin
Yongding He
Lüda
(Dalian)
Miaodao Qundao
Haeju
Kaesong
Ch'unch'ŏn
1708
Kangnŭng
Tonghae

Ba Xian
Po Hai
Penglai
Yantai
Ongjin
Wŏnju
Seoul
Ch'ungju

Cangchow
Yanshan
Laichow Bay
Laiyang
Inch'ŏn
Seoul
Andong

Tehchow
Boxing
Yantai
Cape Chengshan
Ch'ŏngju
SOUTH

Tzepo
Weifang
Shantung
220
Taejon
Yellow Sea
KOREA
Oki

Tsinan
950
Jiao Xian
Laiyang
Kunsan
Chŏnju
Taegu
1860
Ulsan
Tottori
Fukui
2702

35°N
Tai'an
Tsingtao
Masan
1915
Pusan
Matsue
Tsuruga
Gifu

Yanzhou
Liangcheng
Kwangju
Chinju
Korea Strait
Kyōto
Nagoya

Tsining
Lienyunkang
Mokp'o
Yŏsu
Masuda
Yamaguchi
1339
Okayama
Himeji
Kobe
Ōsaka

Tsaochuang
Grand Canal
Tsushima (Japan)
Shimonoseki
Hiroshima
Takamatsu
Sakai Matsusaka
Wakayama

Suchow
Huaibei
1366
Suhsien
Huaiyin
Cheju
Kita-Kyūshū
Ube
Matsuyama
1981
Kōchi
Tokushima
1915
Tanabe

Pengpu
Hwainan
Lake Hungtze
Hongze
Quelpart Island
(Cheju)
Fukuoka
Sasebo
Oita
1791
Shikoku
Nakamura
Kii Strait

Yangchow
Taichow
East China
Nagasaki
Kumamoto
Yatsushiro

Hefei
Nanking
Changshu
Sea
Miyazaki
1700

Lujiang
Wuhu
Wuhsi
Suchow
Kagoshima
Ōsumi Channel
Tanega

Xuancheng
Lake Tai
Kashing
Zhoushan Qundao
Yaku

Tonkling
Anking
1860
1187
120°E
Shanghai
Hangchow
125°E
130°E
135°E

This map shows 1/60 of the earth's surface. Area scale : 1 □ inch on the map ≙ 15,000 □ miles on the ground 1 □ cm on the map ≙ 6000 □ km on the ground

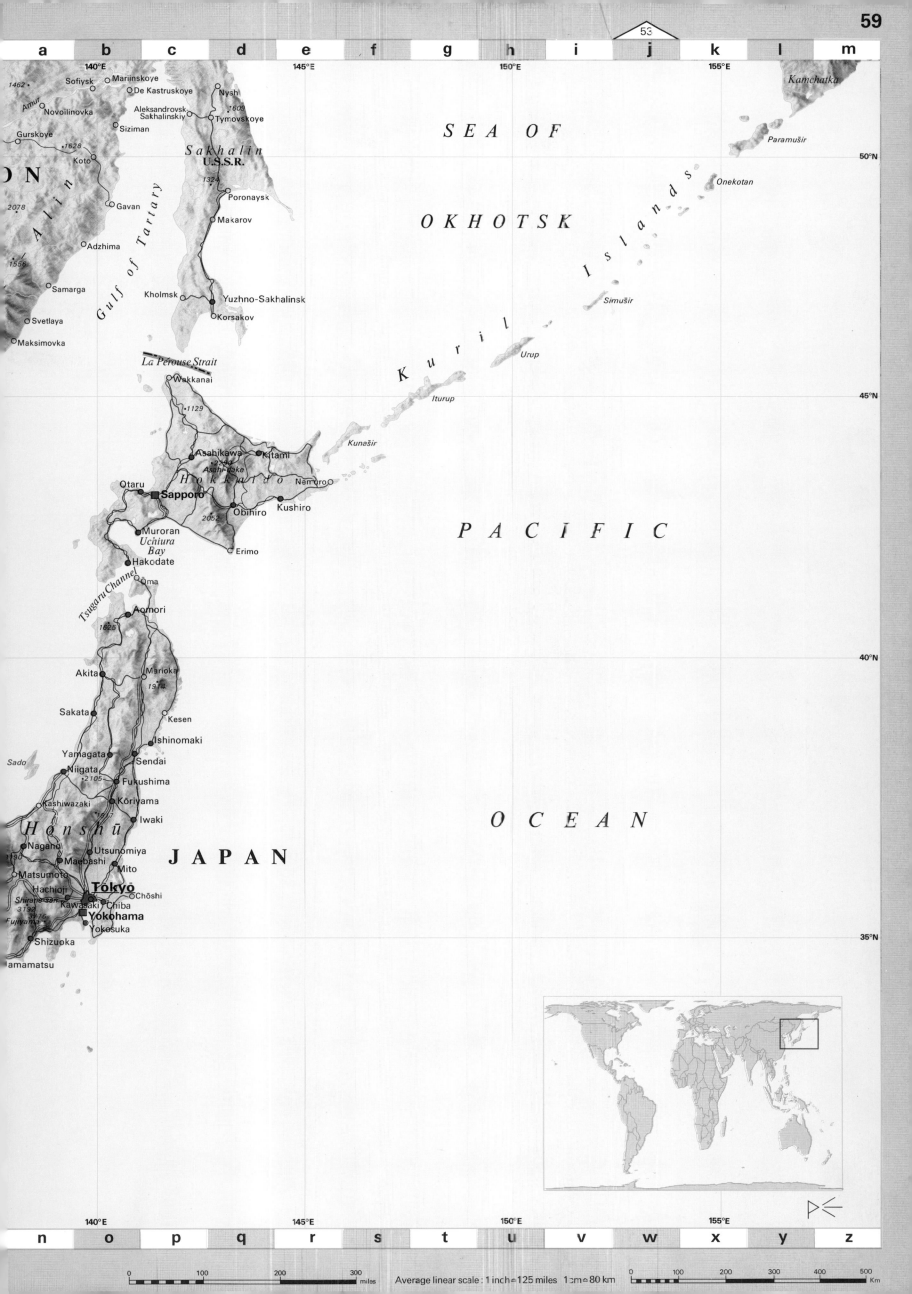

53

1462·
Sofiysk   Mariinskoye
Amur   Novoilinovka   De Kastruskoye   Nysh
Gurskoye   Aleksandrovsk-   ·1609
   Siziman   Sakhalinskiy   Tymovskoye
·1628
Koto   *S a k h a l i n*
   U.S.S.R.
2078   1324·
A l i n   Gavan   Poronaysk
·1556   Adzhima   Makarov

Samarga   *Gulf of Tartary*
   Kholmsk   Yuzhno-Sakhalinsk
Svetlaya   Korsakov
Maksimovka

La Pérouse Strait
   Wakkanai
   ·1129

S E A   O F

O K H O T S K

Kamchatka

Paramušir

Onekotan

Simušir

Kuril   Islands

50°N

45°N

Asahikawa   Kitami
   Asahi-dake
Otaru   *H o k k a i d o*   Nemuro
Sapporo   Kushiro
   2052·   Obihiro
Muroran   Erimo
Uchiura Bay
Hakodate
   Oma
Tsugaru Channel
   Aomori
   1625·

Urup

Iturup

Kunašir

P A C I F I C

Akita   Marioka
   1974·
Sakata   Kesen
   Ishinomaki
Yamagata   Sendai
Niigata   Fukushima
·2105
Kashiwazaki   Kōriyama
Sado   Iwaki
H o n s h ū
Nagano   Utsunomiya   **J A P A N**
Maebashi   Mito
Matsumoto   *O C E A N*
Hachioji   **Tōkyō**   Chōshi
Shirane-san   Kawasaki Chiba
3192·   **Yokohama**
Fujiyama   Yokosuka
Shizuoka
Hamamatsu

40°N

35°N

140°E   145°E   150°E   155°E

0   100   200   300   miles
0   100   200   300   400   500   Km
Average linear scale : 1 inch=125 miles   1 cm=80 km

a b c d e f g h i j k l m

55

SOVIET UNION

Quchan
Mayamey
Sabzevar
Neishabur
Mashhad
Sarakhs
3416
3147
Andkhoy
Aqcha
Mazar-i Sharif
Khulm
Kunduz
Faizabad
Qala Panja
K 55

Bardeskan
Kashmar
Torbat-e Heidariye
Torbat-e Jam
Kuska
Takhta Bazar
Maimana
Sari-i Pul
Sheberghan
Aibak
Baghlan
Taliqan
Zebak
Mastuj
Yasi

Dasht-e Kavir
35°N
Bidokht
Ferdows
Tabas
2578
Ghorian
Quala-i Nau
Tayebad
Jawand
Bala Murghab
Qaisar
Chaghcharan
Daulat Yar
Qarah Taral
3704
Kuh-e-Baba
Behsud
Bamian
Charikar
Kabul
Jalalabad
Asadabad
Besham Qila
Tirich Mir
7690
Drosh
4448

AFGHANISTAN

Aliabad
Khusf
Naiband
2992
Birjand
Sarbisheh
Yazdan
Shindand
Farahrod
Farsi
Sangan
3025
Khurd
3830
Sangan
Uruzgan
Ghazni
Gardez
Matun
Peshawar
Islamabad

IRAN

Bafq
Darband
2438
Ravor
2729
Nehbandan
2488
716
Farah
2560
Dilaram
Lasho Joayin
Khash Rud
Nauzad
Girishk
Kandahar
Arghandab
Tarnak
Qalat-i Chilzai
Tarin Kot
Shahjui
Zarghunshar
Razmak
Kalabagh
Bannu
Lakki
Mianwali
Chakwal
Gujar

Zarand
Baghin
Kerman
Siraj
3143
Namakzar-e Shadad
Nosratabad
1643
Zahedan
Ribat
Zabol
2052
Zaranj
Mirabad
Helmand
1371
Rudbar
Safar
Registan
1314
Chaman
Kand
Sakir
3095
3273
Muslimbagh
Qila Saifullah
Kingri
Loralai
Dera Ghazi Khan
Multan
Sahiwal

Rafsanjan
Hoseinabad
Sirjan
Baft
Laleh Zar
4374
Tahrud
Darzin
Bam
Shurgaz
Mirjaveh
Taftan
3941
Nok Kundi
2333
Sultan
2462
Chagai Hills
2208
Dalbandin
Chagai
Ras Koh
3009
2101
Nushki
Kalat
Sibi
Kahan
Dera Bugti
Rajanpur
Uch
Bahawalpur
Fazilk
Ganganagar
Suratgar

PAKISTAN

Dowlatabad
Hajiabad
3279
Qotbabad
1564
Kahnui
Sabzevaran
Bazman
3503
2548
Khash
Dehak
Saravan
Qila Ladgasht
Besima
Kharan
Surab
Khuzdar
Jacobabad
Shikarpur
Larkana
Sukkur
Khairpur
Tanot
Shahgarh
Sri Mohangarh
Jaisalmer
Pugal
Mahajan
Bikaner
Nagaur
Bap

Bandar Abbas
Minab
Jaghin
Qeshm
1950
Remeshk
Bampur
Bampur
Iranshahr
Kuhak
Panjgur
Patandar
2283
Jebri
Wad
Moro
Sehwan
Sanghar
Myajlar
Phalsund
Balotra
Pokaran
Jodhpur

39
Straits of Hormuz
Al Sha'am
Ras Musandam
2081
2110
Sarbaz
2100
Nikshahr
Awaran
Bela
Kotri
Hyderabad
Mirpur Khas
Gurha
Barmer
Pali
Sirohi
1722
Guru Sikhar

OMAN
Ras al Khaimah
Dibba
Jask
Pishin
Bahu Kalat
Turbat
Hoshab
1454
Kikki
Pasni
Ormara
Hab Chauki
Thatta
Badin
Virawah
Tharad
Udaipur

Sharjah
Dubai
Fujairah
Shinas
Sohar
Al Ain
Al Khaburah
As Suwaiq
As Sib
Muscat
Quraiyat
Bahu Kalat
Chabahar
Ras Kuh Lab
Jiwani
Ras Nuh
Pasni

Gulf of Oman

Karachi

Jati
Rann of Kutch
Radhanpur
Palanpur
Himatnagar
I

Ibri
3019
Nazwa
Izki
Adam
Al Kamil
Sumail
Al Hajar al Sharqi
Sur
Ras al Hadd
Tropic of Cancer
Lakhpat
Rampur
Bhuj
New Kandla
Mandvi
Gulf of Kutch
Morvi
Ahmedabad
Mahesana
Nadiad
Vadodara

OMAN
Ramlat al Wahiba
Al Ashkhirah
A R A B I A N
Dwarka
Jamnagar
Rajkot
Kathiawar
Dhandhuka
Khambhat
Bharuch
Narmada
Godh

Umm as Samim
Masirah
S E A
Porbandar
Junagadh
Bhavnagar
Surat
Tapti
Navsari

Duqm
Veraval
Diu
Gulf of Cambay
(Gulf of Khambhat)
Valsad
1567
Daman
Nasi

20°N

Sharbithat
Ras Sharbithat
Thane
Bombay

Kuria Muria Islands
Pune

Janjira
Bhor
Sata
Koyna Reservoir
Chiplun

Ratnagiri

60°E
65°E
70°E

n o p q r s t u v w x y z

64

This map shows 1/60 of the earth's surface. Area scale : 1 □ inch on the map ≙ 15,000 □ miles on the ground   1 □ cm on the map ≙ 6000 □ km on the ground

a b c d e f g h i j k l m

75°E 80°E 85°E 90°E

Misgar
Mazar
Karakax He
Moyu
Qira
Minfeng
Karasay
Bostan
Aqqikkol Hu
Boluntay

Rakaposhi K2 Kangxiwar
Tekiliktag
Pixa
Pulu
Kerya He
Aktag
Muztag
Muztag
Qumar Heyan

Gilgit
Nanga Parbat
Skardu
Saser
Dahongliutan
Yurungkax
Kunlun Shan
Margai Caka
Xijir Ulan Hu
Luanhaizi
35°N

JAMMU AND KASHMIR
Kargil
Leh
Kizyl Jilga
Tielongtan
CHINA
Ccmo
Dogai Coring
Moron Us He
Tongtianheyan

Wular Lake Srinagar
Pamzal
Chushul
Pangong Tso
Wujang
Tibet
Banvalot
Lhazhong
Do'gyaling
Tanggula Shan
Wenquan

Anantnag
Zangla
Zasar
Ratang
Xungba
Qagcaka
Qma
Gêrzê
Zhaxi Co
Nyima
Dongqiao
Amdo
Nyainrong

Kishtwar
Chenab
Jaggang
Shiquanhe
Gê'gyai
Yar uqu
Nganglar Ringco
Lugu
Kangro
Pa-ding
Baingoin
Naqu

Jammu
Chamba
Dharmsala
Dankhar
Gartsa
Yagra
Lunggar
Coqên
Taagra Yumco
Ombu
Gyaring Co
Xainza
Namco

Sialkot
Pathankot
Gurdaspur
Kulu
Kalpa
Zanda
Moincer
Mapam Yumco
Samsang
Zhari Namco
Tomra
Nam Co
Damxung

Amritsar
Hoshiarpur
Simla
Nilang
Barca
La'nga Co
Burang
Paryang
Raka Zangbo
Yatlung Zangbo Jiang
Kangmar
Yangbajain

Lahore
Jallundur
Ludhiana
Chandigarh
Dehra Dun
Pauri
Karnaprayag
Zhongba
Saga
Ngamring
Lhazê
Zigazê
Gonggar
Lhasa
Nêdong
30°N

Kasur
Firozpur
Ambala
Patiala
Almora
Similot
Daleh
Mustang
Gyirong
Tingri
Dinggyê
Nyêmo
Maizhokunggar

Bhatinda
Karnal
Panipat
Saharanpur
Da'delehura
Dhaulagiri
Annapurna
Pokhara
Xixabangma Feng
Everest
Kangma
Yamzho Yumco

Nohar
Hisar
Rohtak
Meerut
Hapur
Moradabad
Rampur
Pilibhit
Nepalganj
Mukala
Mikalu
Gala
Comai

Delhi
New Delhi
Ghaziabad
Budaun
Bareilly
Butwal
Katmandu
Bhaktapur
Bhojpur
Darjeeling
Timphu
BHUTAN
Tashigang

Churu
Rewari
Aligarh
Etah
Shahjahanpur
Sitapur
Birganj
Sirha
Biratnagar
Shiliguri
Jalpaiguri
Tongsa Dzong
Dirang

Ratangarh
Hodal
Mathura
Farrukhabad
Kannauj
Balrampur
Bettia
Motihari
Raniganj
Koch Bihar
Nowgong

Sikar
Alwar
Agra
Etawah
Lucknow
Faizabad
Gorakhpur
Muzaffarpur
Darbhanga
Purnia
Rangpur
Dinajpur
Dhuburi
Goalpara
Gauhati

Didwana
Bharatpur
Gwalior
Orai
Kanpur
Sultanpur
Azamgarh
Ghaghara
Patna
Bihar
Bhagalpur
Bogra
Jamalpur
Tura
Shillong

Jaipur
Gangapur
Jhansi
Fatehpur
Ghazipur
Arrah
Mongiyr
Ingraj Bazar
Jamalpur
Sylhet
Karimganj

Ajmer
Tonk
Banas
Shivpur
Bande
Allahabad
Varanasi
Mirzapur
Gaya
Kodarma
Dumka
Pabna
Mymensingh
Maulvi Bazar

Beawar
Bhilwara
Kota
Baran
Guna
Chhatarpur
Panna
Rewa
Maihar
Sasaram
Garwa
Hazaribag
Dhanbad
Berhampore
Siuri
BANGLADESH
Dacca
Comilla
Agartala
Aizawl

Rampura
Mandsaur
Raisen
Damoh
Son
Sonhat
Ranchi
Puruliya
Barddhaman
Navadwip
Faridpur
Jessore
Chandpur
Barkal

INDIA
Shajapur
Narsinghgarh
Sagar
Jabalpur
Shahdol
Ambikapur
Jashpurnagar
Jamshedpur
Bankura
Calcutta
Khulna
Barisal
Chittagong

Ratlam
Ujjain
Bhopal
Narmada
Narsimhapur
Mand a
Bilaspur
Sundargarh
Rourkela
Kharagpur
Hugli

Ahod
Indore
Hoshangabad
Harda
Chhindwara
Seoni
Balaghat
Bampada
Balasore
Ganges Delta
Cox's Bazar

Mhow
Barwani
Khandwa
Khargon
Burhanpur
Batul
Katni
Sarangarh
Hirakud Reservoir
Deogarh
Sambalpur
Bhadrakh
Palmyras Point

Barwani
Satpura Range
Nagpur
Bhandara
Raipur
Balangir
Cuttack
BURMA
Kyauktaw

Dhule
Jalgaon
Amravati
Wardha
Raj Nandgaon
Phulabani
Bhubaneswar
Bhanjanagar
Sittwe

Malegaon
Buldana
Akola
Yevatmal
Garhchiroli
Kanker
Makri
Puri
20°N

Aurangabad
Jalna
Nanded
Sirpur
Chandrapur
Indravati
Jagdalpur
Chatrapur
Berhampur

Ahmadnagar
Parbhani
Beed
Adilabad
Jagtial
Sironcha
Jaypur
Parvatipuram

Daund
Barsi
Latur
Nizamabad
Chintalnar
Venkatapuram
Srikakulam
Vizianagaram

Sholapur
Bidar
Karimnagar
Warangal
Bhadrathalam
Khammam
Tuni
Vishakhapatnam

Pandharpur
Gulbarga
Sangareddi
Hyderabad
Nalgonda
Godavari
Kakinada
Rajahmundry

Sangli
Kolhapur
Bijapur
Mahbubnagar
Eluru
Vijayawada
Guntur
Krishna

n o p q r s t u v w x y z

Bay of Bengal

0 100 200 300 miles
Average linear scale 1 inch=125 miles 1 cm=80 km
0 100 200 300 400 500 Km

a b c d e f g h i j k l m

Taiyuan
Suide
Yangchuan
Yutze
Taigu
Singtai
2069
115°E
Tehchow
Fenglai
Yantai
120°E
Laiyang
Cape Chengshan

Yellow
Inch'ŏn
Seoul
Kangnung
Wŏnju
Ch'ŏngju

S O U T H

Huo Xian
Fengfeng
Hantan
Linqing
Box ng
Weifang
Ta'an
Sea
Taejŏn
Andong

Changchih
Anyang
Tsinan
950
Jiao Xian

Shantung

Taegu
K O R E A
Kunsan
Chŏnju
Chŏngju
Masan
Chinju
35°N

Hancheng
2322
Jiaozuo
Sinsiang
Hohpi
Heze
Tsining
Yanzhou
C.Junan
Tsingtao
Liangcheng

Kwangju
Mokp'o
1918
Yosu

Sanmenhsia
Loyang
1440
Chengchow
Kaifeng
Qi Xian
Zhecheng
Suchow
Tsaochuang
Suhsien
Lienyunkang

Cheju
Quelpart Island
(Cheju)

Lingbao
1997
Pingtingshan
Hsuchang
Huaibei
366
Huaiyin
Binhai

Shannan
Nanzhao
Luohe
Shangshui
Pengpu
Lake
Hung'tze
Hongze

Zhenping
Nanyang
Tanghe
Great
Xincai
Fuyang
Lake
Kaoyu

ang Xian
1140
Siangfan
Sui Xian
Xinyang
Huangchuan
Hwainan
Yangchow
Taichow
Nantung

1612
Nanzhang
Yunmeng
Luoshan
Chu Xian
Nanking
Changshu
Nantung

Shiyan
Macheng
Hefei
Plain
Lujiang
Wuhu
Wuhsi

N
A
Yangtze (Chang Jiang)
Xuancheng
Suchow
Shanghai

Ichang
Yidu
Wuhan
1860
Anting
Tonkling
1187
Kashing

Shasi
Mianyang
Hwangshih
1341
Hangchow

Li Xian
Tongshan
Tunxi
Shaohing
Ningpo
Guoju

feng
Changteh
Kiukiang
Xingzi
Xin'anjiang
30°N

Yuan Jiang
Lake
Tungting
1596
Xiushui
Nanchang
Kingtehchen
Quzhou
Kinhwa
Linhai

*Zhoushan
Islands*

E A S T   C H I N A

Anhua
Yiyang
Shangjao
Lishui

S E A

Chenxi
Changsha
Gao'an

Qianyang
Siangtan
Chuchow
Xinyu
Cuixi
2158
Pucheng
Yunhe
Wenchow

Liahyuan
1290
Pingsiang
Zhenghe
Fud ng

Shaoyang
Hengyang
Gan Jiang
Nanfeng
Shaowu
Ningde

1934
Ji'an
1199
Nanping

Wuvi Shan
1871
Sanming
1494
Minqing

Xiang Jiang
Leiyang
Ningdu
Min Jiang
Yong'an

Quanzhou
Ningyuan
Chen Xian
Ruijin
Putian
Foochow

Kweilin
Kanchow
Longyan

Ryūkyū Islands

Okinawa
Naha

Lian Xian
1902
Shaokwan
Changchow
Mei Xian
Zhangpu
Ta oyuan
Ch lung

Pingle
Yingde
1560
Chao'an
Zhangpu
Hsinchu
Taipei
Ilan

Dongnan
Qiu ling
Longchuan
Jieyang
Swatow
Chaoyang
3884
Xueveng

25°N

Pingnan
Wuchow
1282
Amoy
(Xiamen)
Taichung
Changhua
Hualien

Luoding
Si (Xi Jiang)
Foshan
Huizhou
Lufeng
Hengchun
Chiai
3997
TAIWAN

Tropic of Cancer

Xulin
1704
Canton (Guangzhou)
Shun-te
Ta nan
Pingtung

Kongmoon
(Jiangmen)
Chuhoi
Kowloon
Victoria
Kaohsiung
Fangshan

Macao
(Port.)
HONG KONG
(U.K.)

Mowming
Yangjiang

Taiwan Strait

P A C I F I C

Bashi
Channel

Kuwen
Hainan Strait
Haikow

Luzon
Strait
Batan Islands

20°N

O C E A N

Hainan
Wanning

Babuyan Islands

HINA

Cape Bajeador
Laoag
Cape Engaño
Aparri

Luzon
Bangued
Vigan
Tuguegarao

PHILIPPINES

Ilagan

n o p q r s t u v w x y z

0   100   200   300   miles
Average linear scale : 1 inch ≈ 25 miles   1 cm ≈ 80 km
0   100   200   300   400   500   Km

a b c d e f g h i j k l m

Jawhar 75°E Jalna Pengaranga Chandrapur 80°E Makri 85°E Puri
Aurangabad 1646 Parbhani Nanded Adilabad Sirpur Indravati Jagdalpur Berhampur
Thane Ahmadnagar Beed Godavari Sironcha 1240 Jaypur Parvatipuram 1561
Bombay **Pune** Daund Latur Nizamabad Karimnagar Venkatapuram Chintalnar 1680 Srikakulam
Janjira Bhor Barsi Bidar Manjira Jagtial Warangal Vizianagaram
Chiplun Koyna Satara Pandharpur Sholapur Sangareddi **Hyderabad** Khammam Godavari Tuni Vishakhapatnam
Res. Gulbarga Mahbubnagar Nalgonda Bhadrachalam
Ratnagiri Sangli Bijapur I N D I A Rajahmundry Kakinada
Kolhapur Krishna Raichur Nagarjuna Guntur Eluru Kakinada
Belgaum Ramdurg Lingsugur Res. Vijayawada
Goa Gadag Kurnool Markapur Krishna Tenali Machilipatnam
Panaji Dharwar Hospet Adoni Gooty Banganapalle Ongole
Karwar Savanur Tungabhadra Res. 1100 Bellary Kavali
15°N Kotturu Anantapur Cuddapah Penner Nellore
Davangere Chitradurga Kadiri Gudur B E N
Sagar Penukonda Tirupati 1151
Linganamakki Res. Bhadravati 1923 Chik Ballapur Vayalpad Kolar Chittoor
Coondapoor Bhadra Res. Chikmagalur Tumkur **Bangalore** Vellore **Madras**
A R A B I A N Hassan Mandya Krishnagiri Polur Kanchipuram
Mangalore Madikeri Mysore Dharmapur Pondicherry
S E A 1745 Dharmapur 1627 Cuddalore
Cannanore Ootacamund Salem Mayuram
Amindivi (Udagamandalam) Erode Parambalur Coromandel Coast
Islands 2636 Cauvery
Calicut Doda Betta Tiruchchirappalli
Lakshadweep (Kozhikode) Coimbatore Thanjavur
(India) Palghat Pudukkottai
Trichur Anai Mudi Dindigul
Cannanore Ernakulam 2695
10°N Islands Cochin Madurai Palk Strait Jaffna
Alleppey 2019 Virudunagar Rameswaram Mullaittivu
Nine Degree Channel Ramanathapuram Adam's Br. Mannar
Quilon Tenkasi Tuticorin Trincomalee
Minicoy Tirunelveli Gulf of Anuradhapura
Trivandrum 1664 Mannar Puttalam
Eight Degree Channel Nagercoil Cape Comorin Dambulla Batticaloa
Kurunegala **SRI LANKA**
Kandy Piduratalagala
M A L D I V E S **Colombo** 2518 Badulla
2243 Pottuvil
Hambantota
5°N Galle Dondra Head

Male

I N D I A N

0° Equator 75°E 80°E 85°E

n o p q r s t u v w x y z

This map shows 1/60 of the earth's surface. Area scale : 1 □ inch on the map ≈ 15,000 □ miles on the ground 1 □ cm on the map ≈ 6000 □ km on the ground

a   b   c   d   e   f   g   h   i   j   k   l   m

90°E   95°E   100°E

Loikaw

Muang   Chiang Rai

Mekong   Luang Prabang   Ban Ban

Pyinmana

Thayetmyo

Ramree

Cheduba

L A O S

Sayaboury   Vang Vieng   Xieng Khouang

2820   Bia

Toungoo

Phayao   Nan

Pak Sane

Kham Keut

Inthanon   2590   Chiang Mai

Mekong

Prome

Pyu

Phrae

Lampang

1056

Vientiane

Wang Saphung   Nong Khai   Thakhek

Sittang

Myanaung

B U R M A

Irrawaddy

Henzada

Miang   2316

Udon Thani   Sakhon Nakhon

Pegu   Kyaikto

Soai Dao   2102

Kham Keut

Salween

Insein   Thingangyun

Phitsanulok

Chum Phae   Khon Kaen   Kalasin

Basseín   Kanbe   **Rangoon**

Thaton   Mae Sot   Tak

Nakhon Sawan   Phetchabun   Maha Sarakham   Roi Et

O F

Gulf of Martaban

Moulmein

Yasothon

Pyapon

Chaiyaphum

T H A I L A N D

Ubon Ratchathani

Mouths of the Irrawaddy

Ye

Nakhon Ratchasima

15°N

G A L

Tenasserim

Sing Buri   Lop Buri   Buri Ram   Surin

Si Sa Ket

Preparis

Suphan Buri

Khiaw   1282

Prachin Buri   849   Samrong

Cocos Islands (Burma)

Tavoy

Kanchanaburi

Nakhon Pathom

Chao Phraya   Chai Si

Bangkok (Krung Thep)

Ban Pong   Thon Buri

Sisophon   *Angkor*

North Andaman

Mergui Archipelago

Kadan

Mergui

Andaman Islands (India)

Phetchaburi

Chon Buri

Battambang   Tonle Sap

1633

K A M P U C H E A

Middle Andaman

Siracha

Klaeng   Rayong   Chantaburi

Pursat   Kompong Chhnang

1813

South Andaman

Hua Hin

Laem Ngop   Chang

Kut

Andaman

Letsok-Aw

1251   Prachuap Khiri Khan

Hat Lek

Gulf

Kompong Som

Phnom Penh

Little Andaman

Lanbi

756

of   Thailand

Phu Quoc

Ten Degree Channel

St. Matthew's

Chumphon

Isthmus of Kra

10°N

Car Nicobar

Sea

Ranong

Fhangan

Cape Mau

Semui

66

Nicobar Islands (India)

Takua Pa

Surat Thani

Ban Na San

Katchall

Thap Put

Khao Luang   1835

Nakhon Si Thammarat

Little Nicobar

Karbi

Great Nicobar

Phuket

Phatthalung   Thale Luang

Trang

Songkhla

Hat Yai   Pattani

Terutao   Satun

Sai Buri   Yala   Narathiwat

Langkawi

Alor Setar

Sungai Ko-lok   Kota Baharu

Banda Aceh   Sigli

Sungai Petani

Pangkal Kalong

5°N

Bireuen   Lhokseumawe   Idi

Pinang (George Town)   Butterworth

2171   Chamah   Kuala Terengganu

Kelantan

Pinang

Calang   Lhoksukon   285   Geureudong   Peureulak

Taiping   Sungai Siput   Utara

Perak   Tapis   1512

Dungun

Langsa

2131   Kuala Lipis

Ipoh   **M A L A Y A**

Meulaboh

Kampar   Raub   Kuantan

Pangkalanbrandan

Kuala Kubu Baharu   Bentong

Tapaktuan   *Leuse*   3404   Tanjungpura

Kutacana   **Medan**

Tebingtinggi

Petaling Jaya   **MALAYSIA** (WESTERN)

Kuala Lumpur

O C E A N

Kabanjahe   Pematangsiantar

Tanjungbalai   Kelang

Seremban

Tioman

Simeulue   Singkilbaru   Lake Toba

Malacca   Segamat

2300   Sinabunabu   Tarutung

Muar   Blumut   1010

Rantauprapat

Keluang   *Johor*

Tuangku   Sibolga

Dumai   Rupat   Kulai   Johor Baharu

Nias

Padangsidempuan

Duri   **SINGAPORE**

Hutanopan

Panyabungan   Balaipungut

Riau Islands

I N D O N E S I A

Pakanbaru

Pini   Ophir   2912   Lubuksikaping   Payakumbuh

Kampar   *Lingga Islands*

Tanahbala   Bukittinggi   Padangpanjang

Rengat   *Indragiri*   Singkep

90°E   95°E   100°E   0°

n   o   p   q   r   s   t   u   v   w   x   y   z

0   100   200   300 miles

Average linear scale: 1 inch≈125 miles   1cm≈80 km

0   100   200   300   400   500 Km

a   b   c   d   e   f   g   h   i   j   k   l   m

100°E   105°E   110°E

BURMA

Toungoo
Prome
Pyu
Myanaung
Henzada
Pegu
Insein Thingangyun
Kanbe **Rangoon**
Pyapon
Gulf of Martaban
Thaton
Moulmein
Mae Sot
Ye

Irrawaddy
Sittang
Salween

Inthanon 2590
Chiang Mai
Lampang
Phayao
Nan
Phrae
Phitsanulok
Soai Dao 2102
Miang 2316
Chum Phae
Phetchabun

Sayaboury
Vang Vieng Bia 2820
Xieng Khouang
Quynh Luu
Vinh
Dongfang
1879
Yaxian **Hainan**

Gulf of Tongking

Pak Sane
Kham Keut
Napa 2286
Rao Go
Ha Tinh
Dong Hoi

Vientiane
Nong Khai
Wang Saphung
Udon Thani
Sakhon Nakhon
Thakhek
Sepone
Hue
Da Nang

THAILAND

Khon Kaen
Kalasin
Roi Et
Savannakhet

LAOS
VIETNAM

Maha Sarakham
Chaiyaphum
Nakhon Sawan
Nakhon Ratchasima
Khemarat
Yasothon
Ubon Ratchathani
Warin Chamrap
Pakse
2009
B. Thateng
2500 Atouat

Sing Buri
Lop Buri
Buri Ram
Surin
Si Sa Ket
Det Udom
Phiafay
Attopeu
Kontum
Pleiku
1570
An Tuc
Qui Nhon

Suphan Buri
Kanchanaburi
Nakhon Pathom
Ban Pong Thon Buri
Bangkok
Phetchaburi
Khiaw 1282
Prachin Buri 849
Samrong
Angkor
Sisophon
Battambang
Stung Treng
Ban Pu Kroy
Ban Me Thuot
1544
Mdrak

Tavoy
Mergui Archipelago
Kadan
Ban
Hua Hin
Siracha
Chon Buri
Rayong
Klaeng
1633
Chantaburi
Laem Ngop
Pursat
Kompong Chhnang
Kompong Cham
Kratie
Da Lat
Nha Trang
Cam Ranh

Andama
Letsok-Aw
Lanbi
Mergui
1251
Khiri Khan
Prachuap
758
Chang
Kut
Hat Lek
1813
KAMPUCHEA
Bao Loc
1632
Di Linh

Phnom Penh
Phu Chong
Bien Hoa
Saigon (Ho Chi Minh)

Gulf of Thailand
Kompong Som
Kompong Chhnang
Chau Phu
Long Xuyen
My Tho
Vung Tau

15°N

Chumphon
Isthmus of Kra
Ranong
St Matthew's
Phangan
Samui
Sea
Takua Pa
Surat Thani
Ban Na San
Nakhon Si Thammarat
Luang 1835
Thap Put
Karbi
Phuket
Trang
Phatthalung
Thale Luang
Songkhla
Hat Yai
Pattani
Sai Buri
Yala
Narathiwat
Kota Baharu

Phu Quoc
Rach Gia
Can-Tho
Khanh Hung
Nam Can
Cape Mau
Mekong Delta

10°N

Kompong Som

Nanshi
C
Spratly Islands

S
O
U
T
H

Terutao
Satun
Langkawi
Alor Setar
Sungai Petani
Pinang (George Town)
Butterworth
Sungai Ko-lok
Rangkal Kalong
Kuala Terengganu

Banda Aceh
Sigli
Bireuen
Lhokseumawe
Lhoksukon
Idi
Peureulak
Langsa
Pangkalanbrandan
Tanjungpura
Strait of
Taiping
Sungai Siput Utara
Ipoh
Kampar
2131
Kuala Lipis
Raub
Kuala Kubu Baharu
Bentong
MALAYA
2171 Chamah
Tapis 1512
Kuantan
Dungun

Geureudong 2855

North Natuna
Natuna
Natuna Islands (Indonesia)
Binatang
Sibu
Sarikei
Kuching
Bandar Sri Aman

Calang
Meulaboh
Leuser 3404
Kutacane
Kabanjahe
Tapaktuan
Medan
Tebingtinggi
Pematangsiantar
Tanjungbalai
Kuala Lumpur
Kelang Petaling Jaya
Seremban
Malacca
Segamat
Muar
Keluang
Blumut 1010
MALAYSIA (WESTERN)
Tioman
Anambas Islands (Indonesia)

Natuna Islands (Indonesia)
South Natuna Islands
Cape Datu
Datuk Bay
Pamangkat
Singkawang
Sambas
Lupar

5°N

Simeulue
Nias
Lake Toba
Singkilbaru
Tuangku
Sihabuhabu 2300
Tarutung
Rantauprapat
Sibolga
Padangsidempuan
Panyabungan
Hutanopan
2912
Lubuksikaping
Bukittinggi
Payakumbuh
Padangpanjang
Solok
Padang
Pini
Tanahbala
Siberut

INDIAN OCEAN
Equator 0°

Dumai
Duri
Rupat
Pakanbaru
Balaipungut
Rengat
Indragiri
Singkep
Lingga Islands
Berhala Strait
Cape Jabung
Riau Islands
Johor Baharu
SINGAPORE
Kulai
Strait of Malacca
Kelang
Tambelan Islands

Pinang
Ngabang
Sanggau
Sintang
Pontianak
Nanga Pinoh
Kapuas
B
Bengkolan Bay
Maya
Nanga Sokan
O
D
N
I
M

100°E   105°E   110°E

This map shows 1/60 of the earth's surface   Area scale : 1 □ inch on the map ≏ 15,000 □ miles on the ground   1 □ cm on the map ≏ 6000 □ km on the ground

115°E 120°E 125°E

Babuyan Islands

Cape Bojeador
Laoag
Aparri
Cape Engaño

Bangued
Vigan
Tuguegarao

Luzon

Pulog 2934
Bayombong

Lingayen Gulf
Baguio
Lingayen
Dagupan
San Carlos
Masinloc
Iba
Tarlac
Angeles
Olongapo
San Fernando
Caloocan
Quezon
Manila
Pasig
Manila Bay

Cordillera Central

Sierra Madre

Ilagan

San Ildefonso Peninsula

15°N

Polillo Islands

PACIFIC

Laguna de Bay
San Pablo
Lipa
Lucena
Batangas
Calapan
Boac
Halcon *2582
Marinduque
Lubang
Mindoro

Lamon Bay
Daet
Lopez
Naga
Mayon *2462
Legazpi
Sorsogon

Catanduanes
Virac

Baco *2363

Mindoro Strait

Burias
Sibuyan
Tablas
Masbate

Laoang
Catarman
Calbayog
Catbalogan

Calamian Group

Masbate

Samar

P H I L I P P I N E S

Panay
Nangtud *2117

Roxas
Biliran
Tacloban

Zhongye Islands

Cleopatra Needle *1602

Honda Bay
Puerto Princesa

Palawan

San Jose de Buenavista
Iloilo
Silay
Bago
Bacolod
San Carlos
Guimaras
Binalbagan

Cadiz
Bogo
Toledo
Cebu
Mandaue

Cebu

Ormoc
Abuyog
Maasin

Leyte

Dinagat

10°N

Mantalingajan *2085

Negros
Bayawan
Bais
Dumaguete
Siquijor
Tagbilaran
Bohol
Camiguin
Surigao
Siargao

Bugsuk
Balabac

Sulu Sea

Dipolog
Oroquieta
Dapitan
Ozamiz
Tangub
Iligan
Pagadian

Gingoog
Butuan

OCEAN

Cagayan de Oro
Malaybalay
Bislig
Marawi

70

Malayan

Balabac Strait
Banggi

Cagayan Sulu

Jambongan

Basilan
Basilan
Zamboanga

Moro Gulf
Cotabato

Davao
Apo *2954
Digos
Davao Gulf
Koronadal

Mindanao

Tagum

Sea

Kota Kinabalu
Kinabalu *4175
Beaufort
SABAH
Brunei Bay

Labuk Bay
Sandakan

Jolo

General Santos

Sarangani Islands

5°N

Bandar Seri Begawan
Kuala Belait
Miri
BRUNEI

Lahad Datu
Darvel Bay

Sulu Archipelago

Tawitawi
Tawitawi Group

Kawio Islands

LAYSIA (EASTERN)

Mulu *2371
Tawau
Sebuku Bay

Talaud Islands

Sangihe

ARAWAK

*2550
Sesayap
Tarakan

Celébes Sea
(Sulawesi Sea)

Sangihe Islands

Morotai

Guguang *2467
Tanjungredet

Borneo (Kalimantan)

Kayan

Rapak

Menyapa *2000
Liangpran *2240

Manado *2202
Tondano

Tobelo
Akelamo

Jailolo
Ternate
Halmahera

*2913

Buol
Paleleh
Kuandarg
Kotamobagu

Weda
Weda Bay

0°

Mahakam

Samarinda
Muarabadak
Mapaga
Dongkalang
Moutong
Tilamuta
Gorontalo

Molucca

N
*2278

E
Donggala
Palu

Malik
Tongian is.
Teku

Celébes (Sulawesi)
Buol *2217

Gulf of Tomini
S

Dongala
Uebonti
*2420

Sea

Gebe

I

Labuha

A
Bacan

115°E 120°E 125°E

0 100 200 300 miles
Average linear scale : 1 inch ≈ 125 miles   1 cm ≈ 80 km
0 100 200 300 400 500 Km

a   b   c   d   e   f   g   h   i   j   k   l   m

95°E   100°E   105°E   110°E

S   O   U   T   H   C

Trang
Phatthalung
Thale Luang

THAILAND
Hat Yai
Songkhla

Terutao
Satun
Pattani
Sai Buri

Langkawi
Alor
Setar
Yala
Sungai
Ko-lok
Narathiwat

Kota Baharu

S   E   A

Sungai
Petani
Butterworth
Rangkal Kalong

Pinang
(George Town)
Pinang

Kuala Terengganu

North Natuna

5°N

Banda Aceh
Sigli
Lhokseumawe
Lhoksukon

Taiping

Perak 2171
Chamah
Sungai Siput Utara
Dungun

Natuna
(Bunguran)

Bireuen
Idi
Peureulak

Ipoh
Kampar
2131
Raub
Kuala Lipis

Tapis
1512

MALAYA

Calang
2855
Geureudong

Langsa

Kuantan

Natuna Islands
(Indonesia)
South Natuna

Meulaboh
Pangkalanbrandan

Leuser
3404
Tanjungpura

Medan
Tebingtinggi

Kuala Kubu
Baharu

Bentong

MALAYSIA
(WESTERN)

Tapaktuan
Kutacane
Kabanjahe
Pematangsiantar

Kuala
Lumpur

Petaling Jaya
Kelang
Seremban

Tioman

Anambas
Islands
(Indonesia)

Cape Datu
Datuk Bay

Sarike

Simeulue

Lake Toba
Singkilbaru
Tanjungbalai

Sihabuhebu
2300
Tarutung

Rantauprapat

Malacca
Muar
Segamat

Keluang
1010
Kulai
Blumut

SINGAPORE

Kuching
Lup

Tuangku

Sibolga

Barumun
Dumai

Rupat
Duri

Johor
Baharu

Sambas
Pamangkat
Singkawang

Bandar
Sri Aman

Nias
Padangsidempuan
Panyabungan

Balaipungut

Riau Islands

Pinang
Ngabang
Sanggau

0°   Equator
Pini
Hutanopan

Pakanbaru

Kampar

Pontianak

Tanahbala
Lubuksikaping
Ophir
2912
Payakumbuh
Bukittingi
Padangpanjang

Rengat

Indragiri

Lingga Islands
Singkep

Bengolan Bay

Maya

Nanga Soka

Siberut
Padang
Solok

Muarabungo

Hari
Jambi

Berhala Strait
Cape Jabung

Karimata Strait
Ketapang
Karimata

Sipora

Kerinci
3805
Sungaipenuh

65

North Pagai

South
Pagai

Sarolangun

Palembang
Sungaigerung

Muntok
Pangkalpinang
Bangka

Tanjungpandan
Belitung

Gaspar Strait

Lubuklinggau
Perabumulih

Bengkulu

Barisan Mountains

Lahat
Dempo
3159

a

N

D

Bintuhan

Kotabumi
Pesagi
2231

5°S

Enggano

Tanjungkarang
Telukbetung
(Bandarlampung)

J   a

Sunda Strait
Merak

Krakatau

Jakarta

Cape
Cangkuang

Bogor
Sukabumi

Cirebon
Pekalongan

Bandung
Tasik Malaya

Slamet
3418
Purwokerto
Tegal

J

Semarang

Magelang
Surakar

v

Cilacap

Yogyakart

I   N   D   I   A   N

O   C   E   A   N

10°S

95°E   100°E   105°E

Christmas Island
(Australia)

110°E

n   o   p   q   r   s   t   u   v   w   x   y   z

This map shows 1/60 of the earth's surface.   Area scale : 1 ☐ inch on the map ≈ 15,000 ☐ miles on the ground   1 ☐ cm on the map ≈ 6000 ☐ km on the ground

115°E
Balabac Strait
Sulu Sea
120°E
PHILIPPINES
Pagadian
125°E
Davao
Tagum

CHINA
Banggi
Cagayan
Sulu
Zamboanga
Moro Gulf
Cotabato
Apo
2954
Davao
Gulf
Mindanao

Malayan Sea
Jambongan
Basilan
Easilan
Digos
Koronadal

Kota
Kinabalu
4175
Labuk
Bay
Sandakan
Panguturan Group
Jolo
General Santos

Kota
Kinabalu
SABAH
Beaufort
Sarangani
5°N

Brunei Bay
Lahad Datu
Tawitawi
Sulu Archipelago

Bandar Seri Begawan
Darvel Bay
Tawitawi
Group
Kawio
Talaud
Islands

Kuala Belait
BRUNEI
Mulu
2371
Tawau
Celebes Sea
(Sulawesi Sea)
Sangihe

Miri
Sebuku
Bay
Morotai

MALAYSIA
(EASTERN)
Sesayap
Tarakan
Tobelo
Akelamo

Bintulu
SARAWAK
Kayan
Klabat
2022
Manado
Tondano
Jailolo
Saolat
1508
Ternate
Halmahera

Sibu
Guguang
2467
Tanjungredeb
Buol
Palaleh
Kuandang
Kotamobagu
Weda
Weda Bay

Inatang
Rajang
2550
Dondo Bay
2217
Gorontalo
Molucca

Borneo
Liangpran
2240
Manyapa
2000
Rapak
Ogoamas
291
Moutong
Tilamuta
Sea
Bacan
Islands
Labuha

(*Kalimantan*)
Mahakam
Dongkalang
Tongian Islands
0°

Intang
Mapaga
Gulf
of
Tomini
Malik
Teku
Moluccas
Obi

Nanga Pinoh
Raya
2278
Muarabadak
Donggala
Palu
Jebonti
2400
Batui
Peleng
Taliabu
Mangole
Sula Islands M
*Ceram
Sea*

Tumbangsamba
Samarinda
Pasangkayu
Posc
Banggai Islands
Namlea
Buru
Strait
of
Manipa
Ceram

Buntok
Sarempata
1880
Balikpapan
Lumu
Celebes
(Sulawesi)
Watu
M o l u c c a s

Palangkaraya
Tanjung
Muraus Mountains
Besar
1892
Gandadiwata
3074 Masamba
Palopo
Gulf
of
Tolo
Mekongga
2795
Ambon

Sampit
Kandangan
Rantepombalia
3455
Majene
Gulf
of
Bone
Kendari

angkalanbuun
Kotabaru
Parepare
Koaka
Kolono
Kolono

Banjarmasin
Laut
Watampone
Raha
Muna
Butung
5°S

Batakan
Cape
Selatan
Jatisiri
Ujung Pandang
Sinjai
2471
Kabaena
Baubau
Tukangbesi
Islands
Banda Sea

ONESIA
INDONESIA

va Sea
Bawean
Masalembo
Salajar
Tanahjampea
Kalao

Madura
Kangean
Flores Sea
Barat Daya
Islands

Bangkalan
Surabaya
Madura Strait
Lesser Sunda Islands
Wetar

Kediri
Probolinggo
Banyuwangi
Semeru
3676
Alor
Dili
Leti
Islands

Madiun
Malang
Jember
2276
Bali
3726
Sumbawa
Besar
Bata
Ruteng
2400
Maumere
Solor Islands
Atambua
2960
Timor

Denpasar
Lombok
Mataram
Sumbawa
Besar
Ende
Kupang
Besikama

Sumbawa
Flores
Waingapu
Sawu Sea
10°S

Waikabubak
Sumba
Sawu
Roti
Timor Sea

115°E
120°E
125°E

0 100 200 300 miles
Average linear scale: 1 inch≈125 miles 1cm≈80 km
0 100 200 300 400 500 Km

a   b   c   d   e   f   g   h   i   j   k   l   m

130°E   135°E   140°E   145°E

Yap Islands

Faraulep Atoll

Ngulu Atoll   Sorol Atoll

F e d e r a t e d

Palau   Babel Thuap   Woleai Atoll
Islands   ○ Koror   Ifalik Atoll
                                                          • Eauripik Atoll

Palau
(U.S.A.-U.N.)   C a r o l i n e

• Sonsorol

5°N

• Pulo Anna

• Merir   P   A   C   I   F

• Tobi

• Helen Reef

Morotai   O   C   E   A

○ Akelamo
Halmahera   • Mapia Islands

                    Waigeo   O   C   E   A
                                                • Ayu Islands

0°

                    Dampier Strait
                    Cenderawasih   Kwoko
Misool   ○ Sorong   3000   ○ Manokwari   Biak
    990 •   Peg Ariak
                       2939   Yapen
        Steenkool   ○ Sarmi
C   ○ Babo   Van Rees Mountains   ○ Jayapura
e   I N D O N E S I A   ○ Vanimo
r   Fakfak   Gulf of   I R I A N   • Aitape
a   Cenderawasih   Lumi ○ ○ Dreikikir ○ Wewak
C e r a m   Bomberai   Maoke   ○ Wamena   Sepik
   3019 • ○ Bula   m ○ Kaimana   Jaya   Remu
○ Tobo   5029   Mountains   N   e   w
Ambon   JAYA   Telefomin   Bismarck Range
                        ○ Kokonau   G u i n e a   ○ Kopiago ○ Wabag
5°S   Mandala   Mount
        Kai   4702   Mendi ○ Hagen Gore
        Islands   Kubor
                                              Tanahmerah   2895 4355
B a n d a   S e a   Lake
                Aru   Murray
                Islands   Mappi   Digul   Fly   N E W
• Damar   Kikori
    Tanimbar   Strickland
    Islands   Dolak
• Babar   Island
Sermata   Selaru   Cape Vals   Merauke   Gulf o
                                                              Papua
                    A R A F U R A   S E A   ○ Daru

                                              Torres Strait
10°S
                                          Badu ○ Moa
                    130°E   135°E   Prince of Wales 140°E Cape York 145°E
                                                  Island

This map shows 1/60 of the earth's surface. Area scale : 1 □ inch on the map ≙ 15,000 □ miles on the ground 1 □ cm on the map ≙ 6000 □ km on the ground

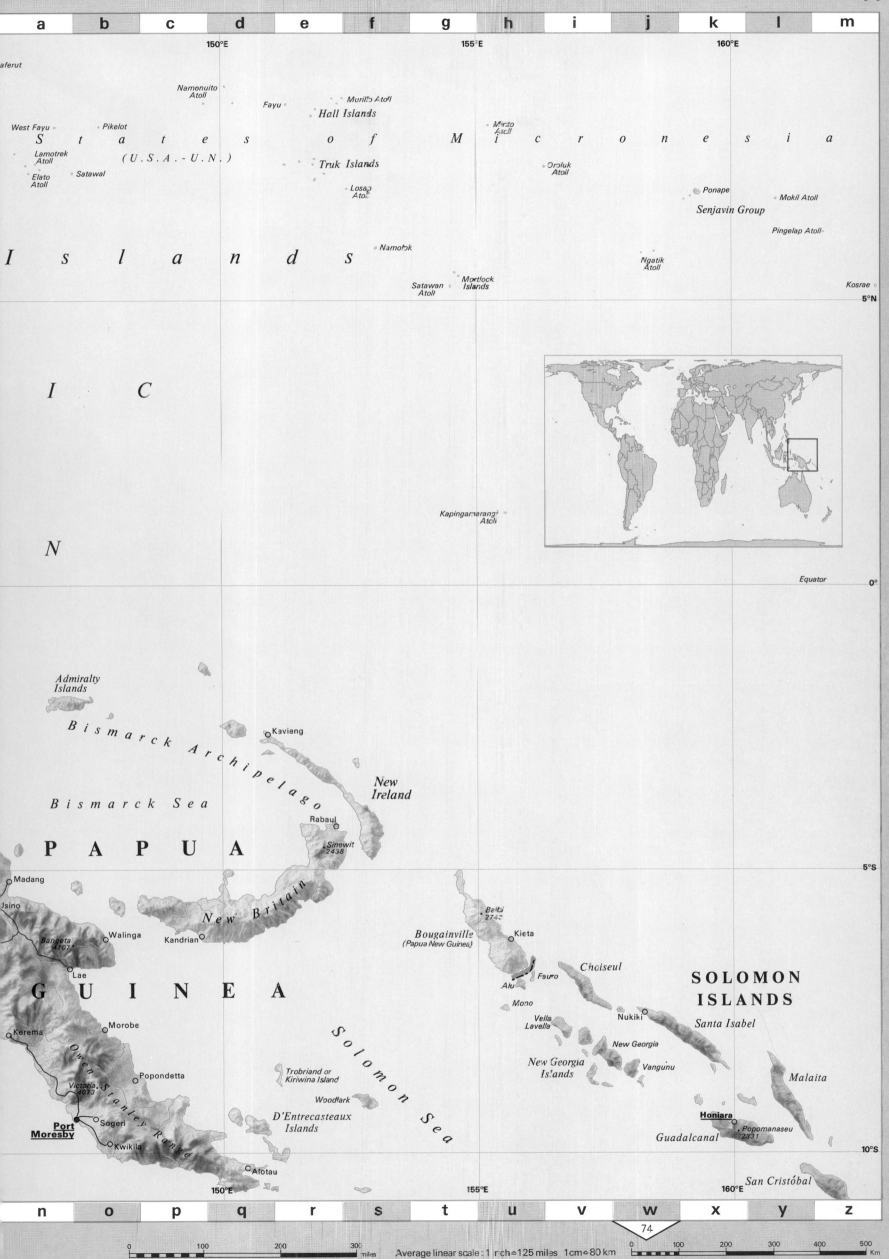

150°E   155°E   160°E

Gaferut

Namonuito
Atoll

West Fayu   Pikelot   Fayu   Murillo Atoll

Hall Islands

S t a t e s   o f   M i c r o n e s i a
Lamotrek
Atoll   (U.S.A.-U.N.)   Truk Islands   Minto
                                                                      Atoll
Elato   Satawal   Oroluk
Atoll   Losap   Atoll
                                               Atoll   Ponape   Mokil Atoll

                                                                                          Senjavin Group

                                                                                                      Pingelap Atoll

I   s   l   a   n   d   s   Namoluk

                                                              Ngatik
                                      Satawan   Mortlock   Atoll
                                      Atoll   Islands   Kosrae

5°N

I   C

N   Equator   0°

                                                    Kapingamarang
                                                    Atoll

Admiralty
Islands

B i s m a r c k   A r c h i p e l a g o   Kavieng

B i s m a r c k   S e a   New
                                                          Ireland

P A P U A   Rabaul
                                   Sinewit
                                   2438

Madang   5°S

Isino

Bangeta   Walinga   Kandrian   New Britain   Balbi
4107   2743
          Lae   Bougainville   Kieta
                                                      (Papua New Guinea)

G U I N E A   Alu   Fauro   Choiseul   S O L O M O N
                                                                                            I S L A N D S
          Morobe   Mono
Kerema   Vella   Nukiki   Santa Isabel
                                                          Lavella
          Owen Stanley Range   Trobriand or   New Georgia   Vangunu
Victoria   Popondetta   Kiriwina Island   New Georgia
4073   Islands   Malaita
Port   Sogeri   Woodlark   Solomon Sea
Moresby   Honiara
          Kwikila   D'Entrecasteaux   Popomanaseu
                                  Islands   Guadalcanal   2331

                                  Alotau   San Cristóbal   10°S

150°E   155°E   160°E

74

0   100   200   300 miles   Average linear scale: 1 inch = 125 miles   1 cm = 80 km   0   100   200   300   400   500 Km

110°E
115°E
120°E
125°E

J a v a
Bali
Denpasar
Mataram
Lombok
3726
Sumbawa
Besar
1400
Sumbawa
Raba
Ruteng
2400
Ende
Flores
Maumere
Solor
Alor
Dili
2960
Atambua
Timor

I N D O N E S I A
Sawu
2427
Besikama

10°S
Waikabubak
Waingapu
Sea

Sumba
1475
Sawu
Kupang
Roti

T i m o r

S e a

Cartier

Cape
Londonderry

Cape
Bougainville
Kalumburu

Bonaparte Archipelago
Theda

15°S
Kuri Bay
Kimberley
Karunjie

Collier
Bay
Mount Hann
778
Plateau

Cape
Lévêque
Beverley
Springs
Mount House
Tableland

I N D I A N
Lombardina
Oobagooma
King Leopold Ranges
923
Mt.
Broome
Mount Ord
736
Glenroy

Beagle
Bay
Derby
Kimberley
Downs

Coulomb
Point
Dampier
Land
Camballin
Fitzroy
Crossing

O C E A N
Broome
Roebuck
Plains
Fitzroy
Myroodah
Mount
Huxley
522
Margaret
River

Dampier
Downs
Nerrima
Christmas
Creek
Bohemia
Downs

Lagrange
247

Frazier Downs

Anna Plains

Eighty Mile Beach

20°S
Wallal Downs
Port
Hedland
Goldsworthy
Great Sandy Desert
Lake
Gregory

Barrow
Island
Dampier
Roebourne
Shay Gap
Yarrie
Mount
418
Elliott

Cooya
Pooya
Whim
Creek
Kangan
Marble
Bar
Bamboo
Creek
Warrawagine
Percival Lakes

North West Cape
Onslow
Yarraloola
Millstream
Mount Florance
W E S T E R N
Nullagine
Lake
Dora
Lake
Auld
Tabletop
427

Exmouth
Pannawonica
Wittenoom
Fortescue
Talawana
Lake
Blanche

Learmonth
Yanrey
Mount
Minnie
Hamersley
Tom Price
1073
Mount Tom
Price
A U S T
Lake
Disappointment
S

Wyloo
Range
1251
Mount
Meharry
Mount
Newman
1053

Winning
Uaroo
Mount
Palgrave
704
Ashburton
Downs
Paraburdoo
Newman
Gibson Desert

Ullawarra
Ashburton

Lyndon
Turee
Creek

Minnie Creek
Bulloo Downs

Cape
Cuvier
Lake
McLeod
Mount
Augustus
1105
Augustus
Mount
Vernon
A U S T R A L I A

Shark Bay
Carnarvon
Warburton Range
Lyons
Three
Rivers
Kumarina
Mount
Essendon
906
Carnarvon Range
Glenayle

Cape
Inscription
Gascoyne
Junction
Dairy
Creek
Gascoyne
Milgun
Neds Creek
738
Granite Peak

Denham
Mount
Seabrook
552
Peak Hill
Lake
Nabberu
Carnegie

Useless Loop
Byro
732
Mount Hale
Karalundi
Warburton
623
Mount
Talbot

Tamala
Hamelin Pool
Curbur
Mileura
Wiluna
Yelma
Lake
Carnegie

Kalli
Meekatharra
Wonganoo

Wannoo
530
Tuckanarra
Gidgee

Yalialong
Big
Bell
Cue
Booylgoo
Springs
594

Billabalon
Murgoo
Great

Kalbarri
Sandstone
Agnew

110°E
115°E
120°E
125°E

This map shows 1/60 of the earth's surface. Area scale : 1 □ inch on the map ≏ 15,000 □ miles on the ground 1 □ cm on the map ≏ 6000 □ km on the ground

a b c d e f g h i j k l m

130°E 135°E 140°E 145°E

PAPUA NEW GUINEA

Leti Islands
Gulf of Papua

Arafura Sea

Torres Strait
Coral

70

10°S

Badu
Moa

Prince of Wales Island
Cape York
Bamaga

Great

Sea

Cape Van Diemen
Cape Croker

Wessel Islands

Murgenella

183.

Andoom
Weipa
Iron Range
Lockhart River
Wenlock

Barrier

Bathurst Island
Melville Island
Van Diemen Gulf

Maningrida
Milingimbi
Galiwinku
Nhulunbuy
Cape Arnhem

Beagle Gulf

Oenpelli
Mount Howiship
385.
Mudginberry
Yirrkala
Camburinga

Aurukun

555.

Reef

Belyuen
Darwin
Noonamah
Darwin River

Arnhem Land

Coen
505.
Princess Charlotte Bay
640.

Cape York

Anson Bay
Batchelor
Adelaide River
Burrundie
Pine Creek
Daly River
Tipperary

El Sherana
366.

Gulf of Carpentaria

Mitchell River
Edward River
Strathmay
213.

Peninsula

Joseph Bonaparte Gulf

Port Keats

Katherine
Bamyili
Mainoru

Umbakumba
Angurugu
Groote Eylandt

Cooktown
Laura
Rossville
Daintree
Mossman

15°S

Forrest River
Ninbing

Willeroo
Elsey
Roper Bar
Roper
Ngukurr
Limmen Bight

Sir Edward Pellew Group

Strathleven
Dunbar
366.
Mitchell

Mareeba
Cairns

Wyndham
Victoria
Timber Creek
Delamere
Larrimah
227.

Nathan River
Bing Bong
Borroloola

Inkerman
Galbraith
Walsh
Chillagoe
Almaden
Atherton
161.
Barron Frere
Innisfail

Lake Argyle

Victoria River Downs
Daly Waters
Hidden Valley
O.T. Downs
McArthur
103.
Robinson River

Mornington
152.
Mornington
Wellesley Islands
Bentinck

Delta Downs
Vanrook
Miranda Downs
Abingdon Downs
Silkwood
Tully

Turkey Creek
Ord River
Mount Remarkable
57.

Top Springs
Mallapunyan

Calvert Hills
Wollogorang
Westmoreland

Karumba
Maggieville
Normanton
Blackbull
Croydon
Gilbert River
Georgetown
Forsayth
Mount Surprise
Einasleigh
Conjuboy
742.
Ingham

Nicholson
Inverway
Wave Hill
Newcastle Waters
25.
Elliott
Lake Woods

Creswell Downs
Benmara
Corinda
Doomadgee
Floraville
Augustus Downs

Wondoola
Claraville
194.
Robinhood
Greenvale

Halls Creek
Gordon Downs

Hooker Creek
288.

Renner Springs
Anthonys Lagoon
Brunette Downs
347.
291.

Lawn Hill
Gregory Downs
Donors Hill
Iffley
Esmeralda
Savannah Downs
Lyndhurst

Sturt Creek

NORTHERN

Alexandria
Alroy Downs

Riversleigh
200.
Herbert Vale
Kamileroi
Thorntonia

Canobie

Maryvale

Lililuna

Tanami

Tennant Creek
436.
Frewena

Wonarah
240.
Camooweal
Yelvertoft

Gunpowder
Millungera

20°S

Balgo

TERRITORY

Mount Davidson
464.
Desert

Avon Downs

Mary Kathleen
Mount Isa
Cloncurry
Dalgonally
Mount Sturgeon
732.
Boonderoo
Lolworth
Mount Stewart
1067.
Pentland

Lake White

Wauchope
Kurundi
Hatches Creek
Elkedra
Warrabri
Annitowa
Austral Downs
Lake Nash

Kajabbi
Julia Creek
Maxwelton
Richmond
Hughenden
Torrens Creek
Lake Buchanan

Lake Wills

Willowra

McKinlay
Kynuna
Whitewood
Aberfoyle

Barrow Creek

Argadargada
339.
Duchess
Corfield
Tangorin

Lake Mackay
808.
Yuendumu

Tea Tree
Utopia
Woodgreen
Ooratippra

Urandangi
Dajarra
380.
Middleton
Chorregon
Winton
Lerida
Corinda
Lake Galilee
Eastmere
Muttaburra
Aramac

RALIA
1067.
Mount Wedge
Aileron

Harts Range
Inciana
Lucy Creek
Marqua

Carandotta
Chatsworth
Linda Downs
Roxborough Downs
Toolebuc
Boulia
392.

Morella

Mount Liebig
1524.
Haast Bluff
Hamilton Downs
1167.

Glenormiston
236.
Marion Downs

Vergemont
Longreach
Barcaldine

Lake Macdonald
901.

Macdonnell Ranges
Glen Helen
Alice Springs
Ringwood

Santa Teresa
Simpson

Coorabulka
Diamantina Lakes
Davenport Downs
Connemara
Arrilalah
Isisford

Lake Hopkins

Lake Neale
Areyonga
Deep Well

Breadalbane
Bedourie

Stonehenge
Yalleroi
Blackall

Giles Meteorological Station
Docker River

Lake Amadeus
Henbury

Desert
Glengyle
Lake Machattie
Monkira
Palparara
Jundah
Yaraka
594.
Emmet

25°S

Curtin Springs
867.
Ayers Rock
Angas Downs
Erldunda

Finke
Engoordina

304.
Galway Downs
Windorah
Listowel Downs
Retreat

Petermann Range

Mount Cockburn
1138.
Mulga Park
Kulgera
Finke
New Crown

Durrie
Betoota
Tonbar
Lynwood
Adavale
329.

Blackstone Camp
1058.
Mount Davies

Musgrave Ranges
1439.
Amata
Tieyon
Abminga

Birdsville

Keeroongooloo
300.
Lake Yamma Yamma
Thylungra
Quilpie
316.
Cheepie
Westgate
Charleville

SOUTH AUSTRALIA
917.
Everard Park
Granite Downs
Welbourn Hill
Fedirka
Alberga
Oodnadatta
Mount Dutton
Lake Eyre

Alton Downs
Pandie Pandie
Goyder Lagoon
Cordillo Downs
120.
Clifton Hills
Innamincka
Cowarie

Eromanga
Toompine
Wyandra
Coongoola

Victoria Desert
130°E 135°E 140°E 145°E

Cooper Creek
Tobermory
Nockatunga
Thargomindah

n o p q r s t u v w x y z

77

0 100 200 300 miles

Average linear scale : 1 inch = 125 miles 1 cm = 80 km

0 100 200 300 400 500 Km

74

145°E 150°E 155°E 160°E

PAPUA
NEW GUINEA

Owen
Port
Moresby
Mount
1925
Suckling
3676
Stanley Range
3329

D'Entrecasteaux
Islands

Baniara

Normanby

Honiara
Guadalcanal
2331

Kwikila

10°S

Robinson
River

Alotau

Louisiade Archipelago

SOLOMON
ISLANDS

Cape
York

183

Iron
Range

Lockhart
River

Wenlock

SOLOMON

e

SEA

l

Rennell
Island

a

Cape
Coen
506
York
Princess
Charlotte
640

Breeza
Plains

Cape
Flattery

P

A

15°S

Peninsula

366

Strathleven

Laura

Cooktown

Rossville

1375

Daintree

Willis Islands

C O R A L

L

Mitchell

Gamboola

Mossman

Walsh

Mareeba

Cairns

Chillagoe

Atherton

Almaden

Bartle
Frere
1611

Innisfail

Abingdon
Downs

Silkwood

Tully

Gilbert
River

Mount
Surprise

Georgetown

Forsayth

Einasleigh

742

Ingham

73

Esmeralda

Greenvale

Robinhood

Lyndhurst

Chesterfield
Islands
(France)

Gregory

S E A

Burdekin

Townsville

Ayr

Mount Elliot
1234

Bowen

Richmond

Mount
Sturgeon

Lolworth

732

Mount
Stewart
1076

Charters
Towers

Pentland

Proserpine

Collinsville

Mount
Dalrymple
1259

Finch
Hatton

Mackay

20°S

Torrens
Creek

Hughenden

Sarina

Whitewood

Aberfoyle

Mount
Coolon

Lake
Buchanan

Mount
Douglas

Nebo

Tangorin

Carmila

Winton

Lake
Galilee

Chorregon

Muttaburra

Eastmere

Blair
Athol

Peak
Downs

St. Lawrence

Cato

Morella

Aramac

Clermont

Marlborough

Fitzroy

Capella

Yeppoon

O

Longreach

Barcaldine

Alpha

Emerald

Rockhampton

Arrilalah

Bogantungan

Duaringa

Mount Morgan

Isisford

Yalleroi

Springsure

Wowan

Gladstone

Q U E E N S L A N D

Barcoo

Stonehenge

Blackall

Rolleston

Baralaba

Banana

Biloela

Miriam Vale

594

Consuelo Peak
1219

Theodore

Monto

Bundaberg

Thomson

Emmet

Tambo

806

Hervey
Bay

25°S

Yaraka

Retreat

Listowel
Downs

A U S T R A L I A

Childers

Fraser
Island

Windorah

Lynwood

Augathella

Taroom

Mundubbera

Maryborough

Adavale

329

Injune

Wandoan

Murgon

Gayndah

Gympie

Thylungra

Charleville

Morven

Mitchell

Miles

Kingaroy

Nambour

Maroochydore

Eromanga

Quilpie

Westgate

Roma

Chinchilla

Yarraman

Moreton
Island

316

Cheepie

Albany
Downs

Surat

Dalby

Esk

Caboolture

Tobermory

Wyandra

Glenmorgan

Toowoomba

Gatton

Ipswich

Brisbane

Thargomindah

Coongoola

Moonie

Clifton

Gold Coast

Bulloo
Downs

Cunnamulla

Bollon

St. George

Westmar

Warwick

Murwillumbah

Eulo

Dirranbandi

Nindigully

Inglewood

Stanthorpe

Casino

Lismore

145°E

n o p q r s t u v w x y z

150°E 155°E 160°E

78

This map shows 1/60 of the earth's surface. Area scale : 1 □ inch on the map ≈ 15,000 □ miles on the ground 1 □ cm on the map ≈ 6000 □ km on the ground

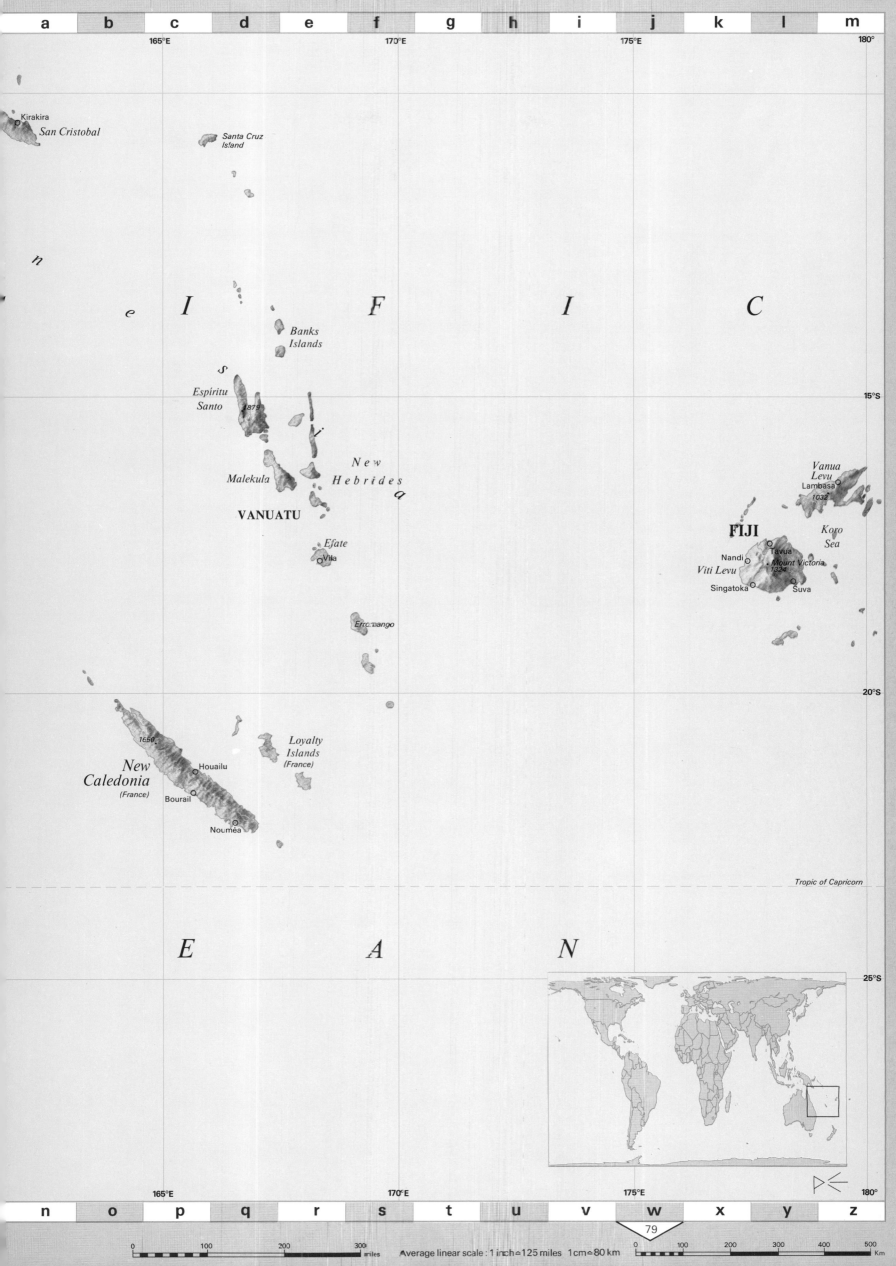

165°E   170°E   175°E   180°

n

Kirakira
San Cristobal

Santa Cruz
Is!and

e   *I*   *F*   *I*   *C*

s

Banks
Islands

15°S

*Espíritu
Santo* 1879

*New
Hebrides*

Malekula

a

VANUATU

Efate
Vila

*Vanua
Levu*
Lambasa
1032

FIJI

*Koro
Sea*

Nandi   Tavua
Mount Victoria
Viti Levu   1324
Singatoka   Suva

Erromango

20°S

*Loyalty
Islands
(France)*

1650

*New
Caledonia
(France)*

Houailu

Bourail

Nouméa

Tropic of Capricorn

E   *A*   *N*

25°S

165°E   170°E   175°E   180°

79

0   100   200   300 miles   Average linear scale : 1 inch≈125 miles   1cm≈80 km   0   100   200   300   400   500 Km

a b c d e f g h i j k l m

115°E | Waldburg Range | 120°E | 125°E | 13

Cape Inscription

Carnarvon
Gascoyne
Junction
Lyons
Dairy
Creek
Gascoyne
Milgun
Kumarina
Three Rivers
Mount Essendon
906•
Mount
Cockburn
1138•
Docker River
Giles
Meteorological
Station
Petermar

25°S

Shark
Bay
Mount
Seabrook
•582
Peak Hill
Neds
Creek
Lake
Nabberu
•738
Granite
Peak
Glenayle
Carnegie

WESTERN

Mount
Davies
1058
Blackstone
Camp

Denham
Useless Loop
Tamala
Hamelin
Pool
Byro
Curbur
Mount Hale
•732
Mileura
Kalli
Karalundi
Meekatharra
Wiluna
Yelma
Wonganoo
Mount
Talbot
623

AUSTRALIA

Wannoo
Yallalong
Billabalon
Murgoo
Big Bell
•530
Lake
Austin
Tuckanarra
Cue
Gidgee
•661

Lake Carnegie

Kalbarri
Northampton
Geraldton
Mullewa
Sandstone
Mount Magnet
552•
Agnew
Booylgoo Springs
Lake Yeo
Lake
Rason
466•

A U S T

Houtman
Abrolhos
Wallabi Group
Easter Group
Pelsart Group
Mingenew
Paynes
Find
Salt Lakes
Leonora
Lake
Carey
•259

Great Victoria

Eneabba
Coorow
Lake Moore
•447
Lake Barlee
Menzies
Lake
Raeside
•393
•389

30°S

Green Head
Cervantes Island
Pithara
Moora
•686
Lake Deborah
Kalgoorlie
Coolgardie
Ponton Creek
Nullarbor Plain
Rawlinna
Loongana
Deakin

Cape Leschenault
Gingin
Swan
Southern Cross
•381

Perth
Fremantle
Mandurah
Peel Bay
Northam
Kellerberrin
Parker Range
Lake Cowan
Hampton Tableland
Eucla
Wilson Bluf

Waroona
Narrogin
Johnston
Lakes
Norseman
Balladonia
Twilight Cove
•19
Eyre
Scorpion Bay

Bunbury
Collie
Wagin
•411
Peak Charles
658
Cape Culver

Busselton
Katanning
Jerramungup
Ravensthorpe
Esperance
Israelite Bay
585
Great Austra

Karridale
Manjimup
Bluff Knoll
•1109
Hood Cape
West Group
Sandy Bay

Flinders Bay
Frankland
Stirling Range
Cape Knob
Recherche-Archipelago
Twin Rocks

Cape D'Entrecasteaux
Albany
Channel Cape
Termination Island

35°S
Cape Nuyts
West Cape Howe
Bald Cape

Victoria Range
Geelvink Channel
Greenough
Darling Range
Avon
Blackwood

Carnarvon Range
Virginia Range
Fraser Range
Russell Range

Gibson Desert

n o p q r s t u v w x y z

115°E | 120°E | 125°E | 1

40°S

INDIAN

45°S

This map shows 1/60 of the earth's surface. Area scale : 1 □ inch on the map ≈ 15,000 □ miles on the ground 1 □ cm on the map ≈ 6000 □ km on the ground

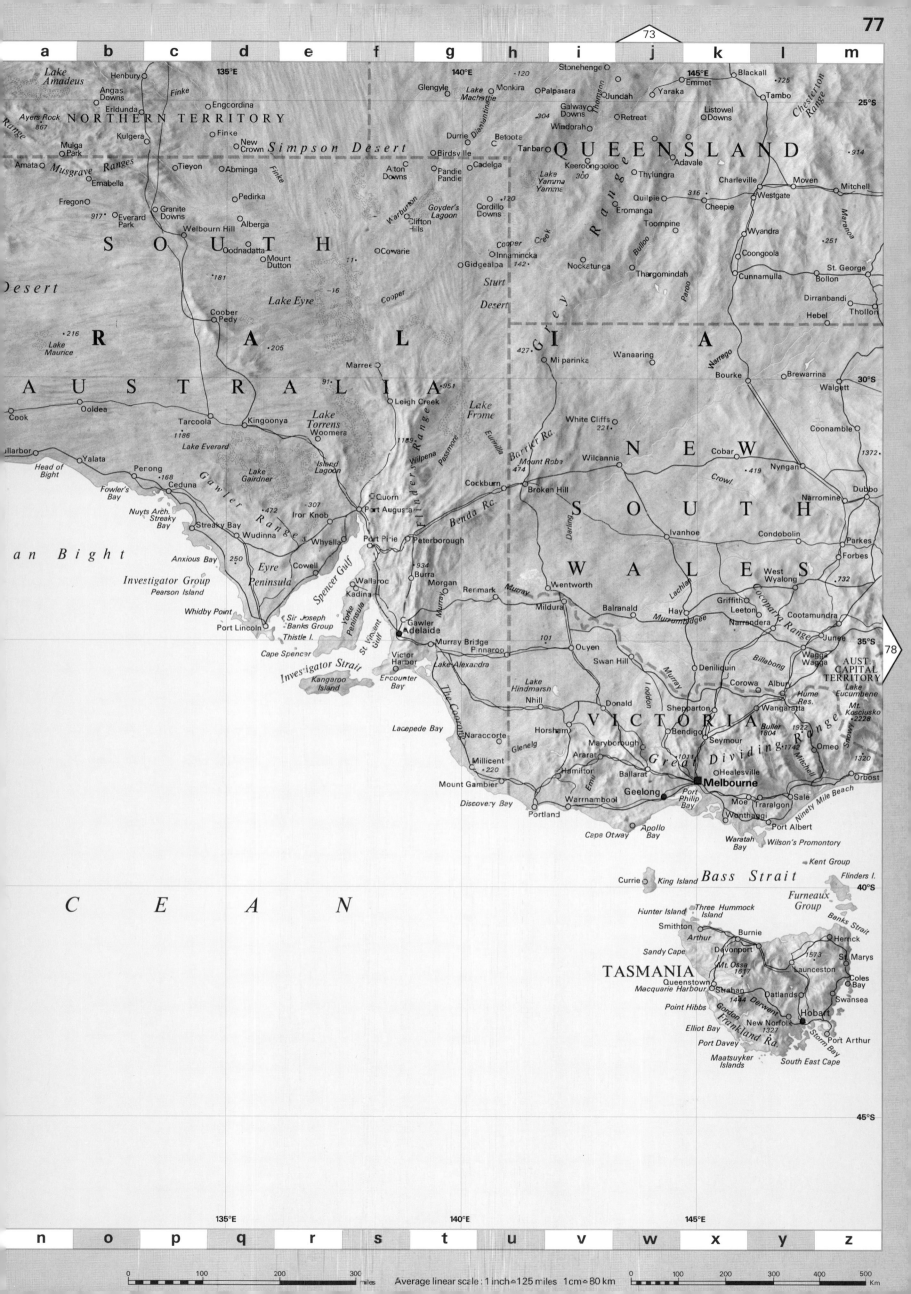

74

a   b   c   d   e   f   g   h   i   j   k   l   m

145°E   150°E   155°E   160°E

Bulloo
Adavale
Augathella
914
Taroom
Mundubbera
Maryborough

Charleville   Morven   Mitchell   Roma   Miles   Gayndah
316   Wandoan   Murgon   Gympie
Quilpie   Cheepie   Westgate   Kingaroy   Yarraman   Nambour
Toompine   Wyandra   QUEENSLAND   Dalby   Esk   Caboolture
Surat   Glenmorgan   Moreton
Coongoola   251   Toowoomba   Island
Cunnamulla   St. George   Bollon   Moonie   Brisbane
Eulo   Clifton   Gold Coast
Dirranbandi   Talwood   Inglewood   Warwick   Murwillumbah
Thallon   Goondiwindi   Stanthorpe   1239
Hebel   Mungindi   Casino   Lismore
Tenterfield

Wanaaring   Gwydir   Moree   Glen   Grafton   Middleton Reef
30°S   Brewarrina   Inverell   Innes   Elisabeth Reef
Bourke   Walgett   Narrabri
AUSTRALIA   Round   P   A
1608
Armidale
Cobar   Coonamble   Tamworth   Kempsey
Nyngan   Gunnedah   Lord Howe
NEW   SOUTH   WALES   1372   Coonabarabran   1494   Port Macquarie   Island
(N.S.W.)
Ivanhoe   Narromine   Coolah   Taree
Condobolin   Dubbo   Barrington   Muswellbrook
Hay   Parkes   Mudgee   1585 Tops
Wellington   Coricudgy   Newcastle
Griffith   Forbes   Orange   1274
West Wyalong   Bathurst   Gosford
Leeton   Cowra   Lithgow
Narrandera   732   Katoomba   Sydney
Junee   1298   Wollongong
Deniliquin   Cootamundra   Goulburn   Nowra
35°S
Wagga   Canberra
Corowa   Wagga   1913   Queanbeyan
77   Albury   AUST. CAPITAL   TERRITORY
Shepparton   Hume   Lake
Reservoir   Eucumbene   Cooma
Bendigo   Wangaratta   Mt. Kosciusko   2228
VICTORIA   Buller   Omeo   Snowy
1804   1320   Orbost
Seymour   Cape Howe
Healesville   Bairnsdale
Melbourne   Sale
Geelong   Moe   Traralgon   Ninety Mile Beach
Port Phillip   Wonthaggi   Port Albert
Bay   Waratah Bay   Wilsons Promontory

Kent Group
Bass Strait
King Island   Furneaux   Flinders Island
40°S   Group
Hunter   Three Hummock   Banks Strait
Island   Island
Smithton   Burnie   Herrick
Devonport   Launceston   St. Marys
Arthur   Ossa   1573
1617   Coles Bay
Queenstown   St. Marys
Strahan   1444   Oaklands   Swansea
Macquarie   New   TASMANIA
Harbour   Norfolk
Elliot Bay   Hobart
Port Davey   Storm Bay   Port Arthur
Maatsuyker   South East
Islands   Cape

Darling   Paroo   Warrego   Balonne   Maranoa
Crowl   Namoi   Great Dividing Range
Lachlan   Macquarie
Murrumbidgee   Cocoparra Range
Murray   Billabong   Dividing   Range
Mitchell   Snowy Mts   Snowy
Gordon   Derwent   Frankland Range

P   A
O   C
TASMAN   S

This map shows 1/60 of the earth's surface. Area scale: 1 □ inch on the map ≙ 15,000 □ miles on the ground   1 □ cm on the map ≙ 6000 □ km on the ground

145°E   150°E   155°E   160°E
45°S

165°E 170°E 175°E 180°E

30°S

*Macauley
Island*
Kermadec Islands *Curtis
(N.Z.)* *Island*

C I F I C C

*Norfolk
Island
(Australia)*

E A N

*Three Kings
Island*

North Cape

35°S

*Ninety
Mile Beach*

Kaitaia
Bay of Islands
774
Whangarei
Dargaville
*Great Barrier
Island*

*Hauraki
Gulf*
Auckland

Bay of Plenty
Te Araroa
Tauranga
East Cape
Hamilton
Waikato
Whakatane
1478
NORTH ISLAND
Tokoroa
Rotorua
Gisborne
Taumarunui
Taupo
New Plymouth
Lake Taupo
Wairoa
Ngauruhoe
Egmont
2291
Hawke Bay
2518
Napier
Hawera
Ruapehu
2797
Hastings
Wanganui
Ruahine Range
Wanganui
40°S
Palmerston
North
Collingwood
Paraparaumu
Tararua Range
1571
Masterton
*Tasman
Bay*
Picton
Cook Strait
Lower Hutt
*Karamea
Bight*
Nelson
Wellington
Richmond Range
Blenheim
Cape Palliser
Westport
*Travers
2337*
Greymouth
Kaikoura
SOUTH ISLAND
Hokitika
*Arthurs
Pass*
Waipara
Southern Alps
Waimakariri
Christchurch
*Arrowsmith
2736*
Canterbury Plains
Cook
3764
*Banks
Peninsula*
Haast
*Lake
Pukaki*
Ashburton
*Canterbury
Bight*
Twizel
Timaru
*Aspiring
3027*
Waitaki
Milford Sound
*Lake
Wakatipu*
Queenstown
45°S
Te Anau
Alexandra
Oamaru
2035
Jane Peak
Clutha
Lumsden
West Cape
Gore
Dunedin
Invercargill
Foveaux Strait
*Stewart
Island*
Southwest Cape
*Bounty
Islands
(N.Z.)*
*Snares
Islands*

NEW ZEALAND

E A

165°E 170°E 175°E 180°E

0 100 200 300 miles
Average linear scale : 1 inch ≏ 125 miles 1cm ≏ 80 km
0 100 200 300 400 500 Km

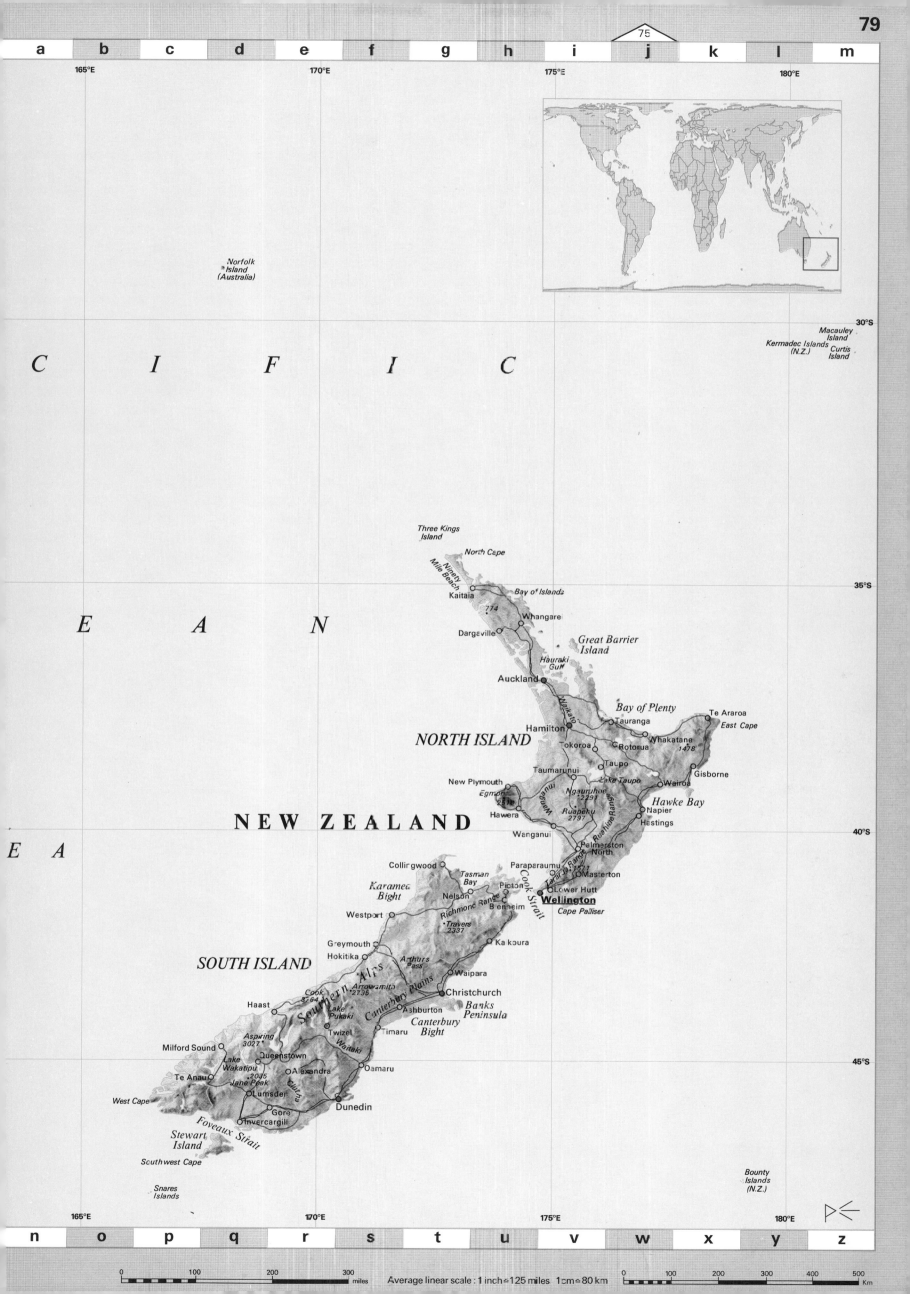

80°W

85°W

90°W

95°W

100°W

105°W

110°W

60°S

65°S

70°S

West of Greenwich

Antarctic Circle

Smyley Island

Eltanin Bay

B E L L I N G S H A U S E N

S E A

Wright 1510

Abbot Ice Shelf

Farewell Island

Sherman Island

Thurston Island

A

Peter Island

S   O   U   T   H   E   R   N   O   C   E   A   N

P   A   C   I   F   I   C

O   C   E   A   N

55°S

115°W   55°S   120°W   60°S   125°W   130°W

This map shows 1/60 of the earth's surface. Area scale : 1 □ inch on the map ≈ 15,000 □ miles on the ground 1 □ cm on the map ≈ 6000 □ km on the ground

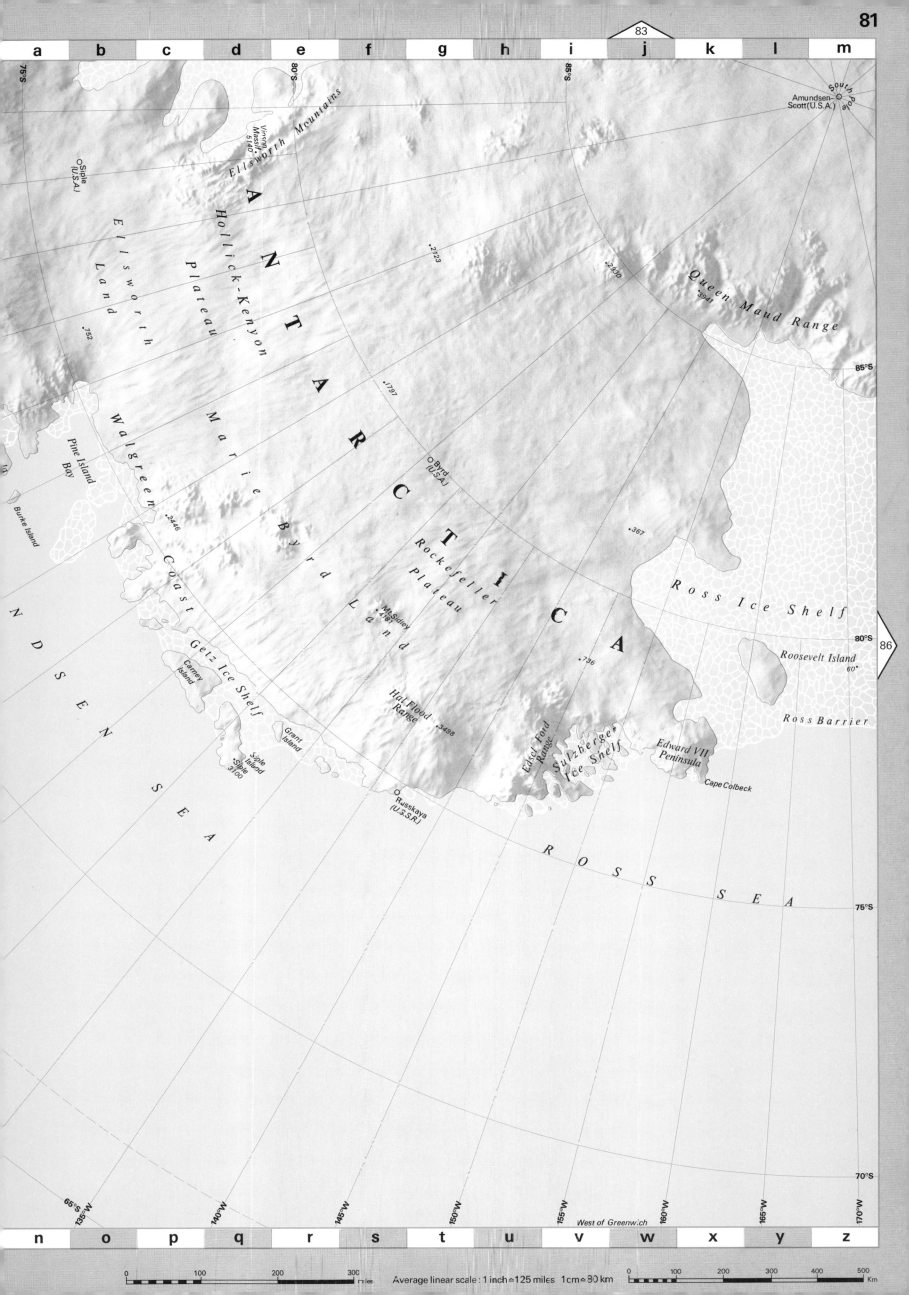

83

75°S

80°S

85°S

Amundsen-
Scott (U.S.A.)

South Pole

Vinson
Massif
5140

Ellsworth Mountains

A

Siple
(U.S.A.)

Ellsworth
Land

Hollick-Kenyon
Plateau

N

.2123

.2520

.3941

Queen Maud Range

T

85°S

.752

.1797

R

Pine Island
Bay

Walgreen
Coast

Marie
Byrd
Land

C

Ross Ice Shelf

Burke Island

.2446

O Byrd
(U.S.A.)

Rockefeller

Plateau

.367

T

80°S

86

Getz Ice Shelf

Carney
Island

Mt.Sidley
.4181

I

.736

Roosevelt Island
60°

A

N

Grant
Island

Hal Flood
Range .3498

C

Ross Barrier

D

Siple
Island
.3100

Edsel Ford
Range

Sulzberger
Ice Shelf

Edward VII
Peninsula

S

O Russkaya
(U.S.S.R.)

A

Cape Colbeck

E

R

O

S

S

N

S

S

E

A

75°S

E

A

70°S

65°S

135°W

140°W

145°W

150°W

155°W

West of Greenwich

160°W

165°W

170°W

0   100   200   300   miles   Average linear scale : 1 inch ≙ 125 miles 1cm ≙ 80 km   0   100   200   300   400   500 Km

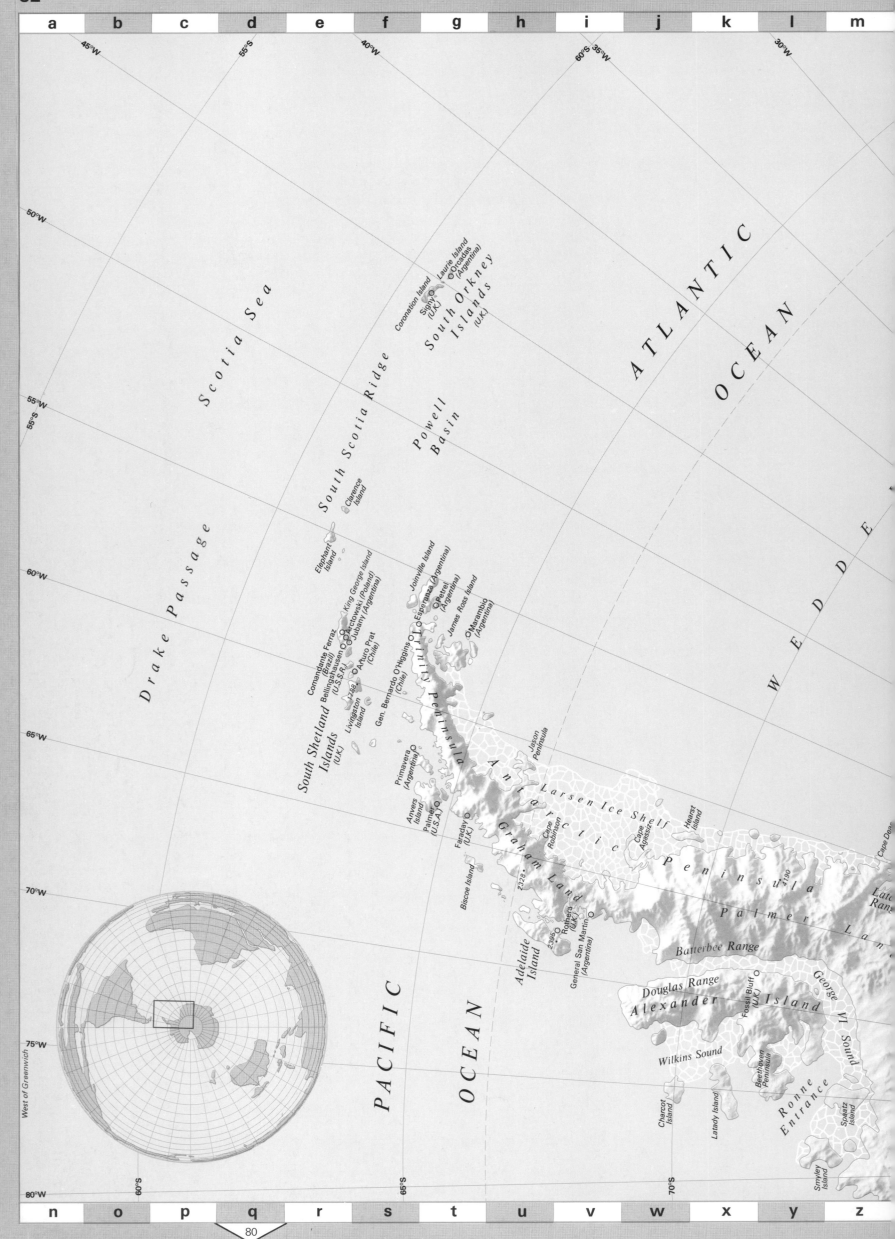

45°W

55°S

40°W

35°W

30°W

50°W

55°W

55°S

Scotia Sea

Laurie Island

Signy ○ Orcadas
(U.K.) (Argentina)

Coronation Island

*South Orkney
Islands*
(U.K.)

ATLANTIC

OCEAN

South Scotia Ridge

*Powell
Basin*

Clarence
Island

**W
E
D
D
E
L
L**

60°W

Drake Passage

Elephant
Island

King George Island

Joinville Island

Esperanza (Argentina)

○ Petrel
(Argentina)

James Ross Island

○ Marambio
(Argentina)

Comandante Ferraz
(Brazil)

Bellingshausen ○ Arctowski (Poland)
(U.S.S.R.) ○ Jubany (Argentina)

Arturo Prat
(Chile)

1288

Livingston
Island

Gen. Bernardo O'Higgins
(Chile)

Trinity Peninsula

65°W

*South Shetland
Islands*
(U.K.)

Primavera ○
(Argentina)

Jason
Peninsula

Larsen Ice Shelf

Hearst
Island

A n t a r c t i c

Anvers
Island
Palmer ○
(U.S.A.)

Faraday ○
(U.K.)

Cape
Robinson

Cape
Agassiz

G r a h a m   L a n d

P e n i n s u l a

70°W

Biscoe
Island

2328

Rothera ○
(U.K.) ○ General San Martin

2190

Palmer Land

Latady
Range

Cape Dean

2395

(Argentina)

Batterbee Range

*Adelaide
Island*

Douglas Range

Fossil Bluff ○
(U.K.)

George VI

75°W

West of Greenwich

Alexander   Island

Sound

Wilkins Sound

Beethoven
Peninsula

PACIFIC

OCEAN

Charcot
Island

Latady Island

*Ronne
Entrance*

Spaatz
Island

Smyley
Island

60°S

65°S

70°S

80°W

This map shows 1/60 of the earth's surface.   Area scale : 1 □ inch on the map ≏ 15,000 □ miles on the ground   1 □ cm on the map ≏ 6000 □ km on the ground

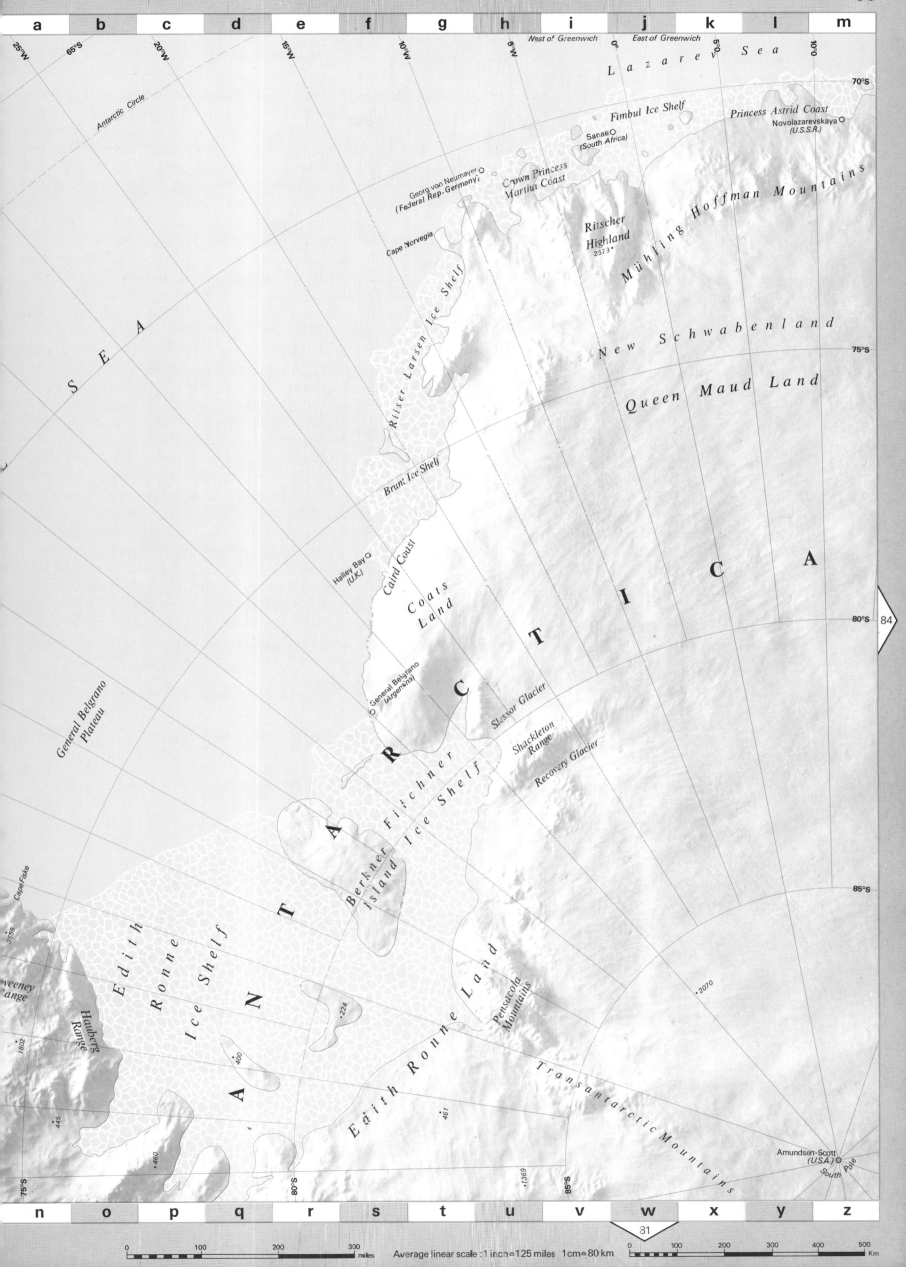

25°W · 65°S · 20°W · 15°W · 10°W · 5°W · West of Greenwich · East of Greenwich · 0° · 5°E · 10°E · 70°S

L a z a r e v   S e a

Fimbul Ice Shelf · Princess Astrid Coast

Sanae ○ (South Africa) · Novolazarevskaya ○ (U.S.S.R.)

Georg von Neumayer ○ (Federal Rep. Germany) · Crown Princess Martha Coast

Cape Norvegia · Ritscher Highland *·2573* · *Mühling   Hoffman   Mountains*

Riiser   Larsen   Ice   Shelf · *New   Schwabenland* · 75°S

Queen   Maud   Land

Brunt Ice Shelf

A   N   T   A   R   C   T   I   C   A

Halley Bay ○ (U.K.) · Caird Coast

Coats Land · 80°S · 84

Stessor Glacier

General Belgrano ○ (Argentina) · Shackleton Range · Recovery Glacier

Fitchner · *Berkner Island Ice Shelf*

General Belgrano Plateau · 85°S

Sweeney Range · Cape Fiske · *·3655*

Edith   Ronne   Ice   Shelf

Hauberg Range · *·1802*

Pensacola Mountains · *·2070*

·224

·445 · *·460* · *·400* · *·461* · *·1369*

Edith Ronne Land

Transantarctic Mountains

Amundsen-Scott ○ (U.S.A.) · South Pole

80°S · 85°S

75°S

31

0 · 100 · 200 · 300 miles · Average linear scale ≙1 inch≙125 miles   1cm≙80 km · 0 · 100 · 200 · 300 · 400 · 500 Km

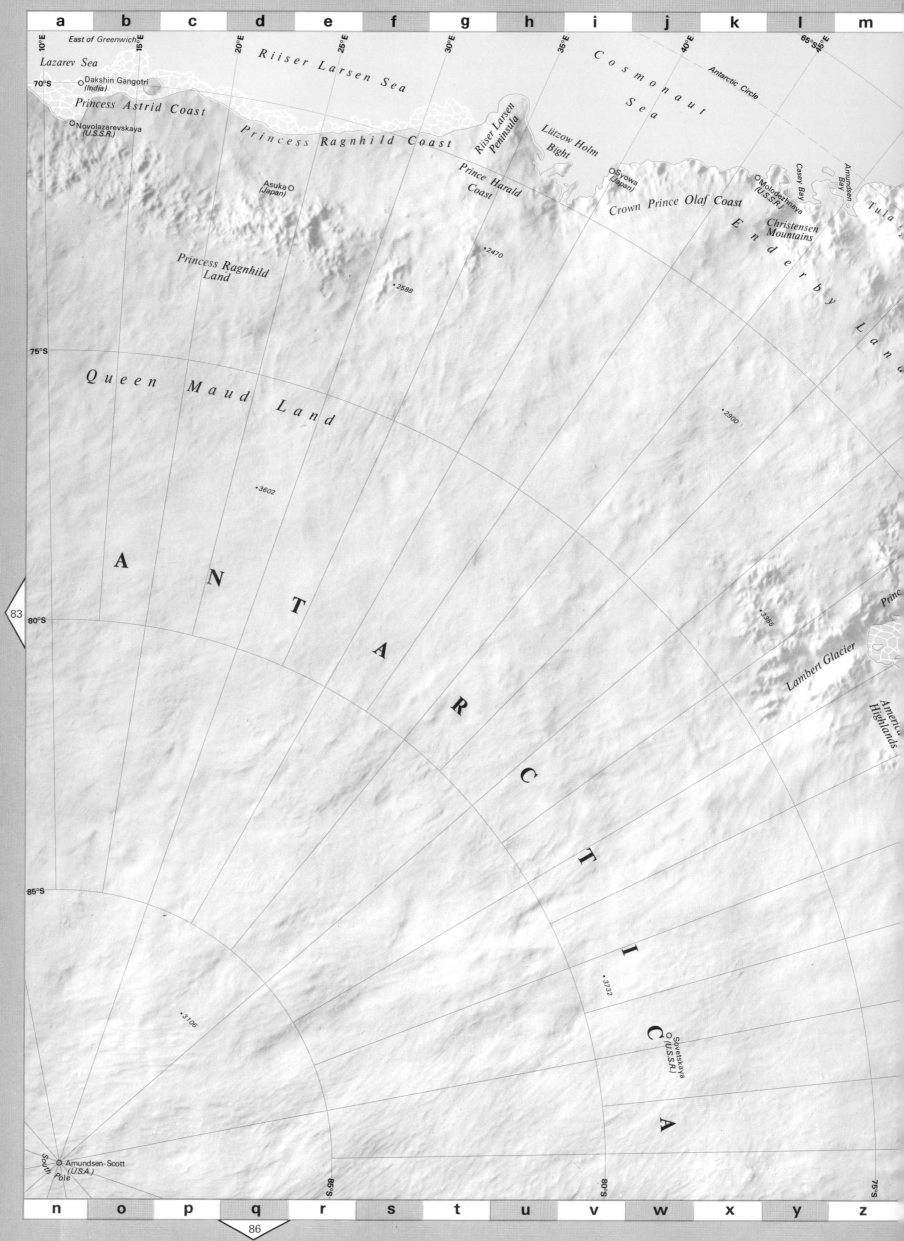

a   b   c   d   e   f   g   h   i   j   k   l   m

East of Greenwich
Lazarev Sea

Riiser Larsen Sea

Cosmonaut Sea

70°S ○Dakshin Gangotri
(India)

Princess Astrid Coast

○Novolazarevskaya
(U.S.S.R.)

Princess Ragnhild Coast

Riiser Larsen Peninsula

Lützow Holm Bight

Antarctic Circle

Asuka ○
(Japan)

Prince Harald Coast

Crown Prince Olaf Coast

Syowa (Japan)○

○Molodezhnaya
(U.S.S.R.)

Casey Bay

Amundsen Bay

Christensen Mountains

Tula

Princess Ragnhild Land

•2470

•2588

Enderby Land

75°S

Queen Maud Land

•2900

•3602

A   N   T   A   R   C   T   I   C   A

•3365

Lambert Glacier

America Highlands

Prince

83 80°S

85°S

•3732

•3106

Sovetskaya
○(U.S.S.R.)

South Pole
○Amundsen-Scott
(U.S.A.)

n   o   p   q   r   s   t   u   v   w   x   y   z

86

This map shows 1/60 of the earth's surface. Area scale : 1 □ inch on the map ≏ 15,000 □ miles on the ground 1 □ cm on the map ≏ 6000 □ km on the ground

a b c d e f g h i j k l m

50°E 55°E 60°S 60°E 55°S 65°E

East of Greenwich

70°E

75°E

80°E

55°S

85°E

90°E

95°E

100°E

I N D I A N

O C E A N

Kemp Land

Cape Boothby

Mac Robertson Land

Mawson (Australia)

...wles Mts.

Cape Darnley

Mackenzie Bay

Amery Ice Shelf

A m e r y   B a s i n

I n g r i d   C h r i s t e n s e n   C o a s t

C o o p e r a t i o n   S e a

Davis (Australia)

Princess Elizabeth Land

•2070

West Ice Shelf

King Leopold and Queen Astrid Coast

D a v i s   S e a

King Wilhelm II Land

Mirny (U.S.S.R.)

Drygalski Island

•2992

Pionerskaya (U.S.S.R.)

Queen Mary Land

Shackleton Ice Shelf

•1380

Denman Glacier

3497 •

Vostok 1 (U.S.S.R.)

Komsomolskaya

70°S 65°S 60°S

n o p q r s t u v w x y z

87

0 100 200 300 miles   Average linear scale 1 inch ≈ 125 miles   1cm ≈ 80 km   0 100 200 300 400 500 Km

a b c d e f g h i j k l m

58°S
58°S
75°S

•3297

Amundsen-Scott
(U.S.A.)
South Pole

3488⊙Vostok
(U.S.S.R.)

•3094

•3102

•2827

•2716

T r a n

Beardmore Glacier

85°S

Mt. Kirkpatrick
•4528

•4282

s a n t a r c t i c

A N T A R C T I C A

Ross Ice Shelf

M o u n t a i n s

•4025

81
80°S

•2675

Scott Base ⊙⊙McMurdo
(U.S.A.)
Terror• •Erebus
3262 3743
Ross
Island

Ross Barrier

•2468

W

Cape
Washington

R O S S   S E A

75°S

Victoria

Coulman
Island

Rennick Glacier

George V
Land

Land

Oates
Land

Hallett⊙
(New Zealand/U.S.A.)

Leningradskaya
⊙(U.S.S.R.)

Cape Hudson

Nimnis Glacier

Cape Adare

Cape Hooker

Cape
Cheetham

International Dateline

70°S

Sturge
Island

Balleny
Islands

170°W
175°W
180°
175°E
170°E
165°E
160°E
65°S

West of Greenwich
East of Greenwich

n o p q r s t u v w x y z

This map shows 1/60 of the earth's surface.   Area scale : 1 □ inch on the map ≃ 15,000 □ miles on the ground 1 □ cm on the map ≃ 6000 □ km on the ground

East of Greenwich

70°S

65°S

Antarctic Circle

Knox Coast

Budd Coast

Casey ○
(Australia)

Cape Poinsett

100°E

105°E

110°E

Sabrina
Coast

W   i   l   k   e   s   L   a   n   d

•2868

Banzare
Coast

Voyeykov
Ice Shelf

115°E

120°E

•2400

Porpoise
Bay

A d é l i e
L a n d

Dumont-d'Urville
O(France)

S   O   U   T   H   E   R   N   O   C   E   A   N

65°S

125°E

Mertz Glaci

Cape
Gray

Dumont d'Urville Sea

•South Magnetic Pole
(1987)

130°E

150°E

145°E

60°S

140°E

55°S

135°E

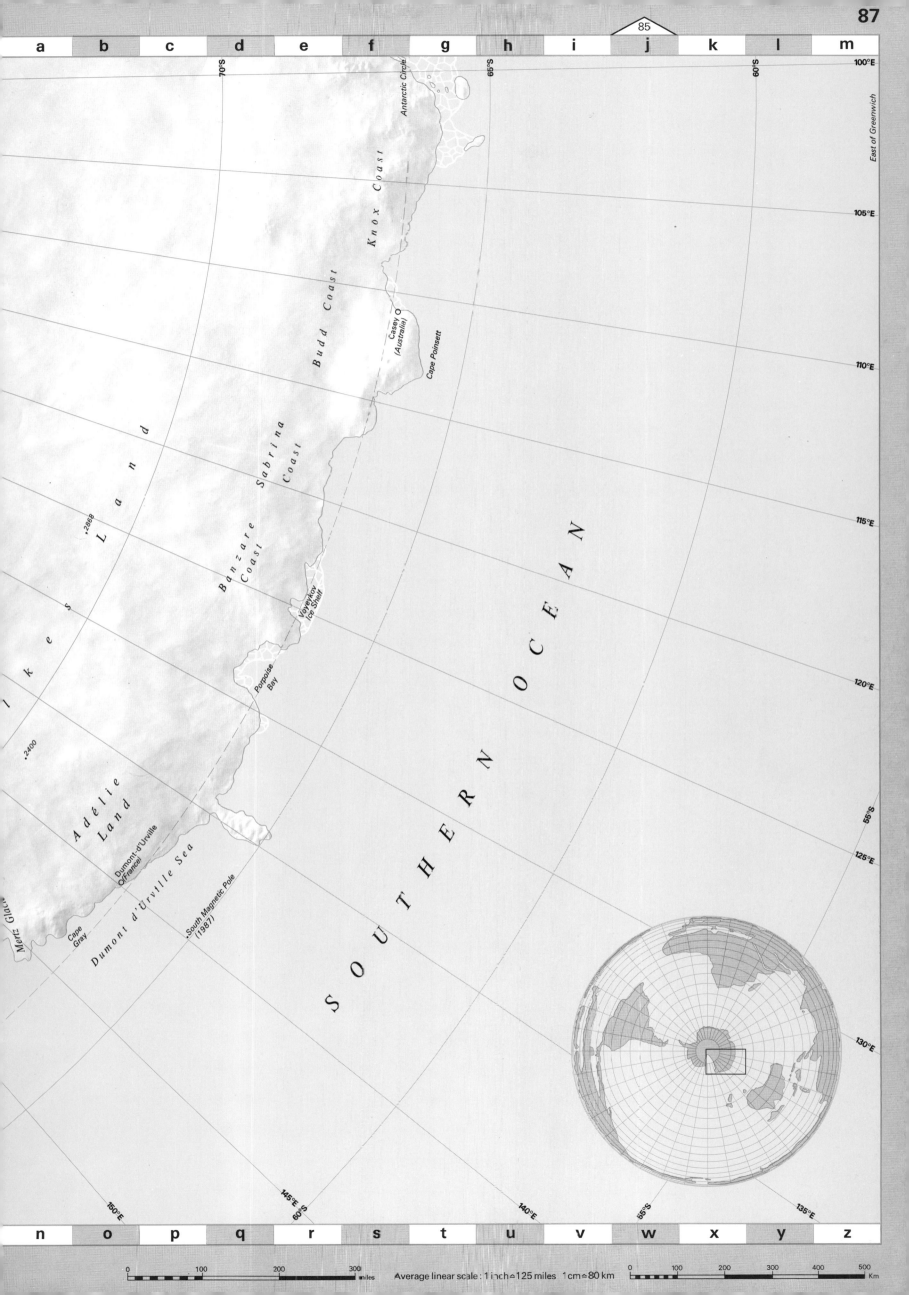

| 0 | 100 | 200 | 300 |
miles

Average linear scale : 1 inch ≃ 125 miles   1 cm ≃ 80 km

| 0 | 100 | 200 | 300 | 400 | 500 |
Km

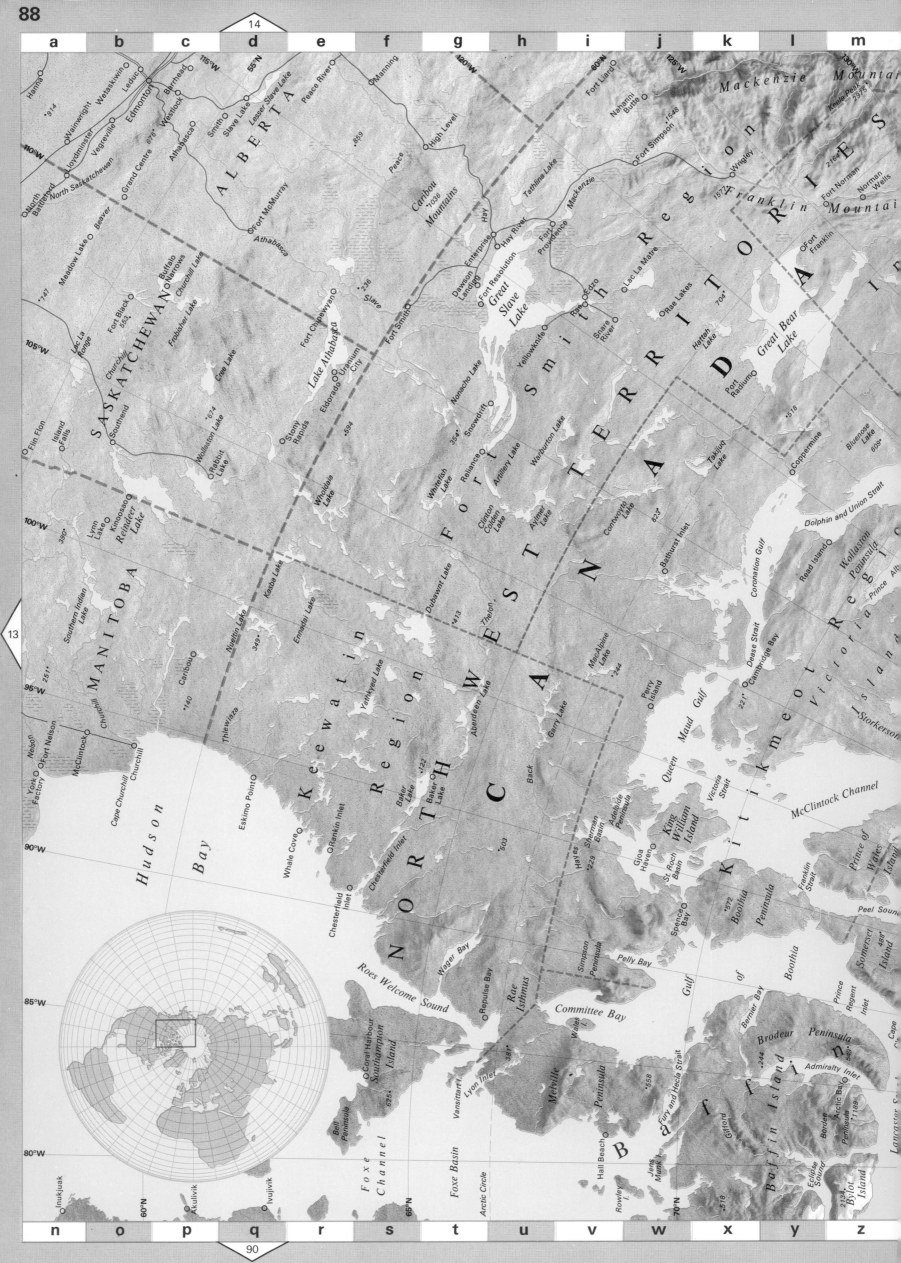

This map shows 1/60 of the earth's surface. Area scale : 1 □ inch on the map ≏ 15,000 □ miles on the ground 1 □ cm on the map ≏ 6000 □ km on the ground

11

YUKON TERRITORY

ALASKA

Brooks Range

Icy Cape

70°N

Eagle Plain

Arctic Village

Ansktuvik Pass

Porcupine
Old Crow

Mount Chamberlin
2438*

Colville

Wainwright

Chukchi Sea

*1931

Fort Good Hope

Mackenzie

Arctic Red River

Fort McPherson

*2236

*749

Deadhorse

Barrow

Colville Lake

Aklavik

Inuvik

Kaktovik

Prudhoe Bay

Cape Barrow

Anderson

*366

*460

MacKenzie Bay

Herschel

Tuktoyaktuk

Cape Dalhousie

B E A U F O R T   S E A

75°N

Paulatuk

Cape Perry

Cape Bathurst

Cape Baring

Amundsen Gulf

Sachs Harbour

*762

Holman Island

Minto Inlet

Prince
Albert
Peninsula

*Banks
Island*

Prince of Wales Strait

Cape Prince Alfred

A R C T I C

O C E A N

80°N

94

*640

McClure   Strait

Hadley Bay

Mould Bay

Prince Patrick Island

*Peninsula

Dundas Peninsula

Melville Island

*1067

Stefansson Island

Viscount   Melville Sound

M e l v i l l e   I s l a n d s

*320

Hazen Strait

MacKenzie King Island

*457

Borden Island

Byam Martin Channel

Lougheed Island

*248

*457

Prince Gustav Adolf Sea

85°N

Bathurst Island

Magnetic North Pole (1987)

Cornwall Island

Ellef Ringnes Island

Amund Ringnes Island

Meighen I.

Resolute

Cornwallis Island

Table I.

Grinnell Peninsula

Belcher Channel

Hassel Sound

Peary Channel

Barrow Strait

*290

Graham I.

Norwegian Bay

Sverdrup Channel

Devon Island

Jones Sound

*1338

Sydkap Ice Cap

Bjorne Peninsula

Axel Heiberg Island

Nansen Sound

Grise Fiord

*1887

Eureka

Greely Fiord

Cape Alert

Cape Discovery

North Pole

North

Lincoln Land

Smith Bay

Agassiz Ice Cap

United States Range

75°N

*2073

*2012

E l l e s m e r e   I s l a n d

*2743

91

0   100   200   300 miles   Average linear scale : 1 inch ≙ 125 miles   1 cm ≙ 80 km   0   100   200   300   400   500 Km

80°W

60°N

Olnukjuak

QUEBEC

Akulivik

Povungnituk

Salluit

Ivujivik

Mansel
Island

Hudson
Bay

Ungava
Peninsula

Nottingham
Island

Salisbury
Island

305

Foxe
Channel

Foxe
Peninsula

Cape
Dorset

411

Nabukjuak

C
A
N
A
D
A

Arctic Circle

Foxe
Basin

Prince
Charles
Island

Jens Munk
Island

Rowley
Island

Foley

Eclipse
Pond Inlet

Sound

Bylot I.
2134

N
O
R
T
H
W
E
S
T

75°W

Purtuniq

Kangiqsujuaq

661

Hudson

Strait

Big
Island

Lake
Harbour

Koukdjuak

Netilling
Lake

Anadjuak
Lake

R
e
g
i
o
n

B
a
f
f
i
n

T
E
R
R
I
T
O
R
I
E
S

Ice Cap

Barnes
Ice Cap
1750

555

Buchan Gulf

Clyde

Baffin

Island

B
a
y

70°W

Kotseak

Kuujjuaq

aux Feuilles

Labrador

390

Cape Hopes
Advance

Ungava
Bay

Akpatok
Island

Frobisher Bay
(Iqaluit)

Meta Incognita

Peninsula

Hall

Peninsula

1148

Frobisher
Bay

C
u
m
b
e
r
l
a
n
d

Kingsa

Nunatak

2591
Penny
Ice Cap

Kivitoo

Henry Kater
Pen.

Home
Bay

Cumberland

Peninsula

Pangnirtung

2134

65°W

Kangiqsualujjuaq

1621

NEWFOUNDLAND

Port
Burwell
Cape
Chidley

Ramah

Resolution
Island

Harper
Island

Labrador Sea

Hoare
Bay

Cape Dyer
Exeter
Sound

Broughton Island

Upernavik

D
a
v
i
s

S
t
r
a
i
t

Svartenhuk
130

Karrats Fj.

Uummannaq
2222
Nuussuaq Halvø

60°N

Fraser

Nutak

1076

Nain

60°N

Qeqertarsuaq
(Godhavn)

Qeqertarsuaq

Disko Bay

Sisimiut

Maniitsoq

Søndre Strømfjord

Søndrestrømfjord

2040

840

50°W

A
T
L
A
N
T
I
C

O
C
E
A
N

Nuuk
(Godthåb)

1767

1780

60°N

e (Kalaa

G

r

55°N

Paamiut

King Christia

55°W

Ivittuut

1643

40°W

35°W

50°W

Nanortalik

Qaqortoq

Narssuaq

Ivittuut

2740

King Frederick VI Coast

K. Løvenørn

Gyldenløves Fj.

Bernstorff's Isfjord

Cape Mosting

Danells Fj.

Ikerasassuaq
(Cape Farewell)

Uummannarssuaq
(Cape Farewell)

Dannebrog
Island

Mt. Forel
3360

Kronprins Frederiks Bjaerge

Ammassalik
Cape Dan

2066

30°W

This map shows 1/60 of the earth's surface.   Area scale : 1 □ inch on the map ≈ 15,000 □ miles on the ground 1 □ cm on the map ≈ 6000 □ km on the ground

a b c d e f g h i j k l m

75°N

Devon Island

·1887

80°N

Smith Bay

North Lincoln Land

·2073

Greely Fjord

Agassiz Ice Cap

85°N

Ellesmere Island

United States Range

·2740

Crane Discovery

North Pole

Baffin

Nares Strait

Hayes Halvø

Inglefield Land

·1500

Kane Basin

Washington Land

Lincoln Sea

ARCTIC OCEAN

Cape Atholl

Hval Sound

Dundas ·796

Qaanaaq (Thule)

Prudhoe Land

Hall Land

Nyeboe Land

Cape York

Melville Bay

Cape Seddon

Knud Rasmussens Land

·945

Nansen Land

·1920

85°N

Holm I.

Steenstrup Glacier

·1310

Peary Land

Melville Land

Frederick E. Hyde Fjord

·1670

Independence Fjord

Wandels Sea

Danmark Fjord

King Frederick VIII Land

·1100· Lambert Land

Crown Prince Christian Land

·765

Nordostrundingen

Ingolf Fjord

G r e e n l a n d

(K a l a a l l i t N u n a a t)

Dronning Louise Land

Germania Land

·250

Sæter Fjord

Île de France

80°N

Greenland

Spitzbergen

1454

West Spitzbergen

92

King Christian X Land

Dove Bay

Store Koldewey

Prince Karls Foreland

Isa Fjord

X Land

Andrées Land

Hudson Land

·1832

Ardencaple Fjord

Shannon

Sea

Scoresby Land

·1900

Kaiser Franz Josephs Fjord

·1604

Clavering I.

Wollaston Foreland

Hold with Hope Pen.

Geographical Society I.

Renland

King Oscars Fjord

Traill I.

75°N

Milne Land

·1740

Jameson Land

Liverpool Land

Gunnbjørn Fjeld

Scoresby Sound

Ittoqqortoormiit

Kangerlussuaq

Cape Brewster

Cape Dalton

Jan Mayen (Norway)

70°N

D e n m a r k   S t r a i t

Isafjördur

Cape Horn

Breidhi Fjord

·961

ICELAND

Húna Bay

25°W

66°N

20°W

65°N

15°W

10°W

5°W

0°

5°E

10°E

0   100   200   300 miles

Average linear scale : 1 inch≏125 miles 1cm≏80 km

0   100   200   300   400   500 Km

North
Pole

A R C T I C

O C E A N

85°N

Ushakova

Vize

West Siberian Sea

Severnaya
Zemlya

Cape Berga
Cape
Peschanyy
Shmidta
Komsomolets
Pioner
.262
Oktyabr'skoy
Revolyutsii
Cape
Mednyy

80°N

Shokal'skogo Str.

Bolshevik

Vilkitskogo
Strait

Russkiy
Nordenshel'da
Arch. Cape
Oskara

Arch.

Taimyr

Byrranga Mountains
.1146

Taimyr Peninsula

Pyasina

.171

.326

Troynoy

Arkticheskogo
Instituta

Mikhaylova

Dikson

Vilkicky

Sokalsky

85°N

Yeva-Liv

Graham
Bell
Island

Rudolf I.

Karla-Aleksandra
Jackson I.
Salisbury I.
Luidzhi

La
Rons'yer
.606
Wilczek
Land

Hell I.   Sar'm

Alexandra
Land

Hooker I.
McClintock I.
.370

Franz Josef Land

George
Land

White
Island

Mys Zelaniya

.1052
Russkaya Gavan

Belyy

Drovyanaya

North East Land

Hinlopenstr.

80°N

.1454

West
Spitzbergen

Spitzbergen

Barents Island

Isa Fjord
Longyearbyen
Barentsburg

Edge Island

.933

B A R E N T S

S E A

N
o
v
a
y
a

Smidovich

Sedova
.1115

Z
e
m
l
y
a

Stolbovoy

Litke

.260

K A R A   S E A

Krasino

Proliv
Karskiye Vorota

.162

Vaigač

Pechora Sea

Chernaya

Dresvyanka
.201

75°N

Bear Island
(Norway)

Kolgujev
.166

Nar'yan
Mar
.106

Malozemel'skaya Tundra

.242

Kanin

Staťanovo

Nonburg

Mezen'
Gulf

Mezen'

Nizhn

Češa
Bay

Velikovisochnoye

N O R W E G I A N   S E A

Tromso

Senja

North Cape

Söröy Hammerfest

Tana

Cape Kiberg

Skibotn

Alta

N
O
R
W
A
Y

Lakselv
.1139
Tana

Kirkenes

Pečenga

.623

Lake
Inari

Ivalo

FINLAND
.636

L
a
p
l
a
n
d

Lotta

Radunskoye
More

Murmansk

.397

K o l a

Cape
Kanin Nos

Volonga

Valonga

Volonga

Mezen'

Azopol'ye

70°N

Moncegorsk

Kirovsk

Arctic Circle

Staťanovo

10°E   15°E   20°E   25°E   30°E   35°E   40°E

n　o　p　33　q　r　s　t　u　v　w　x　y　z

95

Tamyr
Novaya
Lake Khatanga
Khetä
Kheta
Tukalan
Yessey
Changada
Murukta

Verkh. Taymyra
Lake Labaz
Po'kyko
Malinica
Kotuikan
Kochechum

Tareva
Pyasina
Dudypta
Payturma
Volochanka
Kochikha
Boyarka
Kamen 2037
Kamen 1403
Avam
1612

Central Siberian Uplands

Mutoray
Vanavara
636

Taimba
Cadobec
Panovo
Okova

Uchami
Baykit
Kamo A
Korda
UstKamo
Bedoba
Boguchany

100°E

Yenisey Mountains

Lesosibirsk
Strelka
Galanino
Altat

90°E

RUSSIAN S.F.S.R.

S O V I E T   U N I O N   (U. S. S. R.)

80°E

Omsk

Ridge

SIBERIAN

50°E
55°E
60°N

50

0   100   200   300   m ßs
0   100   200   300   400   500   Km

Chukchi

Sea

Mys Shmidta

Long Strait

·1097

Wrangel Island

Retkucha

Krasnoarmeyskiy

Pevek

Illrney

Southern Anyuskiy Mountains

Bol. Anyuy

Kolymskiy Mountains

Korkodon

Kolkodon

Bulun

Oscrovnoy

Mal. Anyuy

Cherskiy

Northern Anyuskiy Mountains

·164

Mal. Ambarchik

Baranikha

Zatishye

Omolon

Berezovka

Zyryanka

Yugo-Tala

Druzhi

Konzaboy

Chernyy Mys

Mys Nerpich'ye

Gorelova

Velochsk

Zhirkova

Srednekolymsk

Sededema

Pastakh

Arga

Chukochye

Lake Nerpich'ye

Balagannakh

Kyrbana

Oysurdakh

Khongseyo

Matava

Shestakova

Kolymskiy Plain

Khara-Tala

Urdakh

East Siberian

Sea

Ulovo

Ilimnlir

Tenail

Kondakovo

·914

Ozhogino

Byvangnyr

Lake Ozhogino

Uyandi

Indigirka

Aleksayeva

Kolesovo

Chokurdakh

Ukta

Tabor

Kiseleva

Chikhacheva

Khroma

Boru

Tenkelji

·221

Kokuora

Kharstan

Balagannakh

Kazachi

Star-Don

Kuagasiak_ha

Uyadey

New Siberian Islands

Novaya Sibir'

Bol. Lyakhovskiy

Chay-Povarnaya

Bennetta

Bol'shoye Zimov've

Fedorovskiy

Kigilyakh

Cape Buzkhaya

Mal. Lyakhovskiy

Stolbovoy

Ambardakh

·320

Koteľnyy

Koteľnyy

Stolbovoy

Berkovskiy

Laptev Sea

Orto-Ayan

Trofimovsk

Antipinsky

A R C T I C

O C E A N

North Pole

Bennetta

Sagastyr

Turkannak

Dunay

Konsomolets

Mal. Taimyr

Cape Peschanny

Oktyabrskoy Revolyutsii

Shokal'skogo Str.

Cape Berga

Bolshevik

Vilkicki Str.

·313

·800

Byrranga Mountains

Cape Begichev

Vezdekhodnaya

Cape Oskara

Lake Taimyr

Niz. Taimyra

This map shows 1/60 of the earth's surface. Area scale : 1 □ inch on the map ≃ 15,000 □ miles on the ground 1 □ cm on the map ≃ 6000 □ km on the ground

Principal Sources for the Thematic Maps: Buch und Buchhandel in Zahlen. Frankfurt 1987. ★ British Geological Survey, Natural Environment Research Council: World Mineral Statistics 1979–1983. London 1985. ★ Dathe, Heinrich und Paul Schöps (eds.): Pelztieratlas. Jena 1986. ★ Deutsche Gesellschaft für Luft- und Raumfahrt: Astronautische Start-Verzeichnisse und Raumflugkörper-Statistiken 1957–1987. ★ Diercke Länderlexikon. Braunschweig 1983. ★ Durrell, Lee: State of the Ark. London 1986. ★ Encyclopedia Britannica. 15th ed. 32 vls. 1985. ★ Encyclopedia Britannica Book of the Year 1986. 1987. 1988. ★ Food and Agricultural Organization of the United Nations (FAO), Rome: FAO Production Yearbook 1985. 1986. FAO Food Balance Sheets 1975–1977. 1979–1981. FAO Yearbook of Fishery Statistics 1983. FAO Trade Yearbook 1986. ★ Fischer Weltalmanach 1986. 1987. 1988. ★ Haack. Atlas zur Zeitgeschichte. Gotha 1985. ★ Herre, Wolf und Manfred Röhrs: Haustiere – zoologisch gesehen. Stuttgart 1973. ★ The International Institute of Strategic Studies (ILSS): The Military Balance 1986–1987. London 1986. ★ International Labour Organization (ILO), Geneva: Yearbook of Labour Statistics 1978. 1979. 1980. 1981. 1982. 1983. 1984. 1985. 1986. 1987. Income Distribution and Economic Development. An Analytical Survey. Geneva 1984. Sixth African Regional Conference. Application of the Declaration of Principles and Programme of Action of the World Employment Conference. Geneva 1983. ★ International Road Transport Union: World Transport Data. Geneva 1985. ★ International Telecommunication Union: Table of International Telex Relations and Traffic. Geneva 1987. ★ Inter-Parliamentary Union (IPU): Women in Parliament 1988. Participation of Women in Political Life and in Decision-Making Process. Geneva 1988. Distribution of Seats Between Men and Women in National Assemblies. Geneva 1987. ★ Jain, Shail: Size Distribution of Income. Compilation of Data. World Bank Staff Working Paper No. 190. Nov. 1974. Washington 1975. ★ Kidron, Michael and Ronald Segal: The State of the World Atlas. London 1981. The New State of the World Atlas (revised ed.). London 1987. ★ Kurian, George Thomas: The New Book of World Rankings. New York 1984. ★ Länder der Erde. Berlin 1985. ★ Meyers Enzyklopädie der Erde (8 vls.). Mannheim 1982. ★ Moroney, John R.: Income Inequality. Trends and International Comparisons. Toronto 1979. ★ Myers, Norman (ed.): GAIA – Der Öko-Atlas unserer Erde. Frankfurt 1985. ★ Nohlen, Dieter and Franz Nuscheler (eds.): Handbuch der Dritten Welt. 8 vls. Hamburg 1981–1983. ★ Ökumene Lexikon. Edited by Hanfried Krüger, Werner Löser et al. Frankfurt 1983. ★ Peters, Arno: Synchronoptische Weltgeschichte. 2 vls. München 1980. ★ Saeger, Joni and Ann Olson: Der Frauenatlas. Frankfurt 1986. ★ Serryn, Pierre: Le Monde d'aujourd'hui. Atlas économique, social, politique, stratégique. Paris 1981. ★ South: South Diary 1987. 1988. ★ Statistisches Bundesamt, Wiesbaden: Statistik des Auslandes. Vierteljahreshefte zur Auslandsstatistik. 1985–1987. Statistik des Auslandes. Länderberichte. ★ Stockholm International Peace Research Institute (SIPRI): SIPRI Yearbook 1987. World Armaments and Disarmament. New York 1987. ★ Taylor, Charles Lewis and David A. Jodice: World Handbook of Political and Social Indicators. New Haven, London 1983. ★ UNESCO: Statistical Yearbook 1974. 1975. 1976. 1977. 1978. 1979. 1980. 1981. 1982. 1983. 1984. 1985. 1986. 1987. ★ UNICEF: The State of the World's Children 1987. ★ The United Nations (UN): UN Statistical Yearbook 1983/84. UN Demographic Yearbook 1972. 1979. 1984. 1985. 1986. National Accounts Statistics. Compendium of Income Distribution Statistics. New York 1985. UN Energy Statistics Yearbook 1984. UN Yearbook of International Trade Statistics 1982. 1983. 1984. 1986. Selected Indicators of the Situation of Women 1985. UN Industrial Statistics Yearbook 1983. 1984. World Conference of the United Nations Decade for Women: Equality, Development and Peace. Copenhagen 1980. Activities for the Advancement of Women: Equality, Development and Peace. Report of Jean Fernand-Laurent. 1983. ★ University of Stellenbosch, Department of Development Administration and the Institute for Cartographic Analysis: The Third World in Maps. 1985. ★ Westermann Lexikon der Geographie. Edited by Wolf Tietze. Braunschweig 1968. ★ World Almanac & Book of Facts 1985. 1986. 1987. ★ The World Bank: World Development Report 1980. 1981. 1982. 1983. 1984. 1985. 1986. 1987. World Labour Report 1984. World Tables 1984. World Atlas of the Child 1979. Social Indicators of Development 1987. The World Bank Atlas 1987. World Economic and Social Indicators. Document of the World Bank. 1980. ★ World Energy Resources 1985–2020. Renewable Energy Resources. The Full Reports to the Conservation Commission of the World Energy Conference. Published for the WEC by IPC Science and Technology Press 1978. ★ The World in Figures. Editorial information compiled by The Economist. London 1987. ★ World Health Organization (WHO), Geneva: World Health Statistics. Annual. ★ Völker der Erde. Bern 1982. ★ Voous, K.H.: Atlas of European Birds. New York 1960.

NATURE, MAN AND SOCIETY
IN 246 THEMATIC MAPS

Each map presents a single subject. As a result, it is possible to dispense with symbols and allow the information to be expressed entirely in terms of colour: dark colours for high values, light for low ones. This makes it easy to see and assimilate the content of the maps – an important feature, since up to 16 maps can be dedicated to a single subject.

The individual subject should not be considered in isolation. The mutual interaction between all spheres of life, the intricacies of nature and culture, of economics, nations and society, mean that each of the subjects can be understood only in connection with the other 45 double-page spreads.

This richness and multiplicity of facts and insights is however the minimum which someone of our time must have in mind if he wishes to form his own opinion on the current situation in the world and in his own country. Without this effort, his own view of the world can never be clear and reliable.

Over 40,000 individual pieces of factual information have been compiled for these 246 thematic world maps. They were obtained almost exclusively from published materials of the United Nations and other international organisations. Their reliability is presumed, and an average of annual data available from 1980 onwards has been calculated. Where official figures were not available, estimates were made in consultation with the leading experts in the various fields concerned. No indication is given of these estimates, since their reliability is no less than that of the official figures.

The names of countries appear also on the small world maps. These can be read with the aid of a magnifying glass or by reference to the large whole-page maps such as that of "States" on pages 112 – 113.

Brief texts on each subject are intended to aid mental categorisation and to make historical connections plain. In addition, they contain the figures of extreme cases which cannot be extracted from the average values given by the colour-coding.

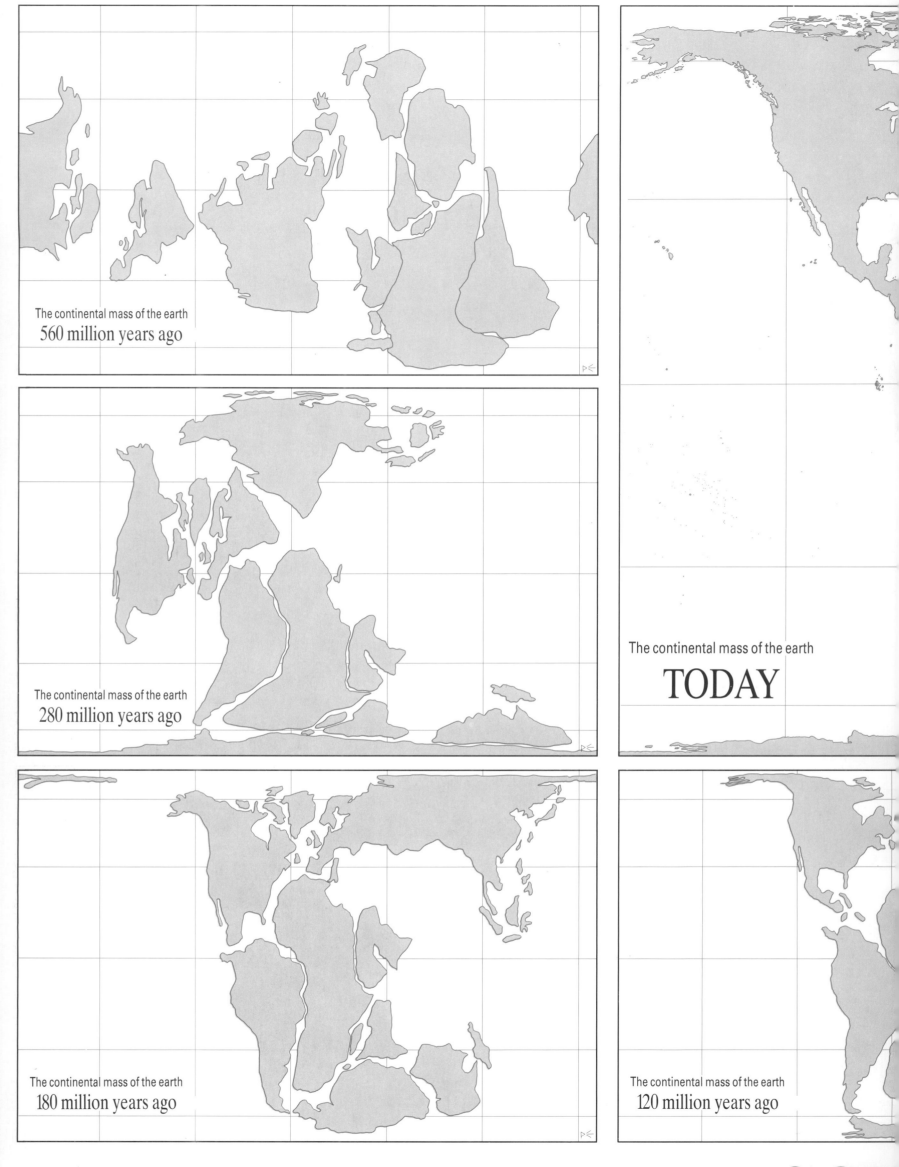

The continental mass of the earth
560 million years ago

The continental mass of the earth
280 million years ago

The continental mass of the earth
180 million years ago

The continental mass of the earth
TODAY

The continental mass of the earth
120 million years ago

THE CON

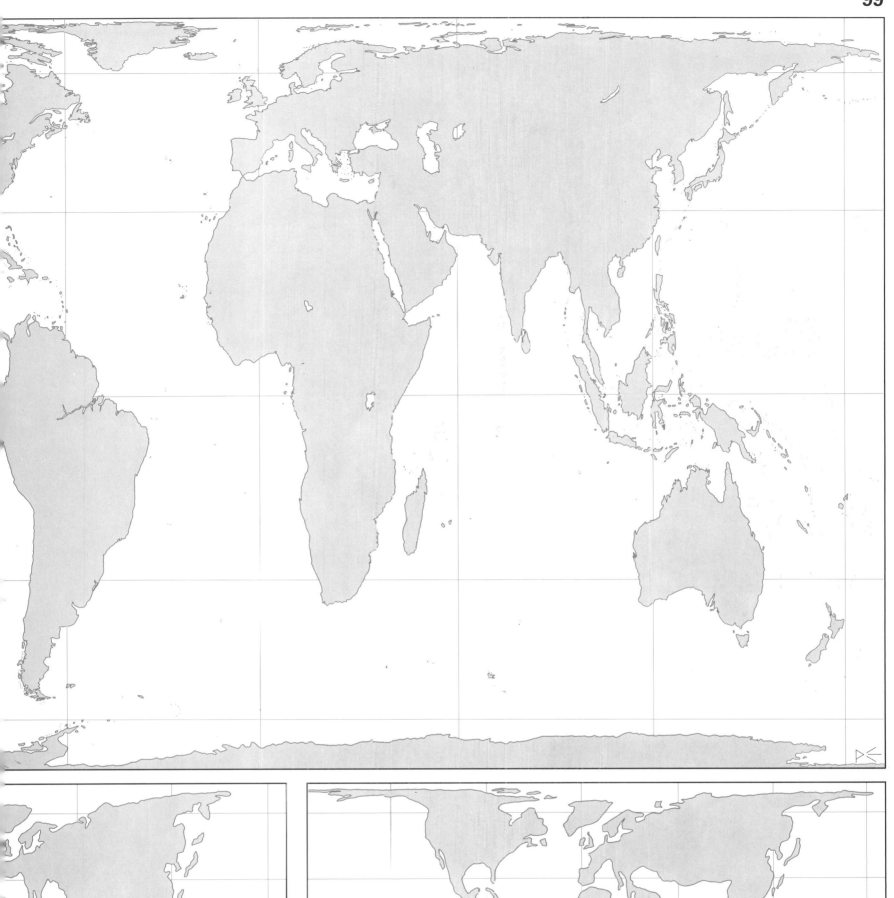

The continental mass of the earth
60 million years ago

TINENTS

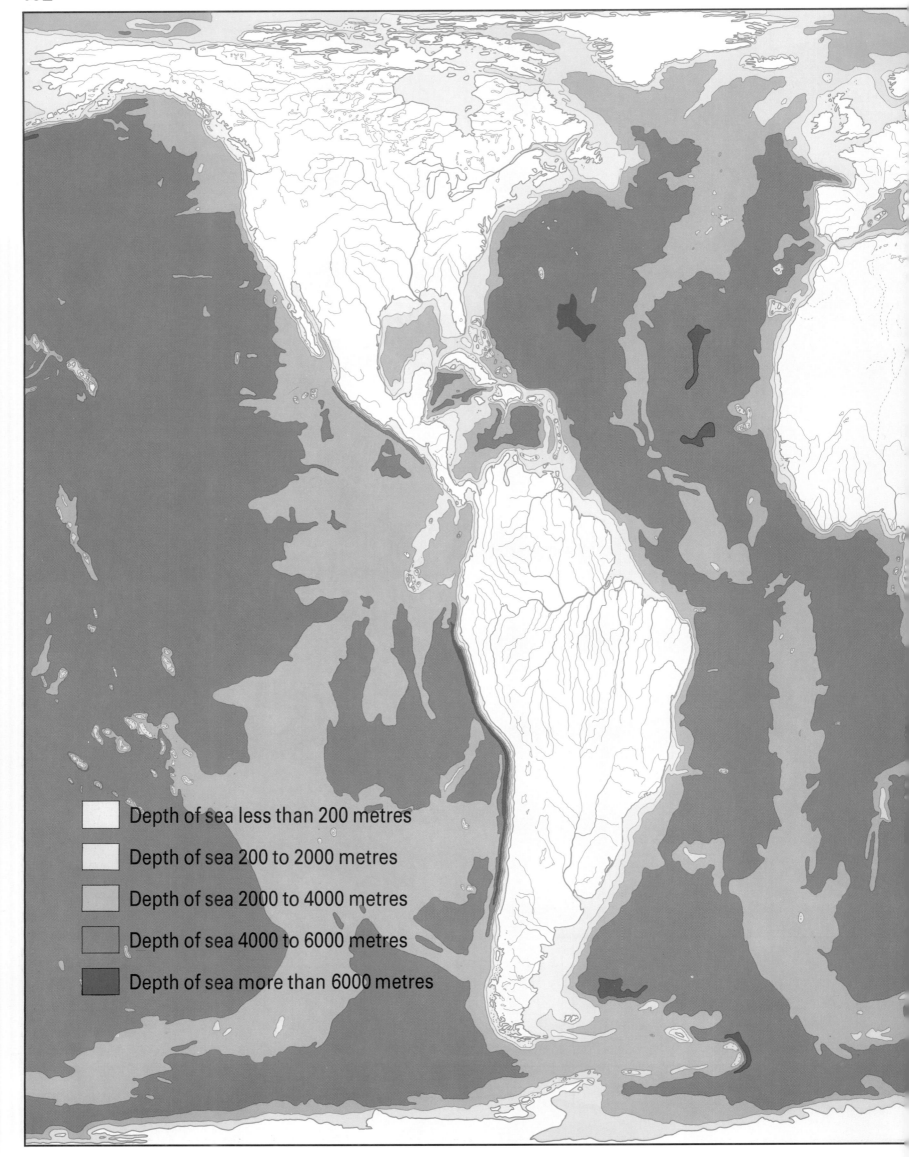

Depth of sea less than 200 metres

Depth of sea 200 to 2000 metres

Depth of sea 2000 to 4000 metres

Depth of sea 4000 to 6000 metres

Depth of sea more than 6000 metres

RIVERS A

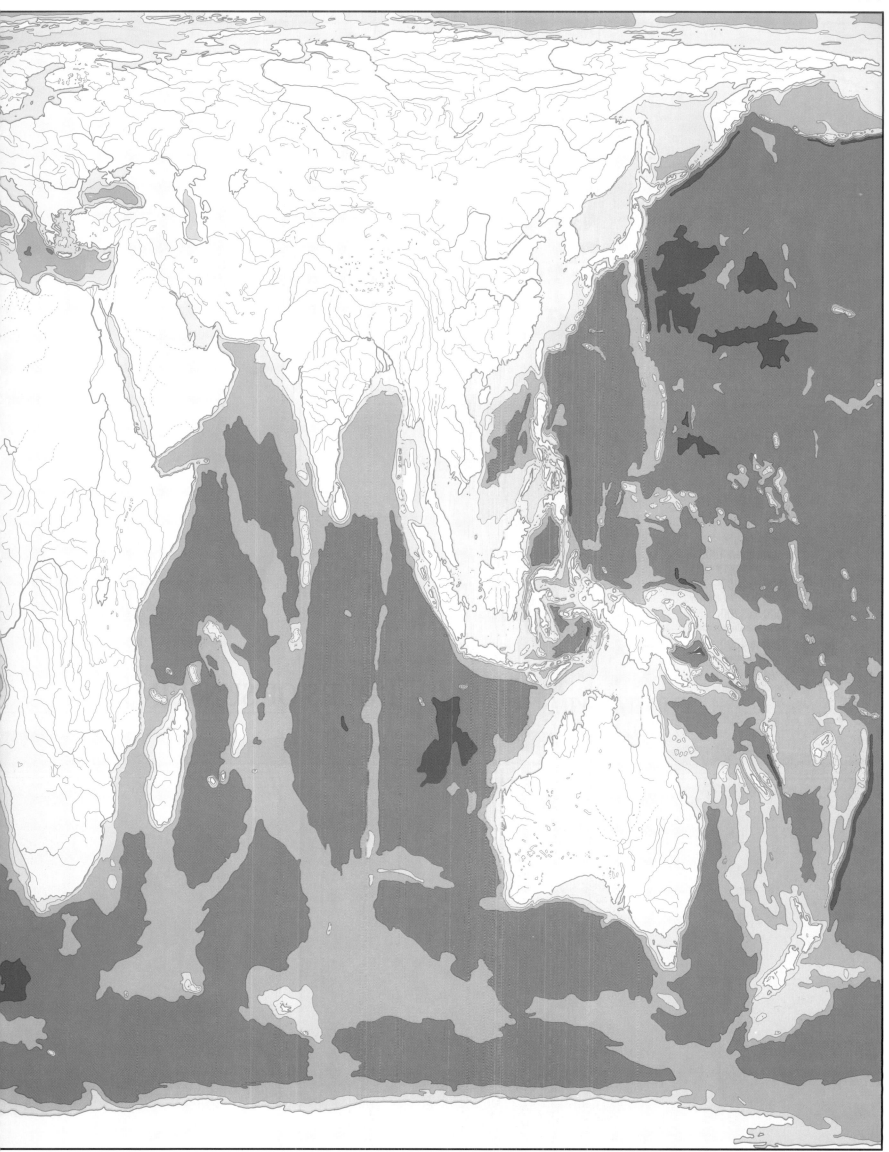

ND SEAS

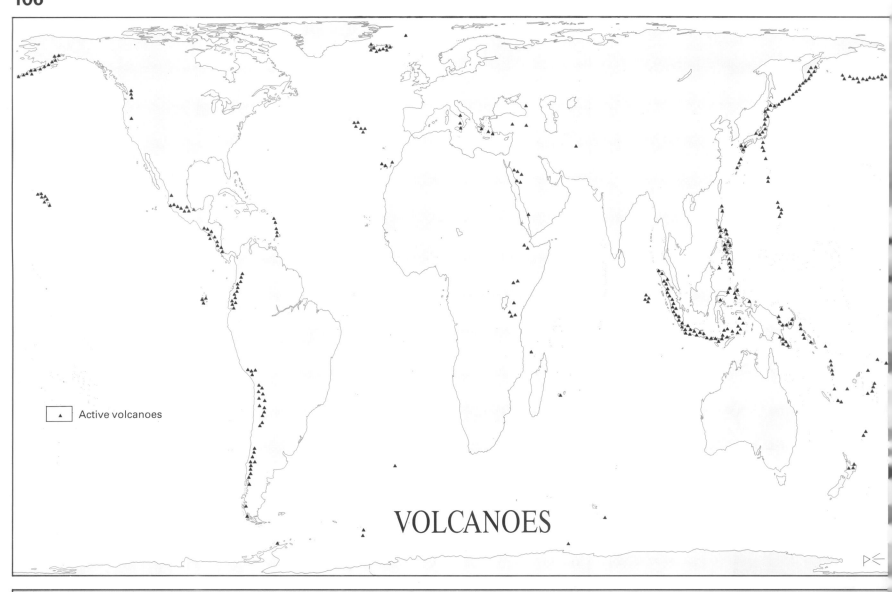

VOLCANOES

▲ Active volcanoes

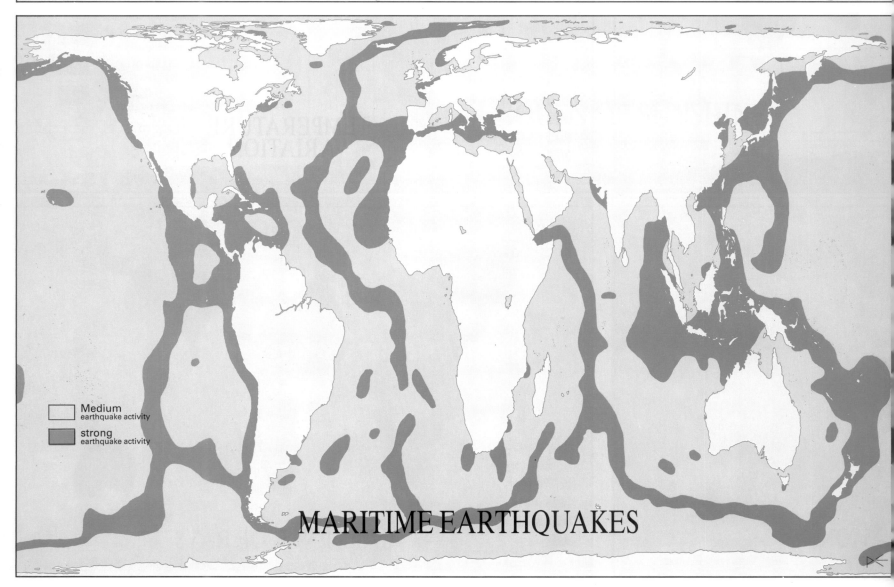

MARITIME EARTHQUAKES

Medium
earthquake activity

strong
earthquake activity

NATURAL

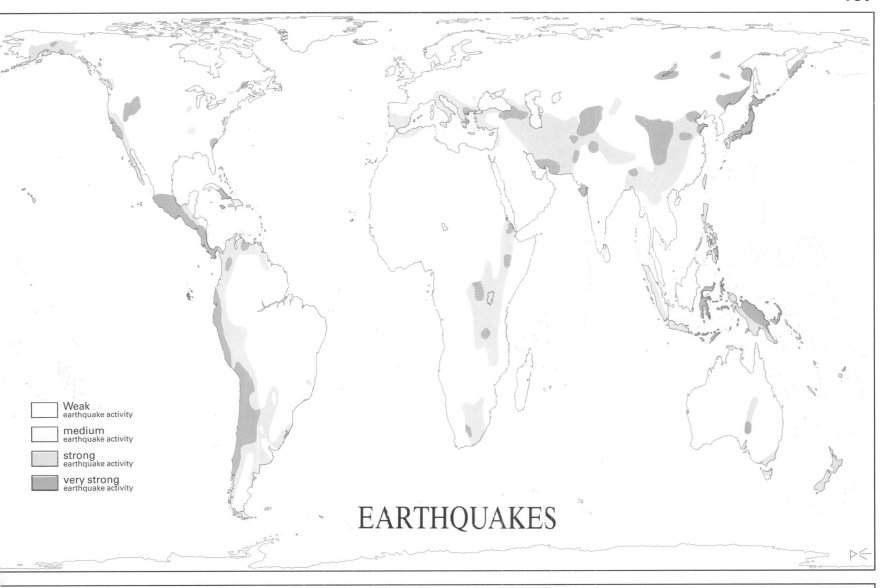

Weak
earthquake activity

medium
earthquake activity

strong
earthquake activity

very strong
earthquake activity

EARTHQUAKES

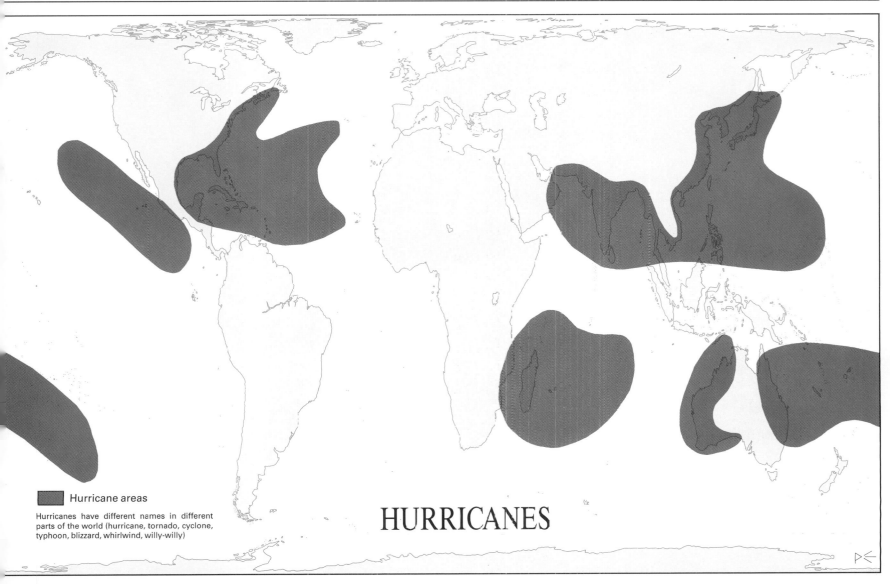

Hurricane areas

Hurricanes have different names in different
parts of the world (hurricane, tornado, cyclone,
typhoon, blizzard, whirlwind, willy-willy)

HURRICANES

DANGERS

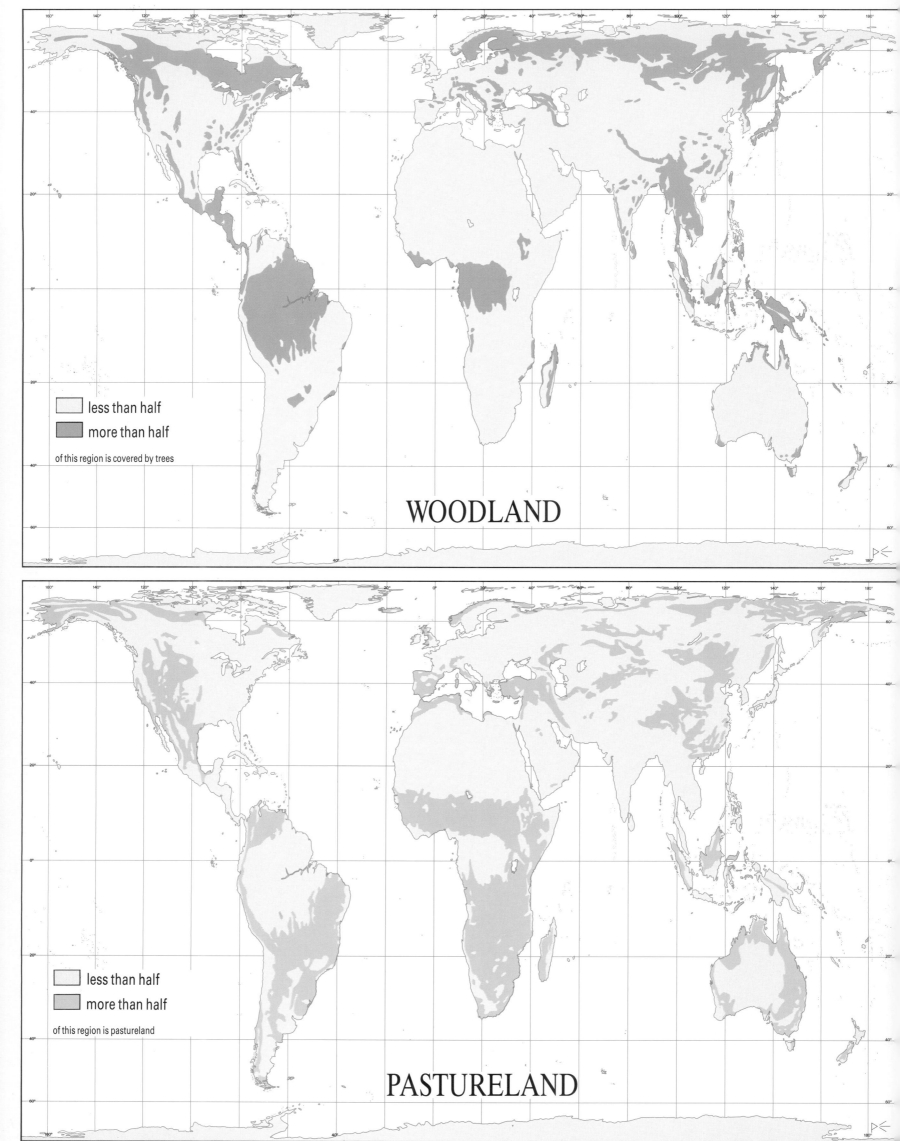

less than half

more than half

of this region is covered by trees

WOODLAND

less than half

more than half

of this region is pastureland

PASTURELAND

VEGET

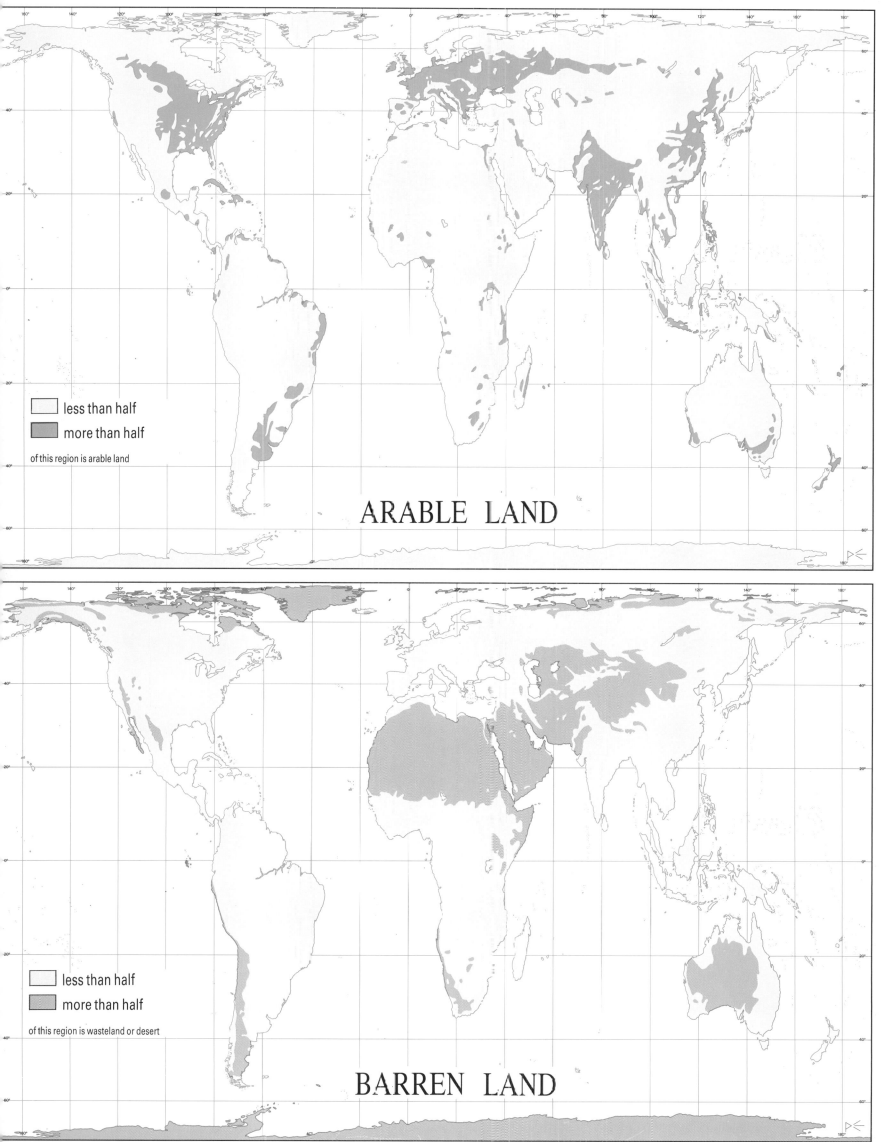

less than half
more than half
of this region is arable land

ARABLE LAND

less than half
more than half
of this region is wasteland or desert

BARREN LAND

ATION

Greenland

Alaska

ICELAND

NORW

C A N A D A

DENMAR

GREAT BRITAIN
& N. IRELAND

IRELAND

NL

BELGIUM
LUX

FRANCE SWI

40°

UNITED STATES OF AMERICA

(U.S.A.)

PORTUGAL

SPAIN

MOROCCO

M
E
X
I
C
O

CUBA

BAHAMAS

ALGERIA

WESTERN
SAHARA

20°

MAURITANIA

JAMAICA

HAITI

DOMINICAN REP.

ANTIGUA AND BARBUDA

CAPE VERDE

SENEGAL

M
A
L
I

N

BELIZE

DOMINICA

GAMBIA

BURKINA
FASO

GUATEMALA

HONDURAS

ST. LUCIA

GUINEA-BISSAU

NIG

EL SALVADOR

ST. VINCENT

BARBADOS

GUINEA

I
V
O
R
Y

C
O
A
S
T

G
H
A
N
A

T
O
G
O

B
E
N
I
N

NICARAGUA

GRENADA

SIERRA LEONE

COSTA RICA

TRINIDAD AND TOBAGO

LIBERIA

PANAMA

VENEZUELA

GUYANA

EQ. GUIN

SÃO TOMÉ & PRINCIPE

C
O
L
O
M
B
I
A

SURINAM

FRENCH
GUIANA

0°

ECUADOR

P
E
R
U

B R A Z I L

20°

BOLIVIA

P
A
R
A
G
U
A
Y

C
H
I
L
E

A
R
G
E
N
T
I
N
A

URUGUAY

40°

60°

STA

SWEDEN
FINLAND

POLAND
CZECH
RIA HUNGARY
ROMANIA
YUGOSLAVIA
ALB
BULGARIA
GREECE
MALTA
CYPRUS
LEBANON
ISRAEL
JORDAN

S O V I E T   U N I O N

(U. S. S. R.)

PEOPLES' REPUBLIC
OF MONGOLIA

NORTH KOREA

SOUTH
KOREA

JAPAN

TURKEY

SYRIA
IRAQ
IRAN
AFGHANISTAN
PAKISTAN
KUWAIT

C H I N A

LIBYA
EGYPT
SAUDI
BAHRAIN QATAR
UNITED
ARAB
EMIRATES
ARABIA
OMAN
YEMEN
P.D.R. YEMEN
DJIBOUTI

NEPAL
BHUTAN
BANGLADESH

I N D I A
BURMA
LAOS

THAILAND

TAIWAN

CHAD
SUDAN

CENTRAL
AFRICAN
REPUBLIC

ETHIOPIA

SOMALIA

SRI LANKA

MALDIVES

CAMBODIA
VIETNAM

PHILIPPINES

UGANDA
KENYA
RWANDA
BURUNDI

CONGO

ZAIRE

SEYCHELLES

BRUNEI
M A L A Y S I A
SINGAPORE

KIRIBATI

NAURU

TANZANIA

I N D O N E S I A
PAPUA
NEW GUINEA

SOLOMON
ISLANDS

ANGOLA
ZAMBIA
MALAWI
COMOROS

TUVALU
WESTERN SAMOA

ZIMBABWE
MOZAMBIQUE
MADAGASCAR
MAURITIUS

VANUATU
FIJI

NAMIBIA
BOTSWANA

TONGA

SWAZILAND
SOUTH
LESOTHO
AFRICA

A U S T R A L I A

NEW ZEALAND

TES

Fewer than 1 inhabitant
per square kilometre

1 to 10 inhabitants
per square kilometre

10 to 100 inhabitants
per square kilometre

100 to 1000 inhabitants
per square kilometre

more than 1000 inhabitants
per square kilometre. The symbols mean
·   500,000 to 1 million inhabitants
•   1 million to 10 million inhabitants
❧   more than 10 million inhabitants

PEOPLE A

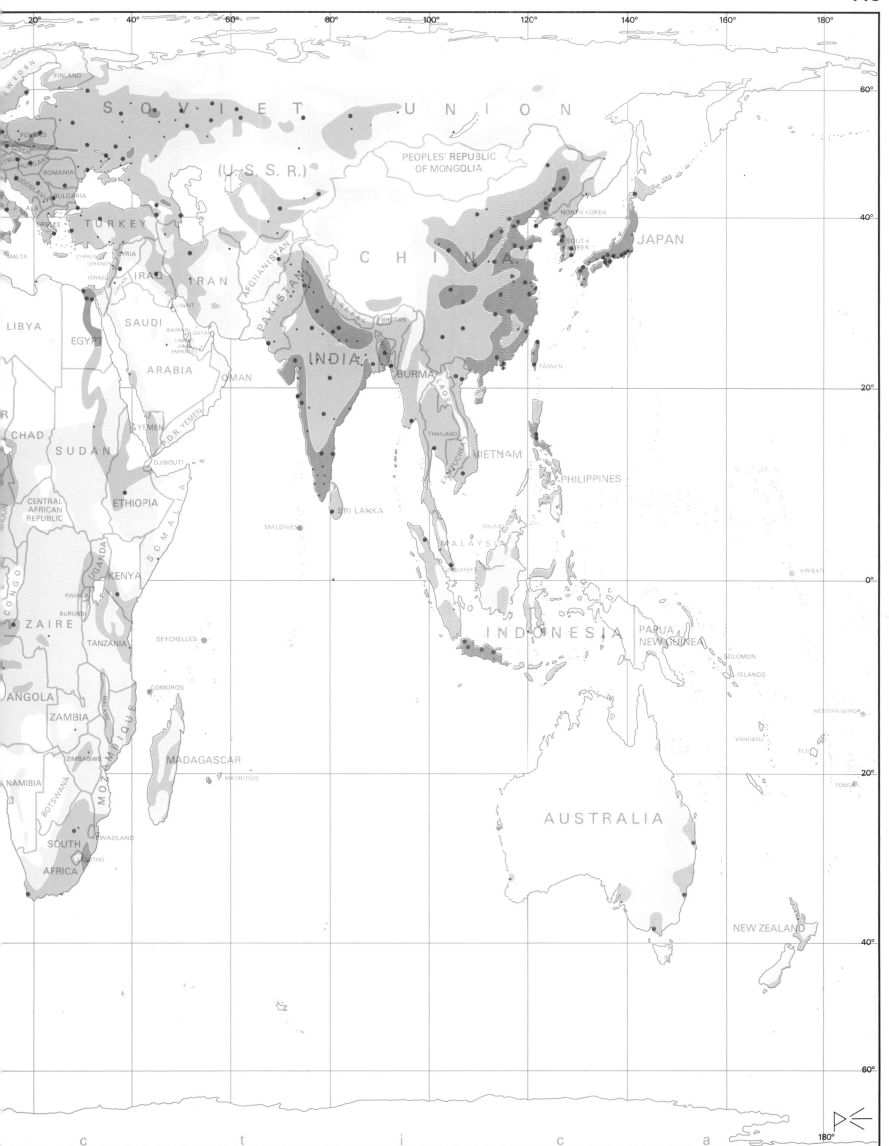

ND CITIES

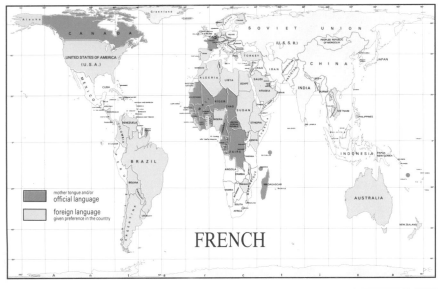

FRENCH

SPANISH

GERMAN

RUSSIAN

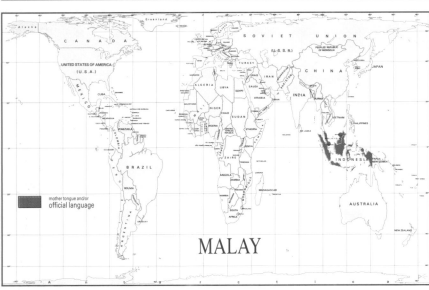

MALAY

PROPORTION OF THE WORLD'S POPULATION SPEA
ONE OF THESE MAJOR LANGUAGES AS THE MOTHE

French	Spanish	Portuguese	English	German	Russian	Italian
2 %	6 %	3 %	10 %	2 %	6 %	1 %

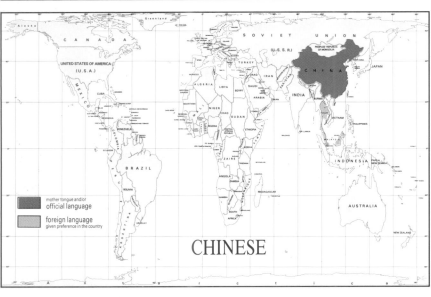

CHINESE

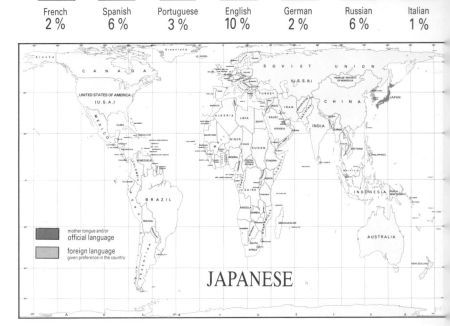

JAPANESE

LANGI

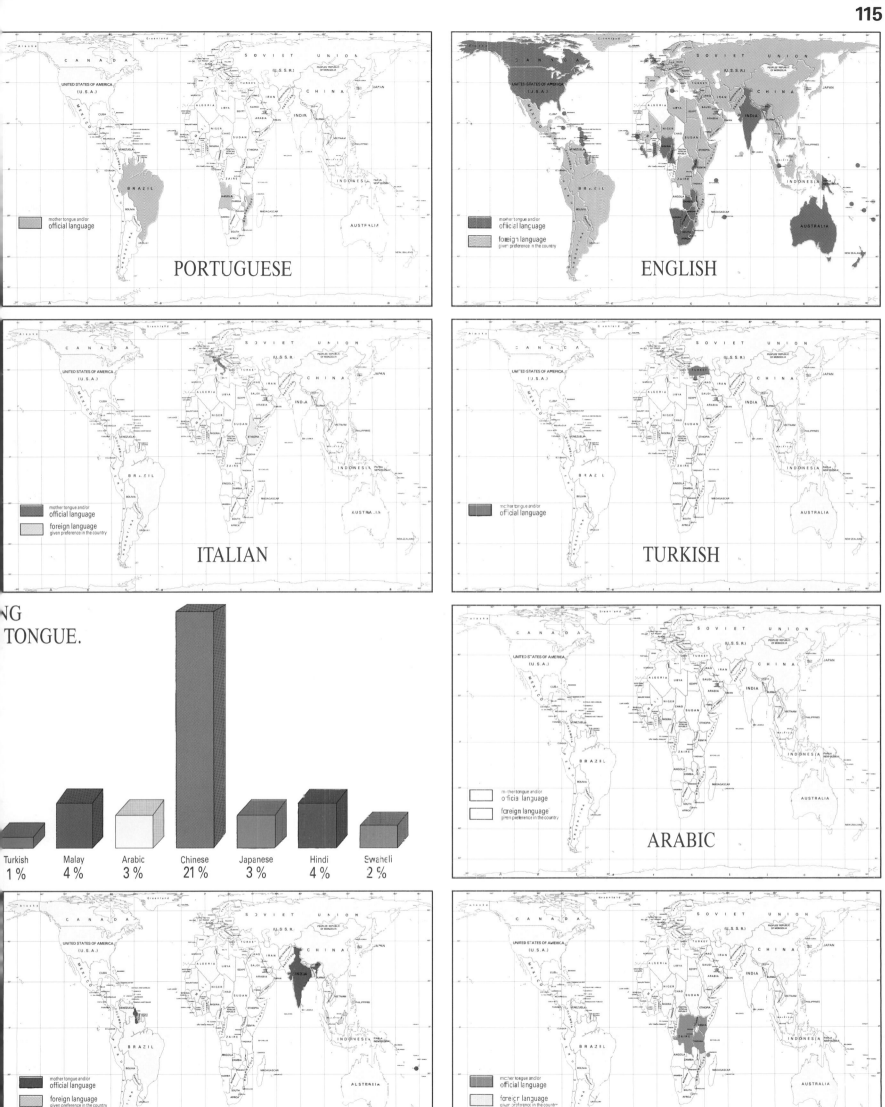

PORTUGUESE

ENGLISH

mother tongue and/or
official language

mother tongue and/or
official language

foreign language
given preference in the country

ITALIAN

TURKISH

mother tongue and/or
official language

foreign language
given preference in the country

mother tongue and/or
official language

NG

TONGUE.

Turkish	Malay	Arabic	Chinese	Japanese	Hindi	Swaheli
1 %	4 %	3 %	21 %	3 %	4 %	2 %

ARABIC

mother tongue and/or
official language

foreign language
given preference in the country

HINDI

SWAHELI

mother tongue and/or
official language

foreign language
given preference in the country

mother tongue and/or
official language

foreign language
given preference in the country

JAGES

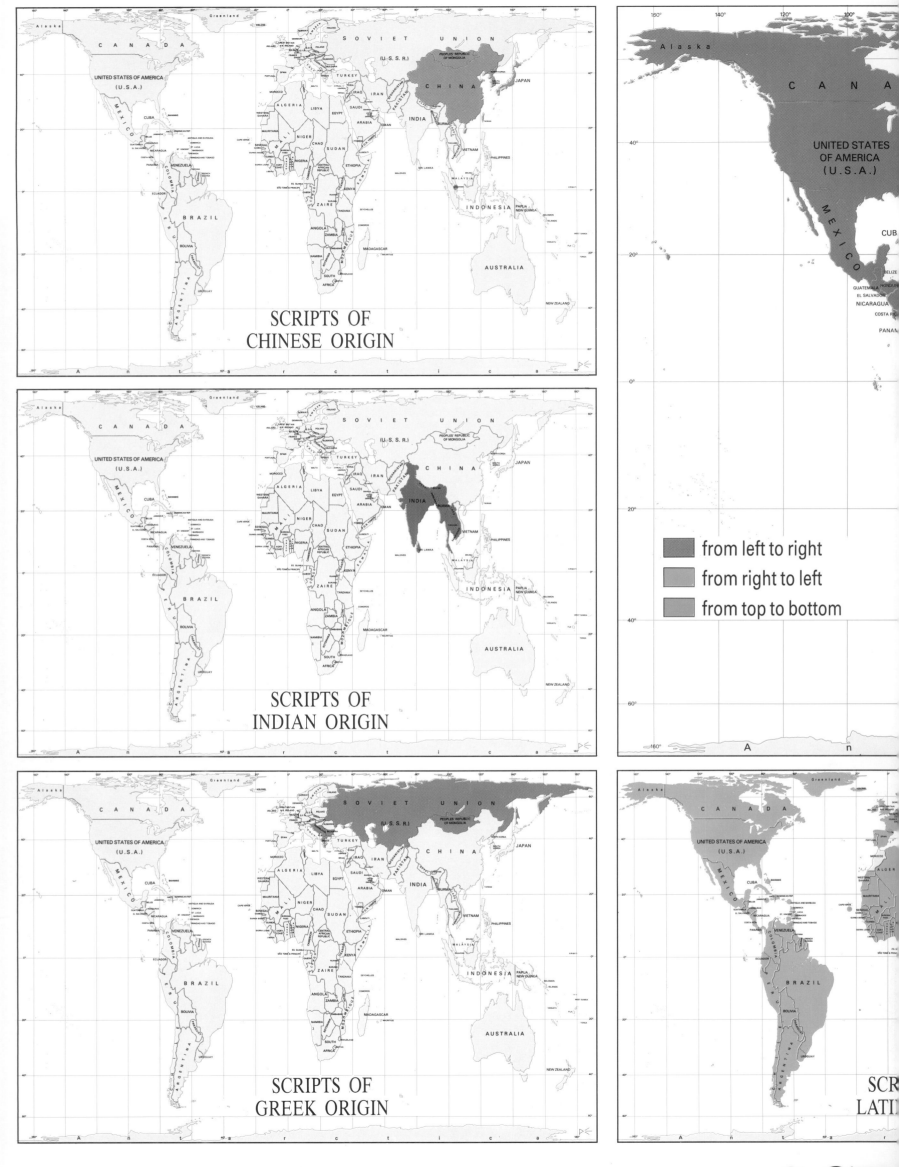

SCRIPTS OF
CHINESE ORIGIN

SCRIPTS OF
INDIAN ORIGIN

SCRIPTS OF
GREEK ORIGIN

from left to right

from right to left

from top to bottom

SCR
LATI

SCR

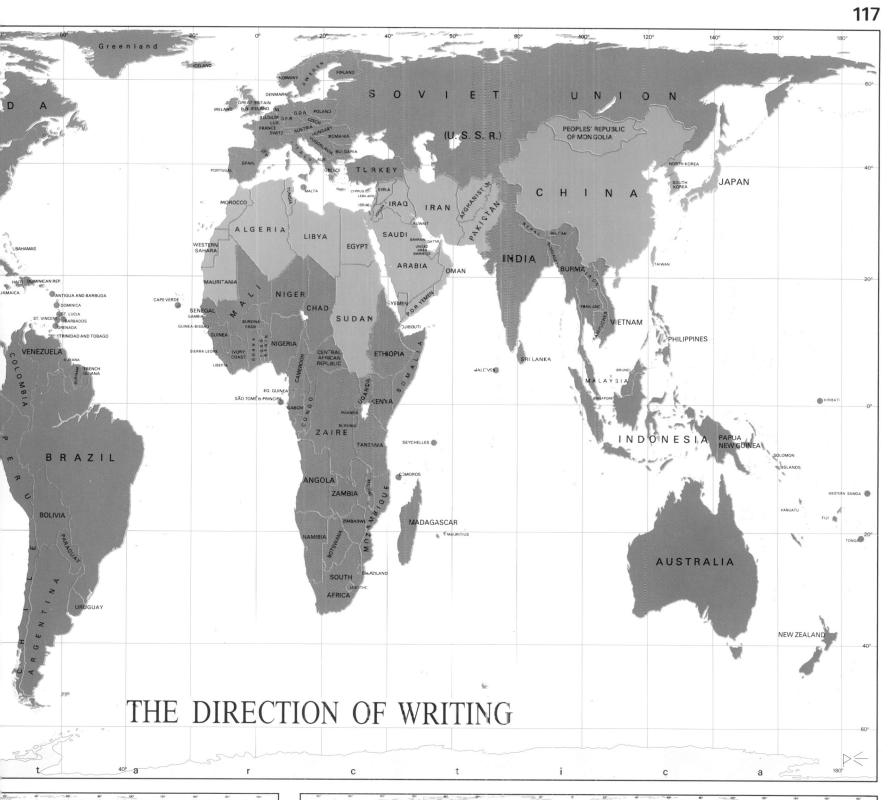

THE DIRECTION OF WRITING

...TS OF
...ORIGIN

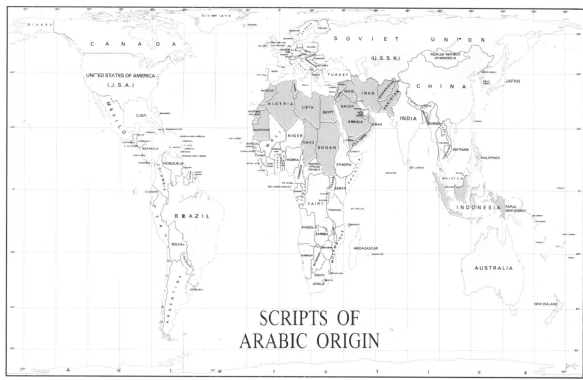

SCRIPTS OF ARABIC ORIGIN

...PTS

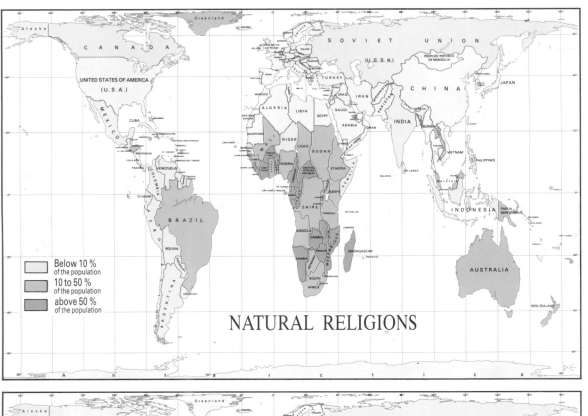

NATURAL RELIGIONS

Below 10 %
of the population

10 to 50 %
of the population

above 50 %
of the population

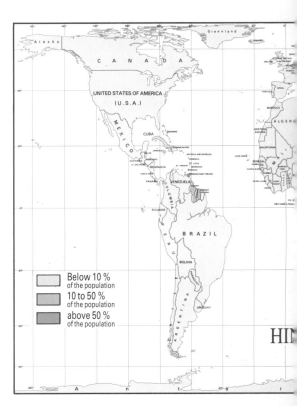

Below 10 %
of the population

10 to 50 %
of the population

above 50 %
of the population

HIN

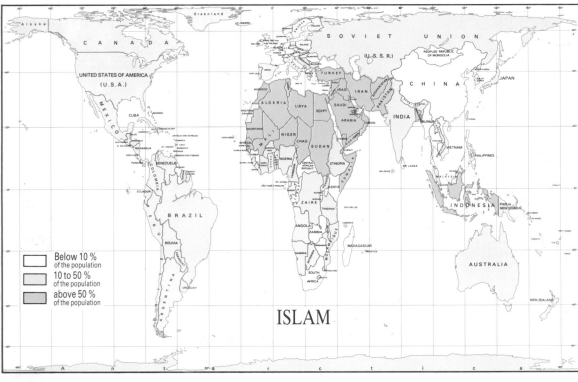

ISLAM

Below 10 %
of the population

10 to 50 %
of the population

above 50 %
of the population

Only religions whose adherents num
population are included or

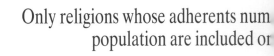

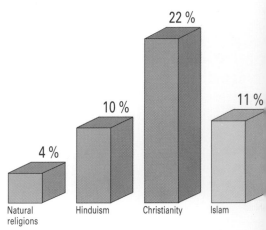

4 %

10 %

22 %

11 %

Natural religions

Hinduism

Christianity

Islam

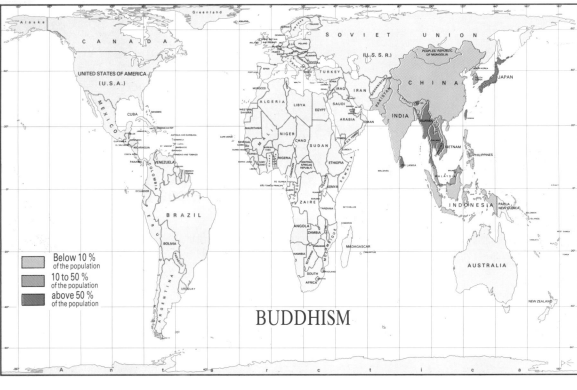

BUDDHISM

Below 10 %
of the population

10 to 50 %
of the population

above 50 %
of the population

Below 10 %
of the population

10 to 50 %
of the population

CON

RELIG

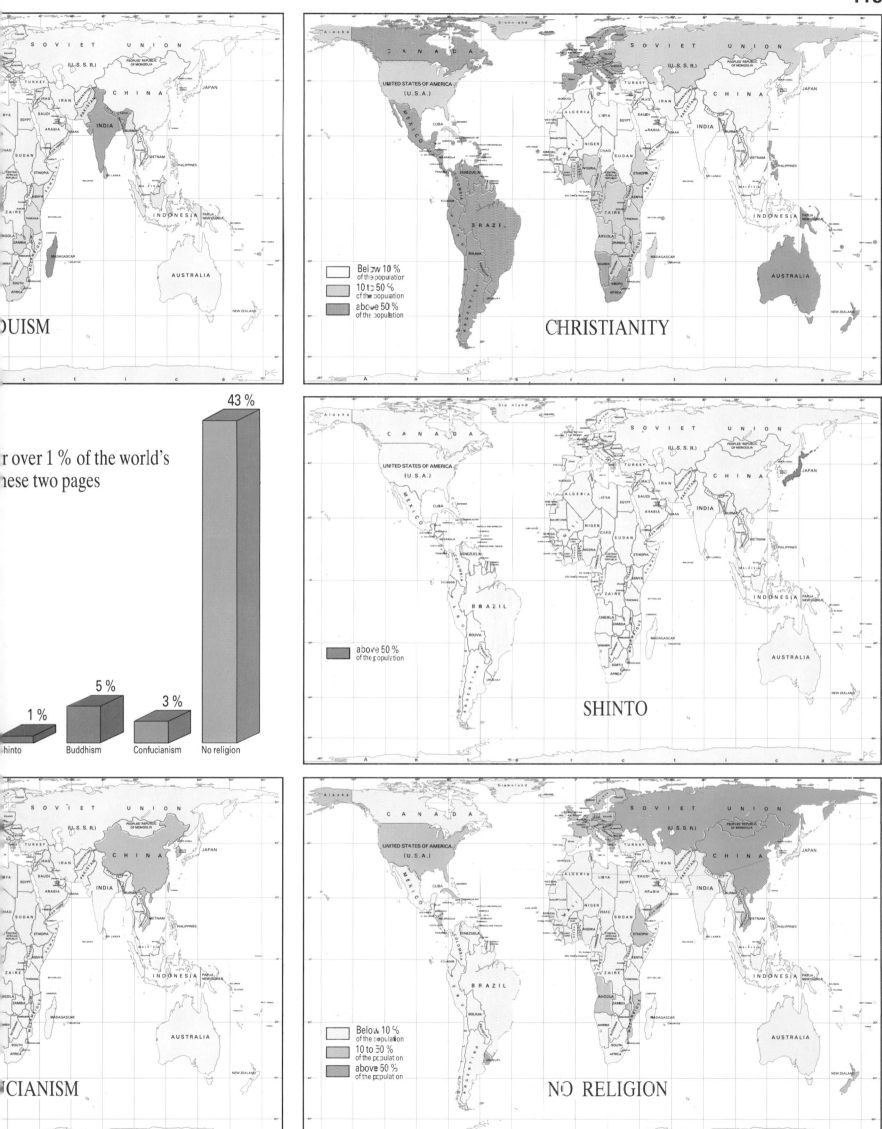

UISM

CHRISTIANITY

Below 10 %
of the population

10 to 50 %
of the population

above 50 %
of the population

r over 1 % of the world's
hese two pages

43 %

5 %

3 %

1 %

hinto

Buddhism

Confucianism

No religion

above 50 %
of the population

SHINTO

CIANISM

NO RELIGION

Below 10 %
of the population

10 to 50 %
of the population

above 50 %
of the population

GIONS

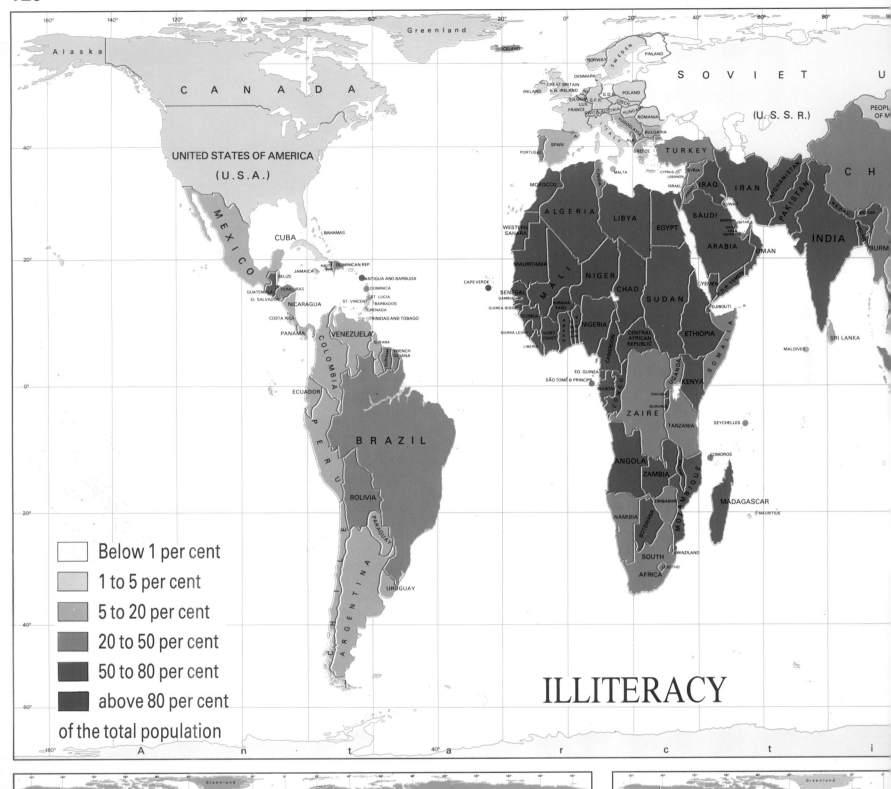

Below 1 per cent

1 to 5 per cent

5 to 20 per cent

20 to 50 per cent

50 to 80 per cent

above 80 per cent

of the total population

ILLITERACY

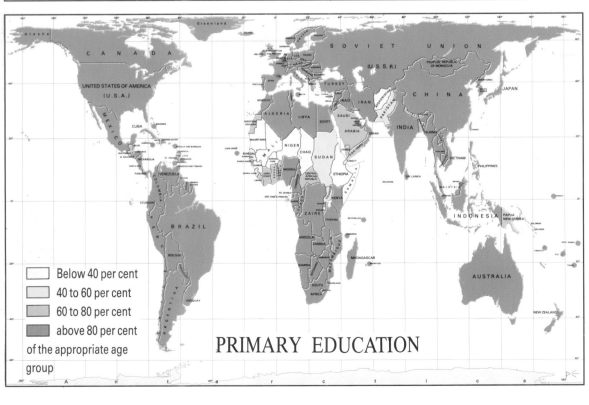

Below 40 per cent

40 to 60 per cent

60 to 80 per cent

above 80 per cent

of the appropriate age group

PRIMARY EDUCATION

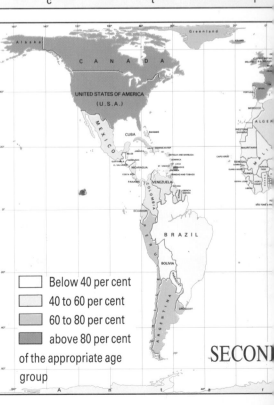

Below 40 per cent

40 to 60 per cent

60 to 80 per cent

above 80 per cent

of the appropriate age group

SECOND

EDUC

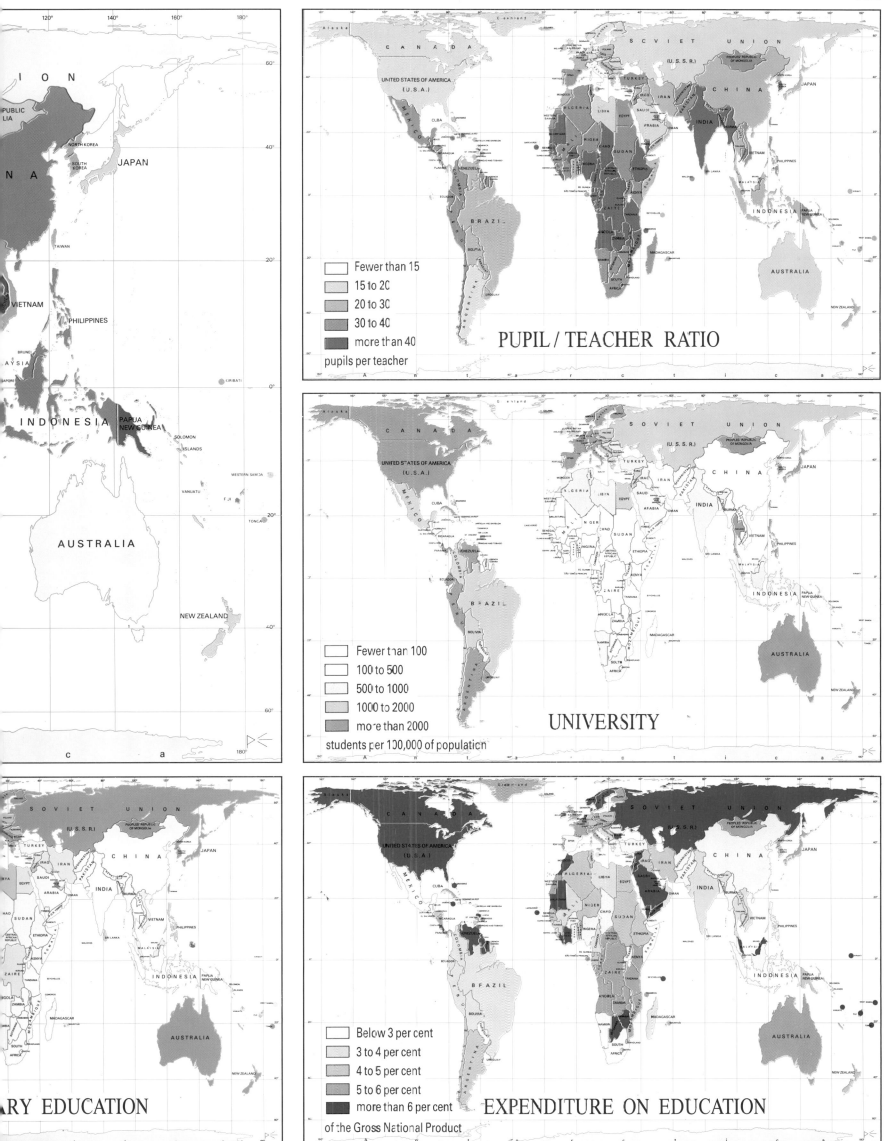

PUPIL / TEACHER RATIO

Fewer than 15
15 to 20
20 to 30
30 to 40
more than 40
pupils per teacher

UNIVERSITY

Fewer than 100
100 to 500
500 to 1000
1000 to 2000
more than 2000
students per 100,000 of population

ARY EDUCATION

EXPENDITURE ON EDUCATION

Below 3 per cent
3 to 4 per cent
4 to 5 per cent
5 to 6 per cent
more than 6 per cent
of the Gross National Product

ATION

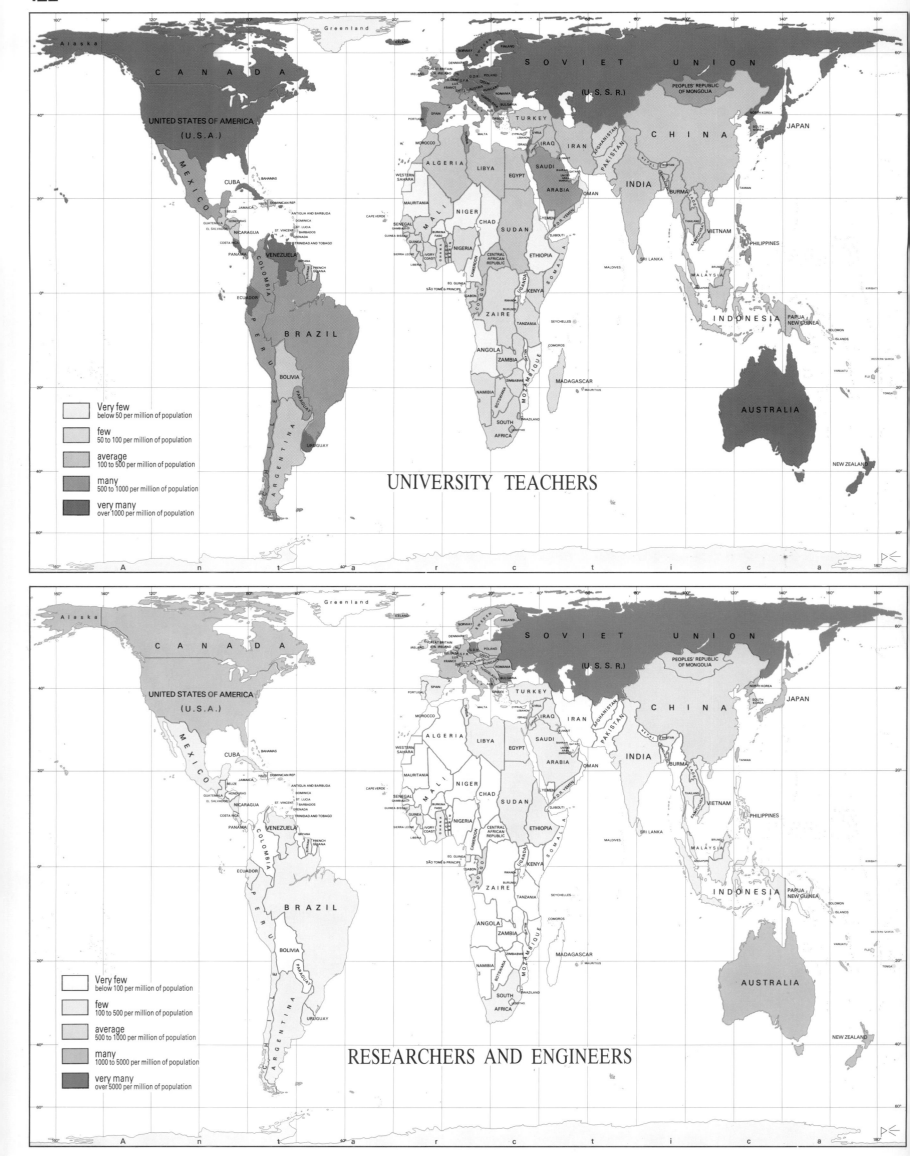

UNIVERSITY TEACHERS

Very few
below 50 per million of population

few
50 to 100 per million of population

average
100 to 500 per million of population

many
500 to 1000 per million of population

very many
over 1000 per million of population

RESEARCHERS AND ENGINEERS

Very few
below 100 per million of population

few
100 to 500 per million of population

average
500 to 1000 per million of population

many
1000 to 5000 per million of population

very many
over 5000 per million of population

THE SC

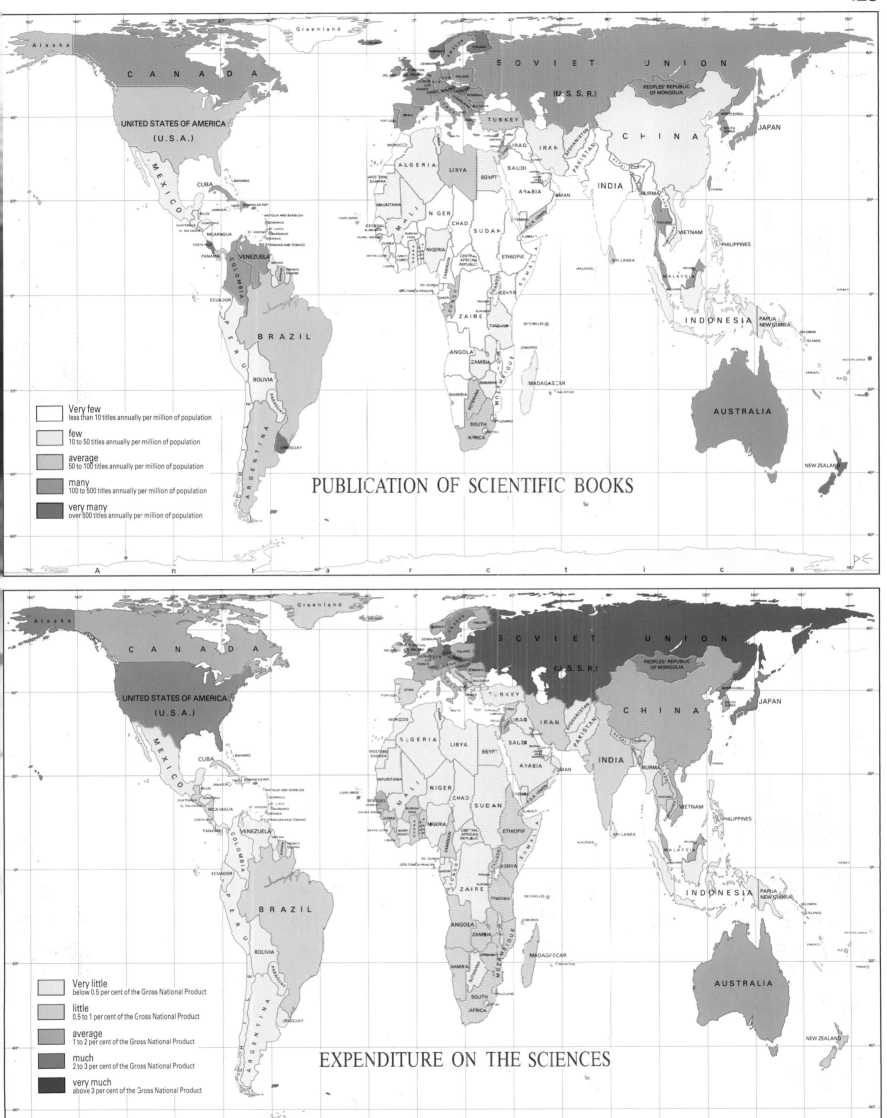

PUBLICATION OF SCIENTIFIC BOOKS

	Very few
	less than 10 titles annually per million of population
	few
	10 to 50 titles annually per million of population
	average
	50 to 100 titles annually per million of population
	many
	100 to 500 titles annually per million of population
	very many
	over 500 titles annually per million of population

EXPENDITURE ON THE SCIENCES

	Very little
	below 0.5 per cent of the Gross National Product
	little
	0.5 to 1 per cent of the Gross National Product
	average
	1 to 2 per cent of the Gross National Product
	much
	2 to 3 per cent of the Gross National Product
	very much
	above 3 per cent of the Gross National Product

IENCES

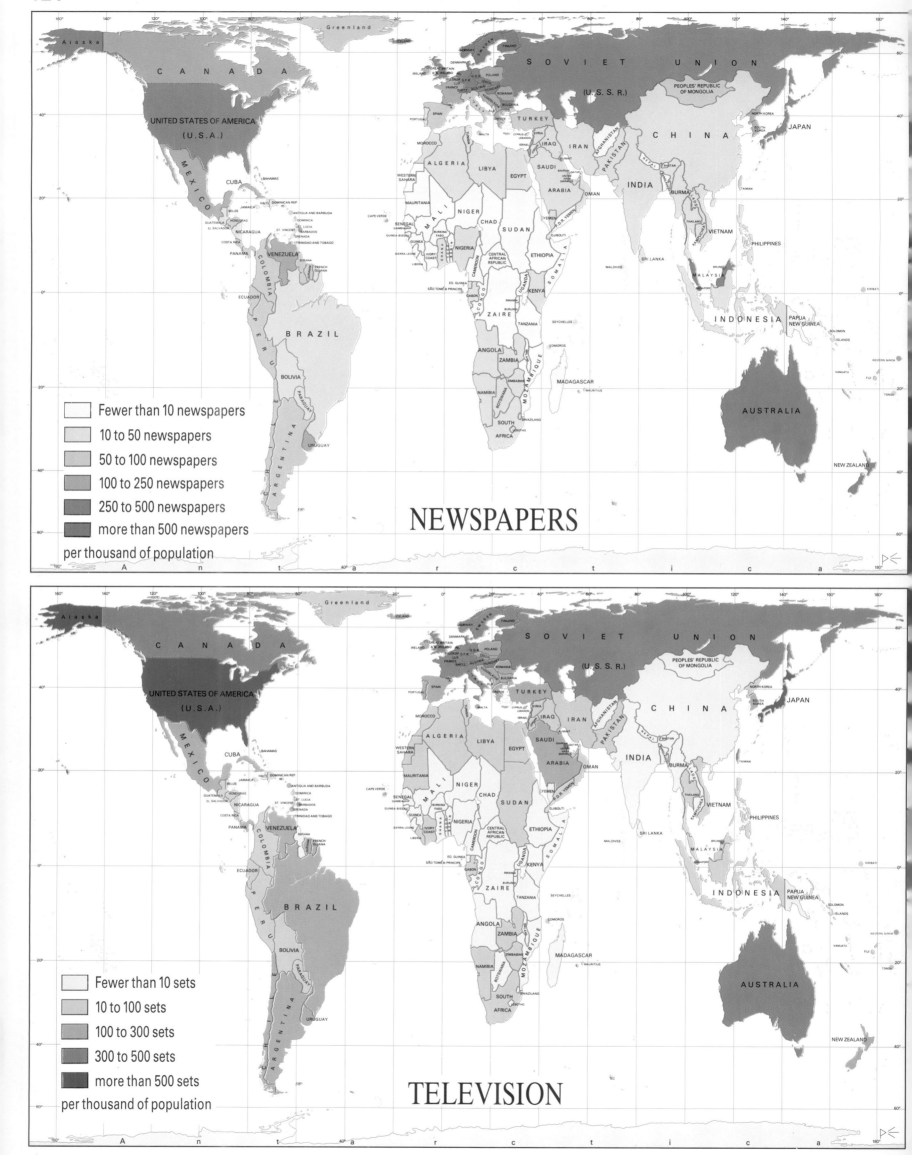

NEWSPAPERS

Fewer than 10 newspapers

10 to 50 newspapers

50 to 100 newspapers

100 to 250 newspapers

250 to 500 newspapers

more than 500 newspapers

per thousand of population

TELEVISION

Fewer than 10 sets

10 to 100 sets

100 to 300 sets

300 to 500 sets

more than 500 sets

per thousand of population

INFORM

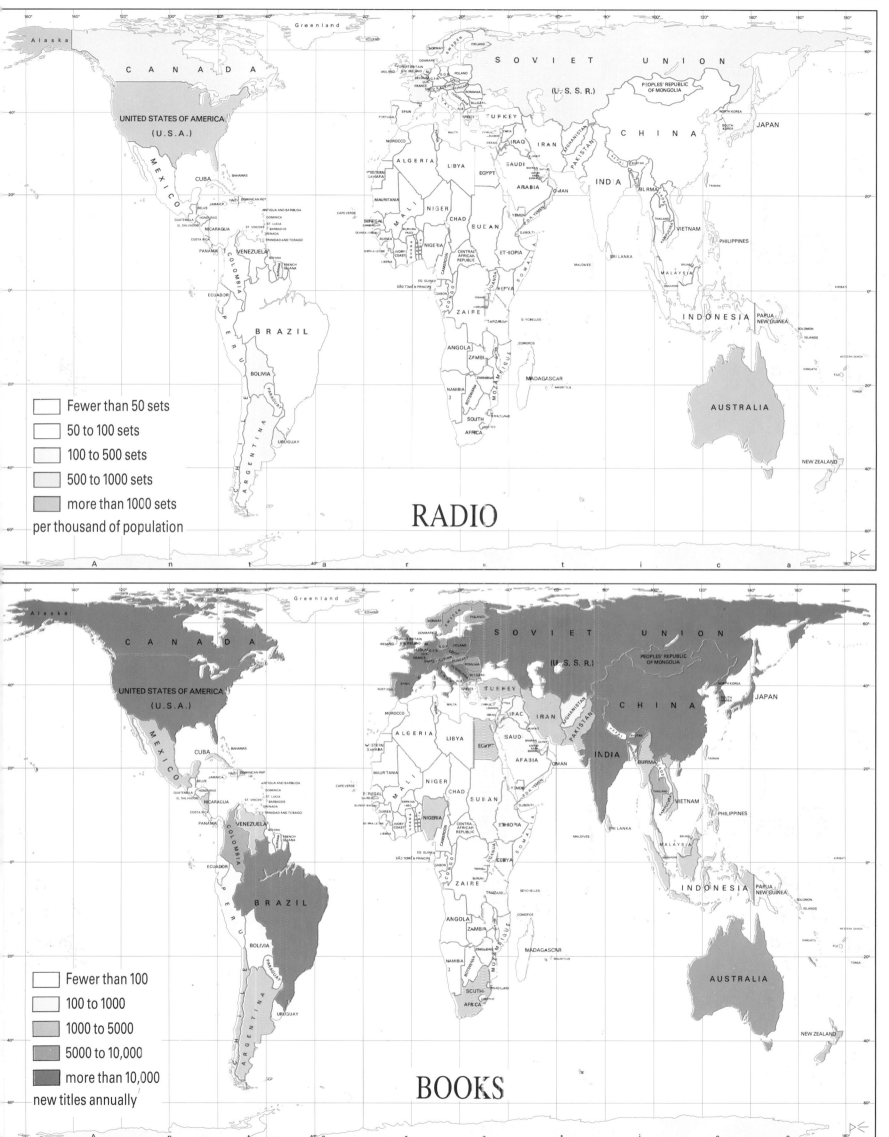

RADIO

Fewer than 50 sets
50 to 100 sets
100 to 500 sets
500 to 1000 sets
more than 1000 sets
per thousand of population

BOOKS

Fewer than 100
100 to 1000
1000 to 5000
5000 to 10,000
more than 10,000
new titles annually

MATION

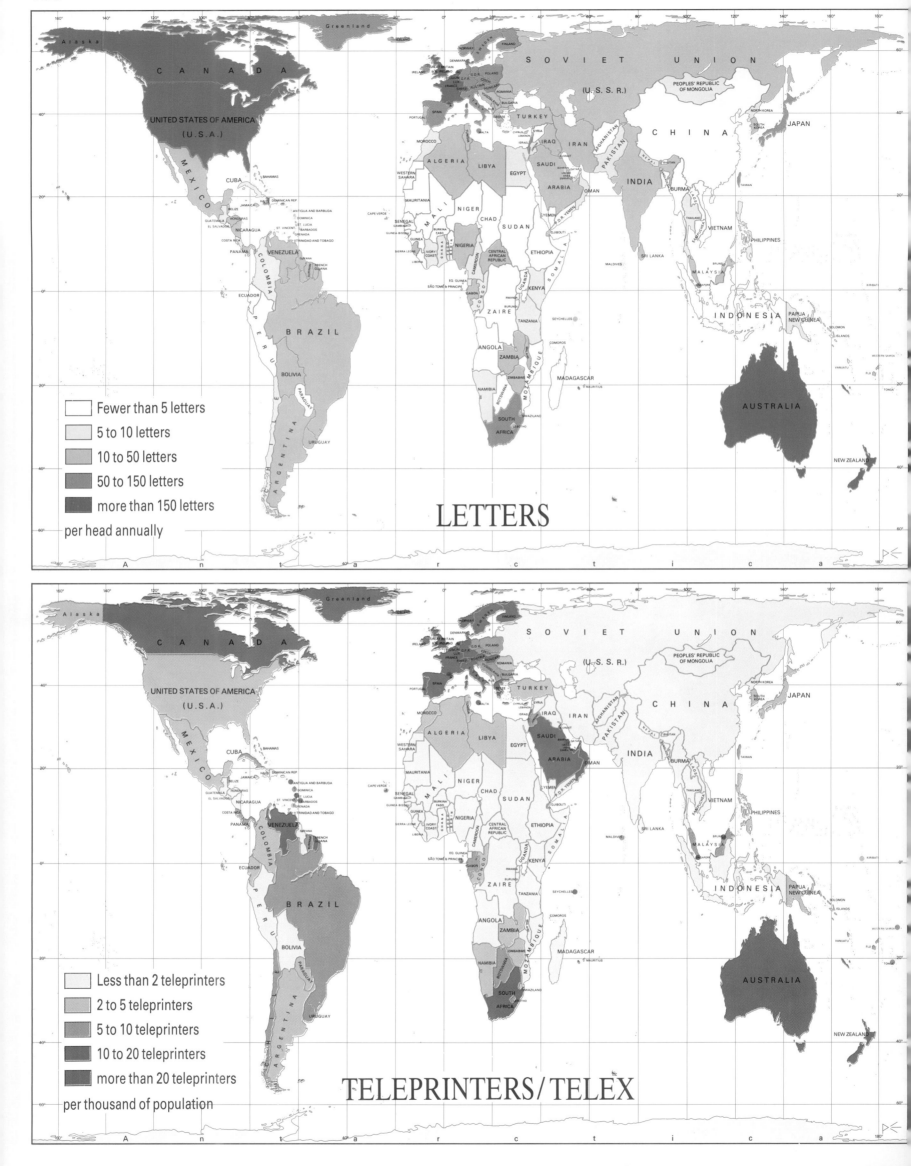

LETTERS

Fewer than 5 letters
5 to 10 letters
10 to 50 letters
50 to 150 letters
more than 150 letters
per head annually

TELEPRINTERS/TELEX

Less than 2 teleprinters
2 to 5 teleprinters
5 to 10 teleprinters
10 to 20 teleprinters
more than 20 teleprinters
per thousand of population

COMMUN

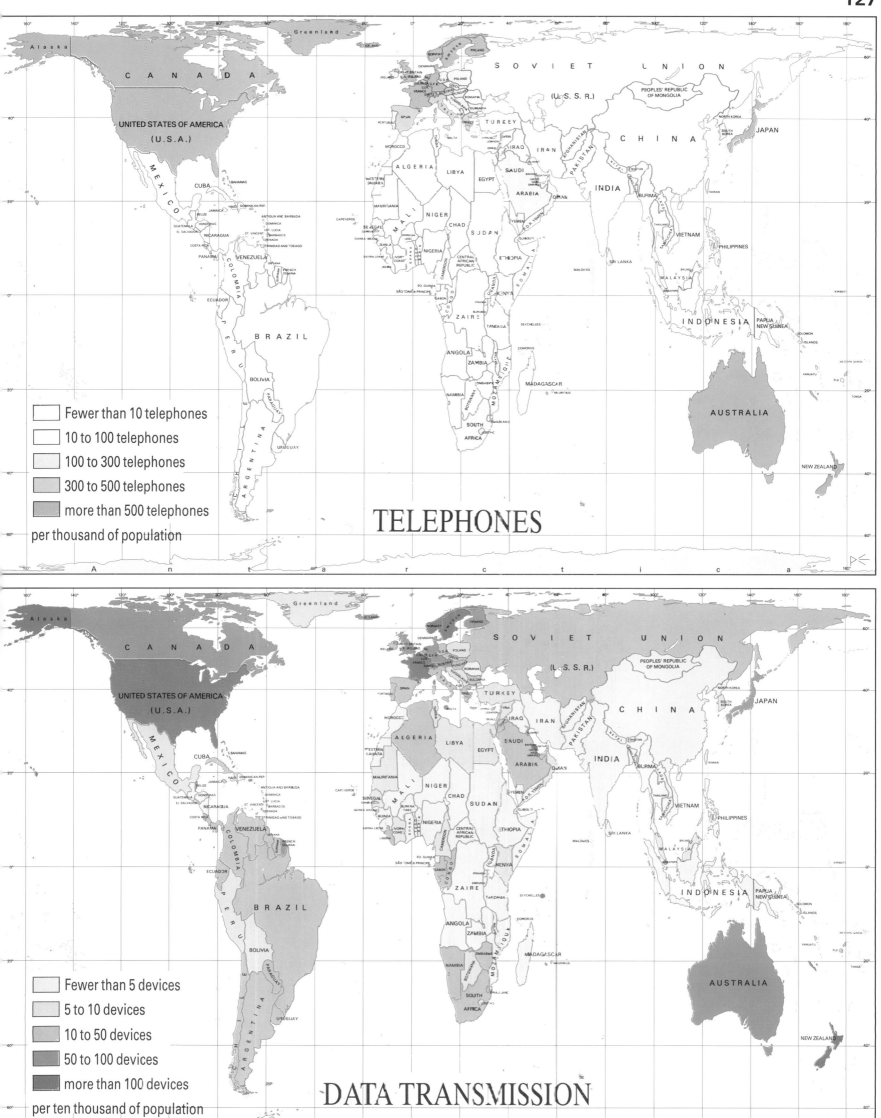

TELEPHONES

Fewer than 10 telephones
10 to 100 telephones
100 to 300 telephones
300 to 500 telephones
more than 500 telephones
per thousand of population

DATA TRANSMISSION

Fewer than 5 devices
5 to 10 devices
10 to 50 devices
50 to 100 devices
more than 100 devices
per ten thousand of population

ICATIONS

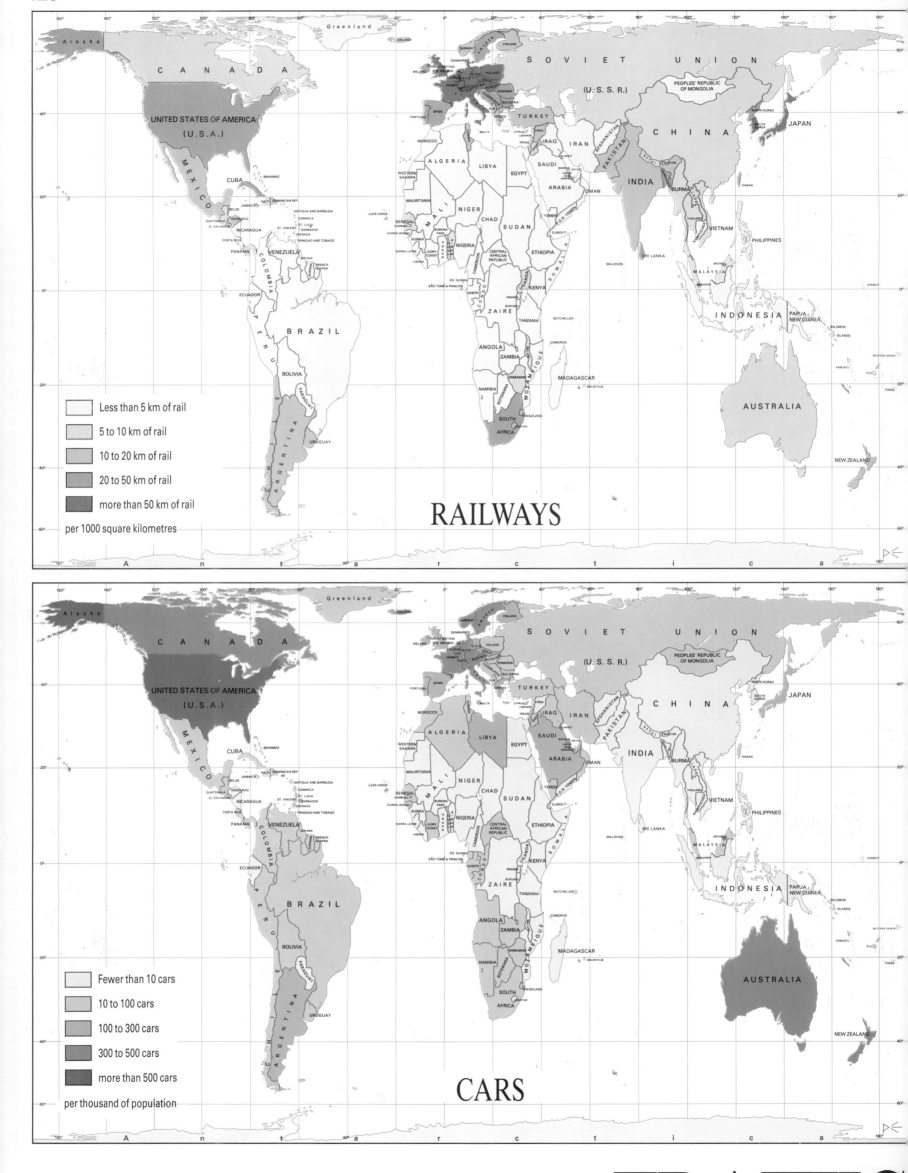

RAILWAYS

Less than 5 km of rail
5 to 10 km of rail
10 to 20 km of rail
20 to 50 km of rail
more than 50 km of rail

per 1000 square kilometres

CARS

Fewer than 10 cars
10 to 100 cars
100 to 300 cars
300 to 500 cars
more than 500 cars

per thousand of population

TRAFFIC

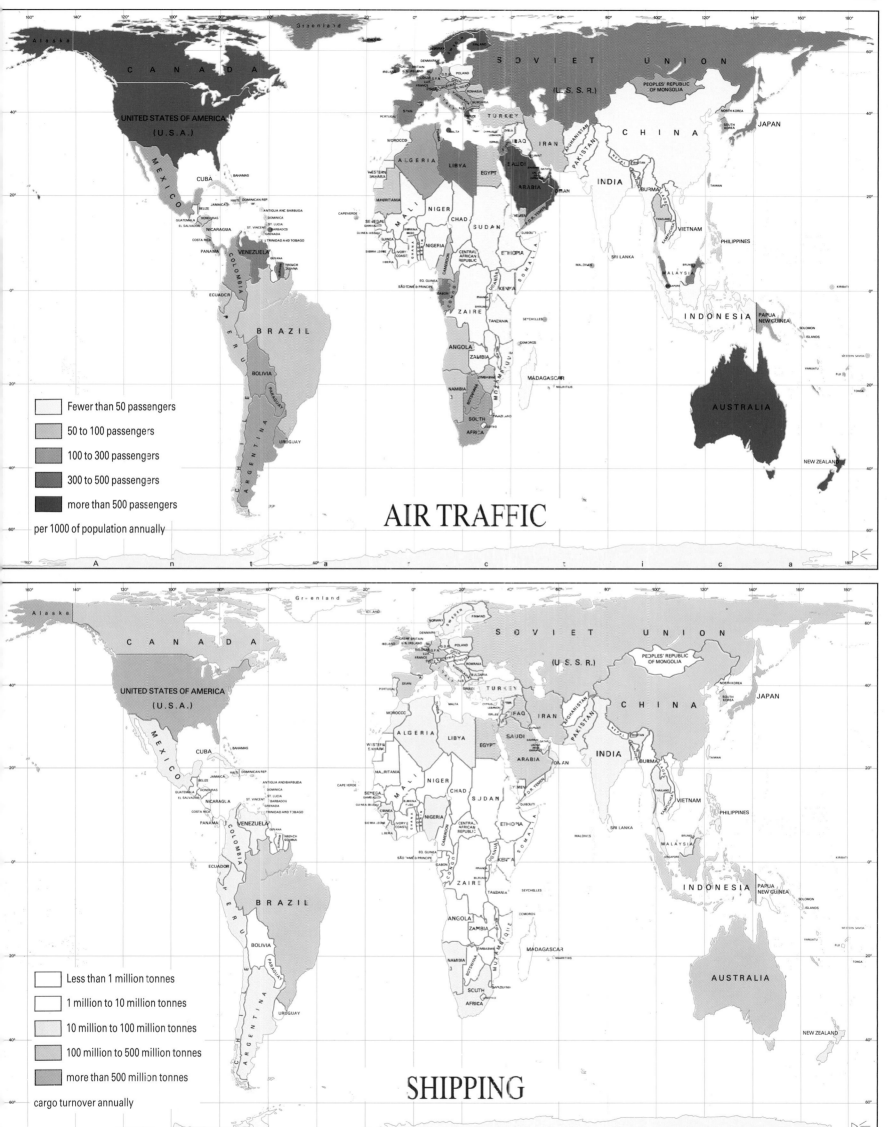

AIR TRAFFIC

Fewer than 50 passengers
50 to 100 passengers
100 to 300 passengers
300 to 500 passengers
more than 500 passengers

per 1000 of population annually

SHIPPING

Less than 1 million tonnes
1 million to 10 million tonnes
10 million to 100 million tonnes
100 million to 500 million tonnes
more than 500 million tonnes

cargo turnover annually

DENSITY

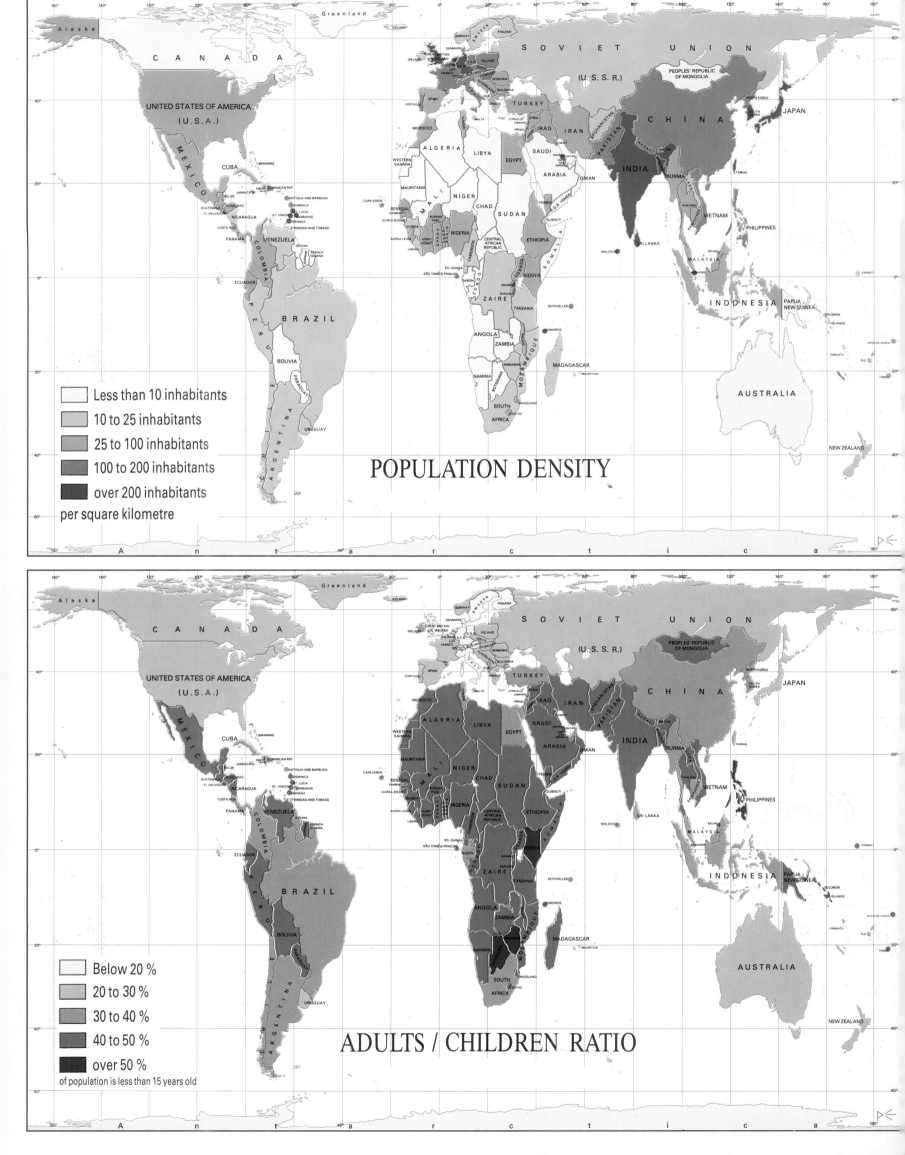

POPULATION DENSITY

Less than 10 inhabitants
10 to 25 inhabitants
25 to 100 inhabitants
100 to 200 inhabitants
over 200 inhabitants
per square kilometre

ADULTS / CHILDREN RATIO

Below 20 %
20 to 30 %
30 to 40 %
40 to 50 %
over 50 %
of population is less than 15 years old

POPULATION

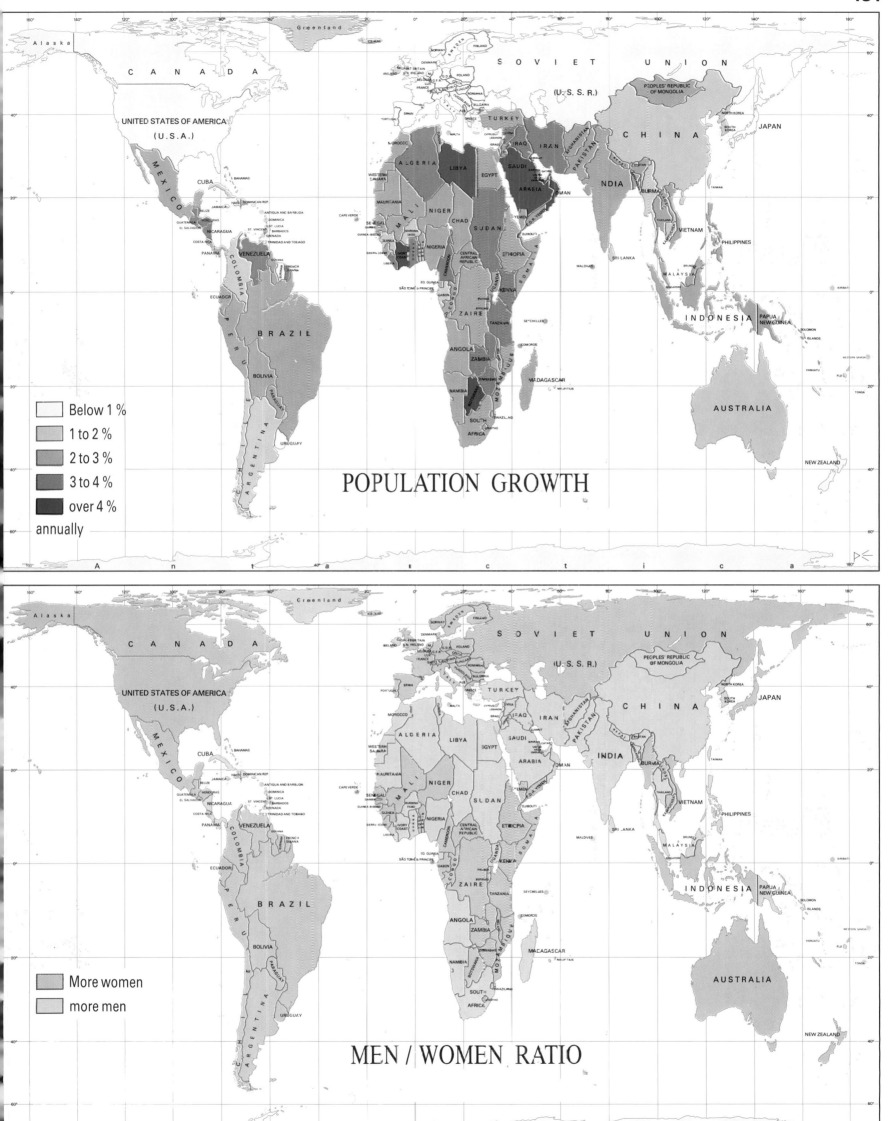

POPULATION GROWTH

Below 1 %
1 to 2 %
2 to 3 %
3 to 4 %
over 4 %
annually

MEN / WOMEN RATIO

More women
more men

STRUCTURE

Less than 45 years

45 to 55 years

56 to 65 years

66 to 75 years

above 75 years

LIFE EXP

ECTANCY

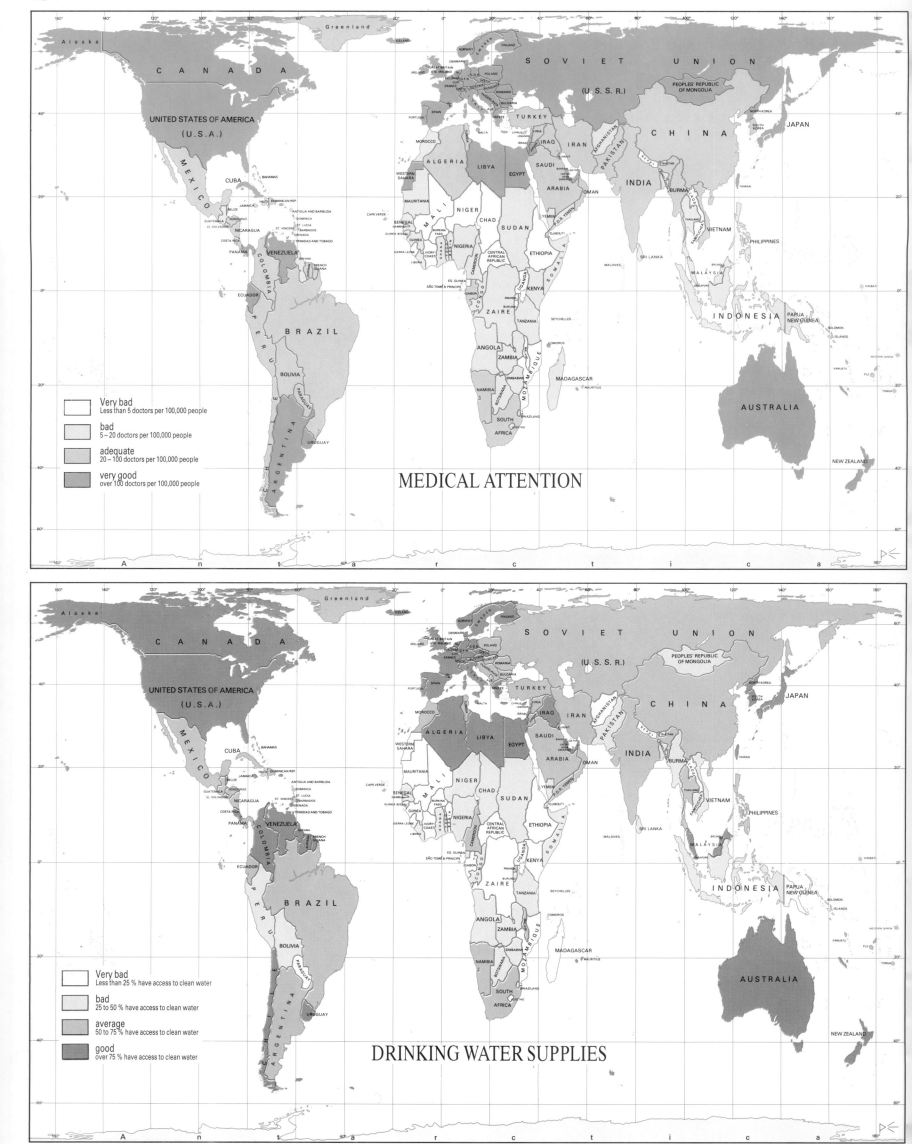

MEDICAL ATTENTION

Very bad
Less than 5 doctors per 100,000 people

bad
5 – 20 doctors per 100,000 people

adequate
20 – 100 doctors per 100,000 people

very good
over 100 doctors per 100,000 people

DRINKING WATER SUPPLIES

Very bad
Less than 25 % have access to clean water

bad
25 to 50 % have access to clean water

average
50 to 75 % have access to clean water

good
over 75 % have access to clean water

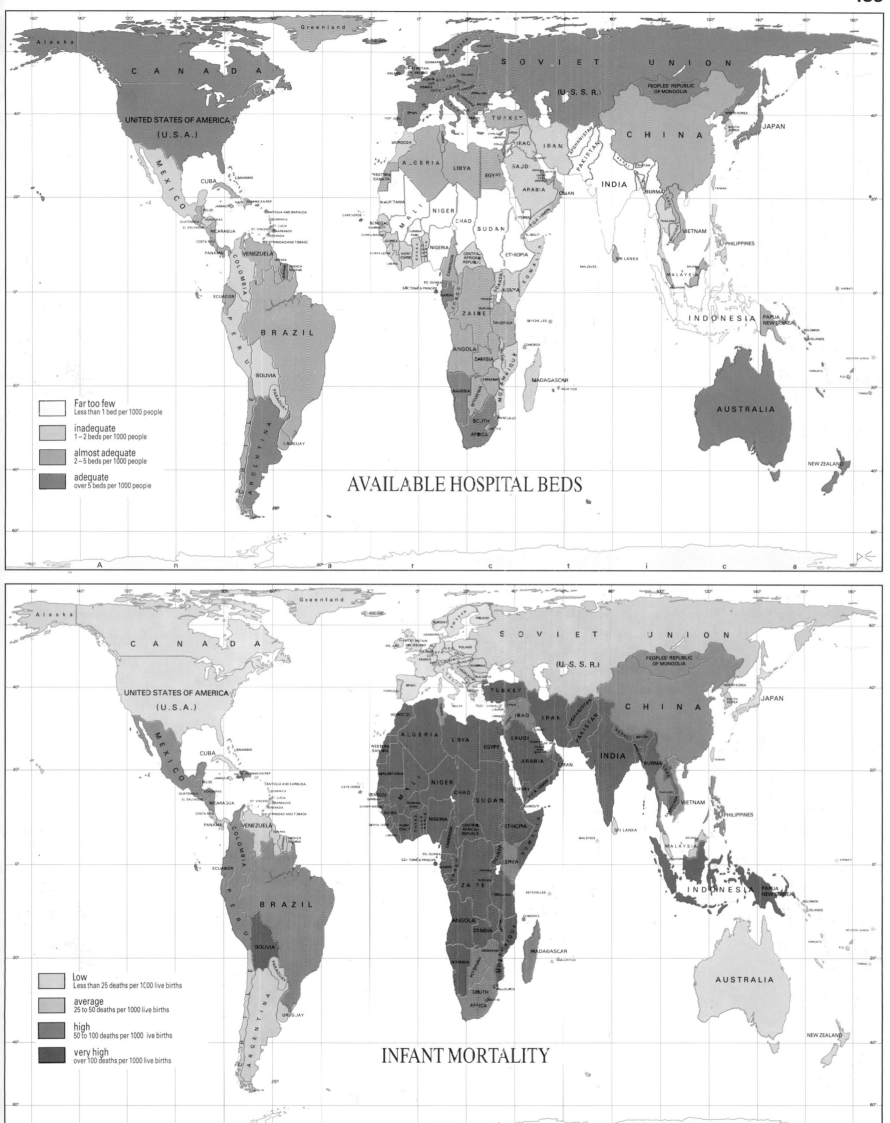

AVAILABLE HOSPITAL BEDS

Far too few
Less than 1 bed per 1000 people

inadequate
1 – 2 beds per 1000 people

almost adequate
2 – 5 beds per 1000 people

adequate
over 5 beds per 1000 people

INFANT MORTALITY

Low
Less than 25 deaths per 1000 live births

average
25 to 50 deaths per 1000 live births

high
50 to 100 deaths per 1000 live births

very high
over 100 deaths per 1000 live births

LTH

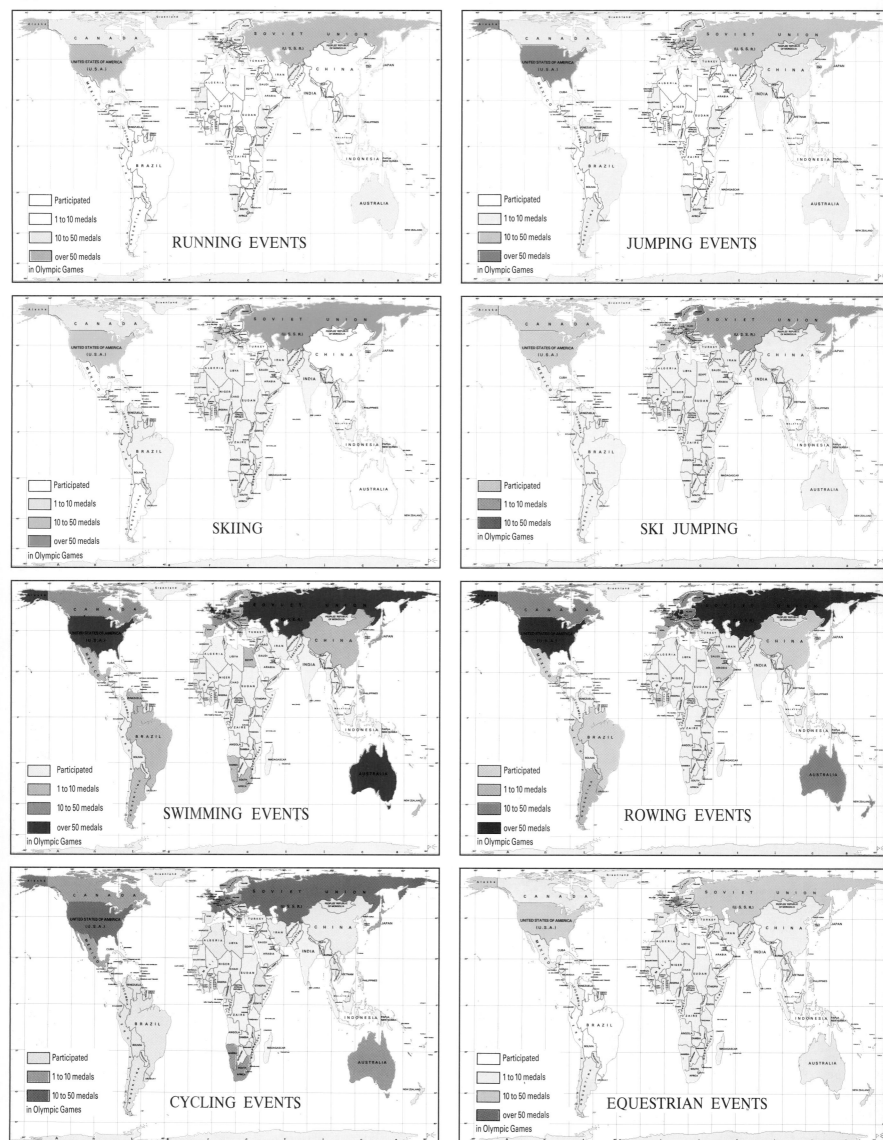

RUNNING EVENTS

Participated
1 to 10 medals
10 to 50 medals
over 50 medals
in Olympic Games

JUMPING EVENTS

Participated
1 to 10 medals
10 to 50 medals
over 50 medals
in Olympic Games

SKIING

Participated
1 to 10 medals
10 to 50 medals
over 50 medals
in Olympic Games

SKI JUMPING

Participated
1 to 10 medals
10 to 50 medals
in Olympic Games

SWIMMING EVENTS

Participated
1 to 10 medals
10 to 50 medals
over 50 medals
in Olympic Games

ROWING EVENTS

Participated
1 to 10 medals
10 to 50 medals
over 50 medals
in Olympic Games

CYCLING EVENTS

Participated
1 to 10 medals
10 to 50 medals
in Olympic Games

EQUESTRIAN EVENTS

Participated
1 to 10 medals
10 to 50 medals
over 50 medals
in Olympic Games

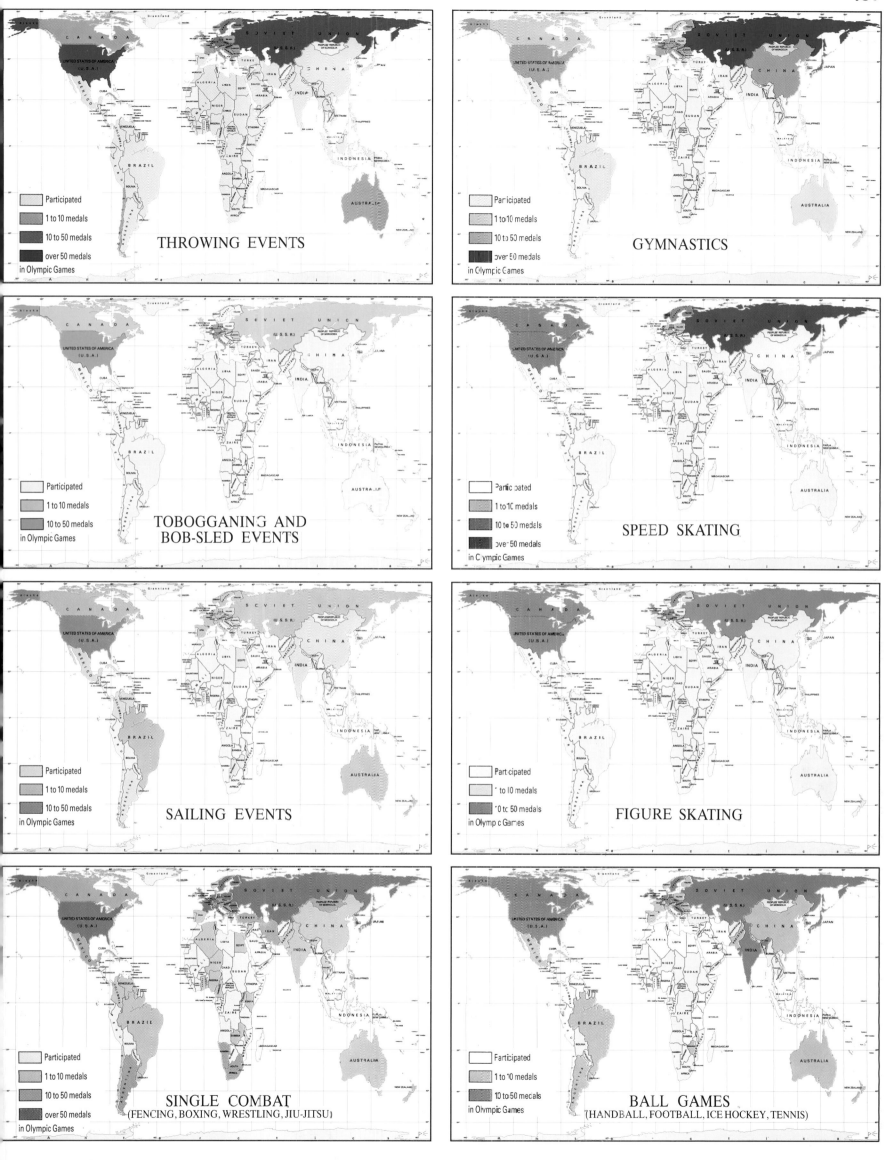

THROWING EVENTS

Participated
1 to 10 medals
10 to 50 medals
over 50 medals
in Olympic Games

GYMNASTICS

Participated
1 to 10 medals
10 to 50 medals
over 50 medals
in Olympic Games

TOBOGGANING AND BOB-SLED EVENTS

Participated
1 to 10 medals
10 to 50 medals
in Olympic Games

SPEED SKATING

Participated
1 to 10 medals
10 to 50 medals
over 50 medals
in Olympic Games

SAILING EVENTS

Participated
1 to 10 medals
10 to 50 medals
in Olympic Games

FIGURE SKATING

Participated
1 to 10 medals
10 to 50 medals
in Olympic Games

SINGLE COMBAT
(FENCING, BOXING, WRESTLING, JIU-JITSU)

Participated
1 to 10 medals
10 to 50 medals
over 50 medals
in Olympic Games

BALL GAMES
(HANDBALL, FOOTBALL, ICE HOCKEY, TENNIS)

Participated
1 to 10 medals
10 to 50 medals
in Olympic Games

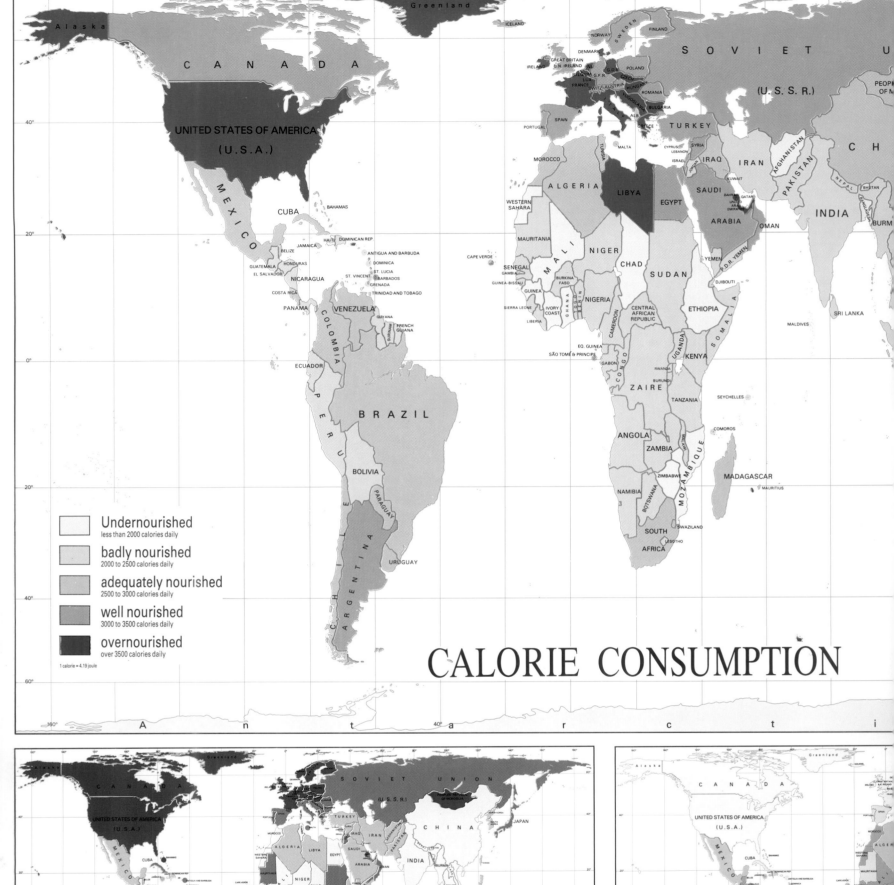

Undernourished
less than 2000 calories daily

badly nourished
2000 to 2500 calories daily

adequately nourished
2500 to 3000 calories daily

well nourished
3000 to 3500 calories daily

overnourished
over 3500 calories daily

1 calorie = 4.19 joule

CALORIE CONSUMPTION

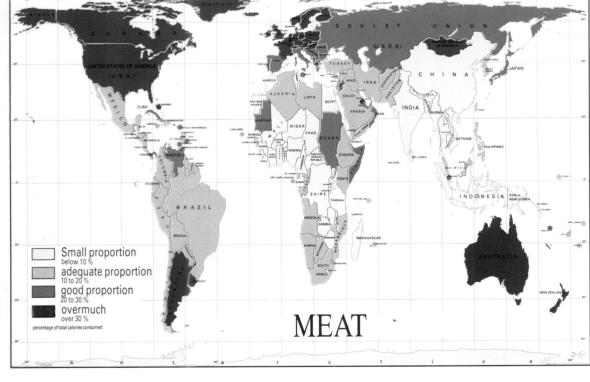

Small proportion
below 10 %

adequate proportion
10 to 20 %

good proportion
20 to 30 %

overmuch
over 30 %

percentage of total calories consumed

MEAT

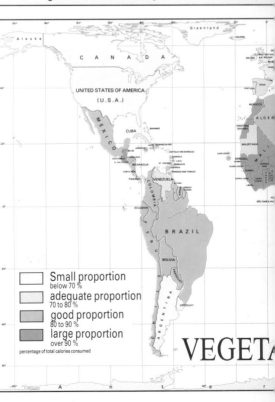

Small proportion
below 70 %

adequate proportion
70 to 80 %

good proportion
80 to 90 %

large proportion
over 90 %

percentage of total calories consumed

VEGETA

NUTR

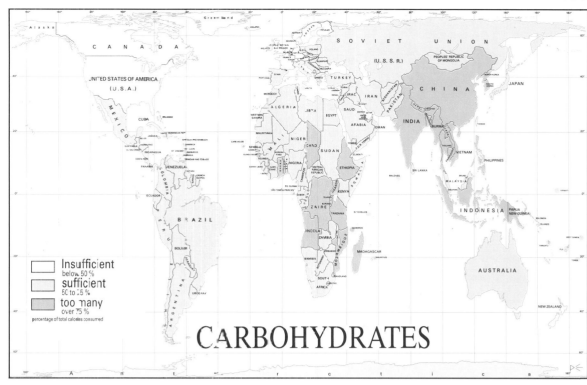

Insufficient
below 50 %

sufficient
50 to 75 %

too many
over 75 %

percentage of total calories consumed

CARBOHYDRATES

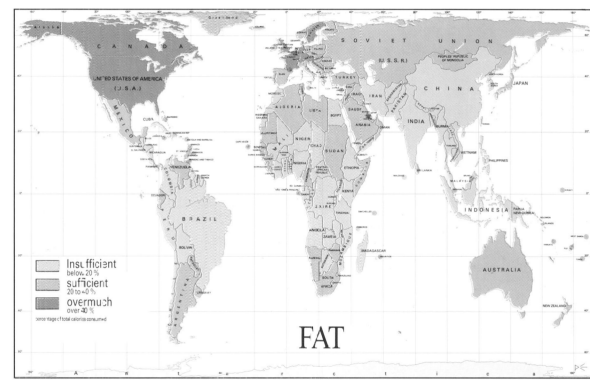

Insufficient
below 20 %

sufficient
20 to 40 %

overmuch
over 40 %

percentage of total calories consumed

FAT

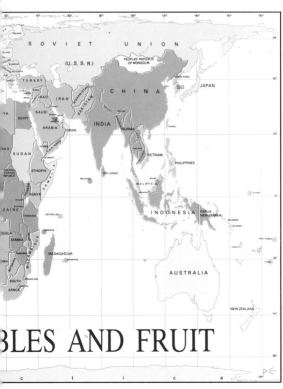

BLES AND FRUIT

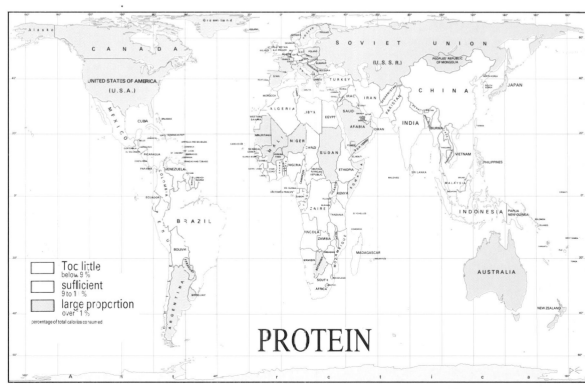

Too little
below 9 %

sufficient
9 to 1 %

large proportion
over 1 %

percentage of total calories consumed

PROTEIN

ITION

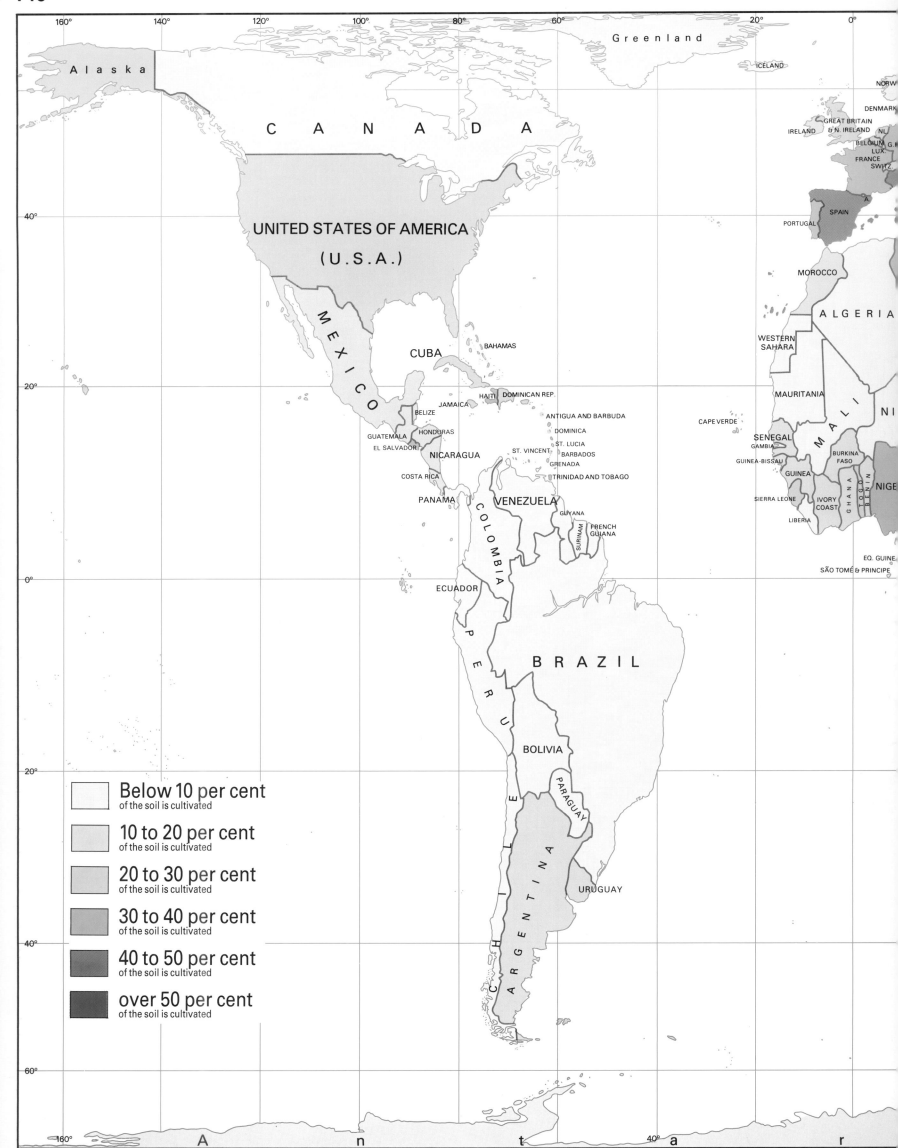

160° 140° 120° 100° 80° 60° 20° 0°

Greenland

ICELAND

NORW

Alaska

DENMARK

GREAT BRITAIN

IRELAND & N. IRELAND NL

BELGIUM G.R.

LUX.

FRANCE

SWITZ.

C A N A D A

40°

SPAIN

UNITED STATES OF AMERICA

PORTUGAL

(U.S.A.)

MOROCCO

A L G E R I A

WESTERN

SAHARA

CUBA

BAHAMAS

20°

M
E
X
I
C
O

MAURITANIA

M
A
L
I

N
I

JAMAICA HAITI DOMINICAN REP.

CAPE VERDE

BELIZE

ANTIGUA AND BARBUDA

SENEGAL

GUATEMALA HONDURAS DOMINICA

GAMBIA BURKINA

EL SALVADOR ST. LUCIA

GUINEA-BISSAU FASO

NICARAGUA ST. VINCENT BARBADOS

GUINEA

GRENADA

SIERRA LEONE

NIGE

COSTA RICA TRINIDAD AND TOBAGO

IVORY

G
H
A
N
A

T
O
G
O

B
E
N
I
N

COAST

PANAMA VENEZUELA

LIBERIA

EQ. GUINE.

C
O
L
O
M
B
I
A

GUYANA

SÃO TOMÉ & PRINCIPE

SURINAM

FRENCH

GUIANA

0°

ECUADOR

P
E
R
U

B R A Z I L

20°

BOLIVIA

P
A
R
A
G
U
A
Y

C
H
I
L
E

A
R
G
E
N
T
I
N
A

URUGUAY

40°

60°

160° A n t 40° a r

SOIL CUl

20° 40° 60° 80° 100° 120° 140° 160° 180°

60°

SWEDEN

FINLAND

S O V I E T   U N I O N

POLAND

CZECH

STRIA

HUNGARY

ROMANIA

YUGOSLAVIA

BULGARIA

ALB.

GREECE

T U R K E Y

MALTA

CYPRUS

LEBANON

SYRIA

ISRAEL

JORDAN

IRAQ

KUWAIT

I R A N

(U. S. S. R.)

PEOPLES' REPUBLIC
OF MONGOLIA

40°

NORTH KOREA

SOUTH
KOREA

JAPAN

C H I N A

AFGHANISTAN

PAKISTAN

NEPAL

BHUTAN

LIBYA

EGYPT

SAUDI

BAHRAIN QATAR

UNITED
ARAB
EMIRATES

A R A B I A

OMAN

INDIA

BANGLADESH

BURMA

20°

TAIWAN

CHAD

SUDAN

YEMEN

P.D.R. YEMEN

DJIBOUTI

LAOS

THAILAND

KAMPUCHEA

VIETNAM

PHILIPPINES

R

CENTRAL
AFRICAN
REPUBLIC

ETHIOPIA

SOMALIA

SRI LANKA

MALDIVES

BRUNE

M A L A Y S I A

KIRIBATI

0°

UGANDA

KENYA

CONGO

RWANDA

BURUNDI

ZAIRE

TANZANIA

SEYCHELLES

SINGAPORE

I N D O N E S I A

PAPUA
NEW GUINEA

SOLOMON

ISLANDS

COMOROS

WESTERN SAMOA

ANGOLA

MALAWI

MOZAMBIQUE

ZAMBIA

VANUATU

FIJI

ZIMBABWE

MADAGASCAR

MAURITIUS

20°

NAMIBIA

BOTSWANA

TONGA

SWAZILAND

SOUTH

LESOTHO

AFRICA

A U S T R A L I A

40°

N E W   Z E A L A N D

60°

c o n t i n e n t a

180°

TIVATION

Below 100 tons
per square kilometre of cultivated land

100 to 200 tons
per square kilometre of cultivated land

200 to 300 tons
per square kilometre of cultivated land

300 to 400 tons
per square kilometre of cultivated land

over 400 tons
per square kilometre of cultivated land

CROP

YIELD

144

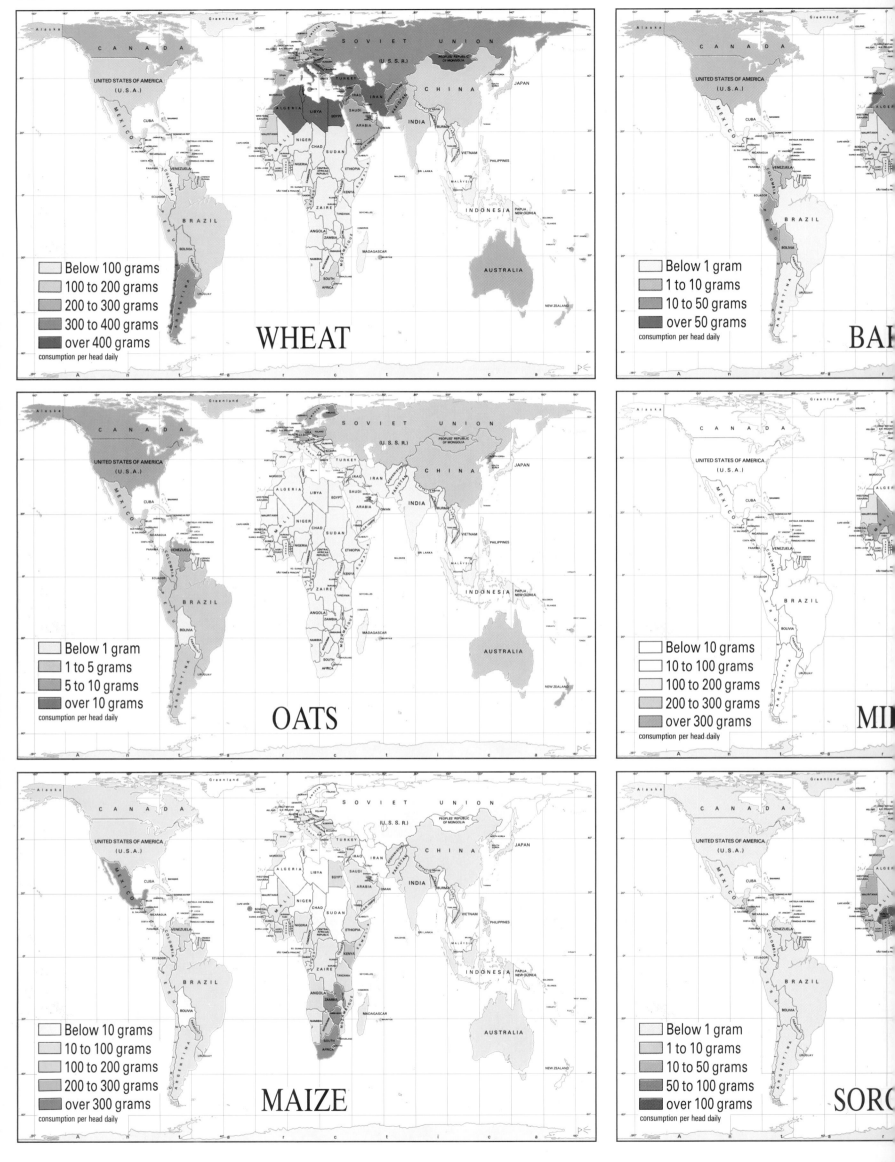

WHEAT

Below 100 grams
100 to 200 grams
200 to 300 grams
300 to 400 grams
over 400 grams
consumption per head daily

BAR

Below 1 gram
1 to 10 grams
10 to 50 grams
over 50 grams
consumption per head daily

OATS

Below 1 gram
1 to 5 grams
5 to 10 grams
over 10 grams
consumption per head daily

MI

Below 10 grams
10 to 100 grams
100 to 200 grams
200 to 300 grams
over 300 grams
consumption per head daily

MAIZE

Below 10 grams
10 to 100 grams
100 to 200 grams
200 to 300 grams
over 300 grams
consumption per head daily

SORG

Below 1 gram
1 to 10 grams
10 to 50 grams
50 to 100 grams
over 100 grams
consumption per head daily

STAPLE FO

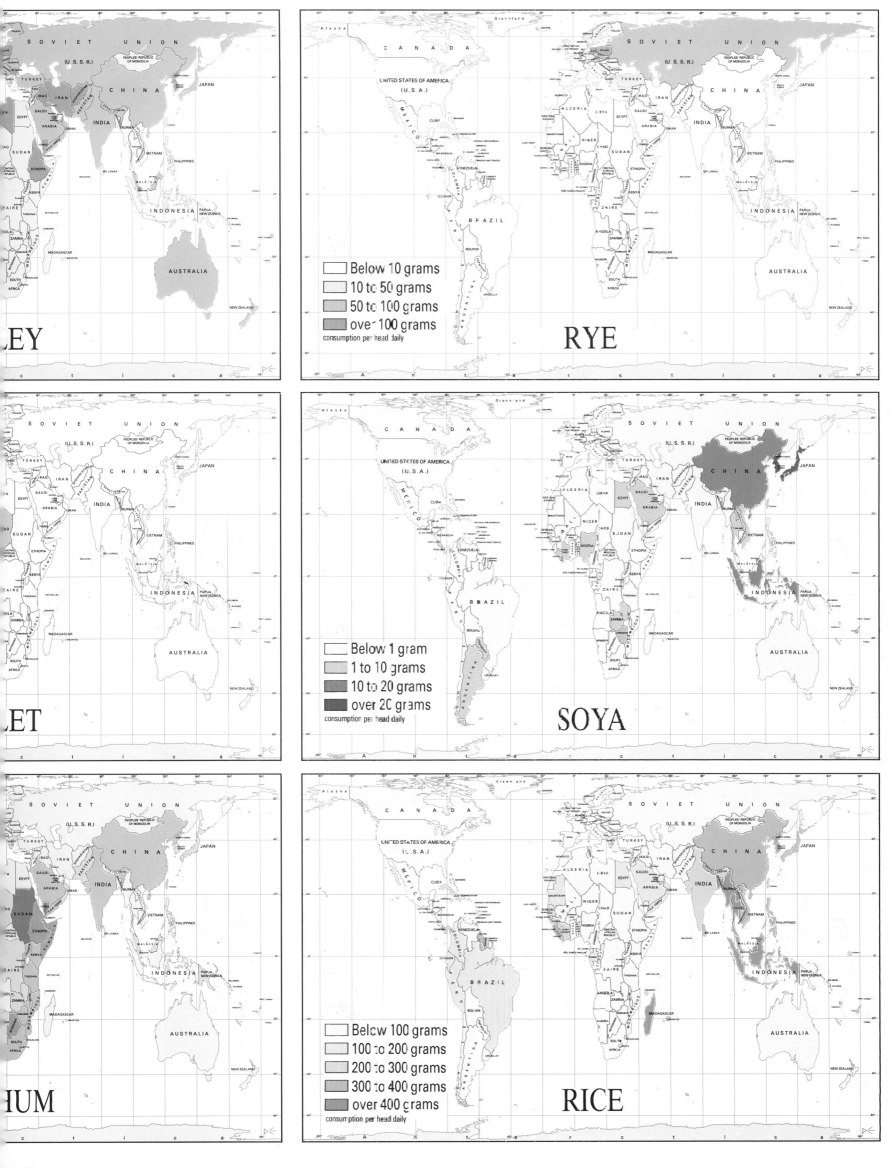

RYE

Below 10 grams
10 to 50 grams
50 to 100 grams
over 100 grams
consumption per head daily

EY

SOYA

Below 1 gram
1 to 10 grams
10 to 20 grams
over 20 grams
consumption per head daily

ET

RICE

Below 100 grams
100 to 200 grams
200 to 300 grams
300 to 400 grams
over 400 grams
consumption per head daily

UM

HUM

ODSTUFFS

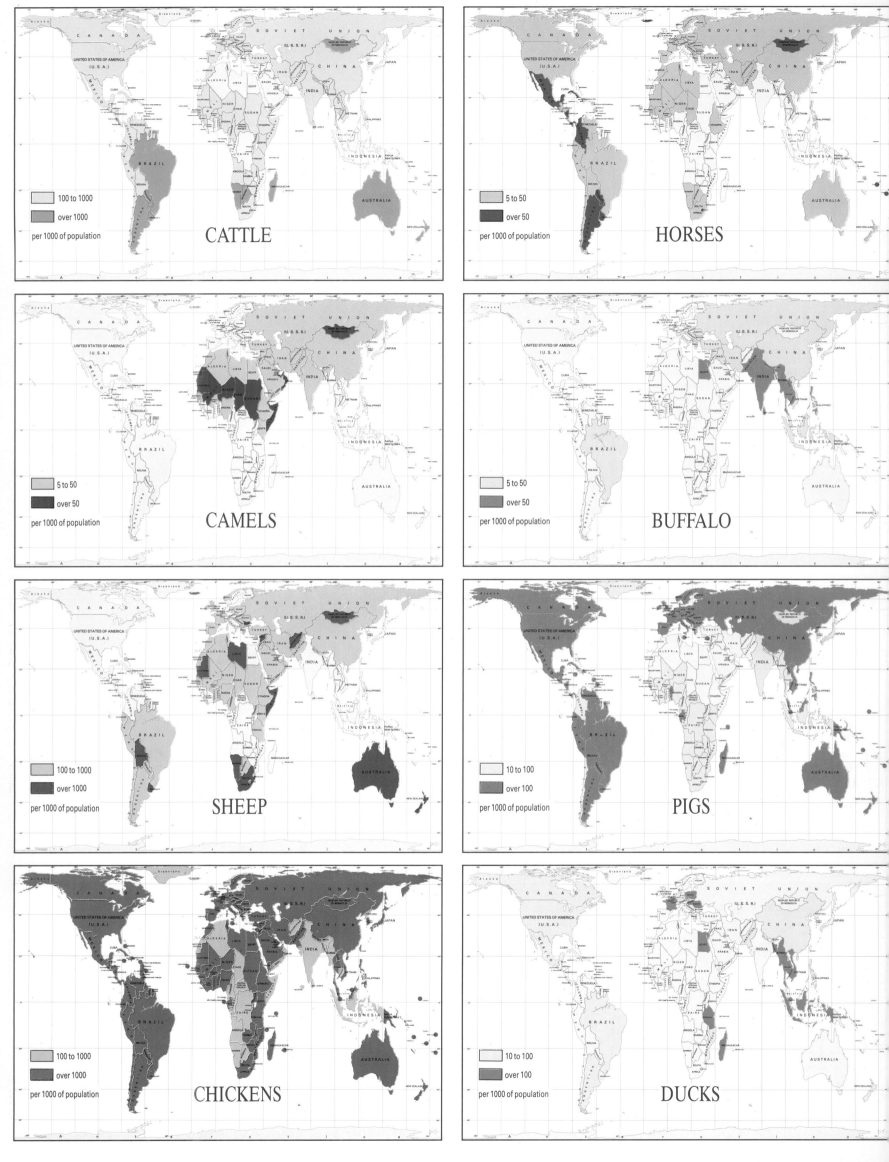

CATTLE

100 to 1000
over 1000
per 1000 of population

HORSES

5 to 50
over 50
per 1000 of population

CAMELS

5 to 50
over 50
per 1000 of population

BUFFALO

5 to 50
over 50
per 1000 of population

SHEEP

100 to 1000
over 1000
per 1000 of population

PIGS

10 to 100
over 100
per 1000 of population

CHICKENS

100 to 1000
over 1000
per 1000 of population

DUCKS

10 to 100
over 100
per 1000 of population

DOMESTIC

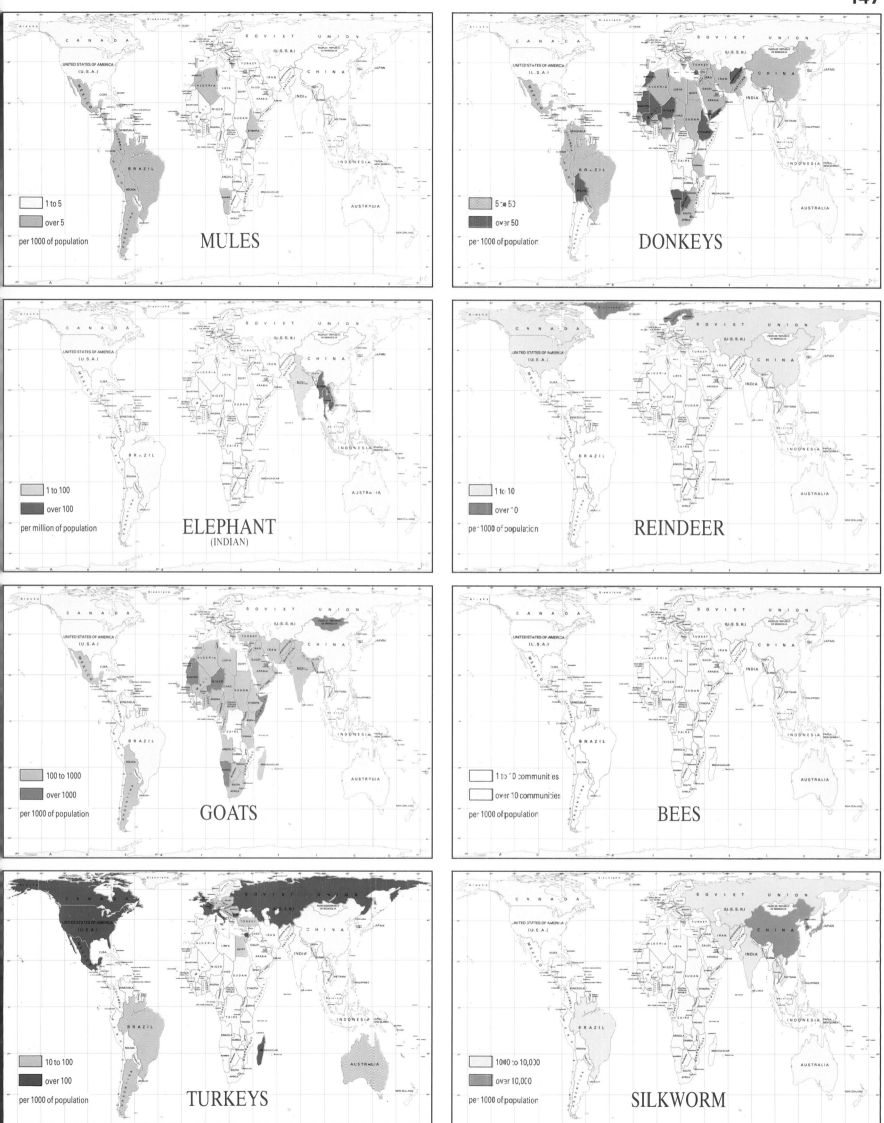

MULES

1 to 5
over 5

per 1000 of population

DONKEYS

5 to 50
over 50

per 1000 of population

ELEPHANT
(INDIAN)

1 to 100
over 100

per million of population

REINDEER

1 to 10
over 10

per 1000 of population

GOATS

100 to 1000
over 1000

per 1000 of population

BEES

1 to 10 communities
over 10 communities

per 1000 of population

TURKEYS

10 to 100
over 100

per 1000 of population

SILKWORM

1000 to 10,000
over 10,000

per 1000 of population

ANIMALS

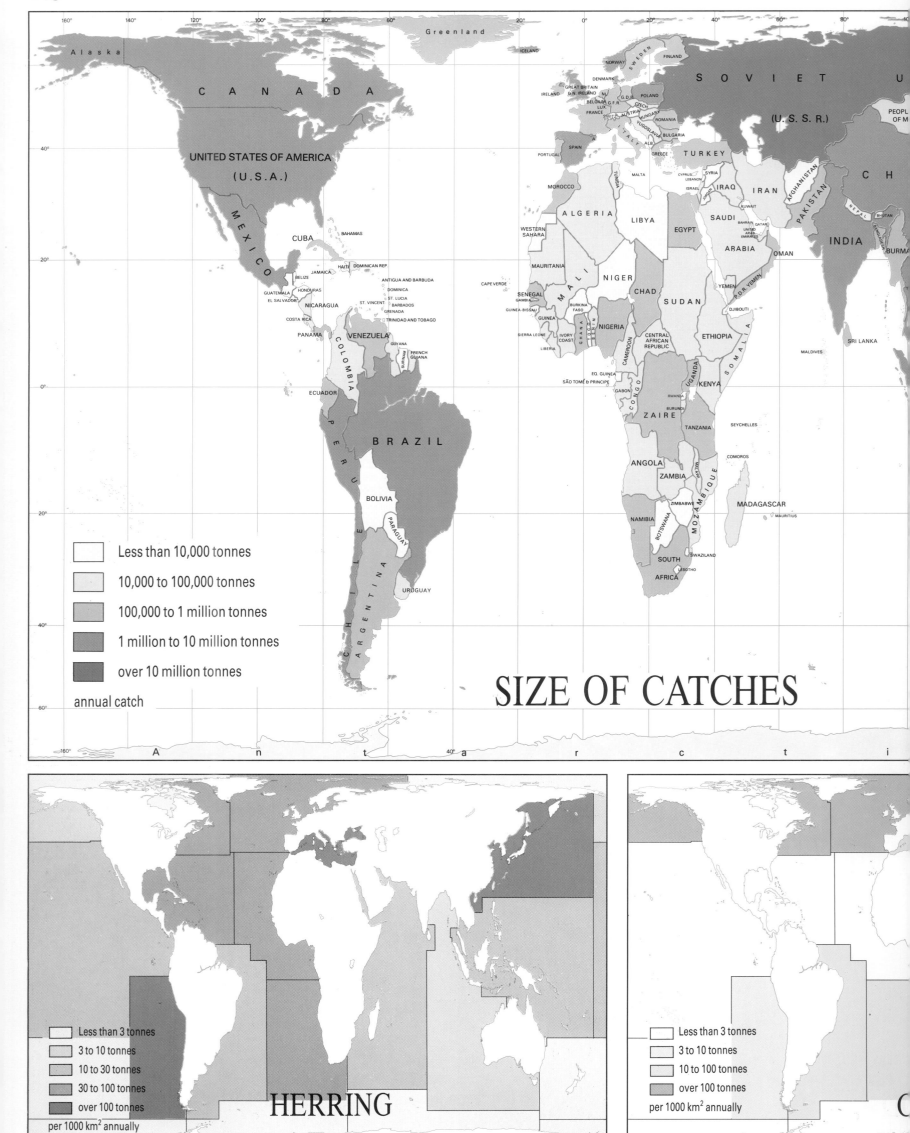

Greenland

ICELAND

C A N A D A

Alaska

UNITED STATES OF AMERICA
(U.S.A.)

MEXICO

CUBA
Bahamas

JAMAICA
HAITI DOMINICAN REP.

BELIZE
GUATEMALA
HONDURAS
EL SALVADOR
NICARAGUA
COSTA RICA
PANAMA

ANTIGUA AND BARBUDA
DOMINICA
ST. LUCIA
ST. VINCENT BARBADOS
GRENADA
TRINIDAD AND TOBAGO

VENEZUELA
GUYANA
COLOMBIA
SURINAM
FRENCH GUIANA

ECUADOR

P E R U

B R A Z I L

BOLIVIA

PARAGUAY

C H I L E

A R G E N T I N A

URUGUAY

S W E D E N
NORWAY FINLAND
DENMARK
GREAT BRITAIN
& N. IRELAND
IRELAND
NL G.D.R. POLAND
BELGIUM
LUX
FRANCE SWITZ AUSTRIA HUNGARY ROMANIA
ITALY YUGOSLAVIA BULGARIA
ALB
SPAIN GREECE
PORTUGAL

S O V I E T   U

(U.S.S.R.)

PEOPL
OF M

TURKEY

CYPRUS LEBANON SYRIA
ISRAEL IRAQ IRAN
JORDAN
KUWAIT

MOROCCO

ALGERIA
LIBYA
EGYPT
SAUDI
ARABIA

AFGHANISTAN
PAKISTAN

CH

NEPAL BHUTAN

INDIA BANGLADESH

BURMA

WESTERN
SAHARA

MAURITANIA

CAPE VERDE
SENEGAL
GAMBIA
GUINEA-BISSAU
GUINEA
SIERRA LEONE
LIBERIA

M A L I

BURKINA
FASO

IVORY
COAST
GHANA TOGO BENIN

N I G E R

NIGERIA

CHAD

SUDAN

BAHRAIN QATAR
UNITED
ARAB
EMIRATES
YEMEN
P.D.R. YEMEN

OMAN

DJIBOUTI

MALDIVES

SRI LANKA

EQ. GUINEA
SÃO TOMÉ & PRINCIPE

CAMEROON
CENTRAL
AFRICAN
REPUBLIC

GABON
CONGO

Z A I R E

RWANDA
BURUNDI

UGANDA
KENYA

S O M A L I A

ETHIOPIA

TANZANIA

SEYCHELLES

ANGOLA

ZAMBIA

MALAWI
MOZAMBIQUE

COMOROS

MADAGASCAR

MAURITIUS

NAMIBIA

BOTSWANA

ZIMBABWE

SWAZILAND

SOUTH
AFRICA

LESOTHO

Size of catches legend

☐	Less than 10,000 tonnes
☐	10,000 to 100,000 tonnes
☐	100,000 to 1 million tonnes
☐	1 million to 10 million tonnes
☐	over 10 million tonnes

annual catch

SIZE OF CATCHES

A   n   t   a   r   c   t   i

Herring legend

☐	Less than 3 tonnes
☐	3 to 10 tonnes
☐	10 to 30 tonnes
☐	30 to 100 tonnes
☐	over 100 tonnes

per 1000 km² annually

HERRING

legend

☐	Less than 3 tonnes
☐	3 to 10 tonnes
☐	10 to 100 tonnes
☐	over 100 tonnes

per 1000 km² annually

C

FISH

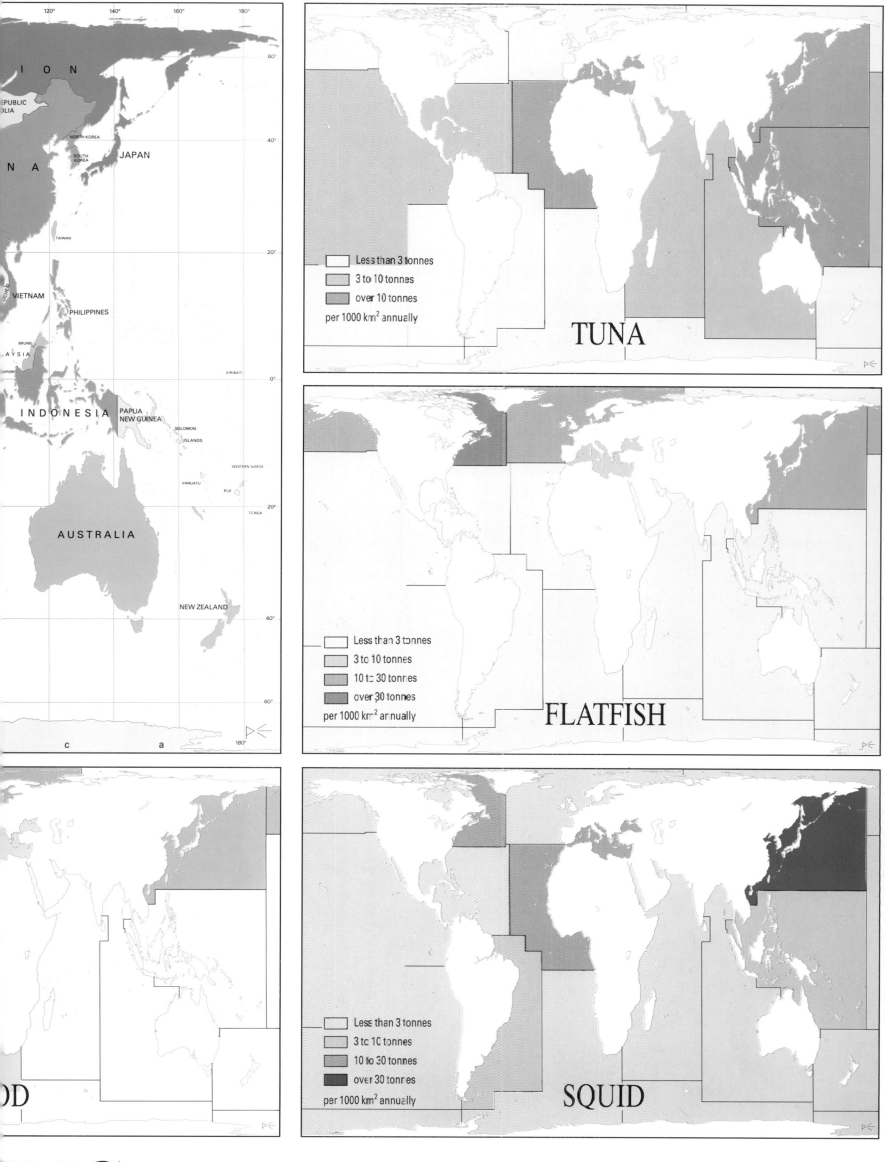

Less than 3 tonnes
3 to 10 tonnes
over 10 tonnes
per 1000 km² annually

TUNA

Less than 3 tonnes
3 to 10 tonnes
10 to 30 tonnes
over 30 tonnes
per 1000 km² annually

FLATFISH

Less than 3 tonnes
3 to 10 tonnes
10 to 30 tonnes
over 30 tonnes
per 1000 km² annually

SQUID

ING

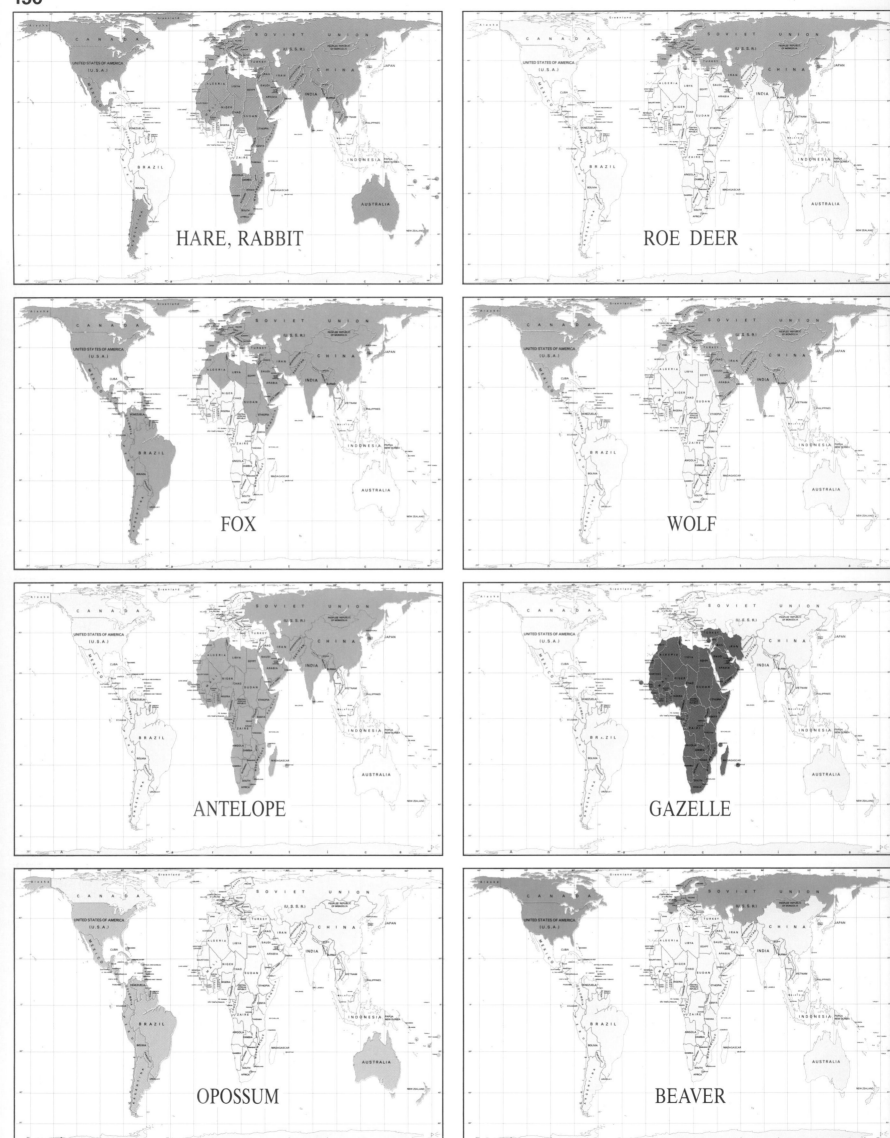

HARE, RABBIT

ROE DEER

FOX

WOLF

ANTELOPE

GAZELLE

OPOSSUM

BEAVER

HUN

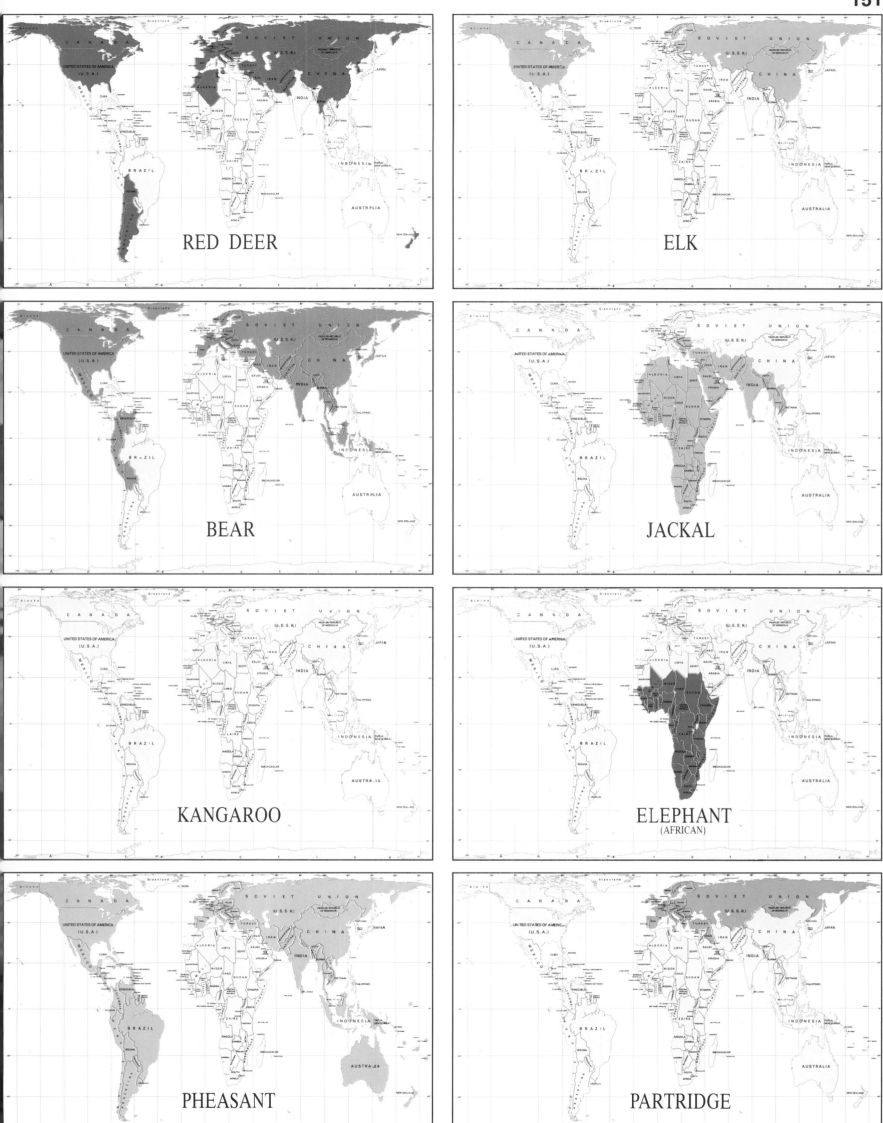

RED DEER

ELK

BEAR

JACKAL

KANGAROO

ELEPHANT
(AFRICAN)

PHEASANT

PARTRIDGE

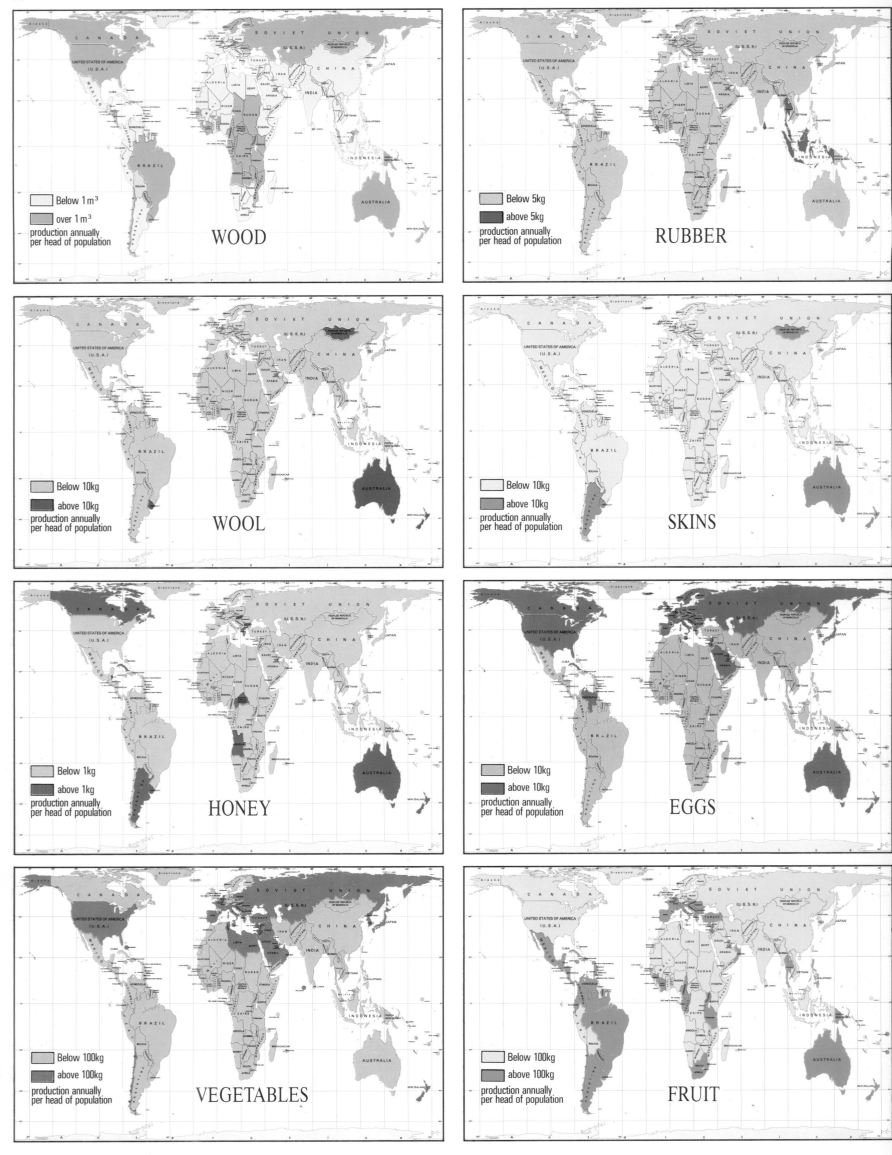

WOOD

Below 1 m³
over 1 m³
production annually
per head of population

RUBBER

Below 5kg
above 5kg
production annually
per head of population

WOOL

Below 10kg
above 10kg
production annually
per head of population

SKINS

Below 10kg
above 10kg
production annually
per head of population

HONEY

Below 1kg
above 1kg
production annually
per head of population

EGGS

Below 10kg
above 10kg
production annually
per head of population

VEGETABLES

Below 100kg
above 100kg
production annually
per head of population

FRUIT

Below 100kg
above 100kg
production annually
per head of population

NATURAL

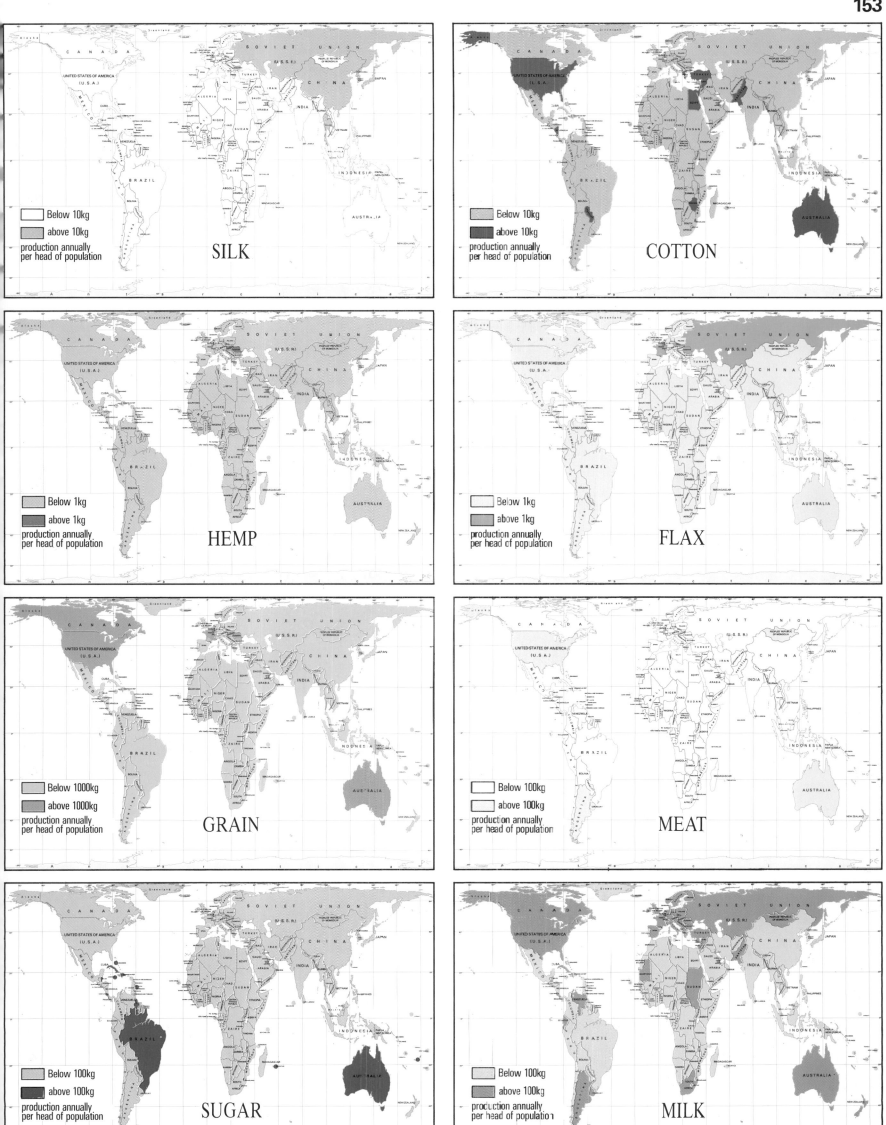

SILK

Below 10kg
above 10kg
production annually
per head of population

COTTON

Below 10kg
above 10kg
production annually
per head of population

HEMP

Below 1kg
above 1kg
production annually
per head of population

FLAX

Below 1kg
above 1kg
production annually
per head of population

GRAIN

Below 1000kg
above 1000kg
production annually
per head of population

MEAT

Below 100kg
above 100kg
production annually
per head of population

SUGAR

Below 100kg
above 100kg
production annually
per head of population

MILK

Below 100kg
above 100kg
production annually
per head of population

PRODUCTS

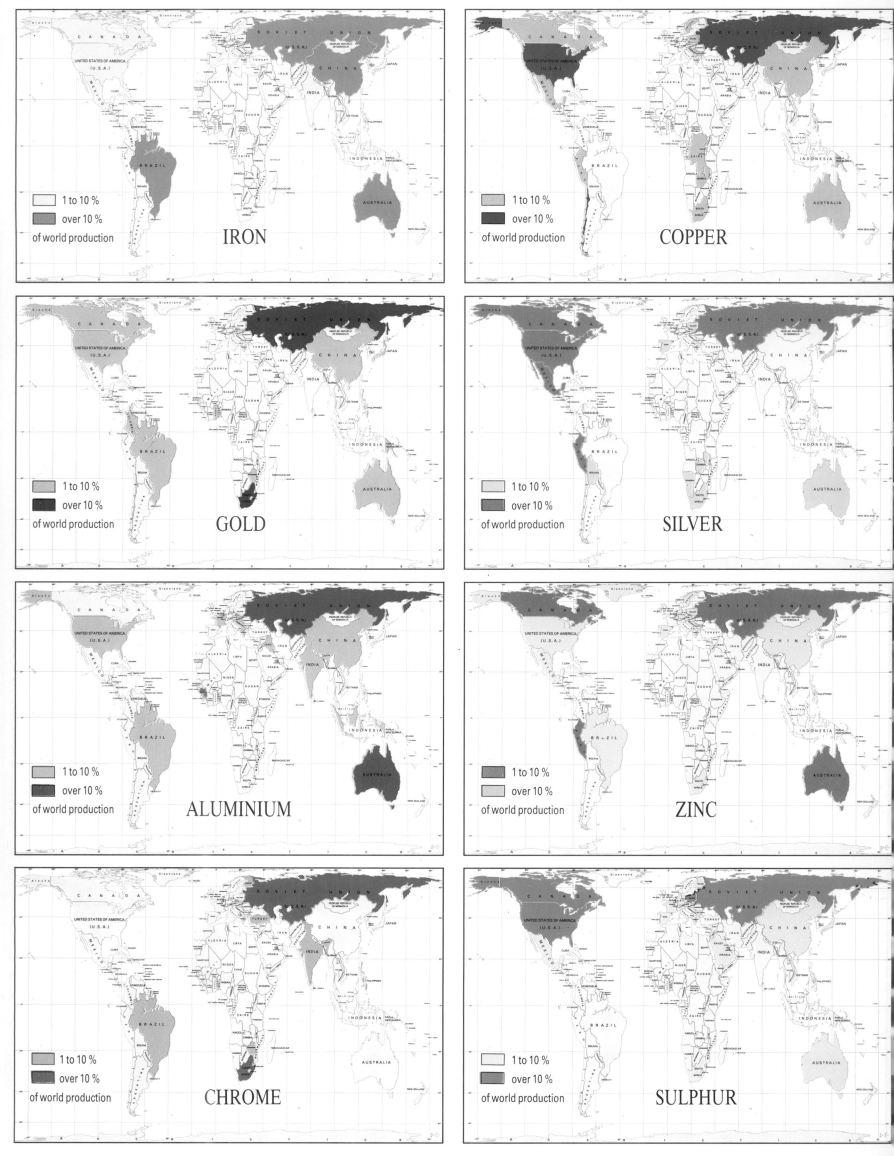

IRON

COPPER

GOLD

SILVER

ALUMINIUM

ZINC

CHROME

SULPHUR

MINERAL

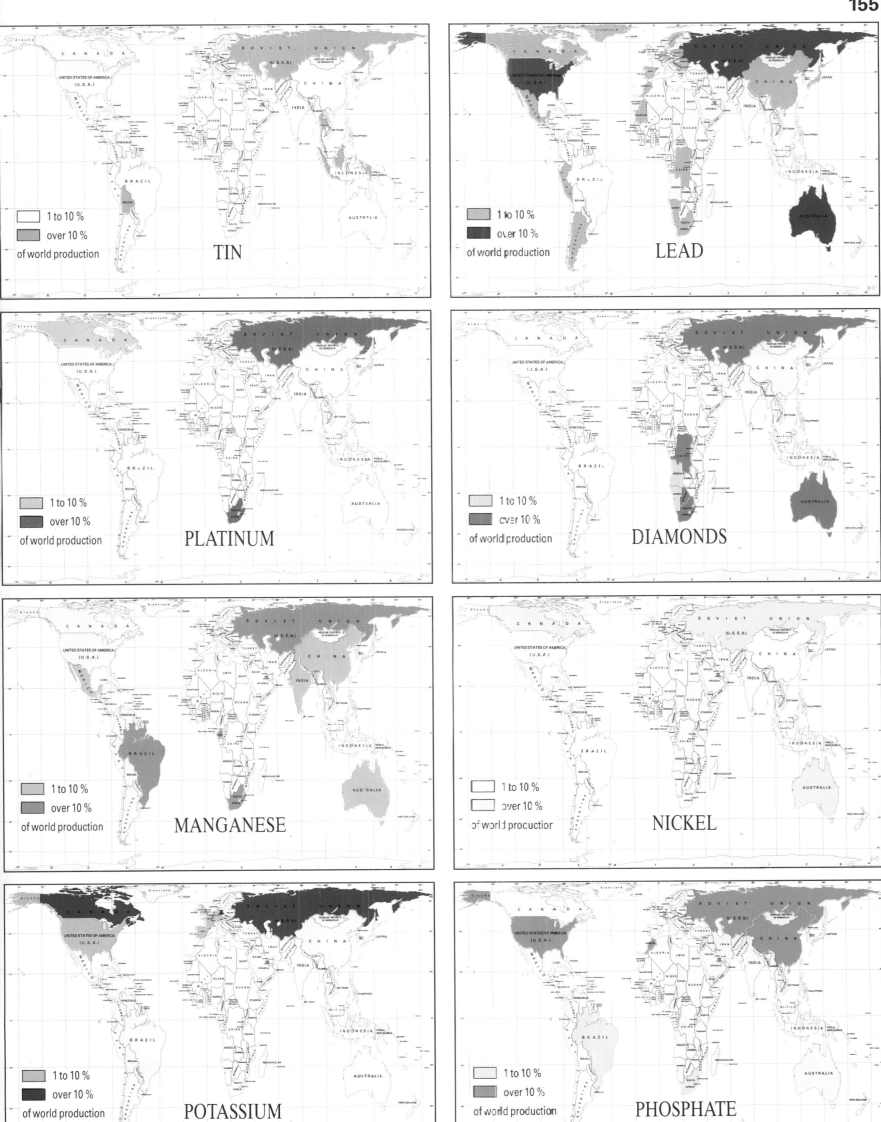

TIN

1 to 10 %
over 10 %
of world production

LEAD

1 to 10 %
over 10 %
of world production

PLATINUM

1 to 10 %
over 10 %
of world production

DIAMONDS

1 to 10 %
over 10 %
of world production

MANGANESE

1 to 10 %
over 10 %
of world production

NICKEL

1 to 10 %
over 10 %
of world production

POTASSIUM

1 to 10 %
over 10 %
of world production

PHOSPHATE

1 to 10 %
over 10 %
of world production

RESOURCES

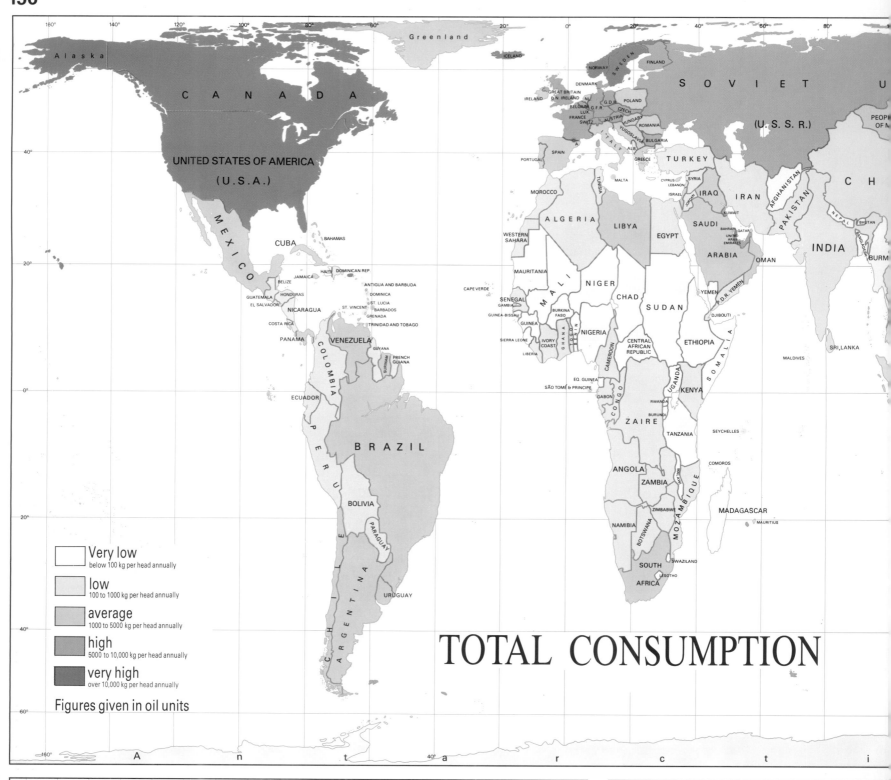

Legend

Very low
below 100 kg per head annually

low
100 to 1000 kg per head annually

average
1000 to 5000 kg per head annually

high
5000 to 10,000 kg per head annually

very high
over 10,000 kg per head annually

Figures given in oil units

TOTAL CONSUMPTION

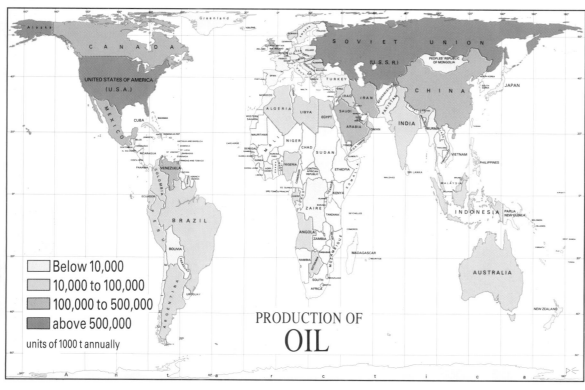

Below 10,000

10,000 to 100,000

100,000 to 500,000

above 500,000

units of 1000 t annually

PRODUCTION OF
OIL

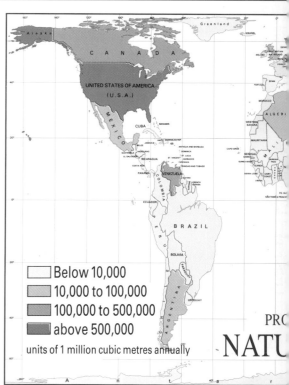

Below 10,000

10,000 to 100,000

100,000 to 500,000

above 500,000

units of 1 million cubic metres annually

PRO

NATU

ENE

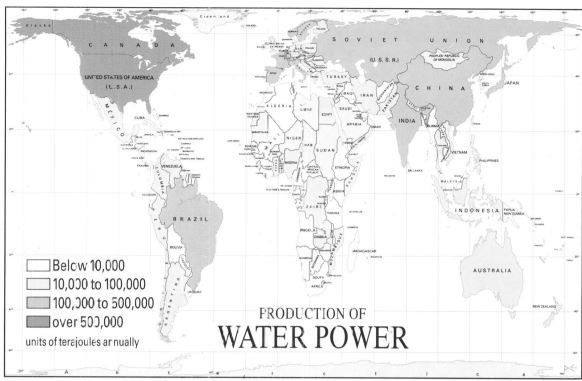

PRODUCTION OF
WATER POWER

Below 10,000
10,000 to 100,000
100,000 to 500,000
over 500,000
units of terajoules annually

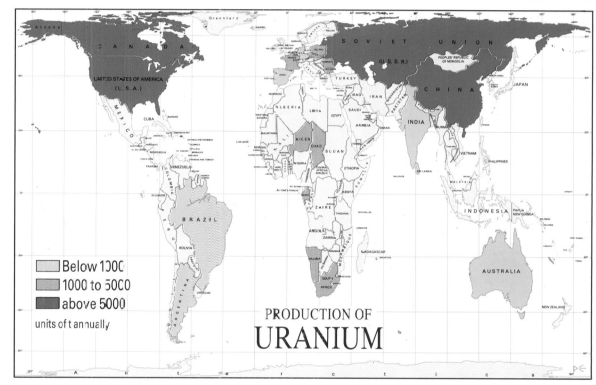

PRODUCTION OF
URANIUM

Below 1000
1000 to 5000
above 5000
units of t annually

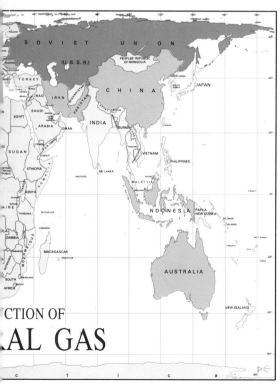

...CTION OF
...AL GAS

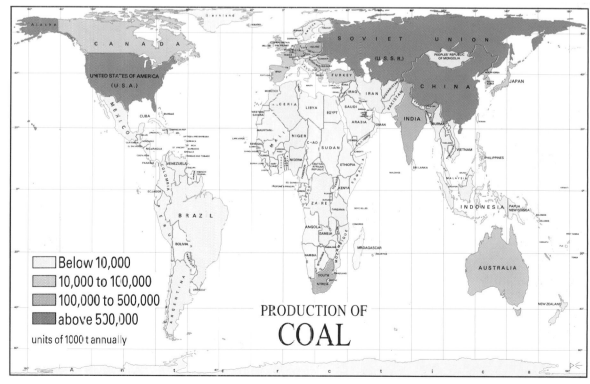

PRODUCTION OF
COAL

Below 10,000
10,000 to 100,000
100,000 to 500,000
above 500,000
units of 1000 t annually

RGY

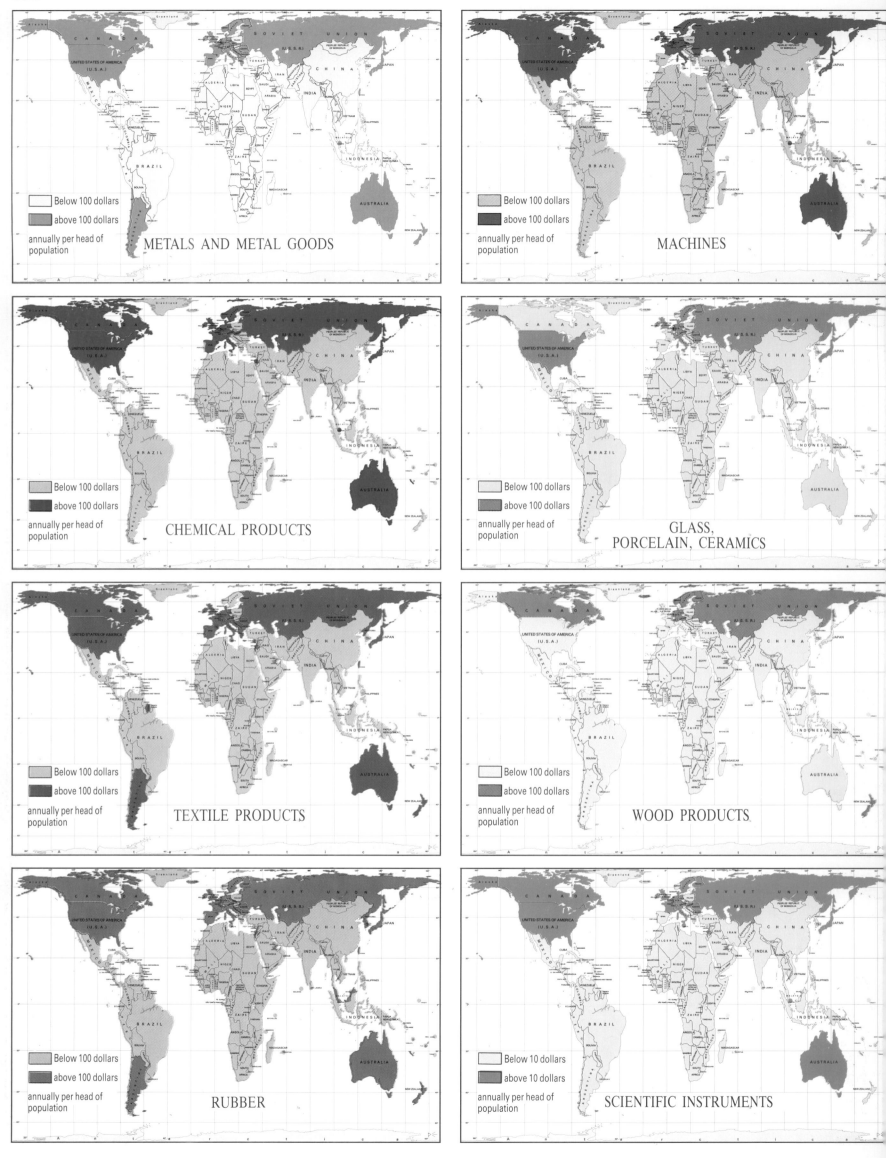

METALS AND METAL GOODS

Below 100 dollars
above 100 dollars

annually per head of population

MACHINES

Below 100 dollars
above 100 dollars

annually per head of population

CHEMICAL PRODUCTS

Below 100 dollars
above 100 dollars

annually per head of population

GLASS, PORCELAIN, CERAMICS

Below 100 dollars
above 100 dollars

annually per head of population

TEXTILE PRODUCTS

Below 100 dollars
above 100 dollars

annually per head of population

WOOD PRODUCTS

Below 100 dollars
above 100 dollars

annually per head of population

RUBBER

Below 100 dollars
above 100 dollars

annually per head of population

SCIENTIFIC INSTRUMENTS

Below 10 dollars
above 10 dollars

annually per head of population

INDUSTRIAL

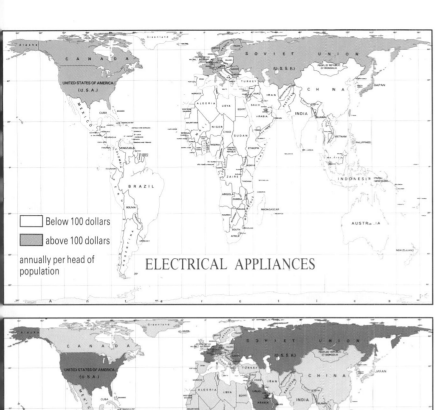

Below 100 dollars
above 100 dollars

annually per head of population

ELECTRICAL APPLIANCES

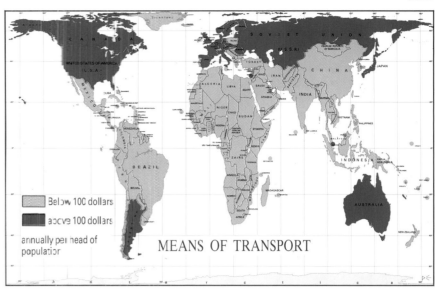

Below 100 dollars
above 100 dollars

annually per head of population

MEANS OF TRANSPORT

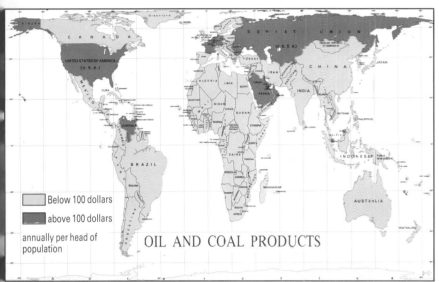

Below 100 dollars
above 100 dollars

annually per head of population

OIL AND COAL PRODUCTS

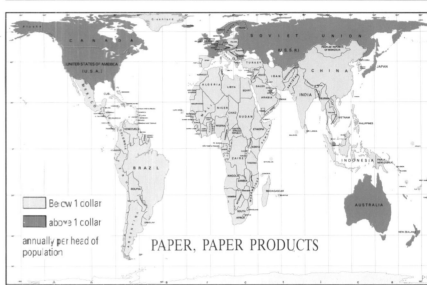

Below 1 dollar
above 1 dollar

annually per head of population

PAPER, PAPER PRODUCTS

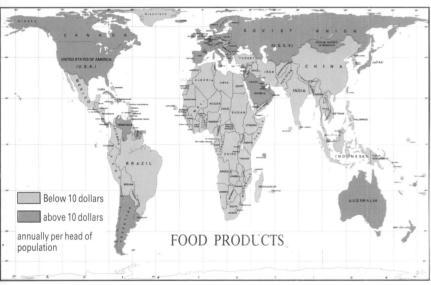

Below 10 dollars
above 10 dollars

annually per head of population

FOOD PRODUCTS

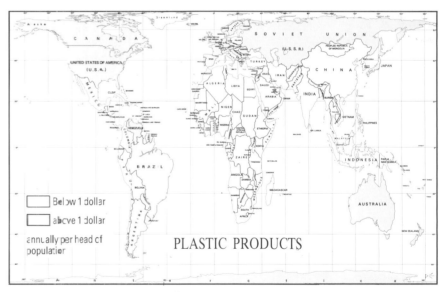

Below 1 dollar
above 1 dollar

annually per head of population

PLASTIC PRODUCTS

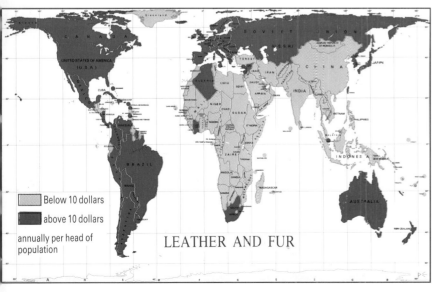

Below 10 dollars
above 10 dollars

annually per head of population

LEATHER AND FUR

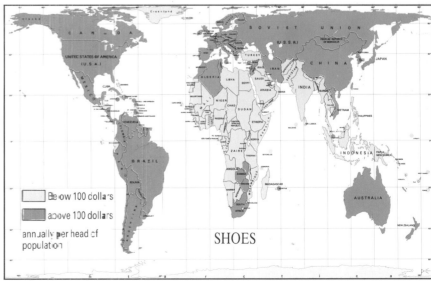

Below 100 dollars
above 100 dollars

annually per head of population

SHOES

PRODUCTS

Fewer than 25 per cent
of the population live in cities

25 to 50 per cent
of the population live in cities

50 to 75 per cent
of the population live in cities

over 75 per cent
of the population live in cities

URBAN

SWEDEN

FINLAND

S O V I E T   U N I O N

(U.S.S.R.)

PEOPLES' REPUBLIC
OF MONGOLIA

60°

POLAND

CZECH

HUNGARY

ROMANIA

YUGOSLAVIA

BULGARIA

ALB.

GREECE

TURKEY

NORTH KOREA

SOUTH
KOREA

JAPAN

40°

MALTA

CYPRUS

LEBANON

SYRIA

ISRAEL

JORDAN

IRAQ

IRAN

AFGHANISTAN

PAKISTAN

C H I N A

LIBYA

EGYPT

KUWAIT

SAUDI

BAHRAIN

QATAR

UNITED
ARAB
EMIRATES

NEPAL

BHUTAN

BANGLADESH

TAIWAN

20°

ARABIA

OMAN

INDIA

BURMA

LAOS

CHAD

SUDAN

YEMEN

P.D.R. YEMEN

DJIBOUTI

THAILAND

KAMPUCHEA

VIETNAM

PHILIPPINES

CENTRAL
AFRICAN
REPUBLIC

ETHIOPIA

SOMALIA

SRI LANKA

MALDIVES

BRUNEI

MALAYSIA

CAMEROON

UGANDA

KENYA

SINGAPORE

KIRIBATI

0°

CONGO

RWANDA

BURUNDI

ZAIRE

TANZANIA

SEYCHELLES

I N D O N E S I A

PAPUA
NEW GUINEA

SOLOMON
ISLANDS

COMOROS

WESTERN SAMOA

ANGOLA

MALAWI

ZAMBIA

MOZAMBIQUE

VANUATU

FIJI

ZIMBABWE

MADAGASCAR

MAURITIUS

TONGA

20°

NAMIBIA

BOTSWANA

SWAZILAND

AUSTRALIA

SOUTH
AFRICA

LESOTHO

NEW ZEALAND

40°

60°

c   t   i   c   a

180°

SATION

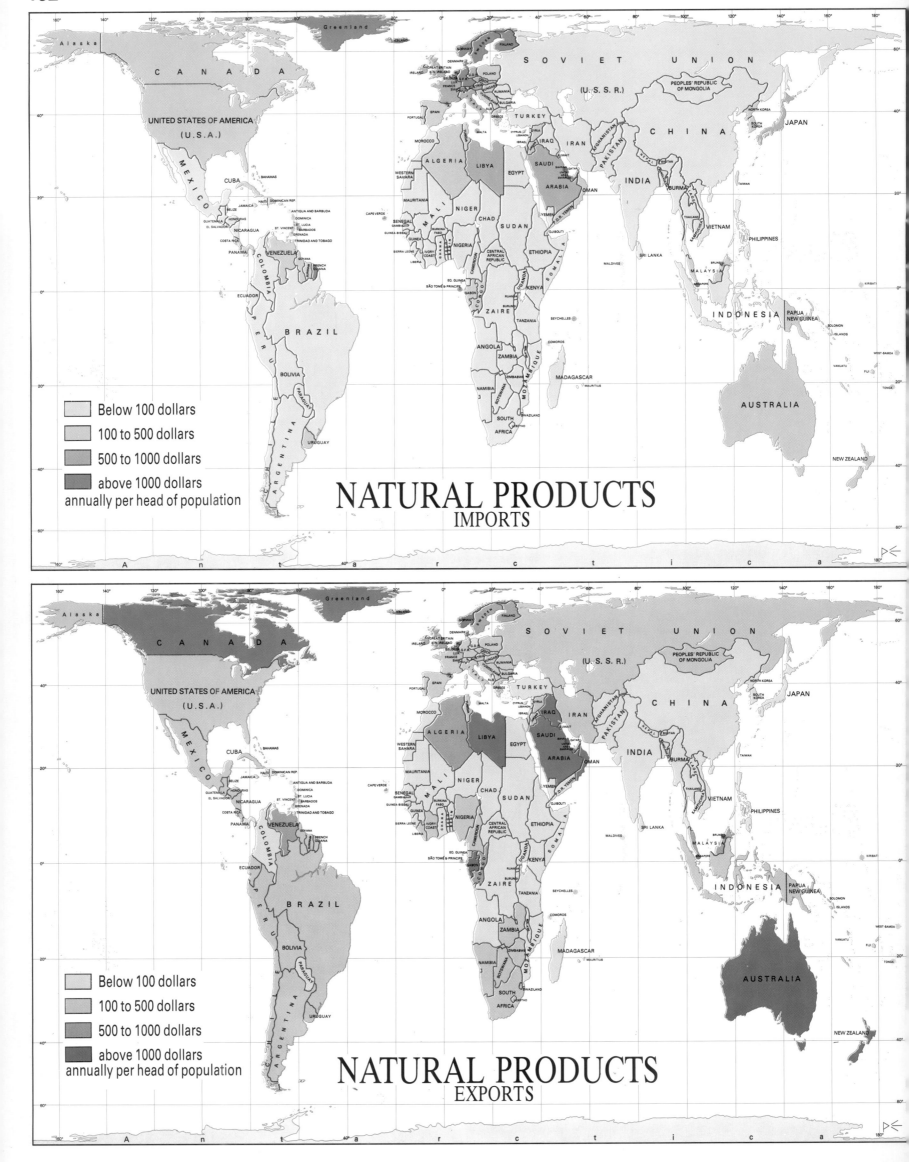

Below 100 dollars
100 to 500 dollars
500 to 1000 dollars
above 1000 dollars
annually per head of population

NATURAL PRODUCTS
IMPORTS

Below 100 dollars
100 to 500 dollars
500 to 1000 dollars
above 1000 dollars
annually per head of population

NATURAL PRODUCTS
EXPORTS

WORLD

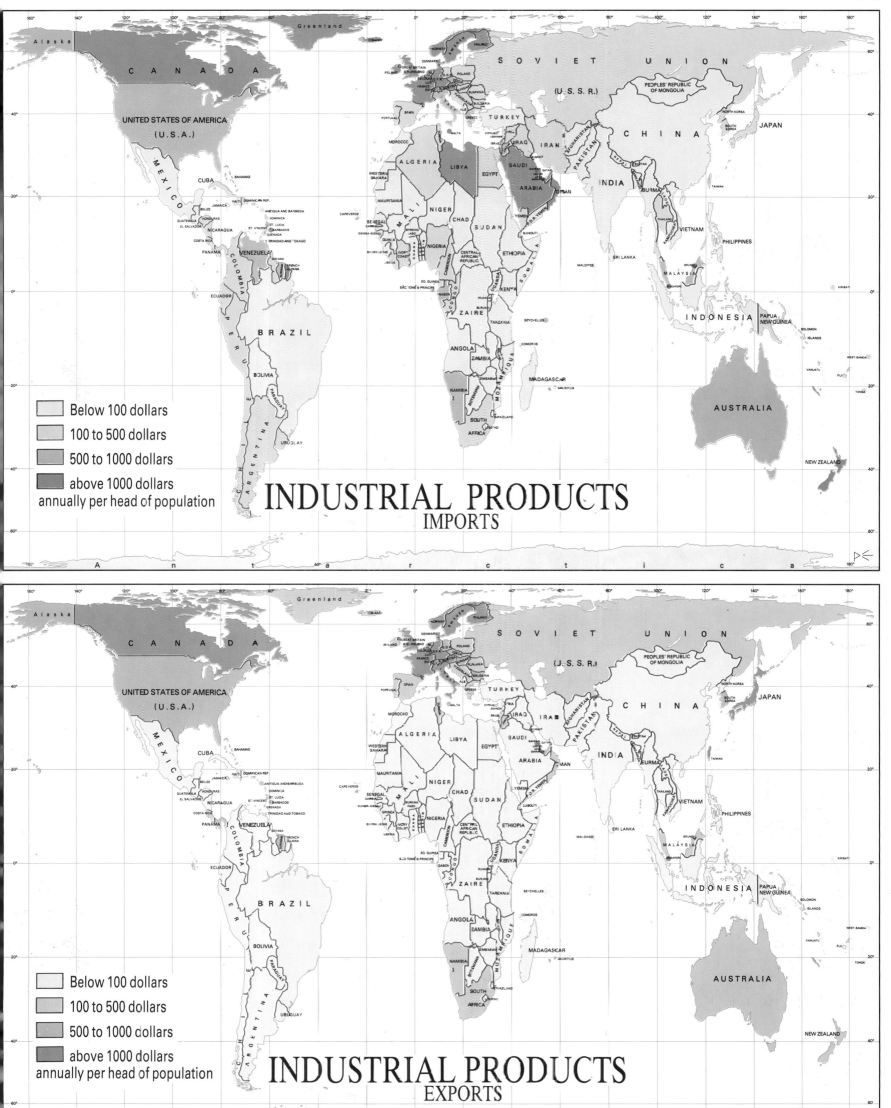

INDUSTRIAL PRODUCTS
IMPORTS

Below 100 dollars
100 to 500 dollars
500 to 1000 dollars
above 1000 dollars
annually per head of population

INDUSTRIAL PRODUCTS
EXPORTS

Below 100 dollars
100 to 500 dollars
500 to 1000 dollars
above 1000 dollars
annually per head of population

TRADE

Average income:

Below 500 dollars
per person annually

500 to 1000 dollars
per person annually

1000 to 5000 dollars
per person annually

5000 to 10,000 dollars
per person annually

over 10,000 dollars
per person annually

POOR NATIONS

RICH NATIONS

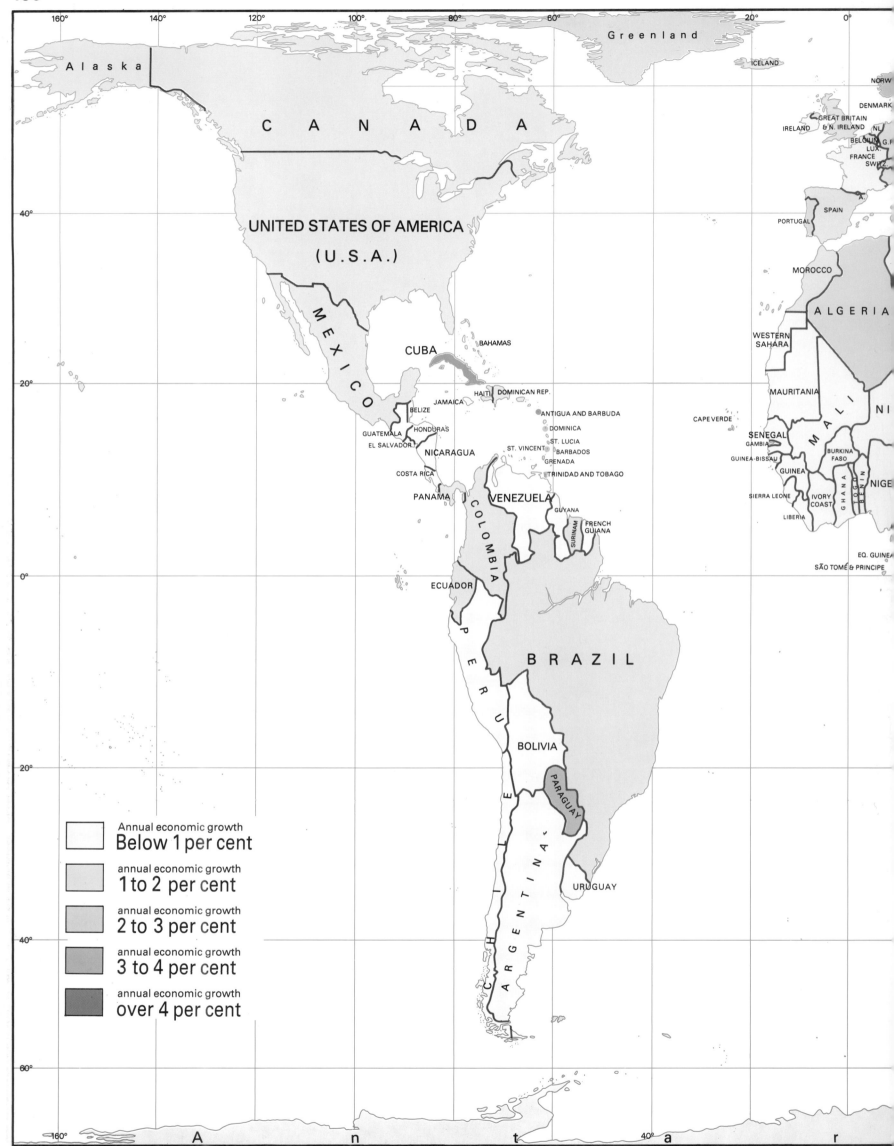

160°   140°   120°   100°   80°   60°   20°   0°

Greenland

Alaska

ICELAND

NORW

DENMARK

C A N A D A

GREAT BRITAIN
& N. IRELAND

IRELAND   NL

BELGIUM G.F.
LUX
FRANCE
SWITZ.

UNITED STATES OF AMERICA

SPAIN

40°

(U.S.A.)

PORTUGAL

MOROCCO

M
E
X
I
C
O

ALGERIA

WESTERN
SAHARA

CUBA

BAHAMAS

20°

MAURITANIA

HAITI   DOMINICAN REP.

M
A
L
I

NI

JAMAICA

BELIZE

ANTIGUA AND BARBUDA

SENEGAL

GUATEMALA   HONDURAS

DOMINICA

GAMBIA

BURKINA
FASO

EL SALVADOR

ST. LUCIA

GUINEA-BISSAU

NIGE

NICARAGUA

ST. VINCENT   BARBADOS
GRENADA

GUINEA

COSTA RICA

TRINIDAD AND TOBAGO

SIERRA LEONE

IVORY
COAST

LIBERIA

CAPE VERDE

PANAMA   VENEZUELA

C
O
L
O
M
B
I
A

GUYANA

EQ. GUINEA

SÃO TOMÉ & PRINCIPE

SURINAM

FRENCH
GUIANA

0°

ECUADOR

P
E
R
U

B R A Z I L

20°

BOLIVIA

P
A
R
A
G
U
A
Y

Annual economic growth
Below 1 per cent

annual economic growth
1 to 2 per cent

annual economic growth
2 to 3 per cent

annual economic growth
3 to 4 per cent

C
H
I
L
E

A
R
G
E
N
T
I
N
A

URUGUAY

40°

annual economic growth
over 4 per cent

60°

160°   A   n   t   40°   a   r

ECONOMIC

C GROWTH

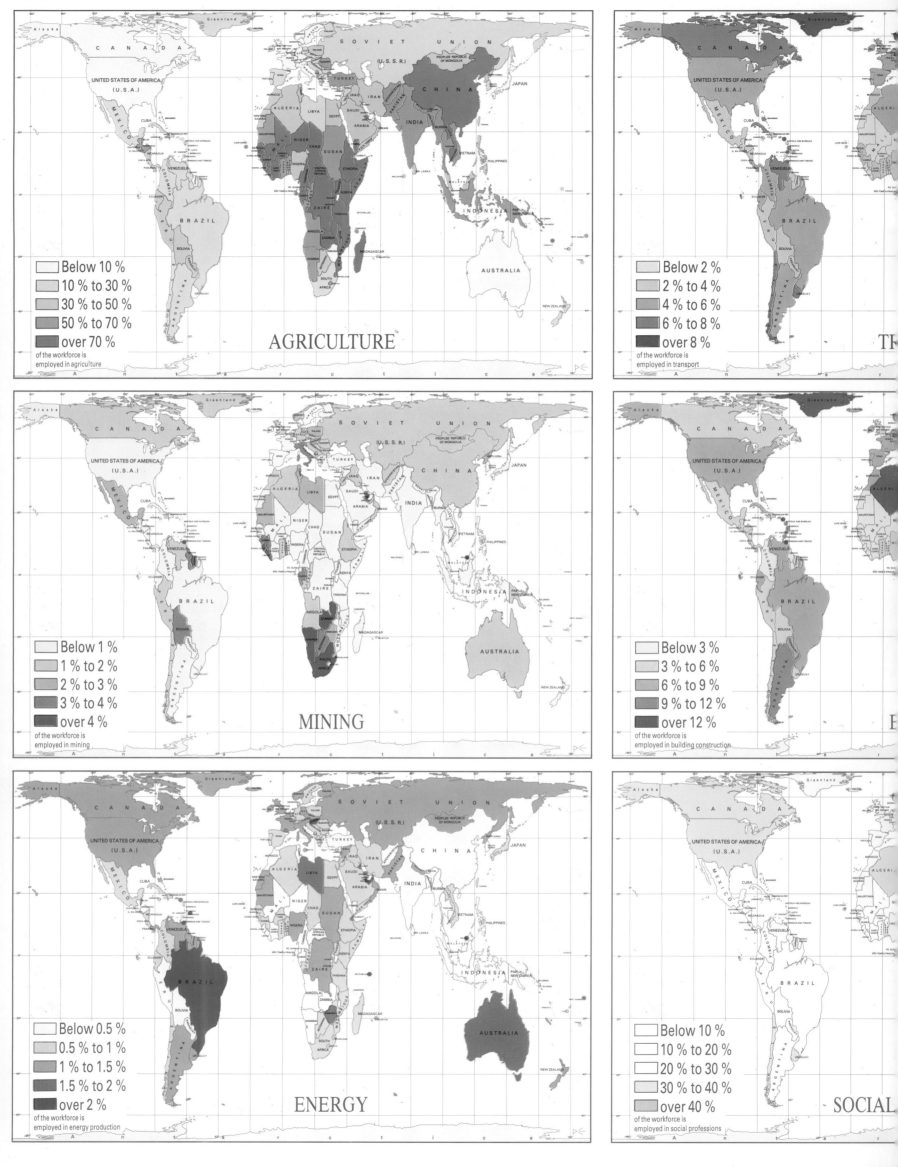

Below 10 %
10 % to 30 %
30 % to 50 %
50 % to 70 %
over 70 %
of the workforce is
employed in agriculture

AGRICULTURE

Below 2 %
2 % to 4 %
4 % to 6 %
6 % to 8 %
over 8 %
of the workforce is
employed in transport

TR

Below 1 %
1 % to 2 %
2 % to 3 %
3 % to 4 %
over 4 %
of the workforce is
employed in mining

MINING

Below 3 %
3 % to 6 %
6 % to 9 %
9 % to 12 %
over 12 %
of the workforce is
employed in building construction

B

Below 0.5 %
0.5 % to 1 %
1 % to 1.5 %
1.5 % to 2 %
over 2 %
of the workforce is
employed in energy production

ENERGY

Below 10 %
10 % to 20 %
20 % to 30 %
30 % to 40 %
over 40 %
of the workforce is
employed in social professions

SOCIAL

EMPLOYMENT

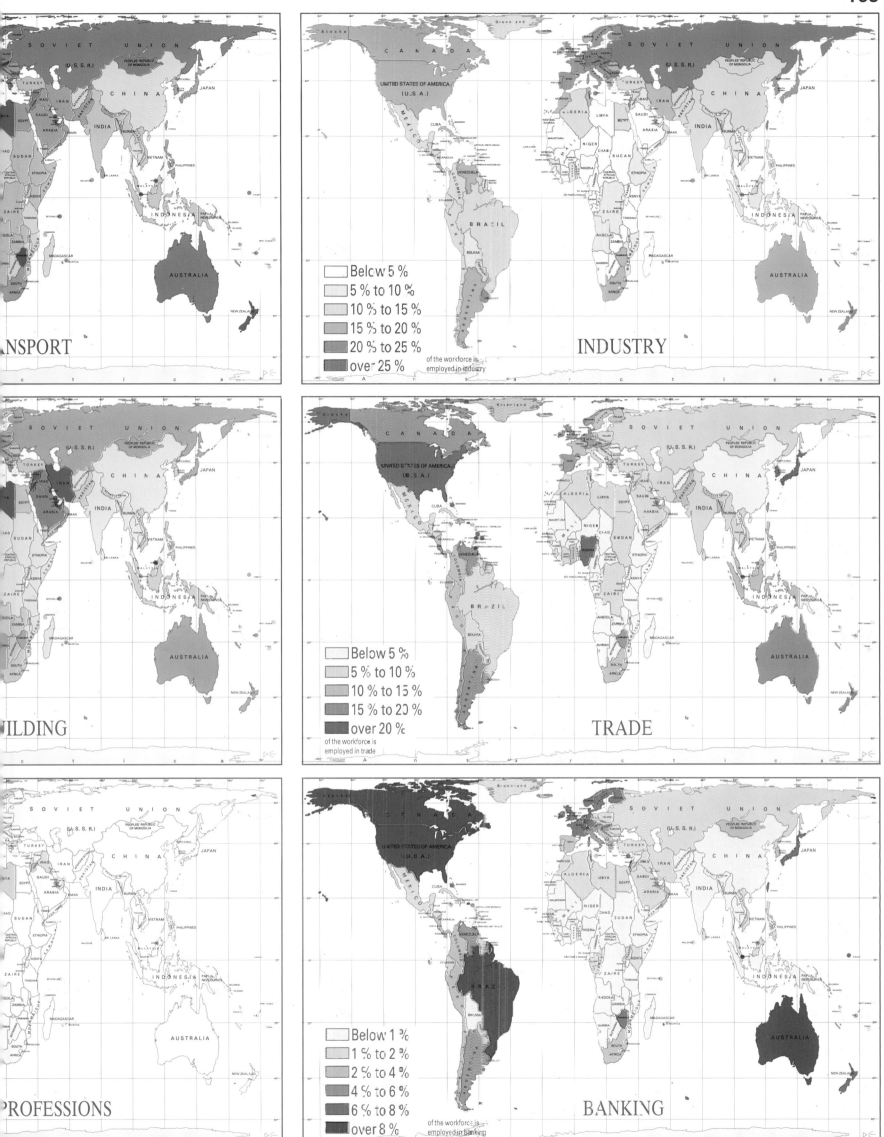

NSPORT

INDUSTRY

Below 5 %
5 % to 10 %
10 % to 15 %
15 % to 20 %
20 % to 25 %
over 25 %

of the workforce is
employed in industry

ILDING

TRADE

Below 5 %
5 % to 10 %
10 % to 15 %
15 % to 20 %
over 20 %

of the workforce is
employed in trade

PROFESSIONS

BANKING

Below 1 %
1 % to 2 %
2 % to 4 %
4 % to 6 %
6 % to 8 %
over 8 %

of the workforce is
employed in banking

STRUCTURE

Capitalist

Marginal

Communist

SOCIAL

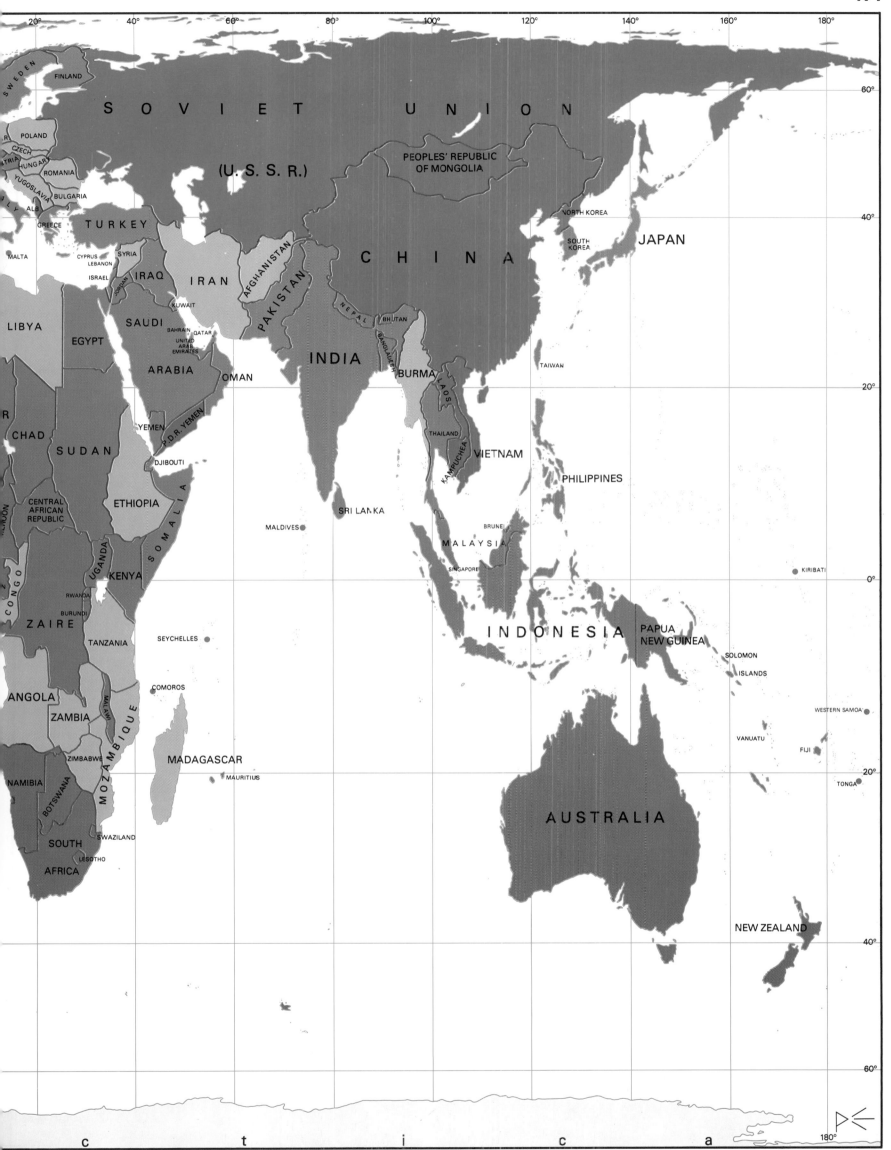

ORDER

Below 1 per cent
of the workforce is unemployed

1 per cent to 5 per cent
of the workforce is unemployed

5 per cent to 10 per cent
of the workforce is unemployed

10 per cent to 20 per cent
of the workforce is unemployed

over 20 per cent
of the workforce is unemployed

UNEMPL

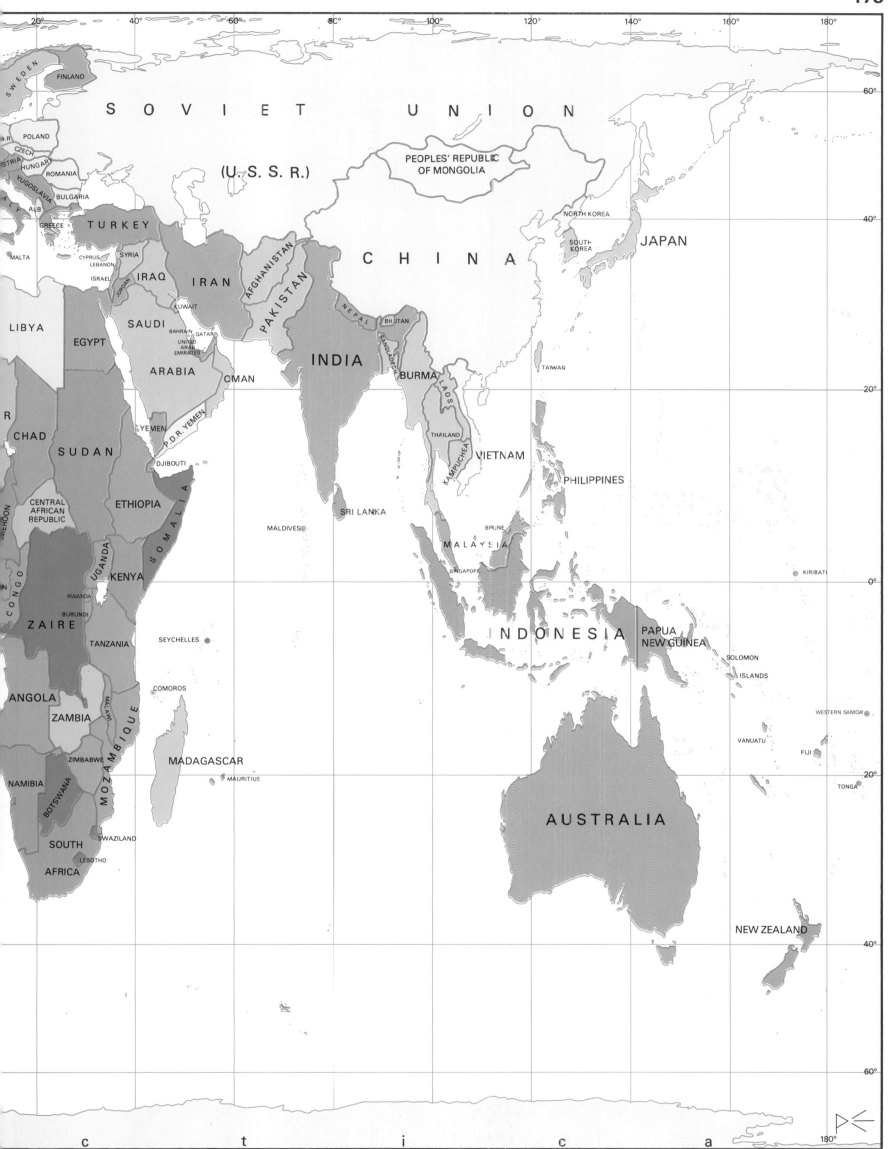

Less than 5 per cent
annual inflation

5 to 10 per cent
annual inflation

10 to 25 per cent
annual inflation

over 25 per cent
annual inflation

INFLA

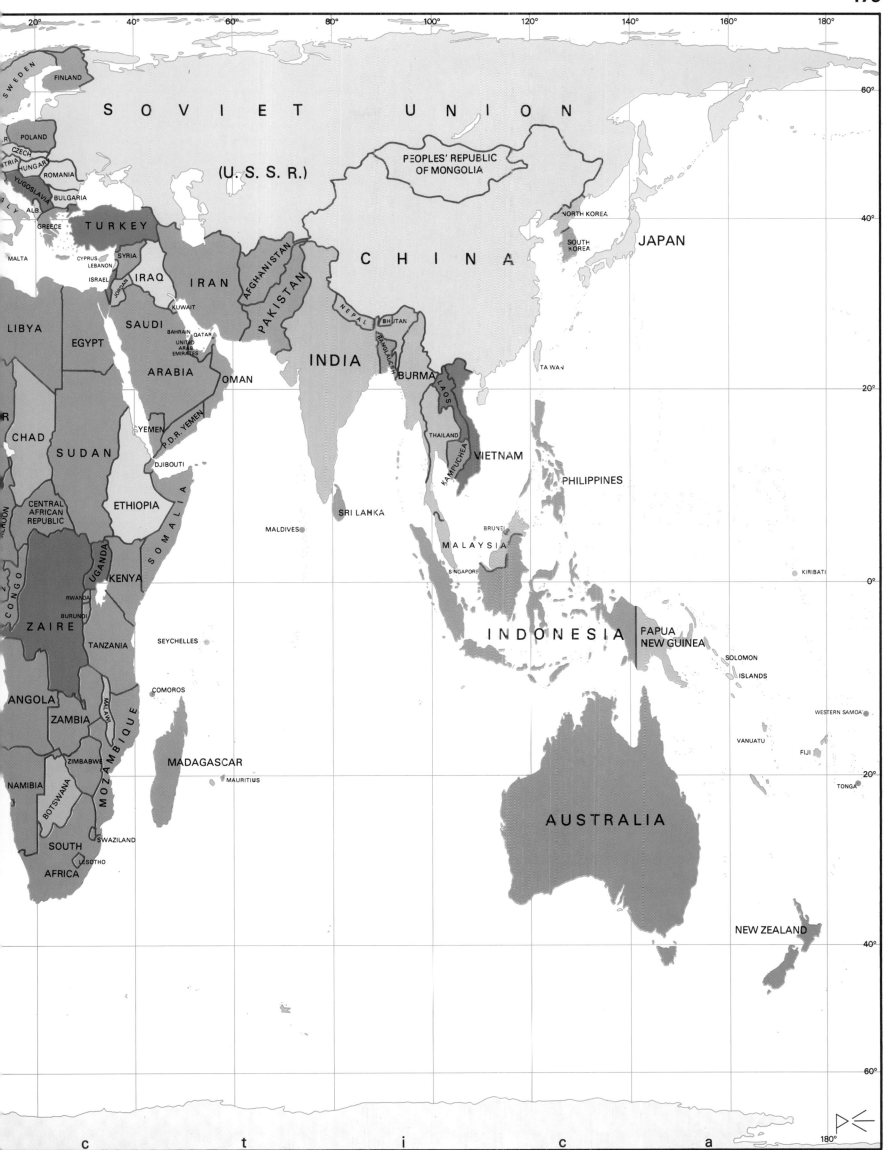

SWEDEN
FINLAND
POLAND
CZECH
STRIA
HUNGARY
ROMANIA
YUGOSLAVIA
BULGARIA
ALB.
GREECE
MALTA

S O V I E T   U N I O N

(U. S. S. R.)

PEOPLES' REPUBLIC
OF MONGOLIA

NORTH KOREA

JAPAN

TURKEY

CYPRUS
LEBANON
SYRIA
ISRAEL
JORDAN
IRAQ
IRAN
AFGHANISTAN
PAKISTAN
KUWAIT

SOUTH
KOREA

C H I N A

LIBYA

EGYPT

SAUDI

ARABIA

OMAN

BAHRAIN QATAR
UNITED
ARAB
EMIRATES

NEPAL
BHUTAN

BANGLADESH

I N D I A

BURMA

TAIWAN

CHAD

SUDAN

YEMEN

P.D.R. YEMEN

DJIBOUTI

LAOS

THAILAND

KAMPUCHEA

VIETNAM

PHILIPPINES

R

CENTRAL
AFRICAN
REPUBLIC

ETHIOPIA

SRI LANKA

MALDIVES

BRUNEI

MALAYSIA

MEROON

CONGO

UGANDA

KENYA

SOMALIA

SINGAPORE

I N D O N E S I A

PAPUA
NEW GUINEA

SOLOMON
ISLANDS

KIRIBATI

ZAIRE

RWANDA
BURUNDI

TANZANIA

SEYCHELLES

ANGOLA

ZAMBIA

MALAWI

COMOROS

MOZAMBIQUE

WESTERN SAMOA

VANUATU

FIJI

ZIMBABWE

NAMIBIA

BOTSWANA

MADAGASCAR

MAURITIUS

AUSTRALIA

TONGA

SOUTH
AFRICA

SWAZILAND

LESOTHO

NEW ZEALAND

20°   40°   60°   80°   100°   120°   140°   160°   180°

60°

40°

20°

0°

20°

40°

60°

180°

c   t   i   c   a

TION

Less than 1 child
per thousand head of population

1 to 5 children
per thousand head of population

5 to 15 children
per thousand head of population

15 to 30 children
per thousand head of population

over 30 children
per thousand head of population

Under 15 years of age are
in paid employment

CHILD L

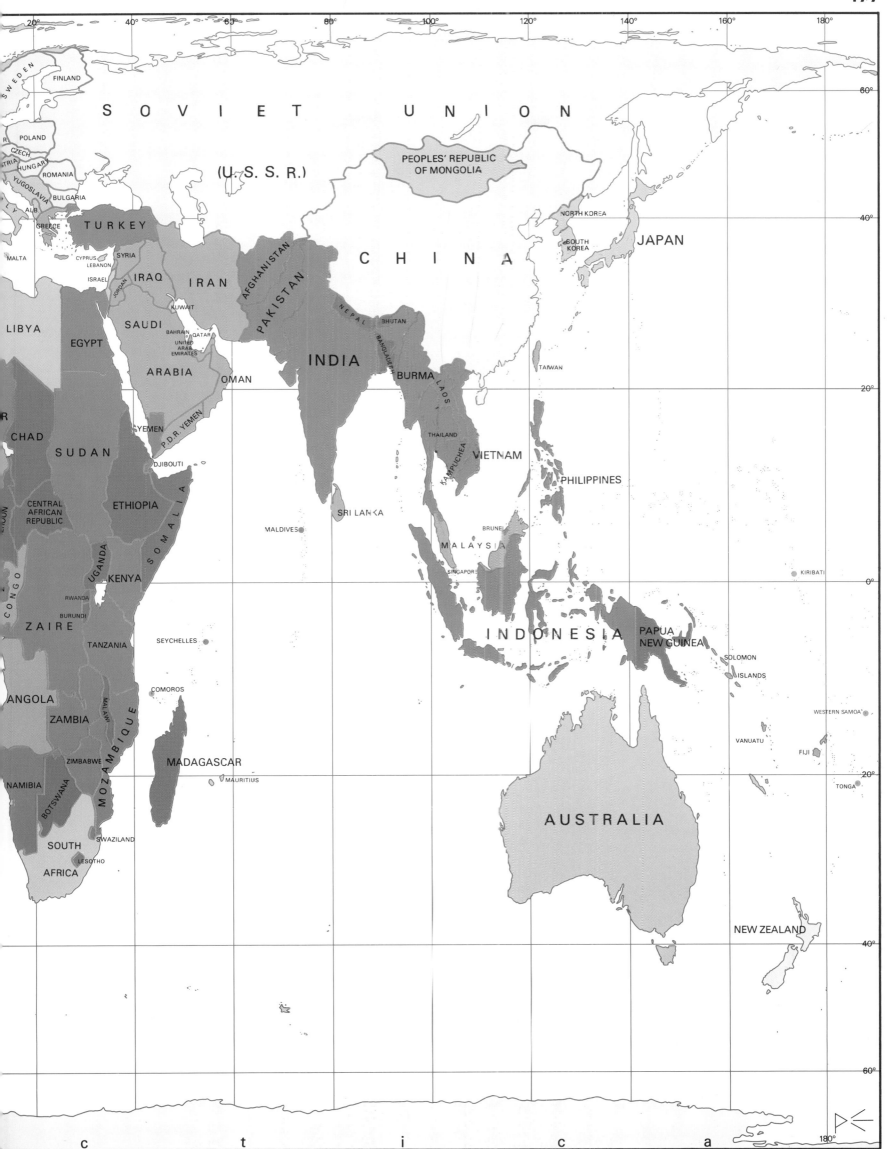

LABOUR

160°   140°   120°   100°   80°   60°   40°   20°   0°

Greenland

ICELAND

NORW

Alaska

DENMARK

GREAT BRITAIN
& N. IRELAND

IRELAND   NL

BELGIUM G.R.
LUX.

FRANCE SWIT.

C A N A D A

40°

UNITED STATES OF AMERICA

(U.S.A.)

SPAIN

PORTUGAL

MOROCCO

A L G E R I A

WESTERN
SAHARA

M E X I C O

CUBA   BAHAMAS

20°

HAITI   DOMINICAN REP.

MAURITANIA

JAMAICA   ANTIGUA AND BARBUDA

BELIZE   DOMINICA

CAPE VERDE   **M A L I**   NI

GUATEMALA   HONDURAS   ST. LUCIA

SENEGAL

EL SALVADOR   ST. VINCENT   BARBADOS

GAMBIA

BURKINA
FASO

NICARAGUA   GRENADA

GUINEA-BISSAU

COSTA RICA   TRINIDAD AND TOBAGO

GUINEA

NIGE

PANAMA   **VENEZUELA**

SIERRA LEONE   IVORY
COAST

GUYANA

LIBERIA

0°

C O L O M B I A

SURINAM

FRENCH
GUIANA

EQ. GUINEA

SÃO TOMÉ & PRINCIPE

ECUADOR

P E R U

B R A Z I L

20°

BOLIVIA

PARAGUAY

Approaching equality
Total income of the richest 10 % = total income of the poorest 20 %

C H I L E

A R G E N T I N A

URUGUAY

Moderate inequality
Total income of the richest 10 % = total income of the poorest 40 %

Severe inequality
Total income of the richest 10 % = total income of the poorest 60 %

40°

Gross inequality
Total income of the richest 10 % = total income of the poorest 80 %

The percentage figures for the poorest refer to average values, which can vary in the individual countries by up to 10 %.

60°

160°   40°

A   n   t   a   r

INEQU

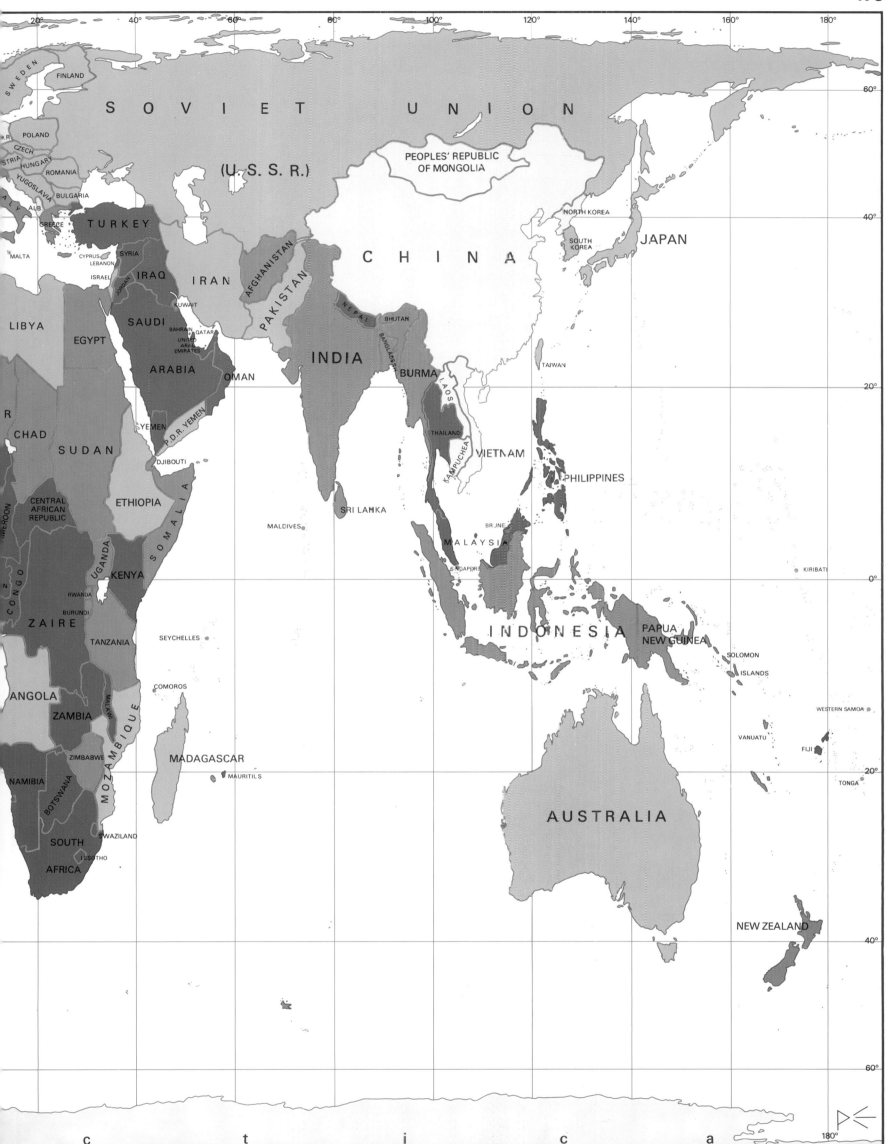

SWEDEN
FINLAND
POLAND
CZECH
STRIA
HUNGARY
ROMANIA
YUGOSLAVIA
BULGARIA
ALB.
GREECE

SOVIET UNION
(U.S.S.R.)

PEOPLES' REPUBLIC
OF MONGOLIA

NORTH KOREA

JAPAN

SOUTH
KOREA

CHINA

TURKEY

MALTA

CYPRUS
LEBANON

SYRIA

ISRAEL
JORDAN
IRAQ

IRAN

AFGHANISTAN

PAKISTAN

KUWAIT

LIBYA

EGYPT

SAUDI

BAHRAIN QATAR
UNITED
ARAB
EMIRATES

ARABIA

OMAN

NEPAL
BHUTAN

BANGLADESH

INDIA

BURMA

LAOS

TAIWAN

YEMEN
P.D.R. YEMEN

THAILAND

KAMPUCHEA

VIETNAM

PHILIPPINES

CHAD

SUDAN

DJIBOUTI

R

CENTRAL
AFRICAN
REPUBLIC

ETHIOPIA

SRI LANKA

MALDIVES

BRUNEI

MEROON

UGANDA

SOMALIA

KENYA

MALAYSIA

SINGAPORE

CONGO

RWANDA

BURUNDI

KIRIBATI

ZAIRE

TANZANIA

SEYCHELLES

INDONESIA

PAPUA
NEW GUINEA

SOLOMON
ISLANDS

COMOROS

ANGOLA

ZAMBIA

MALAWI

WESTERN SAMOA

VANUATU

MADAGASCAR

MOZAMBIQUE

ZIMBABWE

FIJI

NAMIBIA

BOTSWANA

MAURITIUS

TONGA

AUSTRALIA

SWAZILAND

SOUTH

LESOTHO

AFRICA

NEW ZEALAND

c   o   t   i   n   c   a

ALITY

Low amount of prostitution

medium amount of prostitution

high amount of prostitution

PROSTI

TUTION

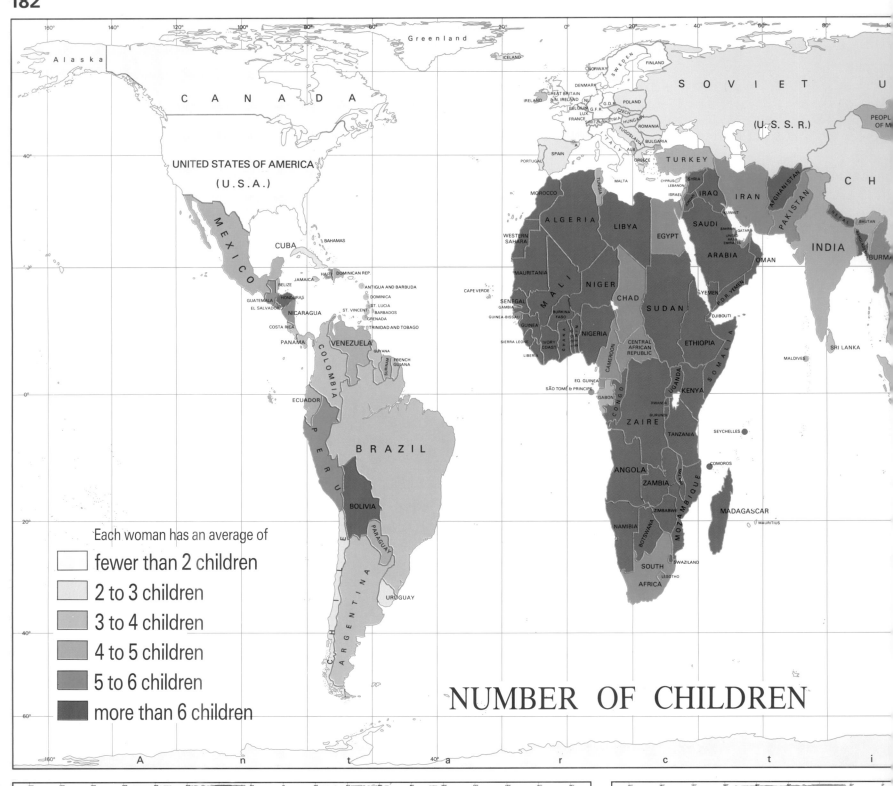

Each woman has an average of

- [ ] fewer than 2 children
- 2 to 3 children
- 3 to 4 children
- 4 to 5 children
- 5 to 6 children
- more than 6 children

NUMBER OF CHILDREN

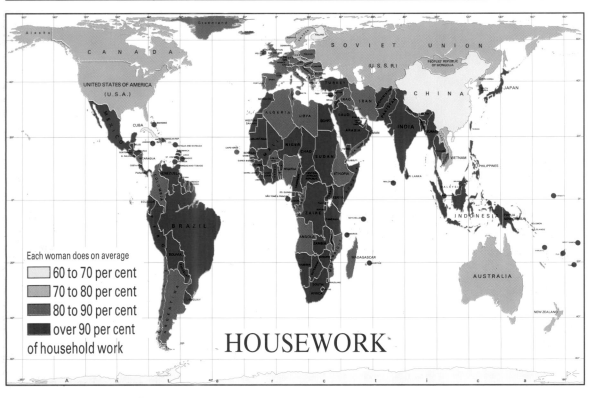

Each woman does on average

- 60 to 70 per cent
- 70 to 80 per cent
- 80 to 90 per cent
- over 90 per cent
of household work

HOUSEWORK

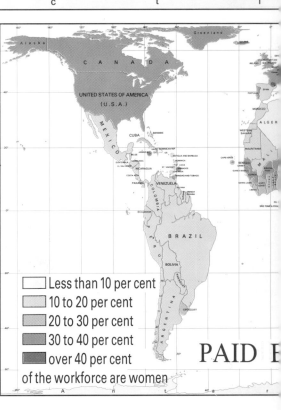

- [ ] Less than 10 per cent
- 10 to 20 per cent
- 20 to 30 per cent
- 30 to 40 per cent
- over 40 per cent
of the workforce are women

PAID E

THE STATUS

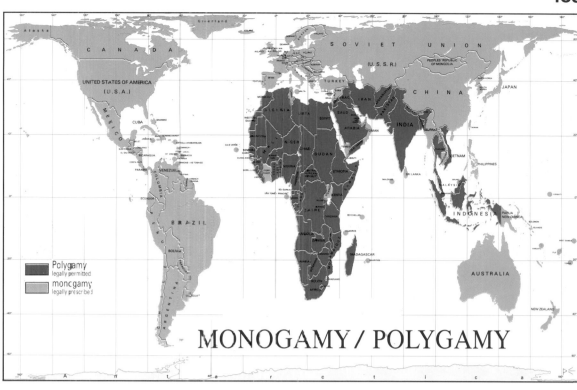

MONOGAMY / POLYGAMY

Polygamy
legally permitted

monogamy
legally prescribed

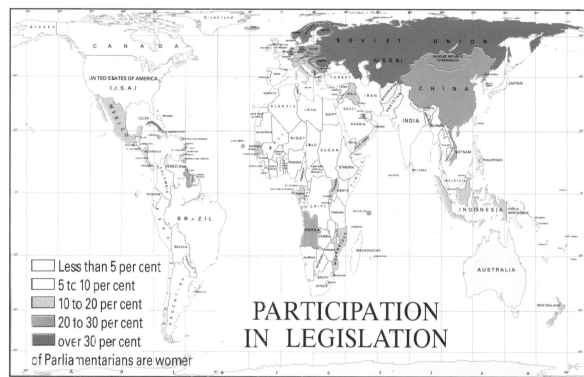

Less than 5 per cent

5 to 10 per cent

10 to 20 per cent

20 to 30 per cent

over 30 per cent

of Parliamentarians are women

PARTICIPATION
IN LEGISLATION

EMPLOYMENT

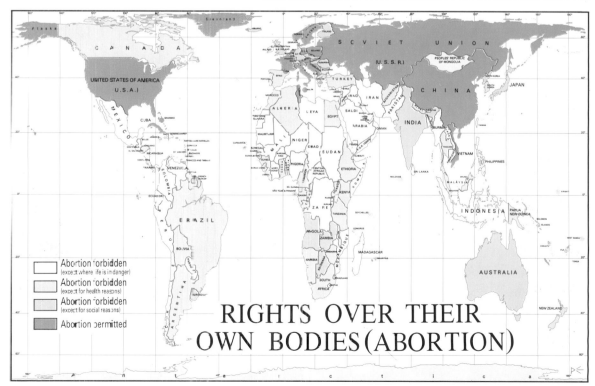

Abortion forbidden
(except where life is in danger)

Abortion forbidden
(except for health reasons)

Abortion forbidden
(except for social reasons)

Abortion permitted

RIGHTS OVER THEIR
OWN BODIES (ABORTION)

OF WOMEN

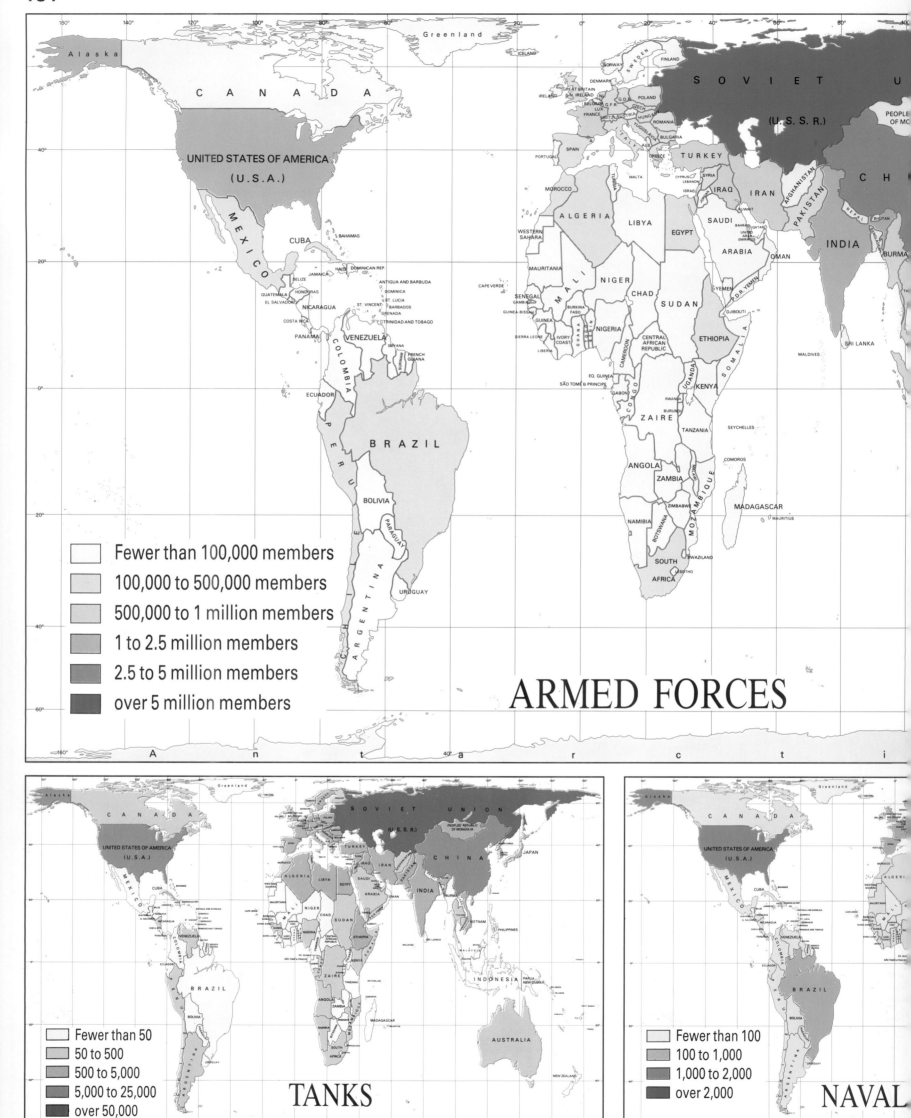

ARMED FORCES

Fewer than 100,000 members
100,000 to 500,000 members
500,000 to 1 million members
1 to 2.5 million members
2.5 to 5 million members
over 5 million members

TANKS

Fewer than 50
50 to 500
500 to 5,000
5,000 to 25,000
over 50,000

NAVAL

Fewer than 100
100 to 1,000
1,000 to 2,000
over 2,000

RELATIVE MILIT

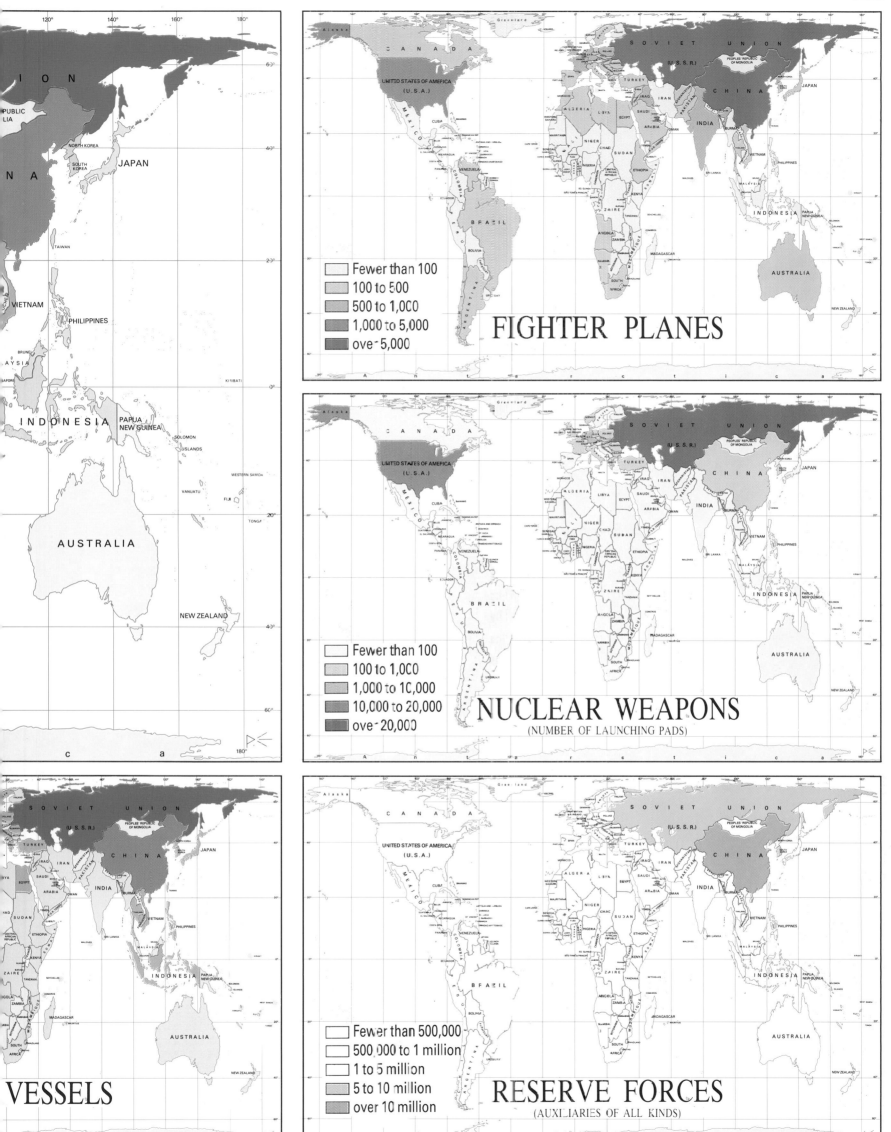

FIGHTER PLANES

Fewer than 100
100 to 500
500 to 1,000
1,000 to 5,000
over 5,000

NUCLEAR WEAPONS
(NUMBER OF LAUNCHING PADS)

Fewer than 100
100 to 1,000
1,000 to 10,000
10,000 to 20,000
over 20,000

VESSELS

RESERVE FORCES
(AUXILIARIES OF ALL KINDS)

Fewer than 500,000
500,000 to 1 million
1 to 5 million
5 to 10 million
over 10 million

ARY STRENGTH

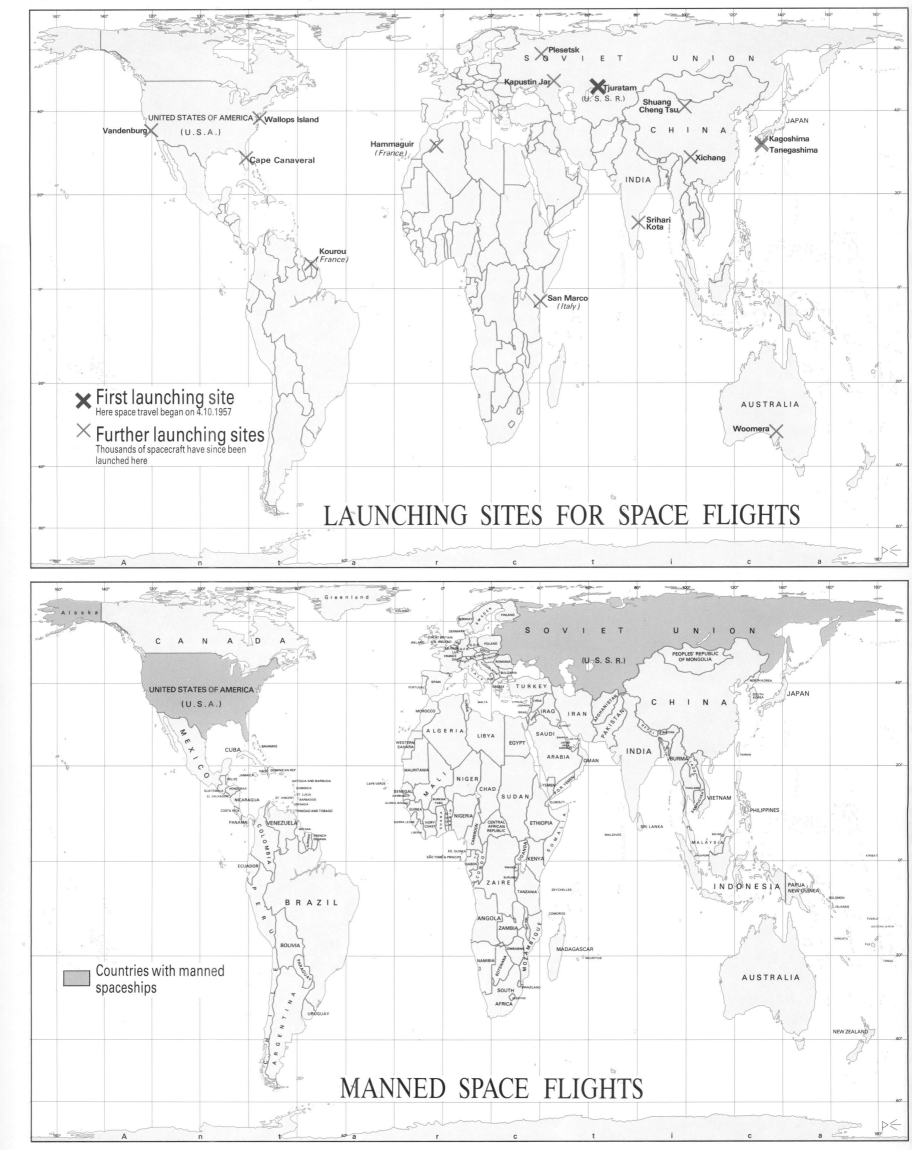

First launching site
Here space travel began on 4.10.1957

Further launching sites
Thousands of spacecraft have since been launched here

LAUNCHING SITES FOR SPACE FLIGHTS

Vandenburg

UNITED STATES OF AMERICA
(U.S.A.)

Wallops Island

Cape Canaveral

Kourou
(France)

Plesetsk

Kapustin Jar

Tjuratam
(U.S.S.R.)

Shuang
Cheng Tsu

SOVIET UNION

CHINA

INDIA

JAPAN

Kagoshima
Tanegashima

Xichang

Srihari
Kota

Hammaguir
(France)

San Marco
(Italy)

AUSTRALIA

Woomera

Countries with manned
spaceships

MANNED SPACE FLIGHTS

THE CONQUI

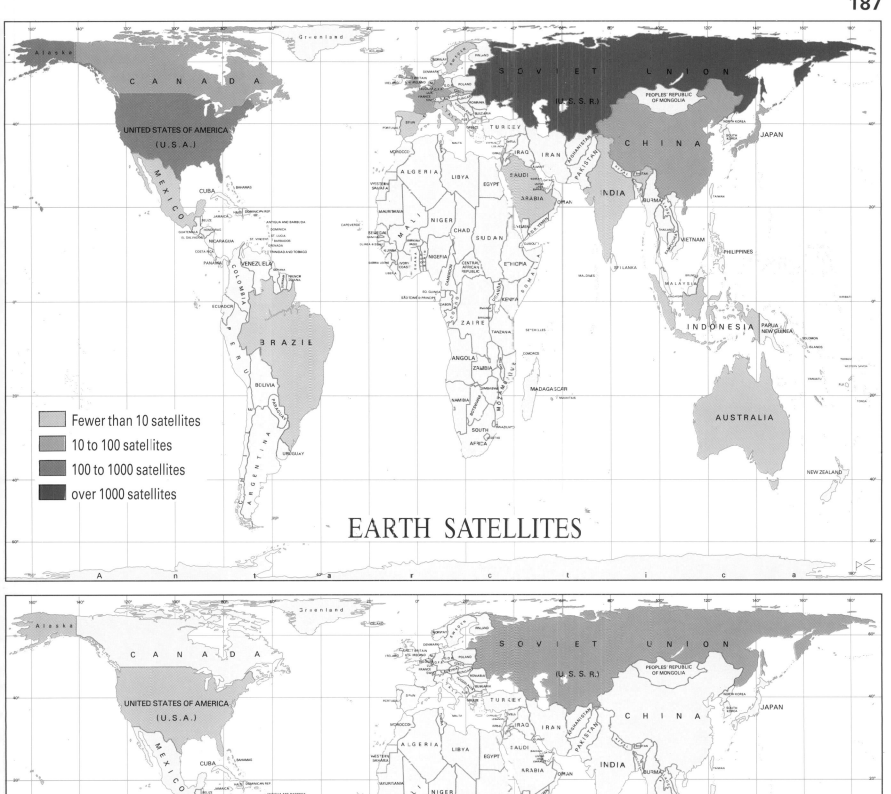

EARTH SATELLITES

Fewer than 10 satellites
10 to 100 satellites
100 to 1000 satellites
over 1000 satellites

INTERPLANETARY SPACE FLIGHTS

Fewer than 50
over 50

EST OF SPACE

INDEX

Each name in the index is followed by a page number and a letter. On the page referred to, the letter can be found either at the top or at the bottom of the map frame. In the first case, the place is in the upper half of the map vertically below the letter; otherwise it is on the lower half of the map vertically above the letter. If a name extends over several letters, the given letter indicates its beginning.

Names such as countries or oceans which cover a large area on the map are listed with their page number only. However, if they extend over two pages, two page numbers are shown – the left-hand and right-hand page numbers being linked with a dash. Names of countries, oceans, rivers and mountains that extend over more than a double page are listed under each separate page. A dash between two nonconsecutive page numbers means that the place appears on all maps between and including those two pages.

The headwords are in alphabetical order. Names with prefixes like "Saint" or "Bad" can be looked up under the initial letter of the prefix. Place names appear on the maps in their widely-used Anglicised form, or in their local spelling or a standard transliteration of that local spelling. The index also includes local forms of names where the Anglicised form has been used on the map. In these cases the local name is followed by the Anglicised name in brackets. This indicates that the place name appears on the map, at the reference given, in the form shown in brackets, not in its local form.

Simikot ...61 f
Simla ...61 c
Simpson Desert ...73 t
Simpson Peninsula ...13 b
Simušir ...59 i
Sinadogo ...43 u
Sinai Peninsula ...38 j
Sinawan ...37 g
Sincelejo ...22 m
Sinclair Mills ...14 h
Sind ...61 f
Sindi ...42 f
Šinedžinst ...57 n
Sines ...34 n
Sinewit ...71 r
Singa ...42 m
Singapore ...66 t
Singatoka ...75 k
Sing Buri ...65 j
Singida ...45 h
Singkawang ...68 l
Singkep ...68 i
Singkilbaru ...66 p
Singtai ...63 c
Sining ...57 o
Sinjai ...69 t
Sinjar ...54 s
Sinkat ...38 y
Sinn ...58 m
Sinnamary ...26 j
Sinop ...35 m
Sintang ...68 m
Sinú ...22 m
Sinugif ...43 j
Sinŭiju ...58 s
Sinyaya ...52 k
Sinyuga ...52 x
Sioux City ...15 v
Sioux Falls ...15 v
Sioux Lookout ...16 c
Siple (Mountain) ...81 b
Siple (Research Sta.) ...81 q
Siple Island ...81 q
Sipora ...68 e
Siquijor ...67 i
Sira ...56 i
Siracha ...65 j
Siraj ...60 b
Sir Edward Pellew Group ...73 g
Siret ...35 h
Sirha ...61 i
Sir James McBrien, Mount 12 o
Sirjan ...60 a
Sir Joseph Banks Group ...77 e
Sirohi ...60 z
Sironcha ...64 h
Sirpur ...64 g
Sirsa ...61 a
Sirte ...35 o
Sirte Desert ...37 k
Sirte, Gulf of ...35/38
Sirwa ...43 h
Si Sa Ket ...66 g
Sishen ...48 z
Sisimiut ...90 i
Sisophon ...66 g
Sisseton ...15 i
Sitapur ...61 e
Sitka ...11 x
Sittang ...65 g
Sittwe ...62 o
Siuri ...61 w
Sivas ...54 p
Siverek ...54 r
Sivuch ...53 v
Siwa ...38 e
Siwa, Oasis ...38 e
Sixtymile ...11 i
Siziman ...59 b
Skagen, Cape ...33 c
Skagerrak ...33 b
Skagway ...11 x
Skardu ...61 a
Skeena ...14 d
Skellefte ...33 g
Skellefteå ...33 h
Skibotn ...33 h
Skikda ...34 w
Sklad ...52 j
Skoer Fjord ...91 u

Skopin ...54 e
Skopje ...35 e
Skovorodino ...52 x
Skukuza ...49 f
Skye ...32 v
Slamet ...68 y
Slana ...11 h
Slave Coast ...41 o
Slave Lake ...14 l
Slave River ...12 u
Slessor Glacier ...83 u
Slidell ...19 i
Sligo ...32 u
Slippers Bay ...48 w
Sliven ...35 h
Slonim ...33 w
Sl'ud'anka ...52 x
Słupsk ...33 s
Slutsk ...33 x
Smallwood Reservoir ...17 f
Smara ...36 r
Smederevo ...35 e
Smidovich ...50 j
Smith ...14 l
Smith Bay ...13 g
Smithfield ...49 o
Smith's Falls ...16 l
Smithton ...77 w
Smolensk ...33 z
Smyley Island ...82 z
Snag ...11 i
Snake ...14 j
Snake River (USA) ...15 a
Snare River ...12 s
Snares Islands ...79 p
Snowdrift ...12 u
Snowy ...78 z
Snowy Mountains ...78 q
Soai Dao ...65 k
Sobat ...42 k
Sobradinho Reservoir ...27 r
Sobral ...27 f
Soči ...54 r
Socompa ...28 q
Socorro (Colombia) ...23 n
Socorro (USA) ...18 j
Socorro (Island) ...18 u
Socotra ...231 c
Soda Springs ...15 a
Söderhamn ...33 g
Södertälje ...33 f
Sodiri ...42 j
Sodo ...43 o
Sofala Bay ...46 v
Sofia ...35 f
Sofiysk ...53 o
Sofiysk (Amur) ...59 b
Sogamoso ...23 o
Sogeri ...71 o
Sognefjörd ...33 a
Sogo Nur ...57 o
Sohâg ...38 i
Sohar ...39 z
Soje ...49 b
Šokalsky ...51 c
Sokcho ...58 v
Sokodé ...41 a
Sokolo ...40 i
Sokoto ...41 d
Sokoto (River) ...41 c
Sokyrbulak ...55 b
So edade ...25 b
Soikamsk ...50 w
Sol Iletsk ...54 m
Solimões ...23 s
Solodniki ...54 h
Solok ...68 f
Sololo ...43 p
Solomon Islands ...71/74
Solomon Sea ...74 k
Solor Islands ...69 v
Solovjevsk ...57 i
Solwezi ...45 n
Somalia ...4 3
Somerset ...16 t
Somerset East ...49 n
Somerset Island ...13 a
Son ...61 t
Sonaly ...55 i
Søndrestrømfjord ...90 w

Søndre Strømfjord (Fjord) 90 w
Songea ...45 u
Songkhla ...65 w
Songo ...45 s
Sonhat ...61 s
Sonoyta ...18 f
Sonsonate ...22 c
Sonsorol ...70 d
Sopo ...42 g
Sorabai ...60 k
Sordongnokh ...53 f
Sordongnokh ...53 p
Soria ...34 e
Sorocaba ...29 f
Sorochinsk ...54 m
Sorol Atoll ...70 j
Sorong ...70 p
Soroti ...42 y
Söröya ...33 i
Sorsk ...56 i
Sorsogon ...67 i
Sortavala ...33 m
Sosna ...52 b
Sosnovka ...57 f
Sos'va ...50 y
Sosyko ...54 e
Souanké ...41 x
Soubré ...40 v
Souk-Ahras ...34 w
Sŏul (Seoul) ...58 u
Sounda ...44 e
Souré ...26 m
Sousse ...34 y
South Africa ...46/48-49
Southampton Island ...13 q
Southampton (UK) ...34 f
Southampton (USA) ...17 n
South Andaman ...65 e
South Anyuskiy Mountains 10 b
South Australia ...77 b
South Bend ...16 s
South Bug ...35 k
South Carolina ...20 m
South China Sea ...66-67
South Dakota ...15 g
South East Cape ...77 y
Southend ...12 w
Southend-on-Sea ...32 y
Southern Alps ...79 r
Southern Cross ...76 f
Southern Indian Lake ...12 z
Southern Ocean ...87 t
Southern Sierra Madre ...19 p
Southern Sporades ...35 u
South Georgia Islands ...31 j
South Horr ...43 o
South Island ...79 r
South Magnetic Pole ...87 p
South Natuna Islands ...68 l
South Orkney Islands ...82 g
South Pagai ...68 r
South Platte ...15 s
South Pole ...81 m
South Saskatchewan ...15 a
South Scotia Ridge ...82 f
South Shetland Islands ...82 r
Southwest Cape ...79 p
Sovetsk ...33 v
Sovetskaya ...84 w
Sovetskiy ...50 z
Soviet Union ...10/33/35/50-59
Soyapa ...18 i
Soyo ...44 a
Spaatz Island ...82 z
Spain ...34/36
Spanish Town ...21 o
Spartanburg ...20 l
Spassk Dal'niy ...58 k
Spearfish ...15 e
Spence Bay ...13 a
Spencer ...15 w
Spencer, Cape ...77 r
Spencer Gulf ...77 e
Spitzbergen ...92 p
Split ...35 b
Spokane ...14 j
Spratly Islands ...66 z
Springbok ...48 w
Springdale ...17 j
Springfield (Colorado) ...15 s

Springfield (Illinois) ...16 q
Springfield (Massachusetts) ...17 n
Springfield (Missouri) ...15 x
Springfield (Ohio) ...16 u
Springs ...46 q
Springsure ...74 r
Spruce Knob ...16 w
Squaw Harbor ...11 n
Sredinnyy Mountains ...53 y
Srednekolymsk ...53 j
Sredniy ...53 w
Sredniy Kalar ...52 t
Sretensk ...57 k
Srikakulam ...64 k
Sri Lanka ...64
Sri Mohangarh ...60 k
Srinagar ...61 a
Stafonovo ...50 f
Stakhanov ...54 d
Stampriet ...48 j
Standerton ...49 r
Stanford ...15 a
Stanley (N.Dakota) ...15 f
Stanley (Uganda) ...42 w
Stannakh-Khocho ...52 i
Stanovoy Mountains ...52 y
Stanthorpe ...78 f
Staraja Russa ...33 m
Stara Zagora ...35 h
Star.Dom ...53 d
Stargard ...33 s
Staritsa ...51 s
Staritsa (Moscow) ...50 n
Star. Kayakhnyy ...52 b
Star. Kheydzhan ...53 s
Staryy Nadym ...51 p
Staryy Oskol ...54 d
Staten Island ...30 z
Stavanger ...33 a
Stavropol' ...54 r
Stavropolka ...55 f
Steamboat ...12 p
Steamboat Springs ...15 p
Steelpoort ...49 e
Steenkool ...70 q
Steenstrup Glacier ...91 b
Stefansson Island ...12 j
Steinhausen ...48 i
Steinkier ...33 d
Steinkopf ...48 w
Stephenville ...17 h
Stepnyak ...55 i
Sterling ...15 r
Sterlitamak ...55 a
Stettin (Szczecin) ...33 r
Stevens Point ...16 d
Stewart (British Colombia) 11 z
Stewart (Yukon Territory) ...11 i
Stewart Crossing ...11 k
Stewart Island ...79 p
Stewart, Mount ...74 p
Stewart (River) ...11 k
Steynsburg ...49 o
Steytlerville ...49 n
Stikine ...11 z
Stilbaai ...48 y
Stirling ...32 w
Stockholm ...33 g
Stockton ...14 u
Stoke-on-Trent ...32 w
Stolbovoy ...50 j
Stolbovoy (Island) ...53 c
Stonehenge ...77 i
Stony Rapids ...12 v
Stony River ...11 z
Store Koldewey ...91 u
Storkerson Peninsula ...12 i
Storm Bay ...77 z
Storm Lake ...16 n
Stors, Lake ...33 e
Storuman ...33 f
Strahan ...77 x
Stralsund ...33 q
Strand ...48 w
Strasbourg ...34 j
Strathleven ...73 k
Strathmay ...73 k
Streaky Bay ...77 z

Strelka ...53 i
Strelka (Yenisey) ...51 w
Strelka-čunja ...52 a
Strezhevoy ...51 q
Strickland ...70 x
Strömsund ...33 f
Stryy ...35 f
Stung Treng ...66 i
Sturge Island ...86 v
Sturgeon Bay ...16 f
Sturgeon Falls ...16 j
Sturt Creek ...73 n
Sturt Desert ...77 h
Stutterheim ...49 p
Stuttgart ...34 l
Styr ...33 w
Suakin ...38 z
Suanhwa ...57 w
Suata ...23 g
Subotica ...35 d
Suceava ...35 h
Süchbaatar ...57 d
Suchow (Xuzhou) ...63 f
Suchow (Suzhou) ...63 h
Suchumi ...54 r
Suckling, Mount ...74 e
Sucre ...28 f
Sucuaro ...23 q
Sucunduri ...25 j
Sucuriu ...29 b
Sucurundi ...25 j
Sudan ...38/42-43
Sudbury ...16 i
Sudd ...42 j
Suddie ...23 k
Sudety ...35
Sudocje, Lake ...55 o
Sudr ...38 j
Sue ...42 u
Suez ...38 j
Suez Canal ...38 j
Suez, Gulf of ...38 j
Sugdža ...57 e
Suglan ...53 a
Sugoy ...53 k
Sugun ...55 y
Suhai Hu ...56 x
Suhait ...57 q
Suhsien ...63 e
Suide ...57 t
Suifenhe ...58 j
Suihua ...58 g
Suileng ...58 g
Suining ...62 k
Sui Xian ...63 c
Suj ...57 r
Sukabumi ...68 w
Sukhana ...52 h
Sukhinichi ...54 b
Sukhona ...50 r
Sukkur ...60 j
Suknah ...37 j
Sulaiman ...60 k
Sulaimaniyah (Iraq) ...39 e
Sulaimaniyah (Saudi Arabia) ...39 t
Sulaiman Range ...60 k
Sula Islands ...69 k
Sulan Cheer ...57 s
Sulawesi (Celébes) ...69 t
Sulawesi Sea ...67 u
Suleya ...55 b
Suli Hu ...56 x
Sullana ...24 y
Sullivan ...16 p
Sulphur Springs ...19 e
Sultan ...60 f
Sultanpur ...61 s
Sulu Archipelago ...67 s
Sulu Sea ...67 s
Sulzberger Ice Shelf ...81 v
Sum ...56 l
Sumaih ...42 i
Sumail ...60 o
Sumarokovo ...51 j
Sumatra ...68 f
Sumba ...69 s
Sumbawa ...69 r
Sumbawa Besar ...69 r
Sumbawanga ...45 f

CONCORDIA COLLEGE LIBRARY
2811 NE Holman St.
Portland, OR 97211